A PRIEST IN PUBLIC SERVICE

Notre Dame Studies
in American Catholicism

Sponsored by the
Charles and Margaret Hall Cushwa Center
for the Study of American Catholicism

A Priest in
Public Service
Francis J. Haas and the New Deal

Thomas E. Blantz, C.S.C.

UNIVERSITY OF NOTRE DAME PRESS
NOTRE DAME   LONDON

Library of Congress Cataloging in Publication Data

Blantz, Thomas E.
  A priest in public service.

  (Notre Dame studies in American Catholicism; v. 5)
  Bibliography: p.
  1. Haas, Francis J. (Françis Joseph), 1889–1953.
2. Catholic Church—Bishops—Biography. 3. Bishops,
United States—Biography. 4. Labor policy—United States—
History—20th century. I. Title
II. Series
BX4705.H125B56   282'.092'4   [B]   81-40452
ISBN 0-268-01547-3   AACR2

Manufactured in the United States of America

Contents

Preface

At his elevation to the bishopric in 1943, Monsignor Francis Haas chose as his episcopal motto *In Christo Justitia*—"Let There Be Justice in Christ." He had lived a full and productive priestly life for thirty years—as parish assistant, seminary professor, university dean, director of a national school of social service, labor mediator, and government administrator; yet in all these activities he seemed to hold his work for social justice the most significant and most satisfying. Christian justice, in fact, was the focus and major interest of his life: it was the subject of his graduate studies, the theme of his teaching, the topic of his numerous speeches, and the motivation of his government service. *In Christo Justitia* summarized his life well: his goal was justice and his motivation was religious.

The emphasis in this biography, therefore, will be on Haas's work for social justice—in education, in his priestly ministry, and especially in government service. Government service was indeed the distinctive characteristic and contribution of his life. He held high government positions on both the state and national levels during the New Deal administration of Franklin Roosevelt; he was a confidential adviser to cabinet officers, members of Congress, presidential assistants, and union executives; he was a frequent speaker at labor conventions and government conferences on industry and unemployment; and he served as mediator in more than fifteen hundred industrial disputes throughout the 1930s. After 1941, he accepted appointments to both state and federal civil rights bureaus and he became one of the nation's leading advocates of fair employment opportunity in government and industry.

As a Catholic priest and student of the social encyclicals of Pope Leo XIII and Pope Pius XI, Haas brought a unique social philosophy to these many offices. His public service was motivated by firm belief in the God-given dignity and eternal destiny of all men and women and by deep concern for the well-being of the poor and the underprivileged. All men and women are equal before God, he insisted, and consequently all have the same inviolable rights in justice to a family wage, reasonable conditions of work, freedom of organization, and equal opportunity for employment. "In all that he said and did in reference to social questions," said Cardinal Edward Mooney in 1953, "no one could fail to discern the mind and the heart of the priest."[1]

The author has incurred many obligations in preparing this study. For their hospitality and professional assistance, he is grateful to Monsignors Anthony Arszulowicz, Edmund Falicki, William Schuit, and the late Hugh Beahan; to Fathers John McGee, Dennis Morrow, Robert Sampon, and Anthony Vainavicz; to Doctors George Hruneni and Anthony Zito; and to Mary Haas Charnon, and Allen, Arthur, and Dorothy Haas. Personal friends of the bishop and numerous government, labor, and religious leaders consented to interviews and these are gratefully acknowledged in the bibliography. All errors that remain, of course, are the author's.

The archivists and librarians of the Catholic University of America, Columbia University, St. Francis Seminary, Georgetown University, Marquette University, the University of Notre Dame, the Diocese of Grand Rapids, the Archdiocese of Milwaukee, the Paulist Fathers Archives in New York, the National Archives, the Library of Congress, the Franklin D. Roosevelt Library, the Harry S. Truman Library, the National Labor Relations Board, the State Historical Society of Minnesota, and the State Historical Society of Wisconsin were all most helpful and accommodating. The author benefited from materials made available by the Amalgamated Clothing Workers of America, the International Brotherhood of Teamsters, the United Mine Workers of America, and the AFL-CIO offices in Washington. The Eleanor Roosevelt Institute assisted with a liberal travel grant during the summer of 1974. The author is also grateful to the editors of the *Catholic Historical Review*, *Minnesota History*, and *Social Thought* for permission to use materials previously published in these journals. James Langford, Ann Rice, and the staff of the University of Notre Dame Press were most generous with their professional assistance. Successive drafts of the manuscript were typed with admirable skill and patience by Patti Hardy, Carol Spurgeon, Catherine Box, and members of the Faculty Stenographic Pool of the University of Notre Dame.

The author owes his deepest debt of gratitude to Professor William E. Leuchtenburg of Columbia University and the late Reverend Thomas T. McAvoy, C.S.C., of the University of Notre Dame for their assistance, their encouragement, and their example. It has somewhere been suggested that writing a good biography is almost as difficult as living one, but all those mentioned above, and many others, contributed generously to make this study both satisfying and enjoyable.

1

Early Wisconsin Years, 1889-1919

When Monsignor John A. Ryan died on September 16, 1945, civic and religious leaders across the country joined to pay tribute to an outstanding theologian, government official, and uncompromising champion of the rights of the poor. President Harry Truman called him "a powerful influence in our American life" and added that "we shall all miss the wise counsel which he gave so generously out of his long and varied experience." Former Secretary of Labor Frances Perkins acknowledged herself a "debtor to his inspiration and practical thought." Bishop Karl J. Alter of Toledo lamented that "in the death of Monsignor Ryan, the Church loses her best-known champion of the cause of social justice." To Senator Robert Wagner of New York, he was "one of God's noblemen. His life, his thoughts, and his deeds will continue to enrich America and its people until the end of time."[1]

Of all the tributes that Monsignor Ryan received that fall, none perhaps was more sincere or more heartfelt than the eulogy delivered three days later before the hundreds of religious leaders, civic officials, labor executives, and personal friends who crowded into the cathedral of St. Paul, Minnesota, to attend the funeral Mass. The preacher on that occasion was the bishop of Grand Rapids, Michigan, a former student of Monsignor Ryan in Washington and a personal friend for more than twenty-five years.

"It is with deep sorrow and yet with a sense of privilege," the bishop began, "that we assist at the solemn obsequies of one of the few great men of our generation, John Augustine Ryan." The bishop recalled the main events of Ryan's career in the service of social justice—his birth on a Minnesota farm and early education in St. Paul, his numerous writings in defense of the rights of workers, his years as professor of moral theology at The Catholic University of America, and his wide influence as director of the Social Action Department of the National Catholic Welfare Conference for twenty-five years. "In all truth," the bishop declared, "his was a full life as priest and scholar. Teacher, thinker, author, lecturer, administrator—his record does not have to be made or to be built up. It is known to all the world. . . . When we recall the vast services that Monsignor Ryan rendered to the American people—to the poor in enabling them to acquire some little property, and to the rich in assuring them that the right to honestly-won property is sacred and inviolable—our entire nation should offer a prayer of thanksgiving to Heaven that John Ryan lived and worked." The bishop concluded with a solemn declaration: "This morning I venture the prophesy; he will stand in our country almost alone, to offset the sentence of condemnation that future generations will justly pass upon our own, that whereas we have made revolutionary advances in scientific research in behalf of things, we have made little if any progress in the high science of social thinking in behalf of human beings."[2]

The bishop had chosen his words well. John A. Ryan was indeed an extraordinary priest and outstanding champion of social justice, but it was one of the great accomplishments of his life that he did not remain "alone." In his writings, lectures, and personal contacts, he had constantly pleaded for co-workers in the field of social justice, and a small but dedicated band of disciples gradually came to share his social philosophy and his deep concern for the welfare of the underprivileged. Some of these had been his students in St. Paul or Washington, others knew him only through his writings and public lectures, but they soon became recognized as the "Ryan School" of economics or social justice—a further tribute to his achievement. The best-known and most influential of these was probably the bishop who delivered that funeral eulogy in St. Paul, Francis J. Haas.

Although Ryan was twenty years older than Haas, their lives were strikingly similar. Both were born of immigrant Catholic ancestry in the upper Midwest, Ryan in Minnesota and Haas in Wisconsin.[3] Neither family was wealthy and both boys, consequently, were raised in an atmosphere of thrift and hard work. Both entered the seminary in their teens, completed the same standard course of seminary studies, and pursued doctoral studies at Catholic University after ordination. They had only limited experience as parish priests, and both served for over ten years on the faculties of their local seminaries, Ryan in St. Paul and Haas in

Milwaukee. At about the age of forty-five, both were reassigned to Washington, where they were affiliated with Catholic University and the National Catholic School of Social Service and where they gained even wider recognition as experts in matters of social justice. They became confidential advisers to government and labor officials, and throughout the 1930s they were the American Church's foremost champions of Franklin Roosevelt's New Deal.

But there was a basic and obvious difference. Ryan was above all a teacher, a writer, a lecturer, while Haas's numerous administrative posts for most of his life, for both the Church and the government, left him little time for the classroom or for personal research. Father Raymond McGowan, Ryan's close associate at the NCWC, called Ryan "primarily a thinker and teacher, a man apart." "His own action," McGowan added, "had to be secondary."[4] Haas, on the other hand, was a man of action, a doer, an influential government official.

In fact, from the start of the New Deal in 1933 until his death as bishop of Grand Rapids twenty years later, Father Haas probably held more important government positions than any other priest of his time, perhaps of all time. He was a member of the National Recovery Administration's Labor Advisory Board, its General Code Authority, and the National Labor Board. He served on the Labor Policies Board of the Works Progress Administration and on the Wisconsin State Labor Relations Board. He was a special commissioner of conciliation for the Department of Labor, served as chairman of several industry committees of the Department of Labor's Wage and Hour Division, and was a member of the National Resources Planning Board's Committee on Long Range Work and Relief Policies. He served as chairman of the President's Fair Employment Practices Committee in 1943, as a member of President Truman's Committee on Civil Rights in 1947, and as chairman of Michigan's Advisory Committee on Civil Rights in 1949. "It would be impossible to assess the influence that this tall, kindly, intense man had on this nation in such fields as labor relations, civil rights, and similar areas," *the Grand Rapids Press* stated in 1953, "but without doubt it was immense and in some instances even crucial."[5]

Father Haas was born in Racine, Wisconsin, in 1889, and his later interests in public life and ecclesiastical service were undoubtedly influenced by both his family background and the age and locality in which he lived. The first thirty years of his life were a time of social agitation and dawning reform throughout the country, and young Francis Haas grew up amid daily conversation of economic uncertainty, the demands of workers, the treatment of immigrants, and governmental remedies for the growing discontent.[6] Farmers complained bitterly of worsening conditions; industrial life seemed dominated by the unchallenged power of a John D. Rockefeller, an Andrew Carnegie, or a J. P. Morgan; and periodic recessions left breadwinners too often unemployed. Jacob Coxey led a protest march of the discontented and unemployed to Washington in 1894, and the People's or Populist Party united the unemployed, the farmhand, and the day laborer behind the unpredictable but charismatic leadership of James Weaver, "Pitchfork" Ben Tillman, Mary Elizabeth Lease, and "Sockless" Jerry Simpson. It was Mary Lease, "the Patrick Henry in Petticoats," who urged farmers to "raise less corn and more Hell." Through their lectures, sermons, and writings, religious leaders like Washington Gladden, Walter Rauschenbusch, and other Social Gospel spokesmen urged concerted effort by government, industry, and private citizens to improve social and economic conditions to make a good Christian life less difficult for the poor. Progress was slowly made. Civil Service reform, anti-trust legislation, and the Interstate Commerce Commission received congressional approval before the turn of the century, prosperity seemed to be returning to agricultural and industrial life, and reform leaders like Mayors Hazen Pingree of Detroit and Tom Johnson of Cleveland, Governors Hiram Johnson of California and Robert La Follette of Wisconsin, and Presidents Theodore Roosevelt and Woodrow Wilson ushered in what would later be called the "Progressive Period" in American history.

The primary interests of Bishop Haas's later life, however, were the problems of workingmen and of racial and religious minorities, and for these the years 1889 to 1919 were unfortunately not years of reform but of waiting. The American Federation of Labor, founded in 1886, had reached a membership of over 1 million in 1900; but workers had suffered bitter defeats at Homestead, Pennsylvania, in 1892 and Pullman, Illinois, in 1894, and the Supreme Court in 1918 invalidated child labor legislation. The voices of Black leaders George Washington Carver, William E. B. DuBois, and Booker T. Washington attracted increasing attention, but segregated schools and transportation, the gradual disfranchisement of Black Americans throughout the South, and an average of thirty lynchings a year seemed more indelible signs of the times. The Statue of Liberty still beckoned to the poor and oppressed of the world, but it failed to warn of the often shameful treatment of Eastern European immigrants on the Atlantic Seaboard, the Indians on the Great Plains, and the Chinese on the West Coast. For these minorities, reform was still to come.

If the age in which Francis Haas was born and raised contributed to his later interests in social reform, so did the locality. Only fifty miles separated Racine from Chicago and the social work of Jane Addams and Florence Kelley; and Madison, the capital of midwestern reform, was only seventy miles to the west.[7] Under the persistent prodding and inspiration of men like Governor Robert M. La Follette and University of Wisconsin educators John R. Commons and Richard T. Ely, the legislative program enacted in Madison from 1889 to 1919 was the most advanced and progressive in the country: the Bennett Law of 1889, outlawing child labor and providing for compulsory education; a state civil rights act in 1895; a corrupt practices act in 1897; laws against industrial spies and imported strikebreakers by 1900; a direct primary law in 1903; a civil service act in 1905; and a minimum wage law for women in 1913.

Racine at the turn of the century was not only close to the centers of agitation and legislative reform but was caught up in the turmoil of social and industrial change.[8] Its two largest industries—the J. I. Case Threshing Machine Company and the Mitchell-Lewis Motor Company—had been founded before the Civil War and had grown rapidly; other businesses sprang up and expanded after the war; and the city soon grew from a farm and marketing community into a predominantly industrial center in the last quarter of the nineteenth century, with the all-too-frequent results of unexpected layoffs, inadequate wages, industrial accidents, labor strife, and violence.

The city's ethnic composition changed even more radically. Racine had been founded on the banks of the Root River in 1834 as a trapping and trading center, and by 1840 it numbered only 300 inhabitants. The potato famine in Ireland, however, and unsettled political conditions on the Continent persuaded over 4 million Irish and German immigrants to seek new homes in America during the twenty years preceding the Civil War, and many of them found their way into the Midwest. Racine's population increased to over 5,000 in 1850 and almost 12,000 in 1870. By 1890, German and Irish immigration had leveled off, but the so-called "New Immigrants" from Poland, Italy, and the land of Austria-Hungary began to arrive in similar numbers. Racine's population expanded to 29,000 in 1900, and to 38,000 ten years later. From the 1880s to 1917, Racine witnessed an urban revolution of its own.

Frank Haas was born of Racine's older immigrant stock, the son of Peter Haas and Mary O'Day.[9] His paternal grandfather, Felix Haas, had been born in Germany in 1829 and had emigrated from Oberweir bei Lahr, Baden, in the 1840s, the decade that saw nearly a million German immigrants enter the United States. He settled first in the small German community of Pottsville in eastern Pennsylvania and then moved to Caledonia, Wisconsin, a few miles northwest of Racine, where in 1860 Peter Haas, the fourth of twelve children, was born. The family moved to nearby Racine in the 1870s and Peter attended Racine High School and worked for a time as a grocer. He was married in Racine in 1885 and two years later, at the age of twenty-seven, opened his own store at 1240 North Main Street—"P. H. Haas, Staple and Fancy Groceries."

In Peter Haas's household, German loyalties competed with Irish, and apparently the Irish won. In spite of his German name, Bishop Haas more often considered himself Irish. His mother, Mary O'Day, was the daughter of immigrants from County Mayo, and Francis was born within a few hours of St. Patrick's Day. He attended St. Patrick's School and grew up in a predominantly Irish neighborhood in Racine's Fourth Ward. Many of his mother's relatives settled near the center of Racine; one of her brothers assisted for a time in the Haas family store and another worked in the J. I. Case plant a few blocks away. It was only natural, consequently, that young Frank, living near downtown Racine, developed closer ties with the O'Days than with his father's relatives, working on farms beyond the city, and that he identified himself in these early years with the Irish factory worker more easily than with the German farmer. This blending of German and Irish cultures in the Haas household was reflected in a lighthearted comment of Francis's younger sister in 1913: "Spring is here! I hear the German band playing the River Shanon [sic]."[10]

Young Francis's earliest years were pleasant and comfortable, although touched with tragedy. The Haas homestead, which Peter Haas had purchased on the corner of North Main and Hubbard Streets, was a wood-frame, two-story, rectangular structure; the Haas grocery and office occupied the first floor and the family living quarters were upstairs. This upstairs apartment was divided into a dozen rooms, with a parlor, living room, dining room, kitchen, and pantry along one wall and six bedrooms along the other. The parlor was in the front, overlooking North Main and its noisy streetcar line, and several of the bedrooms were so small that they contained a bed, a clothes chest, a straight chair, and little else. There was a set of outside stairs along the south side of the building and a second set leading through the store to the coal cellar. In winter these quarters were heated by two stoves, one in the kitchen and the other in the front room. Located on a small hill overlooking Racine's business district four blocks to the south and Lake Michigan about the same distance to the east, the upstairs rooms, despite the stoves, were chilled by cold winds off the lake in winter and, with only a shallow attic overhead, were uncomfortably hot in summer. But space was ample and the grocery business generally good, and Peter Haas made this the family homestead for more than thirty-five years.[11]

It was at this Main Street address that Francis Haas was born on March 18, 1889, the second of seven children and the oldest son. He had been preceded by an elder sister, Margaret, in 1887. Twin brothers, Allen and Arthur, were two years younger than Francis, and Peter, Jr., was born in 1893. A younger sister, Amy, was born a year later and was apparently the object of special care as she struggled to overcome several bouts of serious illness during her childhood years. The youngest son, Joseph, was born in April 1899 but died before the age of eight months.[12]

Religion was an important part of the German and Irish background of both Peter and Mary Haas, and this appreciation for religion they shared early with their children. St. Patrick's parish, on North Erie Street, was only a five-minute walk from the family home and grocery, and it was here that young Francis was baptized, confirmed, and received his First Communion. The family attended Mass regularly, took part in parish novenas and missions, and relied on the advice and counsel of the parish priest in times of difficulty. The children were encouraged to attend weekday Mass on special occasions, and from their early years they were taught to adopt small practices of penance and self-denial during Advent and Lent. Sundays and holy days were special feasts, beginning with High Mass in the parish church, followed by a large family dinner at noon, and closing with vespers in the evening. Peter Haas took an active part in parish life, serving as one of the auditors of church finances on occasion, offering his services to various building and fund-raising drives, and assisting other families from time to time in their religious or financial needs.[13]

Young Francis received his earliest education at the parish school, under the guidance of the School Sisters of St. Dominic, beginning two years behind his older sister. The school offered only the first six grades, and therefore, in 1899, he transferred to Janes Public School for grades seven and eight. This new school, opened in 1897, was in the 1400 block of North Main and was thus even closer to the Haas residence than St. Patrick's. Upon graduation from Janes in 1901, he enrolled for three years in Racine High School, which his father had attended before him, and in 1904 he transferred to St. Francis Seminary in Milwaukee. The future bishop was always a strong supporter of Catholic education and served for more than twenty-five years on the faculties of various Catholic institutions, but he was grateful for the public education he received in his youth, insisting that it broadened his point of view and made him much more tolerant of the opinions of others.[14]

Throughout these early years, the Haas family was never poor, but recurring sicknesses and the responsibilities of the family store rarely left them free of financial worries, especially during recessions. Peter Haas, in fact, proved to be a successful business-man. Years later, he noted in a letter to his son that he had moved to Racine in 1876 with an "enormous forty-seven cents in my pocket."[15] He had opened his grocery in 1887, and by the time Francis entered the seminary (1904) the store was grossing over $17,000 each year, half of it in cash and half on account. Peter Haas loaned money occasionally to others, assisted friends with their mortgages, and from time to time invested in real estate. By the late 1920s he owned five pieces of property within the city, including the family home and store on North Main and a small vinegar and pickle factory next door. Francis Haas was always an outspoken champion of the poor and the wage earner but he could also understand the worries and uncertainties of the inde-pendent merchant, and he was sympathetic from his youth to the many problems he saw troubling his father.[16]

Undoubtedly the saddest remembrance of Haas's early life was the death of his mother in the spring of 1903. Mary O'Day had been born in Racine in 1863, a descendant of one of the earliest families in the area, and was twenty-two years old at the time of her marriage. The O'Days also lived in Racine's Fourth

Ward and the Haas family maintained close contacts with them in the years after Mary's marriage. Her two brothers, Thomas and Charles, were active in local politics and union affairs, and family correspondence often speaks of Uncle Tom serving on the election board or Uncle Charlie walking the picket line. Mrs. Haas suffered periods of poor health and was afflicted for a time with paralysis. She was only forty years old when she died of complications of a kidney ailment, four years after the death of her youngest son and one year before Francis entered the seminary. At the time of her death, a neighbor sent the following tribute to the daily newspaper:

> She was a woman of rare qualities, her disposition being of a kind and noble character, generous to those in need and charitable to all. . . .
> To her children she was kind and looked to their every want and care possible and it was her wish that they obtain the highest education possible so as to make valuable men and women to the world. She was a most loving and devoted wife, a kind and desirable neighbor and one who will be greatly missed.
> Her great esteem in the community was attested when the funeral was held from St. Patrick's Church yesterday morning. Hundreds of friends and neighbors were present, the edifice being packed, to pay a last tribute to a woman loved in life, mourned in death.[17]

Although Francis rarely spoke of his mother in the correspondence that remains, his seminary diaries invariably note the anniversary of her death each year and his remembrance of her at Mass.

With the death of Francis's mother, Peter Haas became the greatest influence on his young son's life. He was indeed a remarkable man. He had arrived in Racine almost penniless, but through dedication and hard work soon became a successful and respected businessman. His working habits were precise; he kept careful accounts of his debts and projected profits, and he tried to instill this same thoroughness and precision—with varying success—in his children. His own father had remained a farmer all his life; he and Francis used to assist with the harvesting each fall, and Peter could converse knowledgeably about land yields and crop prices, in part, of course, because he regularly purchased produce from local farmers for resale in the grocery. He maintained an interest, too, in civic and political life, was familiar with municipal tax bills and spending policies, participated in public meetings, and kept himself and his family well informed on local and national candidates and issues, especially at election time.

His civic and business interests, however, never interfered with what Peter Haas considered his primary responsibility, care of his family. He set an example of honesty, hard work, and concern for others. He had a deep appreciation for education, took a personal interest in his children's school work, and, while ever encouraging them to greater efforts, understood their short-comings. "In regard to helping Amy, Petie, Art or Al," he wrote Francis in 1905, "I don't think the teachers would allow it.... You can't make a peck contain a bushel. They simply haven't got the ability of going any faster than what the sisters and teachers are making them go. They have very young heads on somewhat older shoulders." When Francis's youngest brother decided to quit his job as gardener one summer, his father noted: "Petie hasn't struck the right work yet, or maybe the work don't strike the right boy when they get Petie."[18] With only a high school edu-cation, the elder Haas was proud that three of his children were able to continue their education—Margaret in nurses' training, Allen in pharmacy at Marquette, and Francis in the seminary. Several of the children suffered from poor health in their early years—Francis with tuberculosis and Al and Amy with nervous disorders—and their father was unsparing in his concern and insistence on proper medical care. He kept in close contact with all the children as they grew older and founded homes of their own, and was ever willing to assist with his counsel, with produce from the family store, or with direct financial assistance. The greatest tribute to his success was the genuine friendship and love they shared, which bound them closely together throughout their lives.

Peter Haas also won the deep respect of his family for his unaffected and manly piety. Religion for him was never super-ficial or divorced from daily life. He often rose early to visit the church and assist at early Mass, especially during Lent or on important feasts and anniversaries. He regularly attended parish missions, was conscientious in observing days of fast and absti-nence, and was rarely absent from Sunday vespers, novenas, or other devotions. His belief was simple and unquestioning; all men were created by God and all therefore owed Him the homage of their worship and obedience to His commandments and to those of His Church. He had a deep and genuine respect for the priest-hood. The priest was a chosen minister of God and, despite human failings and mistakes (which Peter Haas never explained away), deserved the respect of his sacred calling. The elder Haas could only be pleased, consequently, when his oldest son decided to enter the seminary in Milwaukee, after his third year at Racine Public High.[19]

St. Francis Seminary, which Haas entered in late 1904, was one of the nation's leading institutions for the training of priests. It had been founded in 1856 by the second bishop of Milwaukee, John Martin Henni, principally to educate a German-speaking clergy to care for the needs of the immigrant groups arriving in ever increasing numbers in the mid-nineteenth century. Approximately four miles south of Milwaukee, the original seminary building, a brick structure four stories high with a chapel wing extending from the center, was constructed on a beautiful rise overlooking Lake Michigan. It housed fewer than 40 students at its opening, but within ten years more than 150 seminarians were enrolled, and a second wing was added at the north end. When the enrollment reached 250 in 1875, a larger wing was constructed at the southern corner of the building, with private rooms for seminarians in philosophy and theology. By the time of Haas's entrance, the seminary complex included this enlarged main building, which housed dormitories, private rooms, the chapel, and refectory; a convent building for the sisters who assisted with the cooking, laundry, and care of the sick; and several farm buildings, since the seminary grew most of its fruit and vegetables and butchered its own livestock. The seminary catalog for 1904 lists its special attractions: "An artesian well, 1300 feet in depth, furnishes an abundant supply of very wholesome water. All the halls, class-rooms and dormitories are heated with steam. The whole Seminary is furnished with electric light and is provided with elegant bathrooms." Board, room, and tuition were $87.50 per semester.[20]

Following the system of education in many Catholic universities in Europe in the nineteenth century and the system adopted by the Third Plenary Council of Baltimore in 1884, St. Francis Seminary offered a seven-year high school and collegiate program and a further four years of theology.[21] The first five years of the collegiate program, combining high school and early college, placed major emphasis on Latin, Greek, modern languages, English grammar and literature, science, history, and mathematics. The

final two years of the program—called First and Second Philosophy—offered logic, cosmology, metaphysics, psychology, and
ethics—in addition to advanced classes in chemistry, physics,
Hebrew, and Church history. By the turn of the century, most of
the collegiate courses were taught in English, although some of the
lectures were in German and the philosophy and theology classes
in Latin.

The order and discipline of student life were strictly regulated. The bell for rising sounded at 5:30 and for retiring at 9:30.
The day began with Mass and morning prayer and closed with a
common night prayer; and other times were set aside throughout
the day for spiritual reading, the rosary, and private devotions.
Approximately nine hours were assigned each day for classes and
study. Smoking was permitted only at prescribed times, and
silence was observed except for three hours of recreation after
lunch, supper, and in midafternoon. The rule discouraged contacts
with the world outside the seminary: "The days on which the
students may be visited are Wednesday and Saturday afternoons,"
the seminary catalog noted. "On other days, such visits are not
desirable, except for urgent reasons." "Students are not permitted
to visit Milwaukee," the directives continued, "except for very
important reasons, or during vacations."[22] This course of study
and rule of discipline were common to most American seminaries
at the turn of the century, since all were guided by the general
directives of the American hierarchy, but St. Francis Seminary
may have been exceptional in the wide influence it exerted on the
Catholic Church throughout the Middle West. Its living alumni in
1906 numbered over twenty bishops and four hundred priests,
serving in forty-three of the nation's ninety dioceses.

Francis's first weeks in the seminary were quite discouraging.
Like other students away from home for the first time, he was
homesick, and like other students, too, he was certain that his
malady was more serious. His father visited the seminary two
weeks after his arrival and diagnosed the trouble. "I never thought
you were suffering from anything except being homesick," he
wrote from Racine, "and I thought Sunday that you had mastered
that quite well. You are on the right path and you are laying the
foundation or cornerstone for a happy future."[23] He reminded
Francis that he would not want to stay at home all his life and
that the break would have to come eventually, and he assured him
of his own loneliness when he arrived in Racine as a young man
under twenty. Mr. Haas or one of the older children visited Francis

on the prescribed days, wrote letters weekly, and sent packages from home, usually fresh fruit or sweets from the family store.

Homesickness, however, was not Francis's only problem. Although he was going on sixteen and had completed three years of high school, the seminary officials placed him in the first year of the academic program, with students who had completed only eight grades. His professors were uncertain of his command of Latin, and since the philosophy and theology courses in the final six years of the program were taught in Latin, they decided that the new student could profitably repeat his high school work. Haas complained of this decision in letters to his father and his parish priest and, more significantly, set out to prove his superiors wrong.[24] Within two months of his entrance into the seminary, he was promoted to the second year, and a few months later to the third year. In September 1905, after one year in the seminary, he entered the fourth year class, having lost only one year of high school in the transfer from Racine and, presumably, having gained a satisfactory mastery of Latin.

His most serious trial during his first year, however, was neither homesickness nor Latin declensions, but his health. Soon after his arrival, he began to suffer from frequent colds, chest pains, and congestion of the lungs, and after each bout his recovery was slower and more difficult.[25] His health seemed to improve during the hot summer of 1905, but the irregular entries in his diary the following year note that he was again spending more and more time in the seminary infirmary. He continued in school until late 1906, when the trouble was finally diagnosed as consumption and he was advised to transfer immediately to a warmer and drier climate. This was a bitter blow for young Francis and his family. They had lost their youngest brother seven years before, their mother four years later, and now the oldest son was perhaps incurably ill. Still, the doctor left them no choice. Although Francis still desired to be a priest, he notified his teachers and classmates in mid-December that he would not return after the holidays. He spent a subdued Christmas with his family in Racine, and at 4:00 on a cold New Year's morning, in 1907, he bade a sad good-bye to his father, brothers, and sisters and, at age eighteen, boarded the train alone for Santa Fe.[26]

At first, the climate of New Mexico did not seem to help. He took a room in a private boardinghouse on a ranch outside the city and placed himself under a doctor's care, but did not improve as quickly as he had hoped. His living conditions were less than agreeable: there was friction with the administrators over agreed-upon costs and services; the noise around the ranch often kept him awake; and the companionship of the elderly, the sick, and the dying was far from pleasant for someone in his teens. He spent several hours each day in the hot sun, hunting small game in the surrounding fields, watching baseball games, and walking the mile or more into town. To ease the burden on family finances, he worked for a time selling groceries and then found employment in a furniture store, and perhaps overtaxed his strength. Alone and discouraged, his cough increasing and the pain in his lungs more worrisome, he contemplated returning to Racine.[27]

Uncertain of his son's condition, Peter Haas in May decided to go to Sante Fe, investigate the situation, and discuss the next step. He was favorably impressed with the progress he discovered but agreed that the boardinghouse contributed little to recovery. He helped Francis move into more comfortable quarters in town and encouraged him to stay a few months longer. Within weeks of his father's return to Racine, the long-awaited signs of recovery began to appear and the boy's spirits improved. "I have no more fevers, bleeding or anything like before," he wrote on May 31, and he immediately began to plan for the approaching academic year.[28] His father was not certain that the cure was complete, however, and in several letters insisted that Francis have a thorough medical examination before arrangements were made to return to school. "So you think you are real well again," his father wrote in late June. "Well, that's certainly good news...but nevertheless I would like to get Dr. Sloan's opinion about that."[29]

Francis received a clean bill of health later that summer but hesitated to return to the cold winters of Milwaukee. He discussed with his father the possibility of continuing his education in San Antonio or Denver, and decided upon Denver, in part because he thought the higher altitude would be healthier. Receiving permission from Bishop Nicholas Matz of Denver to continue his philosophical studies at Sacred Heart College, young Haas took the additional precaution of remaining the full summer in Santa Fe. He arrived in Denver on September 5 but was soon disappointed. He found that the weather was probably no better for his health than in Wisconsin and the seminary atmosphere much less to his liking. Consequently, on October 12, only five weeks after his arrival, he notified his father that he was returning to Racine and St. Francis Seminary.[30]

The nine months in New Mexico had a profound effect on Francis's life. He had been seriously ill and he knew it, and for the rest of his life he took special care of his health. Away from his family and the seminary rules, he had to make decisions for himself, handle his own finances, and accept as maturely as possible the disappointments and frustrations his illness occasioned. The experience left him mature beyond his years. "God willing, I would like to continue my studies," he confided to a friend before returning to Racine, "but you know we must all undergo hardships, which may in truth be nothing but a test of our metal."[31] Haas's "metal" was perhaps best revealed by the fact that, during those trying months in New Mexico, he continued his studies privately, writing to classmates in Milwaukee for weekly assignments, and on his return to the seminary in the fall of 1907 he was able to pass his fifth year examinations and join his former classmates in the sixth year of the collegiate program despite an absence of ten months.

The scattered correspondence and fragmentary diaries which have been preserved from Haas's seminary days suggest that, except for early anxieties about his health, his life and interests were little different from his classmates'. He noted the arrival of packages from home, commented upon the idiosyncracies of his professors, betrayed anxious moments before examinations, described the football fortunes of Marquette and Wisconsin and the heavyweight title bouts of Jim Jeffries and Jack Johnson, criticized the strictures of seminary discipline, and enjoyed free afternoons hiking, swimming, ice skating, or playing baseball. He inquired regularly about business in the grocery and the uncertain health and scholastic progress of his younger brothers and sister. Letters from his sister Margaret kept him informed of engagements, marriages, and other social events in Racine. Popular with his fellow students, he was chosen president of the seminary Temperance Society, the St. Thomas Literary and Debating Society, and the St. Philip Neri Missionary Society during his final year.[32]

Encouraged by his father, Francis maintained an interest in local and national politics. The elder Haas wrote frequently of tax proposals, changes in property assessments, and the campaign promises of local candidates, and Francis's diaries reveal a similar interest in public affairs. "Situation at present outlook is just about even: Bryan-Taft," he wrote in 1908, and two years later: "Socialists carry Milwaukee County." In 1912, he noted that October 12 was "Bull Moose" night, and after the California returns were announced, a month later, he scribbled—with some exaggeration—"Wilson has big majority."[33] Diocesan seminaries—

St. Francis included—were generally built at a distance from urban centers to reduce the distractions of secular life and to permit full concentration on the curriculum, but Francis managed to continue his interest in American politics and public affairs, an interest he was to retain throughout his life.

Haas's academic interests in the seminary varied. He was proficient in foreign languages; he could read French and Latin, and he preached sermons in German in his deacon year. He found theology and the study of Sacred Scripture particularly attractive, and seriously considered continuing for an advanced degree. For most of his seminary years, however, literature seemed to be his favorite subject. His personal library included works of Shakespeare, Macaulay, and other literary masters, and he always enjoyed returning to them for an hour or two after a busy day. He took part in the seminary's dramatic presentations and was active as a debater, and it is perhaps ironic that, in debate, this future champion of social justice seemed most pleased with two victories he won in 1911, opposing a federal income tax and the eight-hour workday.[34]

Frank Haas was also an accomplished musician, although it is uncertain when this interest began. Most of the children apparently played an instrument, as an early letter from his father indicated: "Amy is now taking lessons on piano and Art is making noise on his blow instrument." Francis played the violin throughout his student days, joined the seminary orchestra, and gave occasional lessons to fellow students. His family enjoyed his playing and reminded him to bring his instrument when he returned to Racine for vacations. He took his violin with him to New Mexico, brightened many solitary hours with it, and was invited to play at Sunday Mass in the Santa Fe cathedral. He sang in parish choirs on occasion and developed some skill on the cello, but the violin was always his favorite. Years later, friends and acquaintances recalled his early musical abilities, and it was apparently only in the late 1930s that he found it impossible to continue this interest.[35]

Throughout his seminary days, Francis showed more than average interest in the problems of the workingman. He was employed in the J. I. Case plant in Racine in the summer of 1909, when the workers were making serious efforts to unionize and work was at best unsteady. His diary for that summer notes that he was to "start work at Cases" on June 23, "laid off" on July 30, and "resumed work" on August 23.[36] It was probably in this strike-torn factory in 1909 that he had his first direct experience of job insecurity, layoffs, and a short pay envelope. He engaged in frequent discussions of labor problems and industrial relations with seminary classmates, and when the well-known theologian, Dr. Charles Bruehl, offered an elective course in 1911 on social justice and contemporary problems, Frank Haas was one of the first to enroll. Dr. Bruehl had been educated in both the United States and Europe and had served for several years as a parish priest in the Archdiocese of Philadelphia and in England and Scotland. Young Haas was thus able to benefit not only from the theologian's familiarity with the social teachings of the Church but also from his personal experiences as a parish priest among the poor at home and in London and Glasgow.[37]

An even greater influence than Dr. Bruehl in stimulating Haas's interest in industrial problems was, as might be expected, his father. Peter Haas sympathized with the problems of the workingman and he kept his son informed on local labor disturbances in his weekly letters. "The strike at Cases is in full fling," he noted in January 1905. "They have imported non-union moulders from somewhere but they only had 18 men working today.... I think it will be a long drawn struggle." The news was no better the following week: "In regard to Cases shop, it is not started yet. They have about 40 bum moulders or scabs commonly called, or...strike breakers.... Nearly all the iron comes out bad and has to go to the dump. It must cost Cases at least $500.00 per day and I think the Union will win the strike anyway." Four months later the picture was the same: "The strike at Cases is the same as ever. They have more non-union men working now than they had union men before the strike and still they are not doing the work that the union men did and [it] is of an inferior quality, 1/3 going to the scrap pile."[38] Whenever there was a serious industrial dispute or work stoppage at Case or some other plant in Racine, Peter Haas was sure to note it. Uncle Tom and Uncle Charlie O'Day were often on picket duty, and there was seldom any doubt where the sympathies of the Haas family lay. In an interview granted as a bishop forty years later, Haas gave his father major credit for stimulating his interest in industrial problems. "My father owned a grocery store in Racine," he noted. "I guess I got interested because during a Case strike long ago he supported the strikers, fed them. And he did it strictly because he was a Christian gentleman. Maybe that's what influenced me most."[39]

After nine years of study at St. Francis Seminary, Frank Haas was ordained to the priesthood in the summer of 1913. Although ordinations were usually held in the seminary chapel or in one of the large churches in Milwaukee, Haas and two of his classmates from Racine received permission from Archbishop Sebastian Messmer to be ordained in their home town. Preparations were made, and on June 11 Frank Haas, George Miller, and John Bott were ordained to the priesthood by Auxiliary Bishop Joseph M. Koudelka, assisted by Monsignor Joseph Rainer, rector of St. Francis Seminary, and several other priests of the Milwaukee archidiocese.[40] St. Joseph's Church, the largest in the city, had been chosen for the ceremony and it was filled that morning with the families and acquaintances of the three candidates. The ordination sermon was delivered in English and German, and music was provided by the seminary choir.

The joy of his ordination continued the following day, when the newly ordained priest returned to St. Patrick's parish to celebrate his first Mass, in the church in which he had been baptized, confirmed, and received his First Holy Communion. Despite an unusual heat wave that brought temperatures into the nineties for several days and caused numerous cases of heat prostration, the church was crowded with friends and relatives and a large number of local and visiting clergy. After the Mass, Father Haas was honored with a luncheon in the parish hall, where he received the congratulations and best wishes of over two hundred guests and bestowed his first priestly blessing. He assisted in his home parish for the next few weeks, singing the High Mass on Sundays, presiding at vespers in the evening, hearing confessions on the weekend, and visiting the sick at home and in hospitals. He had looked forward to the priesthood for ten years, but it must have seemed an impossible dream during that difficult year in New Mexico, and so he found deep joy and satisfaction in the priestly ministry among those family friends he had known and loved so long. For Father Haas, these few weeks were remembered as perhaps the most beautiful of his life.[41]

On July 4, less than four weeks after his ordination, Father Haas received a telephone call from Archbishop Messmer, requesting him to serve as assistant to Father Robert Roche, the pastor of Holy Rosary parish in Milwaukee. The two years he spent there, from the summer of 1913 until the fall of 1915, were occupied with normal parish ministry. He offered Mass each morning in the parish church, heard confessions on weekends, officiated at baptisms and weddings, ministered to the sick, instructed converts, and shared his counsel and advice. An organizer of the parish's St. Vincent de Paul Society, he assisted in bringing food, clothing, and other supplies to the needy. This was the only parochial assignment Father Haas ever held and he found it most satisfying. "Father Robert Roche," he confided to a friend twenty years later, "whom you and the parish loved and revered and whose priestly example will continue to live in Holy Rosary Parish, received me as only my own father could have received me. I count it one of the great blessings of my life to have been associated with him in laboring in Holy Rosary Parish."[42]

These two years of daily contact with Father Roche deepened the young priest's interest in social justice and the problems of the poor. Father Roche had long been concerned over the economic injustices suffered by the working people of his parish. He lamented the drift of European workers away from religion and, mindful perhaps of the attractions socialism held for Milwaukee laborers, he repeated that "unless the Church takes an interest in the working men, she is going to lose them." When Father Haas countered that the American Church had John A. Ryan, the older priest replied: "Yes, but we need a hundred John A. Ryans in this country."[43] These words must have made a deep impression on the young assistant, because he recalled them easily years later—and it was perhaps at that time that he began to consider the possibility of following in Ryan's footsteps.

During these years at Holy Rosary, Father Haas also came under the influence of Father Peter Dietz, a priest in the neighboring parish of Sts. Peter and Paul. Father Dietz was probably as well known as Father Ryan among trade unionists in the early twentieth century. He was a frequent delegate to the annual conventions of the AFL (from 1909 to 1922 he missed only one); he was a leading spokesman for the establishment of an International Federation of Catholic Trade Unions, and in 1910 he founded the Militia of Christ, a religious association of Catholic members of the AFL. Father Haas shared the older priest's concern for the spiritual welfare of industrial workers and from 1913 to 1915 worked closely with him in the Milwaukee chapter of the Militia of Christ. Father Dietz was an outspoken champion of the AFL and Father Haas's later sympathy for the work of the Federation was probably influenced by these early contacts with Father Dietz. A basic difference between Dietz and John Ryan, a historian has suggested, was that Dietz was an "organizer" in the social justice movement, not an "academician." Although Father Haas would one day be a disciple of Ryan, his preference for the union convention hall and the collective bargaining table over the seminar room or the faculty lounge might also be due in part to the example of Father Peter Dietz.[44]

In the fall of 1915, an opening occurred on the faculty of St. Francis Seminary and, at the request of Monsignor Rainer, Archbishop Messmer assigned Father Haas to fill it. He held this position four years. He was placed in the "Collegiate Department," corresponding to today's high school and first two years of college, and his duties were varied. He taught English, Christian doctrine, and arithmetic in his first two years, substituted public speaking or elocution in 1917-18, and added history to his schedule in his final year. He also served as moderator of the St. Thomas Literary and Debating Society, directed a major Shakespearean play each year—*Hamlet*, *King Lear*, and *Macbeth*—and contributed occasional articles on literary and theological subjects to *The Salesianum*, the seminary quarterly.[45]

These seminary commitments did not absorb all of the young priest's time. He spent the summers of 1916 and 1917 at the University of Wisconsin in Madison, studying English and American literature—Chaucer, Shakespeare, Browning, and Emerson—and probably attended lectures on economics and social reform by John R. Commons and Richard T. Ely. He interrupted his studies in the summer of 1918 to serve as a volunteer chaplain at Camp Grant in Illinois, a summer camp for boys conducted by the Knights of Columbus, and on his return to Milwaukee that fall, with World War I still raging, he enlisted as a chaplain. He was commissioned a first lieutenant on November 8, but when the armistice was signed, three days later, he was released from active duty.[46]

With the end of World War I, Father Haas determined to continue his education. After teaching full time in the seminary during the 1918-19 school year, he took courses in ethics and history at Marquette University in the summer and received high grades in both subjects. He apparently received permission to transfer credits from St. Francis Seminary and the University of Wisconsin to Marquette, and was accepted as a candidate for a master of arts degree in 1919. During that summer and early fall he completed a master's thesis, "The Marxian Theory of History," but the degree apparently was never granted. Haas had already decided to begin doctoral studies elsewhere that fall, and probably considering the master's degree unnecessary, apparently never returned to Marquette to fulfill the final requirements.[47]

Haas's decision to enroll in Catholic University that fall to pursue a doctor's degree in sociology was not difficult to understand. After four years on the seminary faculty, he was convinced that he wanted to remain in education and, already thirty years old, he knew he would have to continue his studies then or not at all. Sociology, the study of social institutions and relationships, was emerging as his primary interest. He had at one time considered further studies in dogmatic theology but, under the influence of Father Roche, Father Dietz, and his father, he was more concerned with the unequal distribution of wealth, the rights of workers to a living wage, and the government's responsibility for the welfare of the poor. When he decided on an advanced degree, Catholic University was probably his first choice. His bishop almost certainly insisted that he attend a Catholic institution, and Catholic University seemed to offer the best education. It was situated in Washington, the center of much political and economic decisionmaking, and Haas would enjoy there the companionship of numerous other graduate-student-priests with similar interests. The university had an especially strong faculty in the social sciences, including John A. Ryan in ethics and social justice.

2

The Disciple of John A. Ryan, 1919-1933

The Catholic University of America, which Father Haas entered in the fall of 1919, was a complex of a dozen buildings on a rolling, 100-acre tract of land in northeast Washington.[1] It had been established by the American hierarchy in 1889, the year of Haas's birth, primarily as an institution where graduates of other Catholic colleges might come for advanced degrees—the capstone of an educational system comprising a broad network of parish grade schools, diocesan high schools, and independent Catholic colleges. By 1919 the university had a faculty of eighty and a graduate and undergraduate enrollment of almost 600. It was divided into five schools: Theology, Philosophy, Law, Letters, and Science; and as the only predominantly graduate institution in American Catholic education, it probably enjoyed the highest reputation of any Catholic college.

Enrolling in the School of Philosophy, with a major in sociology and minors in economics and social psychology, Haas numbered among his professors several of the American Church's most esteemed educators. His major professor was Father John O'Grady, educated at All Hallows College in Dublin, Catholic University of America, the University of Chicago, and Johns Hopkins.[2] He had joined the faculty at Catholic University in 1915, published *A Legal Minimum Wage* that same year, and was to serve for many years as secretary of the National Conference of Catholic Charities and as dean of Catholic University's School of Social Work. Father Haas's second professor in his major field was Father William Kerby, an official of the National Catholic War Council, a member of the District of Columbia Board of Charities in 1920, and the author of several books on social welfare and social justice. Father Edward Pace, Haas's professor of social psychology, had studied at the North American College in Rome and at the University of Leipzig, had served as dean of the School of Philosophy for eight years, and in 1919 was general secretary of the university. Father Haas's professor of economics was Frank O'Hara, a graduate of both the University of Minnesota and the University of Berlin and the author of *Unemployment in Oregon* (1914). *Introduction to Economics* (1915), and *The Non-Partisan League* (1917). His concern for social welfare may have been a family trait, since his brother, Father (later Bishop) Edwin O'Hara, was one of the Church's early champions of unemployment compensation, a leader in the campaign for state minimum wage legislation, and the founder of the Rural Life Bureau of the National Catholic Welfare Conference.

The greatest influence on Haas during his three years at Catholic University, however, was Father John A. Ryan. Educated in the St. Paul archidiocesan seminary and at Catholic University, he had taught in the St. Paul seminary for several years, partici- pated in a highly publicized debate with Socialist leader Morris Hillquit in 1914, and had published *A Living Wage* (1906), *Distrib- utive Justice* (1916), and *The Church and Socialism* (1919). Ryan's deep concern for the rights of workers, the just wage, and government responsibility for the welfare of all would be mirrored in Haas's later activities, and he never minimized the debt he owed to the man he affectionately called "the great John A."[3]

As earlier at St. Francis Seminary, Father Haas was not a brilliant student at Catholic University but he was conscientious and hardworking. The titles of his courses mirrored his particular interests: Justice and Rights in General, The Sociological Aspects of Poverty and Relief, Labor Problems, Justice in the Distribution of Income, Social Legislation, and The Influence of Environment on Personality. His hours were long. "I actually heard the milk trucks coming in from the country," he confided to a sister-in-law after one late-night session.[4] During his third year he also com- muted to Johns Hopkins University each week for a seminar in political economy, directed by Professor George Barnett. He passed all his courses without serious difficulty, but it was ironic that for one who would be known as a labor-priest for much of his life, he received his lowest grades in economics.

Frequent letters from home brought family news and addi- tional cares and concern. Nieces and nephews suffered serious bouts of illness and the family turned almost instinctively to "Father Frank" for support and assistance. The postwar economic instability of 1919-1921 caused worry and unrest. Unemployment in Racine increased, income from the family business fluctuated, and close relatives were often short of cash for needed expenses or tax assessments. The young priest at this time began his frequent practice of sending small sums of money home to assist in emergencies, then borrowing from priest-friends in Washington for his own needs. He rarely complained but his family realized that he was bearing an additional burden. "I know it must be hard for you to be so far away from home and then get such letters," one family member wrote in the winter of 1920.[5]

By engaging in research and collecting data during his summer vacations and during whatever free time he could arrange during the regular school year, Father Haas was able to complete his course work and dissertation in the minimum of three years. *Shop Collective Bargaining: A Study of Wage Determination in the Men's Garment Industry*, published in 1922, was a detailed analysis of the collective bargaining agreements signed by the clothing workers and the garment industry between 1910 and 1919, agreements especially important for setting up arbitration machinery and "courts of first instance" to resolve serious disputes. Although the study was chiefly historical in its treatment of sweatshop conditions in the late nineteenth century, the organization of the United Garment Workers and the Amalgamated Clothing Workers of America, and the provisions of the four major agreements themselves, Haas made little attempt to conceal his pro-labor sympathies and his approval of the principle of arbitration. "In view of the peculiar history of the men's ready-made industry," he stated, "it can hardly be doubted that if the influence of the union were to be diminished to any considerable extent, the industry would tend to fall back into its earlier practices of 'sweating' and long hours." In praise of the industry's arbitration procedures, he suggested that "the trade board by its very presence in the district exercises a silent but potent influence in standardizing local earnings." Proof of this was evident, he added, from the number of disputes formally settled and "from the great mass of potential disputes that are obviated" by the existence of an objective and impartial court of arbitration. The final chapter summarized his conclusions: workers under these agreements were better protected from arbitrary discharge, reduced wages, and unreasonable conditions of work; employers were protected from an unstable labor market and from work stoppages and slowdowns; and the public was protected from any "monopolistic collusion" by labor and industry through the presence of an impartial chairman on each arbitration board.[6] Since they attempted to guarantee the economic rights of both labor and industry and contribute to the common good by promoting full employment and production, the agreements could only meet with Haas's approval.

Father Haas's years in Washington were most successful. He had completed a four-year doctoral program in three years and had become expert in an area—labor relations and social welfare— to which he had long been attracted. He was also well acquainted with Catholic University and many of its faculty and it was to be at this university, and affiliated with this faculty, that he would spend some of the most productive years of his life. His dissertation had made valuable contacts for him among union leaders and government arbitrators, especially Sidney Hillman, William Leiserson, and Harry Millis, and it had convinced him further of the need for arbitration and conciliation machinery in industrial relations.[7]

Leaving Catholic University in the summer of 1922, he returned to St. Francis Seminary and remained there until 1931. He had been away for only three years and was thus rejoining a faculty and student body he knew well and with whom he had worked closely before his departure. His interest in scholarship had deepened and he was anxious to share his interests with others in the classroom. His return to Milwaukee also brought him closer to his family in Racine, and these were to be difficult years for them. A major disappointment—and probably the reason for a brief hesitation before accepting the seminary assignment—was that his classmate and friend of many years, Father Aloysius Muench, was also returning to the seminary faculty with a Ph.D., from the University of Fribourg, and Father Muench had been selected to teach the social sciences.[8]

Father Haas was assigned once again to the Collegiate Department and for the first five years taught the history of philosophy, religion, and English literature. There were at that time approximately 320 students in the seminary and each class numbered about twenty-five. During these years he also taught a course in homiletics (a course in public speaking and the preparation and delivery of sermons). Father Haas, in ever increasing demand as a preacher since his ordination nine years before, found this assignment particularly satisfying. In the fall of 1925 he was appointed dean of the Collegiate Department and Father Muench was named dean of the Seminary or Theological Department. In this position, Father Haas served as a principal adviser to the rector, was responsible for arranging academic schedules, and was able to add some of the social science classes to his schedule, relinquishing his courses in religion and in the history of philosophy. He also served as professor and head of the Department of Sociology at nearby Marquette University from 1922 to 1925, and after 1925 remained at Marquette in a part-time capacity. Although he was disappointed that he was not teaching more of the social sciences at St. Francis Seminary, he saw advantages in his appointment to Marquette. He wrote to Father O'Grady in the fall of 1923:

> My time during the next year will again be divided between Marquette University and the Seminary. I have charge of the Sociology at the University, and am teaching but five hours per week here at the Seminary. From the standpoint of convenience this is not the most satisfactory arrangement, but it keeps me in contact with the city and with people that I would otherwise be out of touch with.[9]

On his return to Milwaukee in 1922, Father Haas was also appointed editor of the seminary quarterly, *The Salesianum*. The journal was officially the publication of the seminary's Alumni Association but it contained scholarly articles and news notices of interest to both alumni and students. Haas retained his earlier interests in literature, philosophy, theology, and other academic disciplines, but the magazine, under his editorial direction, gave increasing emphasis to the social sciences. Unsigned editorials discussed "Unemployment Prevention," "Family Life and Industry," "The Holy Father and World Peace," and "The Child Labor Amendment;" Father Muench contributed several articles on the social teachings of the Church, and Haas himself published at least one major address or article in the journal each year: "The Ethics of Agricultural Cooperative Marketing" in 1925, "Setting Minimum Wages according to Minimum Quantity Standards" in 1926, "The Church, Public Opinion, and Industry" in 1927, and "Social Insurance and Health" in 1928.[10]

At both St. Francis Seminary and Marquette, Father Haas was a popular but demanding teacher. He was well read in both classical and contemporary works in the social sciences—and also in philosophy and theology—and he demanded serious reading from his students. A visitor to one of his classes in 1927 remarked on his "ease in dealing with his students" and his insistence that both sides of each question be examined objectively and honestly and that his students form and defend their own opinions. He was an exacting examiner and, as Bishop William O'Connor, his close friend on the seminary faculty for many years, remarked, "he exercised a strong sense of justice in his marking."[11] His infectious enthusiasm, his wry sense of humor, and his approachability usually guaranteed his classes a good enrollment.

During these nine years on the faculties of St. Francis Seminary and Marquette University, Father Haas retained his attraction for the parish work he had found so satisfying earlier as assistant to Father Roche. He assisted with Saturday confessions and Sunday Masses in local parishes as needed and he was frequently invited to preach parish missions or retreats or deliver evening sermons during Lent. Whatever the request, Father Haas was conscientious in his response. He prepared his sermons diligently, writing them out in longhand, occasionally in several drafts. He consulted the standard works of great preachers and commentaries on Holy Scripture and he noted in the sermon margins the sources of quotations and direct references. Whatever the source of his ideas, his examples and illustrations were often from economic life and social justice, indicative of both his major interest and the influence of his professor of theology, John Ryan. But Haas never confused the pulpit with the classroom and only rarely selected social justice as the theme of his sermons. By the close of the decade, he had compiled a collection of almost two hundred sermons, most written in longhand and many with careful notations of dates and churches where each had been delivered[12]

When Father Haas decided to relinquish his full-time teaching position at Marquette in the fall of 1925 and continue on a part-time basis, it was not only because of his additional responsibilities as dean at St. Francis Seminary. After giving the matter considerable thought, he had decided to prepare a textbook in sociology. His graduate and undergraduate courses at the seminary and the university, his articles and editorials in *The Salesianum*, and the various conferences and conventions he attended throughout the 1920s combined to clarify his views on the nature of man, his rights and responsibilities, the obligations of justice and social welfare, the relations between labor and capital, the problems of agriculture, and the purpose of the state, and these he brought together and summarized in *Man and Society*.

Completed in late 1929 or early 1930, the work, in the author's words, was "the outgrowth of eight years of college work at Marquette University and St. Francis Seminary" and was intended "primarily for college courses in sociology." "The book lays no exaggerated claim to originality," he admitted. "Indeed, it is doubtful whether there is very much that is new to be said regarding man's relations to his fellow man." As a former student of John A. Ryan, the author emphasized the ethical context of social and economic problems and he did not shy away from moral evaluations. "The purpose throughout," he noted, "has been to examine the facts and trends of contemporary society in their moral setting, and to show their agreement or disagreement with sound principles of social welfare."[13]

The book was divided into six major sections. The first, on the individual, included chapters on "The Origin of Man" and the "Human Personality." Haas found the arguments for evolution challenging but inconclusive, but saw no theological difficulty in accepting the theory if scientific evidence were to warrant it. "It is to be emphasized," he stated, "that Catholic teaching insists that mankind has descended from a single pair, and that consequently the human race possesses essential unity. This position is dictated by the Catholic doctrines of Original Sin and the Redemption. . . . So long, therefore, as the scientist admits descent from a single pair, he will find nothing in Catholic teaching to prevent him from holding any theory he chooses regarding the bodily evolution of man." Whatever the origin of the human body, Haas insisted that man's soul is created by God, and it is this immortal soul that gives man his unique dignity. "The sacredness of every person," he stated, "flows from the fact that he possesses a human soul."[14]

The second section, on social virtues, contained chapters on "Rights and Duties," "Justice," and "Charity and Equity." If justice were the basis of all human society, Haas saw charity as its perfection, binding all persons together in love and cooperation as children of God and members of one family. Charity, of course, was not a substitute for justice, and Haas criticized "the pseudo-charity of the philanthropist who donates public parks or libraries out of the fortune which he has amassed by underpaying his workers or by exercising unjust monopoly control over foodstuffs, fuel, and other necessities of life."[15] It was a theme to which Haas would return constantly throughout his life: unless founded on justice, other social virtues are inadequate.

The third section was devoted to the family. Haas reviewed the history of the family from earliest times to the present and concluded that "all existing evidence points to the fact that monogamy, strict or dominant, has existed from the beginning of human history." He strongly defended the indissolubility of marriage, insisting that the granting of "divorce and the legal right to enter a new marriage tends to unsettle even the most firmly established homes, with the result that many husbands and wives are tempted to renounce their family obligations to one another and to their children." "If society permits a divorce and remarriage for any reason whatsoever," he said, "it inflicts a grave injustice on itself, inasmuch as it imperils, and ultimately destroys, the monogamous family."[16]

The fourth section discussed the state—its origin, its obligations to its citizens, and its relations with other states. Rejecting the "social contract" theory on the origin of the state espoused by Hobbes, Locke, and Rousseau, Haas saw the state as ordained by God. "The organization of the state has its foundation in the needs of human beings," he wrote. "Assuming man's creation by God, and taking man as he is found, it follows also that civil society has been established directly by God. Because He created man and placed in him the need, capacity, and inclination to enter into orderly relations with his fellow beings, God is the author of the civil organization called the state." Because he accepted this divine origin of the state, it is not surprising that Haas viewed public service as a valid exercise of a priestly calling. Although the League of Nations was out of favor with many Americans, Haas supported international association and spoke of the "necessity of a world organization of nations."[17]

The final two sections of the book addressed more strictly economic questions: the foundations of private property, the worker's right to a living wage, the problems of the farmer in an industrialized society, and the government's responsibilities toward industrial and agricultural workers.[18] Haas rejected communism and state socialism and insisted that private property was necessary to assure individuals and families the autonomy and security that their God-given dignity demanded. The government, however, could not be indifferent to economic conditions, and the author advocated a national minimum wage law, less reliance on property taxation, lower tariff rates to enable foreign nations more easily to purchase farm produce here, and government assistance to agricultural cooperatives.

Although *Man and Society* was adopted in more than a hundred colleges and was sufficiently successful to warrant a second edition in 1952, it was not a "traditional" introduction to sociology, even for that time. Partly for reasons of space, Haas had been forced to omit discussions of mental health and hygiene, crime and punishment, and immigration; instead, he emphasized areas of his own special interest—justice, the rights of workers, the responsibility of the government for the economy, and international relations. The methodology of the book was not induction or generalization from sociological investigations but more often the application of principles of Christian ethics to social and economic situations. Haas condemned abortion and divorce, found little objection to the arguments of St. Thomas justifying a defensive war, lamented the need for married women to seek employment outside the home, and accepted as his basic tenet the inherent dignity of every person as a child of God. Because of its methodology and its theological and ethical emphases, a contemporary Catholic sociologist pronounced the book "an excellent background for the study of sociology."[19] It is not surprising that the book's index contained more references to the works of John Ryan, a moral theologian, than to any other source, past or contemporary.

A few months after leaving Catholic University, Father Haas received a letter from Father William Kerby which not only indicated the fine impression he had made in Washington but offered a scholarly challenge:

> You have left only the most honorable and creditable memories behind you here. I think that there is much promise of a most useful career, in your character and in your industry and talent. This impression of you which is on my part, most sincere, leads me to offer you one suggestion in line with it. Fight to keep your pen active. Do a research problem every year. You have a rich field in Milwaukee and you now have enthusiasm. If you permit it, duties will multiply, distractions will rob you of concentration. Only a settled determination to remain a scholar and to do scholarly work can save you against the pressure toward practical things found universally acting on efficient priests.[20]

The warning was justified. The pressures and distractions which Father Kerby predicated soon appeared, and Father Haas could seldom refuse. He became a member of the Examining Board of the Milwaukee County Civil Service Commission, a lecturer for Milwaukee's School of Social Work, and secretary of the Milwaukee County Association for the Promotion of Old Age

Pensions. He served on the Catholic Rural Life Conference, the National Conference of Catholic Charities, the National Conference of Social Work, the advisory council of the American Association for Social Security, and he was one of the founders of the Catholic Conference on Industrial Problems. He was also a member of the national advisory board of the League of Nations Association, a director of the Carnegie Peace Foundation, and for a time president of the Catholic Association for International Peace.[21] In all these activities, his two most absorbing interests were the rights of workers and international peace.

After three years of study under John Ryan, it was to be expected that Father Haas would become involved in labor problems on his return to Milwaukee. In 1923 he addressed a group of striking railway switchmen on their rights and responsibilities, and that same year he and Father Aloysius Muench appeared before an assembly of molders to urge them to organize and affiliate with a national union as the best way to strengthen their position at the bargaining table. In late 1924 he was asked to serve as impartial chairman of an arbitration board set up to settle a wage dispute between the typographical union's Milwaukee local and the Milwaukee Newspaper Publishers' Association. The panel heard evidence from both sides, discussed various awards, and after three weeks of deliberation granted the workers a wage increase of approximately 4 percent. The award was apparently satisfactory to both sides, since it was not challenged, and in fact was signed without dissent by all five members of the arbitration panel.[22]

Soon after his return to Milwaukee in the fall of 1922, Father Haas also began to campaign for a state unemployment compensation law. State Senator H. A. Huber introduced such a bill the following year and Haas immediately supported it through articles in secular and religious journals.[23] On February 20, he joined University of Wisconsin Professor John R. Commons and others in testifying before the Senate Judiciary Committee in Madison. He insisted that "our theory of government is essentially one of equality of opportunity" and "where...we have the condition that over eight per cent of Wisconsin wage earners are normally unemployed... it is clear that we are confronted with a matter of fundamental justice." He admitted that the dollar-a-day compensation in the bill was in no way sufficient for livelihood, but he emphasized that the purpose of this compensation was to prevent unemployment rather than assist those out of work. "Its aim," he stated, "is to ultimately eliminate paying the dollar-per-day benefits and to have industry regulate itself so that the worker is given an opportunity to work." In light of the Depression, which struck six years later, one portion of his testimony was particularly significant:

> The Huber bill goes to the root of the evil of unemployment.... It will require the employer to estimate more carefully the demands for his product and will prevent him from unwise enlargement of his plant when everyone is talking of high prices and high profits. Quite clearly prices cannot move upward indefinitely during such times, and moreover, the higher the swing, the deeper the fall, and the deeper the fall, the greater the reduction of income to the employer, and the more widespread the suffering of unemployment among wage-earners.[24]

Although it failed of passage that year, Father Haas often used the Huber bill of 1923 as an example of legitimate government intervention in the economy.

At the same time that Father Haas was campaigning for unemployment compensation in Madison, he was assisting in the foundation of a national organization whose purpose was to make American Catholics more aware of the social teachings of the Church. On December 29, 1922, he and approximately one hundred other participants met at Loyola University in Chicago under the auspices of Father John A. Ryan and the Social Action Department of the National Catholic Welfare Conference to found the Catholic Conference on Industrial Problems. Its membership was to be open to all Catholics, annual dues were $1, and its goal was "to discuss and promote the study and understanding of industrial problems." Professor David R. McCabe of Princeton was elected president and Father Raymond McGowan, of the NCWC, secretary-treasurer.[25] In an editorial in the next issue of *The Salesianum*, Father Haas elaborated on its purpose:

> It is generally admitted that the ethical doctrines of the Church must be known and accepted before there can be any permanent peaceful relations between capital and labor. Socialism emphasizes the differences between the employer and the wage-earner, and would keep them apart through the medium of the class struggle. The Church stresses the interests they have in common and endeavors to bring them

together in harmonious cooperation. This is precisely the work that the Catholic Conference on Industrial Problems will seek to do in a practical way.[26]

The constitution of the Catholic Conference provided for "annual meetings for the discussion of industrial problems" and "the formation of local conferences and other organizations for industrial study and discussion." Through the efforts of Father Haas and on the invitation of Archbishop Sebastian Messmer, the first national convention was held in Milwaukee in June of the following year, with "Wages," "Collective Bargaining," "The State and Industry," "The Worker and Ownership," and "Women in Industry" as general topics of discussion.[27] From this Milwaukee conference, the CCIP gradually expanded into other areas of the country and Father Haas was rarely absent from its national and local conferences over the next twenty-five years. He felt it was one of the urgent needs of the times to bring Christian moral teachings to bear on American social and economic life and he saw the Catholic Conference on Industrial Problems as one means of furthering this. Whenever he was called on in later years to submit autobiographical data, he almost invariably noted that he was a "Founding Member of the Catholic Conference on Industrial Problems."

A second major interest of Father Haas during these years was world peace and international economic cooperation. He published editorials in *The Salesianum* on international justice and morality, addressed civic and religious groups in Milwaukee on disarmament, and was a member of the Carnegie Church Peace Union and the League of Nations Association in the 1920s and the World Alliance for International Friendship through the Churches in the 1930s.[28] His most significant achievement in this area, however, was his leadership in the newly organized Catholic Association for International Peace.

Under the sponsorship once again of John A. Ryan and the Social Action Department of the NCWC, this organization had been founded at Catholic University in 1927 "to seek to educate Catholics and non-Catholics on the Catholic point of view on international affairs, as drawn from what the Holy Fathers, the Bishops of the United States, and Catholic scholars had said on the principles of attaining world peace through justice and charity." It hoped to do this through publicizing papal pronouncements on world peace, circulating pamphlets and articles, and sponsoring local and national conferences. Other early leaders of the CAIP included Bishop Thomas Shahan, rector of Catholic University, Fathers Robert Lucey and John LaFarge, S.J., George Shuster of *Commonweal*, and historians Parker Moon and Carlton J. H. Hayes.[29]

For the first three or four years of its existence, the activities of the CAIP occupied a considerable portion of Father Haas's time. Judge Martin Manton of New York, elected president for 1927-28, was succeeded by Carlton J. H. Hayes, and then Father Haas was elected president for two terms, 1929-31. He was the first priest elected to the association's highest office and the first president to be reelected to a second term. For two years he represented the association at peace parlays across the country, strove to bring the principles of disarmament and international peace before a wider circle of priests and laity, and encouraged Catholic colleges and secondary schools to establish annual Peace Days, perhaps during Armistice Week, for lectures, readings, and group discussions on the Church's teachings on justice and international cooperation. He attended international peace conferences at Frankfort in the summer of 1929 and Geneva in 1930, and he returned to Geneva in the summer of 1932 for a meeting of the board of directors of the Church Peace Union. Never neglecting his interest in labor, he arranged his European trips to permit visits to Berlin, Paris, and London in order to study economic conditions and the wages and hours of labor firsthand in these major industrial centers.[30]

Father Haas's views on disarmament, economic cooperation, and the attainment of international peace were spelled out in several speeches he delivered as president of the CAIP from 1929 to 1931. He insisted that war could no longer be considered a reasonable alternative in international policy. "The sanctity of the human person," he stated in 1931, "and its inherent rights to development must be safeguarded at all costs. Organized life in society is possible on no other assumption. Goods, lands, mines, forests, and factories, are immeasurably less valuable than any one person, to say nothing of thousands of persons; and hence it is not only murder, but multiplied murder, to undertake a war, merely for the sake of oil, coal, rubber, or diamonds."[31]

The alternative, however, was not strict pacifism. "War may be necessary in some instances," he admitted in a 1930 speech. "I am not a pacifist—I believe there are certain things that are more sacred than my life. There are things that I would rather die than submit to. Every reasonable man must take this position:

his family and their honor he must be ready to die for; and men do die for these sanctities." But twentieth-century warfare might have made this position purely theoretical. "War, like a surgical operation, may be necessary in some cases," he suggested, "but when it is certain that the operation means death for the patient, it is not allowed. Likewise when a whole race will be exterminated by war, war is not allowed." "War today," he noted in the same address, "means extinction.... A city of the size of New York can be blotted out in a single air raid in less than an hour."[32]

Unable to accept absolute pacifism, Father Haas championed collective security. War could be avoided, he insisted, only if all nations, including the United States, shed their isolationism and agreed upon increased economic cooperation and less political autonomy. "What moralists in too many instances have failed to consider sufficiently," he stated in 1926, "is the economic character of war among civilized peoples." Nations were so dependent upon each other economically that war among a few immediately affected all, and eventually every nation of the world had a serious economic stake in final victory or defeat. "Today the nations are suffering from a degenerate and perverted form of patriotism called nationalism," he declared in an Armistice Day address in 1930. "In practical life it is the attempts of peoples to make themselves economically and culturally self-sufficient—an impossible task in the integrated world of the twentieth century." Some form of world integration was necessary. He championed the Kellogg-Briand Pact, the League of Nations, the permanent Court of International Justice, and the arbitration of international disputes. "Sooner or later," he predicted, "all nations, and especially the United States, must come into the League; and if not into the League, into something identical with the League bearing some other name." The only alternative to international cooperation was wasteful and foolish arms competition, and that, he suggested, was like trying to assure safety on the highways by building ever faster, heavier, and wider cars. The ultimate goal of all political and economic cooperation, of course, was world peace, "a state of order, governed by reason and justice tempered with the charity of Christ. For the realization of these high ideals the world in its better moments is yearning."[33]

If Father Haas's life was not sufficiently occupied in the years after his return from Washington with his teaching and administrative duties at St. Francis Seminary and Marquette, his public lectures and writings, and his numerous activities in labor mediation and international peace, responsibilities to his family in Racine absorbed whatever leisure remained. His father had sold his grocery business on the corner of North Main and Hubbard in 1919 and opened a pickle and vinegar processing plant in the brick building he owned next door. For almost three years the Haas family continued to live above the corner store, while renting the first floor to others who operated the grocery. In 1922, Allen and his father decided to convert the grocery into a pharmacy and the new store was opened in early May, with Allen's brother-in-law, William Sweetman, as manager. The pharmacy prospered initially, but remained an additional source of worry and uncertainty.[34]

Despite economic instability throughout the decade, Peter Haas's financial situation remained comfortable. He took little interest in the drugstore and left its operation almost entirely to Allen and his brother-in-law. The pickle factory absorbed most of his attention. He rose early each day and began work at about 5:30 with one or two assistants. Either he or Margaret or Peter drove to Milwaukee and Kenosha each week to take orders and make deliveries, and he took personal charge of the large sales in Racine. Many hours each week went into office work and bookkeeping: how many bushels of pickles or "cukes" to buy from each farmer, how many to dill, how many barrels of vinegar to put up, how much credit to extend, and how to collect back bills in times of economic slowdown and unemployment. His life, of course, was not all work, and if family, business and politics were Peter Haas's chief interests, rummy and solitaire were not far behind. He liked to spend the evenings playing rummy with Pete or a neighbor or one or two grandchildren, and if no one else was home he enjoyed playing solitaire by the hour. By the middle of the decade he had learned the German favorite, *Schafkopf* or Sheepshead, and this replaced rummy as the regular evening pastime.[35]

Allen Haas, after graduating from Marquette University with a degree in pharmacy, returned to Racine and worked for eight years as an assistant pharmacist. He married Elizabeth Sweetman in St. Patrick's Church in early 1917 and the following year opened a drugstore in the 1800 block of Northwestern Avenue, approximately a mile from the Haas homestead. Allen and Bess eventually had six children—Jeanette, Allen, Jr., James, Robert, Dorothy, and Arthur—although Jeanette, the oldest daughter, died before her second birthday.[36] In that age of home remedies, most of the family turned instinctively to Al in times of sickness and he seemed ever willing to provide the proper tonics, pills, and advice. As time went on, Allen, inheriting much of his father's business acumen, took on more responsibility for the family finances and frequently offered his counsel on questions of tax assessments, insurance premiums, and credit rates. Allen and Francis became particularly close, not only because of their ages, their association with Marquette, and their mutual friends, but because, as their father's health began to fail in the late 1920s, they shared greater responsibility for family decisions.

Allen's twin brother, Arthur, had married Elizabeth Noe in the spring of 1912, the year before Francis's ordination, but misfortune and tragedy struck their lives with cruel regularity. Four children were born to them—Frances, Mary, Billy, and Dick-- but the eldest died at the age of five months. Arthur worked in his father's grocery, and it was on a business trip to Milwaukee in 1919 that tragedy struck for the second time. While standing beside his car in a service station, he was hit by a truck and dragged several feet before the driver realized what had happened. He was rushed to a Milwaukee hospital, and though one leg was amputated immediately, his condition deteriorated. He languished in the hospital for two weeks and Father Frank was summoned from his studies in Washington to be at his side. Despite the doctors' efforts, gangrene could not be checked and, with his family gathered in the sickroom, Arthur died in early May. His young widow could never forget: "I could see his poor suffering face," she wrote Francis a year later, "the way I saw it when I was down that Saturday when he was so bad and I could just feel him take my face in his hands and tell me I would have to carry all the burdens alone. I was glad no one was home with me so I could cry."[37]

With Arthur's death, Elizabeth and the three children moved in with Mr. Haas, Margaret, and Peter, Jr., in the flat above the grocery. Father Haas was still a student at Catholic University and Liz's letters, although tributes to his concern and devotion, must have added to his burdens. "I only wish you could finish soon and be nearer the children," she wrote in 1921. "They really seem better when they see you once in a while." On another occasion, shortly after Father Haas had returned to Washington from a Christmas visit to Racine, she wrote: "After you went yesterday he [Billy] said to me, 'Mother, I like you best of anybody and then I like Father Frank. I wish he didn't have to go away all the time.' Then he started to cry and I said, 'Never mind, Billy, someday Father Frank will stay with you but he has to study now.'" Billy, in fact, never enjoyed good health. He suffered a nervous disorder during these years, lost at least two years of school, and spent long periods in hospitals and sanitariums, some as far away as Madison. Arthur's death, of course, increased the family's financial difficulties and Father Haas was called on more and more to assist from his limited resources.[38]

Living conditions in Racine were far from ideal. The three lively children found the second floor accommodations crowded and restrictive, neither Margaret nor her father were accustomed to small children that close, and friction soon developed between Margaret and Liz. After two years of painful negotiations, the Federal Rubber Company, whose truck had struck Arthur, paid his widow and children $7,700 in compensation, and using part of this money, Liz and her father-in-law purchased a larger home on Barker Street, about two blocks from the pickle factory and the drugstore. Margaret apparently did not move with them but decided to enter nurses' training at St. Catherine's Hospital in Kenosha. From that time on, Liz was further bothered by the thought that she and her children may have been the cause of the family breakup, and these and other fears she confided in her almost weekly letters to Father Frank. "I do everything I can for him [Mr. Haas]," she wrote in 1922, "to make up for Margaret being away but I always did that, even when she was home, and he said to me right after I bought this place, 'Well, Lizzie, no matter who goes back on you, I'll always stick with you,' and believe me it made me feel good."[39]

Liz never seemed to recover from the shock of Arthur's death. "I was telling Margaret yesterday," she wrote in 1920, "that so often during the day I think that Art is just gone like he use to go when he took orders and when it gets near supper time I begin to look and wait for him and then I begin to realize he is not coming and I get such a longing for him that sometimes I think I can't stand it another minute. . . . Father Frank, I know I can never be happy again until I am with him so please pray hard for me as I am afraid I am getting worse instead of better. It just seems as though my heart is aching all the time." Liz's health finally broke in the late 1920s and she died of tuberculosis in February 1930, only a few years younger than Francis's mother when she died. Before her death, Liz had appointed Francis guardian of her three children and she left her estate to him in trust. Billy and Richard continued to live with their grandfather in the Barker Street home, but life was not always pleasant. Peter Haas was then seventy years old; Margaret, at home again, was forty-three and unmarried, and neither was well suited to guide two young teenagers who had recently lost their parents. Mary lived with her maternal grandmother in Racine for short periods each year, after enrolling as a boarding student in Mount Mary College in Milwaukee in the fall of 1931. Financial responsibility for his brother's children during these early Depression days was an additional burden on Father Haas's strained budget, but he remained a source of support and family joy. His coat pockets bulged with Hershey bars on each visit, he always had new and fascinating stories to share, and he thoroughly enjoyed the antics of each growing child.[40]

Margaret, Francis's older sister, continued to offer assistance. Never married, she remained at home to take care of the house for her father and to assist in the grocery or with the pickle and vinegar sales. She had been thirty-four years old when she entered the three-years nurses' training program in Kenosha in 1921, and upon graduation she served chiefly as a private nurse, often on special duty in the Catholic hospitals in Kenosha or Racine, living sometimes at home and sometimes away. She remained close to her father and to all the Haas and O'Day relatives throughout her life, assisted them in periods of illness, and regularly kept her brother informed of local and family events through frequent, newsy letters.[41]

Amy, Father Frank's younger sister, had married Joseph Kloss in 1917 and moved to Kenosha, where her husband was employed by the Simmons Manufacturing Company. They had four children—Francis, Jane, Donald, and Judith—although Francis died in infancy. Their early years were difficult also and Father Haas was able to advance small loans to assist them over periods of illness or other emergencies. Despite the distance, Amy kept close contact with the rest of the family. Margaret or Peter generally visited Kenosha once a week to take orders for pickles and vinegar, and Amy and the children would often return to Racine to spend a day or two with her father. Slightly removed from day-to-day events in Racine, she could view the family situation more objectively, and her brothers and sister, consequently, often relied on her advice.[42]

Peter Haas, Jr., the youngest in the family, had graduated from Racine High School in 1911 and remained at home for several years, working in the grocery until it was sold and then assisting in the pickle factory. His health was not robust and his frequent bouts of illness kept him occasionally from work. He married in the mid-1920s, and he, Irene, and their two children lived for a time in the apartment above the grocery before moving into their own home a few blocks away. Peter continued to work in the factory, handling accounts, taking orders, and making deliveries, and he gradually assumed more and more responsibility as his father's health declined.[43]

In the spring of 1929, while teaching and serving as dean of the Collegiate Department and completing the draft of *Man and Society*, Father Haas was recommended for appointment to the Faculty of Theology at Catholic University in Washington. A second professor was needed to share moral theology courses with John Ryan, and Ryan suggested Haas. The two discussed the proposal in Washington that April and, deeply honored by the recommendation of one he esteemed so highly, Father Haas requested and was granted a leave of absence from the seminary in Milwaukee. "Let me assure you," he wrote Ryan in late April, "that I deeply appreciate the initiative that you have taken in this matter and that I shall do my best not to disappoint you." Ryan was equally pleased. "I am sure," he replied, "that I do not need to express again my great satisfaction that you are to be affiliated with The Catholic University and [become] a fellow worker in my department."[44]

After these preliminary steps, however, the rector of the university, Monsignor James Hugh Ryan, began to hesitate. He had given tentative approval to the appointment, but on receiving the unanimous recommendation of the department faculty in Haas's favor, he raised the objection that Haas's degree was not in theology but in sociology. "In my last letter," John Ryan wrote, "I said that I thought the Rector would accept the recommendation of the Faculty of Theology that you be engaged as Instructor in Moral Theology next year at the University. However, I was mistaken in that assumption." Ryan then asked if Haas would spend the next year in Rome, studying for a doctor's degree in theology, and return to the university the following September. After further discussion, Father Haas agreed. "I have been delighted," he confided to Ryan, "at the prospect of working in your department from the first moment that you suggested the idea. Leaving St. Francis Seminary means some sacrifices for me, but I was willing and am willing to make them in view of the great amount of work to be done in social ethics and the fewness of the priests to do it."[45]

It was discovered, however, that the rector had only promised to place his name on the list of eligible applicants on his return from Rome, and Father Haas considered this unacceptable. "I have thought over the contents of your last letter," he wrote to Father John Ryan in June, "and have come to the conclusion that under the conditions laid down by the Rector, I do not wish to go to Rome next year. The conditions that the Rector makes are such, it seems to me, that he is not held to much of anything a year hence. I would be binding myself, whereas he would be binding himself to practically nothing." But Haas did not give up hope: "Somehow I feel that conditions at the University will change, so that you will be given some degree of freedom in building up your department. When that time comes, if you are still interested in what I may be able to do, let me assure you that my sentiments will be no different then from what they are now."[46]

Father Haas noted in that same letter, however, that at a recent meeting of the American Catholic Philosophical Association the rector had commented on the liberal economic views he had expressed during one of the sessions. "It was an innocent remark," Haas admitted, "but perhaps was significant of his position." Ryan thought it significant too. The rector was fearful, he wrote to Father McGowan, "that with Father Haas at the University there would be an increase in the amount of economic discussion and teaching in the institution. That might discourage big donations. Every time when we discussed the subject the Rector said that if Father Haas should come to the University he would have to confine himself to Moral Theology and refrain from economic activities. The terms upon which he finally consented to consider the appointment of Father Haas were clearly intended to be impossible of acceptance. . . . Obviously the reply given by Father Haas is the only one that a self-respecting person could give."[47]

Father Haas was undoubtedly disappointed with this turn of events, but the situation was remedied two years later. In the summer of 1931, probably on the recommendation of Ryan, O'Grady and Kerby, Father Haas was appointed director of the National Catholic School of Social Service in Washington, succeeding Father Karl J. Alter, who had been appointed bishop of Toledo.[48] The School of Social Service had been founded under the auspices of the National Catholic War Council in 1918 by

Father John J. Burke, C.S.P., originally to train young women for
social work during the World War.[49] Called at first the National
Service School for Women, the school was located on the spacious
Clifton estate in the Georgetown Heights section of Washington,
just off Massachusetts Avenue, but its formal opening, unfortunately, did not take place until November 25, two weeks after
the armistice was signed. Father Burke, executive secretary of the
NCWC, assumed overall direction of the school, and Miss Maud
Cavanaugh of the NCWC's New York office was hired as dean.
The school's first academic program was brief—only a five-week
session—and by mid-January 1919, the first twenty-eight "graduates" were ready for public service. Nine of these women—"Father
Burke's girls," as they were affectionately called—were sent to
France that March to assist NCWC's European offices in bringing
relief to the suffering and homeless in war-torn countries, and
nineteen remained at home to work in military establishments,
community centers, and girls' clubs along the East Coast.

In June 1919, Father Burke received permission from the
NCWC to continue the new school on a permanent basis, without
reference to war-time service. Although he and others would have
preferred formal academic affiliation with an established college
or university, Catholic University was not a coeducational institution at that time and thus the new school had to be established
independently; it eventually received authority to grant its own
degrees. From the very beginning, however, several of Catholic
University's most outstanding professors, John Ryan and John
O'Grady among them, also taught part time at the Service School.
In 1921, the newly founded National Council of Catholic Women
assumed sponsorship of the school and assisted in transferring it
from the Clifton estate to the old Bristol School complex on
19th Street, along Rock Creek Park. Two years later it gained
much-needed academic recognition when Catholic University
agreed to accept the young school as an affiliate and award a
master of arts degree to qualified graduates. That same year,
three outstanding Catholic scholars—Carlton Hayes of Columbia,
Robert Lord of Harvard, and David McCabe of Princeton—accepted appointments to the school's board of trustees.[50]

The duties of director, which Father Haas assumed in 1931,
were summarized in a letter he received from Father Burke:

> The office and responsibility of the Director of the School
> is as follows: the care of the School is in his hands. He has
> charge of the faculty, the curriculum, the admission of

students, the finances; and is responsible to no one except the Board of Trustees of the School. The Director must be willing to teach at the School also, and take a leading interest in those matters that concern the welfare of the School's future—funds for endowment and Scholarship.... The Director has full charge of the finances of the School within the budget he himself compiles and submits for the approval of the Board.... He also has the duty of recommending the professors and instructors and of arranging the salaries thereof.[51]

Father Haas held this position during four Depression years, 1931 to 1935, although, because of his government work after the summer of 1933, he could then devote less time to the school's daily administration. The school at this time, known as the "N-C-Triple-S," was a well-regimented academic and residential institution. It comprised three separate but interconnected buildings on the two-acre property overlooking Rock Creek Park: the four-story main classroom and residence building on 19th Street; a smaller, three-story building, called Mintwood, housing the dining room, faculty residences, and by the 1930s a few student rooms; and a house on 20th Street which served as a residence and business office for Father Burke and other members of NCWC's administrative offices. Although most of the students were in their twenties and were college graduates, hours for rising and retiring were strictly prescribed. Students were not to be out after eleven o'clock, or midnight on special occasions, and latecomers were admitted through locked doors by a faculty member. Since Father Burke, chaplain of the school since 1918, was beginning to suffer from the poor health that would cause his death five years later, the director by 1931 had to assume more and more of the chaplain's duties, including the offering of daily Mass, which most of the students by long custom attended.[52]

The school offered a two-year academic program, leading to a diploma in social service at the end of the first year and, on submission of a thesis, to a master's degree from Catholic University at the end of the second, although less than one-third of the school's fifty students were able to return for the second year in the early 1930s. Classes were taught on four mornings—Monday, Tuesday, Friday, and Saturday in 1933-1934, for example—with most classes meeting twice each week. Wednesdays and Thursdays were set aside for directed field work. A full-time supervisor of field work was hired in 1933 and students were assigned to various social welfare agencies in the Washington area for first-hand observation and practical experience: the Juvenile Protective Association, the Bureau of Emergency Relief, the Bureau of Public Welfare, St. Elizabeth's Hospital, Georgetown University Hospital Clinic, the Christ Child Settlement, and the Washington Mental Hygiene Association. Most afternoons and evenings were set aside for class preparation and individual study. In his annual report of 1934, Father Haas noted proudly that all the students who had left the school the preceding June, after one or two years of study, had found regular employment almost immediately.[53]

As director of the school from 1931 to 1935, Father Haas presided over a dual faculty. Fathers John Ryan, William Kerby, Thomas Verner Moore, and Paul Hanly Furfey retained their positions on the faculty of Catholic University but offered basic courses each year at the School of Social Service in moral philosophy, sociology, psychiatry, and social research. The full-time faculty, often women who also accepted accommodations at Mintwood House, offered service-oriented courses in public health and hygiene, community organization, and social group work, and assisted in supervision of the students' case work and community service. Father Haas offered courses in economics, emphasizing the basic principles of economics and the specific contributions organized labor and government agencies could and should make toward a more equitable economic order. During his tenure as director, Father Haas introduced significant revisions in the academic curriculum; he insisted on an A.B. degree for admission and instituted comprehensive examinations for the master's degree in 1932, added formal religion courses to the curriculum in 1933, and introduced five major areas of specialization for students in their final year: family welfare, child welfare, hospital social service, psychiatric social service, and community organization.[54]

Father Haas's responsibility as director of the NCSSS was further complicated in the fall of 1934, when Catholic University announced establishment of its own School of Social Work, with Father John O'Grady, Father Haas's major professor twelve years earlier, as director. Since the affiliation in 1923, Catholic University had been awarding master of arts degrees to graduates of the National Catholic School of Social Service, and it was now proposing to offer a master of science degree to graduates in its own School of Social Work. The American Association of Schools of Social Work, a professional accrediting agency, questioned this duplication of degrees but did not order changes. A principal reason for establishing the new School of Social Work was the need to provide a program in social work for men, both priests and laymen, preparing for positions in social agencies, and the NCSSS admitted only women. Since 1930, however, Catholic University accepted graduate women, and Father O'Grady envisioned his new school as coeducational. Some preferred to merge the NCSSS with the new School of Social Work, but the deed of incorporation seemed to stipulate that, on loss of its independent status, the school's buildings and other assets would return to the National Council of Catholic Women. At meetings and discussions throughout the spring and summer of 1934, agreement was reached whereby the university's School of Social Work would admit only men and religious women, while lay women would continue to be admitted exclusively into the National Catholic School of Social Service.[55]

Father Haas's major concern as director of the NCSSS from 1931 to 1935, however, was not caused by Father O'Grady and Catholic University but by the economic upheaval of the Depression. Operating expenditures averaged over $55,000 annually, and since tuition receipts rarely exceeded $35,000, between $20,000 and $30,000 had to be solicited in gifts to maintain a balanced budget. With other jobs scarce and social workers in wide demand, applications for admission increased and student enrollment rose from thirty-five to over fifty in the early 1930s, but almost all students needed financial assistance and scholarship funds were never sufficient. Father Haas continued the program, begun by Father Alter, of transferring scholarship funds into loans, hoping that, as loans were paid back in succeeding years, additional funds could continually be made available. Father Haas also opened the school to more part-time and nondegree students, since city and federal employees, seeking additional course work, could bring in needed revenue without seriously increasing costs. For example, an extension course was opened in March 1934 for case workers in the Federal Relief Administration and more than one hundred and fifty registered immediately. The NCSSS had begun a significant publication program in the late 1920s but this had to be curtailed due to lack of finances, a decision especially difficult for the former editor of *The Salesianum*. But Father Haas refused to let financial difficulties interfere with his students' community service. "Despite its own precarious position during the crisis of the 30's," one historian has written, "the School never relaxed in its own imperative sense of community respon-sibility." As its name suggested, the primary goal of NCSSS was social service, and Father Haas, devoting more and more of his own time to public service, insisted on that priority.[56]

During his four years as director, Father Haas made several lasting contributions to the school's organization and structure. He inaugurated reform in the school's system of scholarships and financial aid, interested the Daughters of Isabella in establishing a $100,000 foundation at the school, relaxed the school's resi-dence requirements to permit admission of interested Washington social workers as part-time students, and raised the school to full graduate status by requiring a bachelor's degree or its equiva-lent for admission.[57] During these years, also, Father Haas gave evidence of a characteristic that he was to exhibit for the rest of his life—an ill-disguised dislike of administrative duties. Although he proved to be a competent and effective administrator in his ecclesiastical posts, he never felt at ease behind an executive desk and he delegated his administrative duties to others whenever possible.

Despite the many contributions Father Haas made to the School of Social Service during his four years as director, it is possible that the school made even more to him. Although well known among Catholic educators as a respected sociologist, he had little national reputation before 1931. In the public eye, his appointment to the National Catholic School of Social Service gave him official stature, similar to that of John O'Grady of the National Conference of Catholic Charities and John A. Ryan of the NCWC's Social Action Department. When Franklin Roosevelt began recruiting officials and advisers for his New Deal programs in the spring of 1933, Father Haas, director of the National Catholic School of Social Service, was not only close at hand but was becoming recognized, along with Father O'Grady and Father Ryan, as one of the nation's leading authorities in social justice and social reform.

3

The Philosophy of a New Dealer, 1933

The band of presidential advisers and government administrators that descended upon Washington with the election of Franklin Roosevelt in 1932 was a curious and controversial lot. "A plague of young lawyers," George Peek called them. "They floated airily into offices, took desks, asked for papers and found no end of things to be busy about. I never found out why they came, what they did, or why they left." A cynical John T. Flynn described them as Washington's "Great Minds and Deep Thinkers—youthful pundits from Harvard and Yale and Princeton and especially Columbia, with charts and equations; cornfield philosophers from Kansas and California and of course, the unconquerable champions of all the money theories." New Deal historian Basil Rauch considered them "a corps of experts," but to Forrest Davis they were "the Commissariat of the New Deal, a rising clique busily absorbing power." The *Literary Digest* found them "impractical most of the time, too much devoted to untried theories and to certain disquieting 'isms,'" but in general "an intelligent, an unselfish, an honest, and a loyal lot."[1]

Loyal or subversive, experts or pundits, these New Deal advisers formed an exciting, disorganized, and wholly unlikely political team. They ranged from the brilliantly educated Rexford Tugwell to the self-made Louis Howe, from immigrant labor leader Sidney Hillman to millionaire industrialist Gerard Swope, from Bull Moose Progressive Harold Ickes to Wilsonian Democrat Homer Cummings and Harding Republican William Woodin, from the youthful James M. Landis to the septuagenarian Claude Swanson, and from Lee Pressman on the left to Lew Douglas on the right. They had been recruited from every section of the country, from different social classes, from a variety of educational backgrounds, from both major parties and several minor ones, and their social and economic theories were understandably as conflicting and controversial as the New Deal itself.[2]

It was into this bewildering swirl of contradictory policies and incompatible personalities that Father Haas was gradually drawn in the 1930s. Although Wisconsin newspapers later referred to him on occasion as a member of the early Brain Trust, Father Haas was never one of the president's close advisers.[3] He was primarily a man of action, not ideas, an implementer, not an originator. One is reminded of Justice Oliver Wendell Holmes's appraisal of the president himself: "A first-class temperament, but a second-class intellect." Haas was in no sense a second-class intellect but his intellectual contribution to the New Deal always remained secondary. His influence during the 1930s was chiefly that of a public servant, assisting and implementing the government policies that other officials—the Brain Trusters and the idea men—had formulated.

Father Haas undoubtedly possessed a first-class temperament. He was an impressive man physically: six feet tall, broad shouldered, and weighing over two hundred pounds. His full head of sandy hair earned him the name "Red" Haas long before conservative industrialists adopted it to reflect what they thought were socialistic labor views. His face, large and full, was lined with wrinkles, "as though he carried the worries of the whole world," one secretary remarked, but they added to the warmth of his friendly smile and ready wink.[4] As a seminary professor of public speaking, he possessed a deep, resonant, well-disciplined voice, and his diction was precise and unhurried. Like his close friends John Ryan and Raymond McGowan, he was less than fastidious about pressed suits and shined shoes; one longtime associate suggested that he seemed to "cultivate sloppiness."[5] His favorite pastime was reading, especially history, biography, and the classics of English and American literature. His love of books, in fact, was almost an addiction, and even on his busiest government trips he would steal away for an afternoon to browse through second-hand bookstores. He appreciated good cigars and an occasional drink and, like his father, he liked to relax for an evening of cards with close friends, especially if a few pennies rode on each hand. He followed major league baseball and college football and enjoyed an occasional round of golf. He had a quiet though ready sense of humor and a disarming modesty, and he was one of those rare individuals who seem to have an instinctive interest in everyone they meet. Sympathetic and unassuming, he remained above all a priest, dedicating his life to the service of God and his fellow men. In a public servant, this was undoubtedly a "first-class temperament."

Despite his years as university professor and his numerous publications, however, Haas's intellectual or scholarly contributions to the New Deal were probably secondary. He was a serious student of social questions but he did not possess the brilliant or creative mind of a Rexford Tugwell, an Adolf Berle, a Jerome Frank, or a John Ryan. He was comfortable and at home in the world of ideas, but they were usually ideas that others had originated. His governmental and ecclesiastical appointments, furthermore, combined to deny him the leisure that a creative intellectual life requires. In addition to his many government positions from 1933 until his death in 1953, he served as director of the National Catholic School of Social Service, rector of St. Francis Seminary, dean of the School of Social Science at Catholic University, and bishop of a sprawling midwestern diocese. Even if Father Haas had the time and the talent, however, it is unlikely that he would have devoted himself primarily to scholarship. His chief concern throughout the 1930s and 1940s was more and more with the social and economic injustices suffered by American wage earners; and the remedies for these injustices, he felt, had already been suggested by liberal social philosophers like Pope Leo XIII, John Hobson, Richard T. Ely, and John A. Ryan. Haas's published works, consequently, are often popularizations of the teachings of others—textbook surveys of Catholic social doctrine, pamphlets intended for parish book racks and wide distribution among the Catholic laity, and public addresses reprinted in popular journals. But Haas did possess a consistent and well-thought-out philosophy of social justice, no less real because it was derived from others, and in the possession of this consistent philosophy he probably differed from most other New Deal advisers, and even from the president himself.

The greatest influences on Father Haas's social and economic thought in the 1930s were undoubtedly the encyclicals *Rerum Novarum* of Pope Leo XIII and *Quadragesimo Anno* of Pope Pius XI.[6] *Rerum Novarum* had been issued in 1891, when the spread of laissez-faire liberalism and the concentration of financial and industrial power in the hands of a few made the economic conditions of workingmen more and more intolerable. The pope had defended the right of private ownership against the attacks of socialism, but he had insisted that workers had equally inviolable rights—to a living wage, reasonable hours, and respectable conditions of work—and these rights, he declared, could be adequately secured chiefly through "workmen's associations" and social legislation. Forty years later, Pope Pius XI published his encyclical *Quadragesimo Anno*, "On the Reconstruction of the Social Order." He restated Pope Leo's teachings on wages, hours, unions, and legislation, but noted that recent events—the Crash of 1929 and the Depression that followed—had revealed further weaknesses in modern economic life which the recommendations of his predecessor alone could not cure. As an additional step, the pontiff proposed the reorganization of society according to the "Occuptional Group System," a program whereby conditions of work, production schedules, and other economic factors would be determined by tripartite boards from industry, labor, and the public. Insisting that society must be founded upon the virtues of justice and charity, both pontiffs concluded their encyclicals with a plea for the moral and religious conversion of mankind to accompany social and economic reform.

Papal encyclicals, however, like political constitutions and judicial decisions, are subject to conflicting interpretations, and the writings of Popes Leo and Pius were no exception. American Catholics were divided over the compatibility of capitalism with Pope Pius's "New Social Order." Conservative Catholics insisted that the American economic system already conformed in essentials to the teachings of the social encyclicals. Throughout the 1930s, Cardinal William O'Connell of Boston and Patrick Scanlon of the *Brooklyn Tablet*, among others, saw the threat of communism principally in efforts to tamper with the free-enterprise system. There was "complete recognition" in *Quadragesimo Anno*, one author stated, that "freedom of private initiative, the accumulation of resources and values, and individual rights are the very springs of social well-being and progress." "Why then should we be afraid," he asked, "of the inevitably greater accumulation of capital in the hands of those fitted to use it, and, after all, eventually bound to use it more for the common good than for their own?"[7]

The voices on the left, however, were equally insistent. Dr. Charles Bruehl, Father Haas's professor at St. Francis Seminary, published an article in 1935 titled "The Case against the Capitalistic System," and he spoke of capitalism's "inherently evil nature." Dom Virgil Michel, of St. John's University in Minnesota, declared: "Capitalism is precisely an economic system in which capital (or goods used in the production of further goods) plays the predominant part. Hence the system is vicious, both ethically and ontologically." John F. Prince, a prominent Catholic layman, held the opinion that "as for the practice of capitalistic industrialism, Pope Pius XI denounces it every bit as vigorously as Communism." German-American Catholics like Frederick P. Kenkel, William Engelen, and Edward Koch were equally insistent. The Pope's New Social Order, they declared, could not be realized until the free-enterprise system, founded on the profit motive, was superseded by a religiously oriented cooperative movement.[8]

Father Haas rejected these opinions and followed the interpretation of John A. Ryan. In an article written in 1931, Ryan had insisted that "despite his denunciations of the evils of present-day capitalism, Pope Pius declares that the system is not 'vicious of its very nature.'"[9] The Pope's defense of private property, the wage contract, trade associations, and the unionization of workers, Ryan added, gave at least implicit approval to the free-enterprise system. He admitted, however, that there were serious defects in American economic life—low wages, long hours, unreasonable working conditions—and that important changes were needed to bring it into conformity with the Pope's plan for social reconstruction. Such changes, however, could be made without destroying the system. The influence of the social encyclicals was apparent in all of Father Haas's work and writing in the 1930s and thereafter, but they were always the encyclicals as interpreted by John A. Ryan.

Following the example of Pope Leo XIII in *Rerum Novarum* and John Ryan in *A Living Wage*, Father Haas founded his social and economic philosophy on a belief in the inherent, God-given dignity of man. "From the Christian point of view," he wrote in *Man and Society*, "human life cannot be measured in terms of a money equivalent. According to Christian teaching, a human being has intrinsic value. This means that a human being is valuable in himself, apart from any relation to other human beings or to material things." This belief stemmed principally from his religious convictions. According to Holy Scripture, only man is created "in the image and likeness of God," only man ranks "a little less than the angels," and only man is destined for eternal happiness with God. "The ultimate basis of human dignity," he noted, "is man's eternal destiny... and the spirituality of the human soul."[10]

Father Haas realized, however, that many could not accept this theological foundation for man's special dignity and he turned occasionally to other arguments. "As far as scientific experiment has been able to discover," he wrote, "abstract thought, as manifested in articulate speech and in the manufacture of tools, is possessed by man alone." Only man is able to distinguish between right and wrong, only man is able "to give expression in some form or other to religious sentiments," and only man is able to make continual progress against the often hostile forces of nature. In the opinion of Father Haas, natural science, even without the aid of Divine Revelation, could sufficiently demonstrate man's "place of pre-eminence in the world above all visible created things."[11]

Because of this God-given dignity, every human being possesses certain natural and inviolable rights. Father Haas divided these rights into two general classes: "those which protect a person against sudden or violent death by an unjust aggressor" and "those which protect his title to normal growth and development, both physical and moral." This natural rights doctrine had been expounded by countless theologians since St. Thomas Aquinas in the thirteenth century, and was similar to that suggested in the Declaration of Independence, but Father Haas's treatment was different in that he almost invariably drew his illustrations from industrial ethics[12] :

> By virtue of the right to life, everyone is obliged to avoid exposing himself or others to unusual physical hazards. Ordinarily, the primary instinct of self-preservation impels the individual to protect and safeguard his own life. But there is no primary instinct in the individual impelling him to respect the life and bodily integrity of others. ... The responsible heads of a factory who know that the machinery in their plant is extremely dangerous, and who refuse to install the necessary guards, render themselves guilty of murder, in case a worker dies as a result of an accident suffered while operating a defective or unguarded machine. These conclusions are immediately deducible from the right of every individual to freedom from unjust attacks on his life.
>
> The second group of natural rights includes the rights to normal human growth and development, both physical and moral. ... The disregard of the rights to normal growth and development is exemplified in the case of low-wage families in which the father's earnings are insufficient to

secure the quantities of food, housing, clothing, medical care, and recreation, necessary for physical and spiritual well-being. As a result, the health of the family is impaired, and its resistance to disease and death is abnormally reduced.

From the teachings of earlier theologians and from the social encyclicals of Popes Leo XIII and Pius XI, Father Haas derived his conviction that every human being has an inalienable right to private property. As early as the thirteenth century, St. Thomas Aquinas had taught that private ownership was not only permissible but necessary for man to live a full and satisfying life. In *Rerum Novarum*, Pope Leo stated that "every man has by nature the right to possess property as his own. This is one of the chief points of distinction between man and the animal creation." Pope Pius XI added that it was the "unanimous contention" of Church authorities that "the right of owning private property has been given to man by nature, or rather by the Creator Himself." Father Haas devoted two chapters of *Man and Society* to discussion of private ownership. "The institution of property is rooted in man's nature," he wrote, "and therefore willed by its Divine Author." "The natural necessities of every individual," he added, "demand that he own goods sufficient for present and future needs, and, in addition, that he be free to increase his goods indefinitely up to a limit fixed by the needs of others."[13]

This right of private property, however, was not absolute and unrestricted. "The right of ownership," he noted, "is not merely individual; it is also social. The right of any person to own property is limited by the right of every other person in the community." "Vast aggregations of capital are necessary for large-scale production," he admitted, but "the control of such capital must be restricted or limited in the public interest." When such restrictions are not observed, "large sections of the weaker economic groups are held in a condition of dependency, and the great mass of the people suffer serious impairment of their personal and political freedom."[14] The principal limitation on the right of private property, Haas insisted, is the right of everyone in the community to an adequate family wage. No one has the right to increase his personal wealth while depriving others of the means of a normal livelihood.

Many Americans at that time, however, rejected this doctrine in favor of the view that wages should be set solely by the law of supply and demand, regardless of the needs of the individual

worker. Professor Augustus Dyer of Vanderbilt University summarized this more popular opinion in an address in Milwaukee in
late 1923:

> When you have paid the farmer the price fixed by the
> law of demand and supply, whether it is high or low, for
> wheat or corn, you don't feel you owe him another cent,
> and nobody else feels so. And the same is true when you pay
> the newspaper for advertising and pay the telegraph company
> for sending your telegrams. It is strange that we try to
> make an exception when it comes to labor; there is no
> ground for exception. When an employer has paid the price
> fixed by the law of supply and demand to his labor, he
> doesn't owe them a single other penny, not another penny.
> He has fulfilled every possible industrial obligation.[15]

A few months earlier, in *Adkins* v. *Children's Hospital*, the
Supreme Court had given this doctrine its official approval. Speaking for the majority in declaring the minimum wage law of the
District of Columbia unconstitutional, Associate Justice George
Sutherland had declared: "In principle there can be no difference
between the case of selling labor and the case of selling goods.
If one goes to the butcher, the baker or the grocer to buy food, he
is morally entitled to obtain the worth of his money but he is
not entitled to more. If what he gets is worth what he pays he is
not justified in demanding more simply because he needs more;
and the shopkeeper, having dealt fairly and honestly in that
transaction, is not concerned in any peculiar sense with the
customer's necessities."[16]
     Father Haas emphatically rejected this attempt to equate
human labor with a bushel of wheat or corn. "This revolting
doctrine," he asserted, "totally ignores the important fact that the
worker is a human being, intended for a level of earthly existence
immeasurably above that of animals; and the further important
consequence that virtuous living, which is the *sine qua non* of
eternal happiness, is rendered extremely difficult, and sometimes
impossible, because the breadwinner of the family is forced to
accept less than a living wage." "Every human being," he stated a
few years later, "is intrinsically valuable. He bears the image of
the Eternal God, and is placed in the world to realize an immortal
destiny. As a consequence, he may not be looked upon as a mere
material thing, and his wages, which to him mean life, may not be
decided by the mere accident that there are either a large or a

small number of individuals ready to do the same work." America should "shrink in horror," he wrote in 1931, at the thought that family happiness and the birth of children are "to be determined by the uncontrolled haggling of the labor market."[17]

In a study completed in 1925, Father Haas suggested that the basic minimum wage for a family of five should be in the area of $1,700 a year, but he noted that recent statistics indicated that at least 75 percent of Americans received less.[18] The effects of this were critical. Infant mortality rates were higher among low-income families, sickness among adults was more prevalent, and low-wage families were denied opportunities for adequate education and recreation. "It should be remembered," he added, "that human dignity requires more than the preservation of physical well-being and bodily integrity. It includes also the maintenance of self-respect and independence."[19] The life of the low-income family was in no way compatible with man's innate dignity as a child of God.

Father Haas based his demand for higher wages not only on man's inherent dignity as a child of God but also on the need for economic stability. He recalled that American economic life since the Civil War had been governed by the laissez-faire individualism of Adam Smith, John Stuart Mill, David Ricardo, and Herbert Spencer, and since labor had been unable to attain equal strength with industry at the bargaining table, a disastrous imbalance had set in. Monopolies had sprung up, industrial profits had soared, the work week had lengthened, unemployment had spread, child labor had increased, and wages had not kept pace with prices. Such conditions could not continue indefinitely. As profits and production ran away from wages and consumption and as demand lagged far behind supply, the heavily unbalanced economic structure finally collapsed in 1929. The reasons for this crash, Father Haas asserted in 1933, were not difficult to discover:

> The depression, its why and whither, resolves itself into a question of distribution. Essentially the problem is like cutting a pie. If four persons are to get a piece, one way of cutting it is to divide it into four equal parts. Another way is to cut it unequally. Obviously if one gets more than a quarter the others must be satisfied with less than the other three quarters. The larger the share one person gets the smaller the share remaining for the rest, and vice versa.
> The pie to be cut is the national income, which consists of the goods produced in a country in one year, and valued

in the United States in 1933 at $40 billion and in 1929 at
$85 billion. Clearly the pie is much smaller in 1933 than in
1929.

The four classes of persons getting the whole national
income each year are landowners, wage and salary workers,
interest receivers, and profit receivers. Mainly because the
nation's yearly income has been divided disproportionately,
that is because too little of it went to wage and salary workers and too much to the other three groups, the total amount
in 1929 has shrunk to less than one half, and 60 million
persons are suffering varying degrees of want and privation.

In economic language the cause of the depression was the
failure before 1929 of the purchasing power of the workers
to keep pace with the rapidly increasing output of mech-
anized industry. Since 1913 the rate of consumption increased less than one-third as rapidly as the rate of production. Workers received far from sufficient income to purchase
the goods of factories and, for want of customers, factories
shut down.

Less than fifty-five per cent of American business is now
operating. Clearly there can be no revival and permanent
recovery until workers, who constitute the principal market
for goods, have enough of income to buy all that factories
and farms can turn out. Put simply, business must have
customers who have money.[20]

This was obviously an oversimplification of a complex
problem. Father Haas was well aware that other factors contributed to the Wall Street Crash and Depression—wild speculation in
securities, easy credit, excessive savings, a short-sighted tariff
policy—but he saw the chief cause of the collapse in the unequal
distribution of income and the subsequent inability of consumption to keep pace with production. "The national wealth of the
United States," he wrote before the Crash of 1929, "is increasing
rapidly—more rapidly than the population. This means that a
larger volume of goods is produced each year than is consumed."
"Manufacturers produce, or are ready to produce, goods," he
declared a few years later, "but buyers for lack of sufficient
income cannot take them off their hands."[21]

For Father Haas, the fundamental question was how to
guarantee that the national pie was more equitably divided and
how the purchasing power of the American consumer could be
increased by raising the wages of industrial workers. Pope Leo

XIII had suggested in *Rerum Novarum* that there were two principal means of guaranteeing workers an adequate wage—voluntary associations of workers or intervention by the state—and John Ryan repeated the same view fifteen years later in *A Living Wage.* "The features of our industrial system," Ryan wrote in 1906, "that render organized action indispensable to the welfare of the laborer, and the large, numerous, and varied gains that organization has brought him, are so obvious that only the densely ignorant or the hopelessly prejudiced can escape their cogency." If organization proves ineffective, Ryan noted, "the state has both the right and the duty to compel all employers to pay a Living Wage."[22] Father Haas was in full agreement. "The instrumentalities for securing adequate income and proper working standards for wage-earners," he declared in 1927, "can be narrowed down to two: collective bargaining and legal enactment."[23]

Despite this general agreement, Father Haas and Monsignor Ryan differed slightly in the emphasis they placed on each of these means. Monsignor Ryan's interest in social justice had been shaped chiefly in the years before World War I, a period in which organized labor had been weak and ineffective and in which social progress had been achieved principally through legislative action, especially under reformist governors like Robert La Follette, Hiram Johnson of California, and Albert B. Cummins of Iowa. Ryan was always an outspoken champion of the worker's right to organize, but he was cool to some unions because of their socialistic leanings, and maybe to the AFL because of its opposition to positive social legislation. As one recent authority has stated: "Despite his general support of labor unions since his abandonment of compulsory arbitration in the twenties, Ryan was never excited by the labor movement as were many of his fellow Catholics. . . . His awareness of the power of business led him to continue to rely on the state as the only institution with sufficient leverage to bring any basic change in the social structure."[24] Father Haas did not share these views of his former professor. Twenty years younger than Ryan, he saw no serious danger of socialist domination of the American labor movement in the post-World War I decades and little hope for effective labor legislation from the conservative lawmakers assembling in Washington and most state capitals in the 1920s. As a result, he placed his greatest hope for industrial reform in a strong labor movement.

"It is not too much to say," Father Haas declared in 1931, "that if all American wage earners had been organized during the past forty years, at least seventy or eighty per cent of their number, the present tragic condition of employment and business stagnation could not exist."[25] He declared elsewhere, a few years earlier:

> In order, therefore, that the benefits of rationalization may continue to be enjoyed and at the same time the working classes may not suffer, it is necessary that the workers be organized in unions, so that their representatives may speak for them on a basis of equality when they negotiate with the spokesmen of integrated capital and management.... With the overwhelmingly [sic] bulk of American goods manufactured by corporations of organized capital and less than 20 per cent of the 16 million wage-earners organized in trade unions it is only through collective agreements negotiated for workers on a scale paralleling the organization of the particular industry in which they are employed that wage justice can be secured to the individual worker. It is only in this way that he will be able to purchase the goods that will enable him to live as a human being and to provide for the normal vicissitudes of sickness, accident, unemployment, and old age. Again, it is only under a system of collective agreements that family life can be properly safeguarded and promoted.... Incidentally, under a system of collective agreements justice will be maintained because an approximately equal bargaining power will be exercised by both sides.

In a pamphlet titled *The Why and Whither of Labor Unions*, published later in the 1930s, he emphasized the same arguments:

> Workers organize because they know that they must organize to better their lot.... They fully realize that individual bargaining is a futile performance because, notably in the mass production industries, the individual withholding of labor is futile. In addition, they see that as a rule the lowest wages are paid and the longest hours are worked in the non-union industries, and that in the unionized industries the opposite is true.
> It is notorious that the yearly share of the national product which goes to labor is too small.... there is no surer way for workers to obtain a fairer share of the goods and services produced than by organizing into unions. In addition, in organization they have the most efficacious instrument to reduce working hours generally, especially in the industries

in which hours are immoderately long. Unquestionably the reduction of hours will require more persons to be employed and consequently reduce the number of those unable to find jobs.[26]

In taking this stand in support of the unionization of workers, Father Haas was again repeating the teachings of the papal encyclicals. Pope Leo XIII had declared that it was "greatly to be desired" that workmen's associations "should multiply and become more effective," and Pope Pius XI praised his predecessor for "encouraging Christian workingmen to form unions according to their several trades" and for "teaching them how to do it."[27] Both pontiffs had insisted that since the worker's right to associate with others in labor unions was a natural right, the state had no more authority to deny or abridge it than to deny or abridge a citizen's right to associate with others in marriage or in religious worship. But Father Haas went a step further. Workingmen, he insisted, had not only the right to join a union but a solemn obligation to do so. "Every worker," he declared in a Labor Day address in 1933, "has the duty to himself and to his fellow men to join his union and to be proud of his membership. . . . Given two men of equal ability, one a union man and the other non-union, unquestionably the union man is the better. He recognizes his obligations to himself, his family, and his country." Union membership was a "sacred obligation in justice and charity," he declared in 1935, and he elaborated on this a few years later:

Sometimes non-union workers who receive fairly good incomes ask: "Why should we join a union?" The answer is, either justice or charity or both require them to do so. If they are in an industry which is partially organized, it is entirely likely that they are enjoying good conditions because their non-union employer in order "to keep the union out" meets or nearly meets the higher wage and hour standards prevailing in union establishments. Clearly such non-union employees are eating the fruit not of their own but of others' sacrifices and contributions. The workers in the union shops perhaps risked their jobs to get their union recognized, and they pay monthly dues to keep it a going concern. Simple justice requires non-union employees who enjoy the common benefits to carry their share of the common burden.

On the other hand, if non-union workers who are receiving good wages are in an industry in which there is little or no unionization, it is their obligation to join with their low-wage fellow workers and assist them in raising their standards. The better paid violate charity when they say coldly: "We can take care of ourselves. The company needs us. Let the unskilled look out for themselves." Charity requires the strong to help the weak and it assuredly obliges the better paid to share their strength with the poorer paid by combining with them to assist them.[28]

Such a doctrine aroused heated opposition from less liberal members of the Church. "Christ tells us to hear the Church," one layman wrote, "but where, oh where, did He say to join a union?" "We of the Catholic laity," another wrote, "are beginning to question the honesty and motives of some of our clergy who have championed the cause of labor racketeers at the expense of the workingman." A Catholic mother in New York echoed the same sentiments. "You must realize," she wrote, "the enormous cost in money and sacrifice to Catholics, in the building, upkeep, tuition, etc. of our Catholic schools and colleges. If you think we Catholic parents, after these huge sacrifices, are going to turn our children over to gangsters, racketeers, hoodlums and communists, who so often run these various unions, you are greatly out of step with the Catholic parents of America." "Stick to religion," another suggested. "You don't even know the definition of it." Even fellow priests objected. A parish priest from Cleveland wrote "just to let you know that all Catholic priests do not agree with your method of arguing about a laboring man's obligation to join a labor union. If you had paused a moment before making the statement, you would never have made it."[29]

But Father Haas was not only unwilling to alter his position; he expanded it into other areas. He saw lack of organization and collective activity as a principal reason for the economic difficulties confronting American farmers. In *American Agriculture and International Affairs*, published in 1930, he wrote:

> As commerce is now carried on between cities and farms, the agencies of the urban population enjoy an undue advantage over rural dwellers.... Urban buying agencies—the grain and cotton brokers, dairy associations, and the meat packers —are generally organized, and buy from farmers, who must sell as individuals. Urban selling agencies—the farm-machinery manufacturers, mail-order houses, and railroads—are likewise organized, and sell to farmers, who must buy as individuals.[30]

The obvious solution, according to Father Haas, was organization through agricultural cooperatives. "Under the prevailing system of mass production, mass capitalization, and mass merchandising in cities," he wrote, "cooperation among farmers in selling and buying is the only practicable means of maintaining just exchange relations between agriculture and city agencies. The cooperative seeks to meet organization with organization. It aims to match strength with strength."

Despite his enthusiastic support of organization and collective action, Father Haas realized that there were economic problems which these could not solve. "It should not be concluded," he wrote in the late 1930s, "that collective bargaining, essential as it is, will solve all the ills of workers, to say nothing of those of the whole country. Collective bargaining is not a panacea. It has definite limitations. It can help wage earners only up to a certain point." Beyond that point, social legislation was necessary. "Until the time comes," he had written in 1924, "when employers through their representatives and workers through their representatives negotiate the terms of the wage contract, the various States and the Federal Government will continue to pass laws regulating the trade relations between employers and workers. The former method is certainly by far the more desirable arrangement of the two, but when private initiative fails, as it has up to the present time, the State is in duty bound to intervene in order to protect the interests of the community and particularly those of the weaker classes."[31]

Father Haas singled out four principal areas in which he felt government intervention was necessary in the 1920s—unemployment compensation, minimum wage, child labor, and medical insurance—but he insisted that government intervention must always be the last resort.[32] "Private action is always preferable to government activity in correcting social wrongs," he stated in *Man and Society*; and elsewhere in the same work: "The situations in which the state must intervene include all those cases in which groups of persons are powerless to protect or help themselves, and no remedy but state intervention is available." He continued:

> The limits, therefore, which public welfare sets for state intervention are defined by the answer to the question: Can individuals be adequately protected and their needs provided for either by themselves or by those responsible for them? If the answer is affirmative, the state should not intervene.

If the answer is in the negative, the state should intervene. In considering whether or not a particular field of action is a legitimate one for state intervention, the presumption favors the negative, for it must be assumed that the great majority of individuals are able to take care of themselves.[33]

Father Haas insisted, however, that not even increased government intervention and wider acceptance of collective bargaining were, of themselves, sufficient to cure the economic ills of the early 1930s. These remedies were too often "merely patchwork," he declared in 1932, "and the patching at one spot may increase the strain at others and make the entire fabric weaker than before." Reconstruction of the economic structure was needed, and the program he proposed was the Occupational Group System of Pope Pius XI's *Quadragesimo Anno*:

A good deal is said today about the need of partnership between worker and employer with the government acting as a chairman. In broad outline, this is the "Occupational Group" System of Pope Pius XI. All the people, workers and employers, in all establishments in all industries and callings would be organized. Taking the textile industry as an illustration, the textile workers throughout the country would unite, and without intimidation or coercion from either government or employers select their representatives. The textile owners, exercising like freedom, which incidentally has never been denied any employer group, would likewise, without restriction, select their representatives. The two groups of freely chosen agents, with equal voting power, would sit as the permanent council for the textile industry and, with the aid and guidance but not with the dictation of government, establish wages, hours, production quotas, and profits for the industry. Mining, metals, service, and all other industries and callings would organize on the same basis and for the same purpose.

Moreover, all the organized groups—mining, metals, service, and all the rest—would be united and represented in a single national council to which each organized group would send its representatives. These representatives of employers and employees, in equal number, would with the guidance and assistance but not with the dictation of government, constitute a super-body to manage the entire economic life of the country.

One of the duties of this national body would be to seek to maintain a reasonable relationship in wages among the separate industries and callings so that one is not overpaid and another underpaid. Equally important, it would aim to preserve something like a proper balance of prices among the separate industries and callings so that in proportion to their respective contributions, one would not get too large, and another too small, a share of the aggregate volume of goods and services produced.

The advantages of this arrangement are evident. As *Quadragesimo Anno* points out, it promotes cooperation and good will by uniting men "not according to the position they occupy in the labor market but according to the diverse functions which they exercise in society"; it places restraints on competition among workers and thereby restrains class warfare; it enables the economic regime to function for the only national purpose it can have—to produce for all and each, all the necessaries and conveniences which the wealth, resources, technical achievements and enterprises of the people can yield.[34]

Father Haas returned to this Occupational Group System in numerous addresses and writings throughout the 1930s and 1940s. In September and December 1932, he discussed the program in addresses before the National Conference of Catholic Charities and the Catholic Conference on Industrial Problems; in *The American Labor Movement*, published in 1937, he inserted a special section, "Pius XI on Occupational Organization of Society"; he touched briefly on the topic in an address before the American Association for Labor Legislation in Philadelphia in 1940; in an article written in 1944, his first year as bishop, he insisted that the tripartite system of Pope Pius XI be the basis of "Christian Planning for Post-War Reconstruction"; and when asked to deliver the first John A. Ryan Memorial Lecture in Chicago in February 1949, he thought no topic more appropriate than the reorganization of modern society according to the Occupational Group System.[35] For Father Haas, the Occupational Group System would preserve the free-enterprise system, guarantee labor's right to organize, and assure the consumer, through the government representative, a voice in determining economic policy. The system was not a panacea, he admitted, but it was the most effective and consistent means of eliminating industrial conflicts, maintaining economic balance and stability, guaranteeing the rights of workers, employers, and consumers, and inaugurating a more just and harmonious social order.

If one phrase could summarize this complex structure of Haas's thought, it might be "justice through organization." Justice was undoubtedly the preoccupation of his life. He frequently quoted the remark of Frederick Ozanam, the French social reformer, that "charity is the Good Samaritan pouring oil into the wounds of the traveler that has been attacked, but justice prevents him from being attacked."[36] He insisted that justice, not charity, was the primary responsibility of government. "The right to a decent family income in return for useful labor," he wrote in 1930, "is a right conferred by justice on farm and city workers. If this right is allowed to be violated, no system of public charity in the form of cash aid to farmers, or poor relief to city dwellers, can take its place."[37] Like Father John Ryan, he dedicated his life to the crusade for social justice, striving to guarantee adequate wages, hours, and working conditions to industrial laborers and civil and economic rights to religious and racial minorities. When he was appointed bishop of Grand Rapids in 1943, he chose for his episcopal motto *In Christo Justitia*, "Let There Be Justice in Christ."

Father Haas argued throughout his life that the most effective means of promoting social justice was the greater organization of all levels of American society. In the 1920s, he had championed agricultural cooperatives, urging farmers to organize and pool their resources in order to improve their economic position. Throughout the 1930s, with millions of industrial workers unemployed and further millions underpaid, Haas insisted that workers had not only a right but a moral obligation to unionize. Reconstruction of the social order, which Pope Pius XI strongly urged, presumed the organization of workers in labor unions and the organization of employers in trade associations. International organization, Haas further believed, was essential for world peace. He was an active member of the International Labor Organization, the World Peace Union, the League of Nations Association, and, after 1945, a strong supporter of the United Nations. For Father Haas, social justice was possible only in an organized society. As friends used to comment: "He couldn't even preach a sermon on the Good Shepherd without first organizing the sheep."[38]

Such a consistent social and economic philosophy was in many ways unique among government officials in the 1930s. Influenced by the social encyclicals of Popes Leo XIII and Pius XI and by the teachings of John A. Ryan, Father Haas founded this philosophy on the innate, God-given dignity of every human being. From this dignity flowed fundamental and inalienable rights to life, liberty, private property, and a living wage sufficient to provide each worker and his family with the necessities of life, a minimum ŏf comfort, and reasonable security for the future. Each worker's dignity as a child of God demanded at least this much, regardless of the size of industries, the state of the economy, or the number of unemployed competing for jobs. The two principal means of guaranteeing this living wage, according to Haas, were collective bargaining through unionization and social legislation. Unionization and collective bargaining were preferable because they were more directly controlled by workers, but if these proved insufficient, the government had a solemn obligation to intervene. This broader unionization and increased government intervention in the economy could also lead, according to Haas, to the further goal of the reorganization of society, according to the Occupational Group System of Pope Pius XI, whereby economic policy in each industry and in a nation as a whole would be determined jointly by tripartite boards from labor, management, and the public represented by government. Such a consistent social philosophy, though unique among government officials, was to harmonize well with the New Deal programs inaugurated by President Franklin Roosevelt in 1933.

4

First Months in Government Service: The NRA, 1933-1934

On a chilling and overcast March 4, 1933, four years into the most devastating depression in American history, Franklin Roosevelt stood firm and erect on the East Portico of the Capitol to deliver his first inaugural address. "This is pre-eminently the time to speak the truth," he began solemnly, "the whole truth, frankly and boldly."[1] His voice was clear and confident but his words were grim: "Values have shrunken to fantastic levels; taxes have risen; our ability to pay has fallen; government of all kinds is faced by serious curtailment of income; the means of exchange are frozen in the currents of trade; the withered leaves of industrial enterprise lie on every side; farmers find no markets for their produce; the savings of many years in thousands of families are gone. More important, a host of unemployed citizens face the grim problem of existence, and an equally great number toil with little return."

Despite the bleakness of this description, the president remained optimistic and self-assured: "This Nation asks for action, and action now. Our greatest primary task is to put people to work. This is no unsolvable problem if we face it wisely and courageously. It can be accomplished in part by direct recruiting by the Government itself, treating the task as we would treat the emergency of a war, but at the same time, through this employment, accomplishing greatly needed projects to stimulate and reorganize the use of our natural resources."

"We do not distrust the future of essential democracy," the president concluded. "The people of the United States have not failed. In their need they have registered a mandate that they want direct, vigorous action. They have asked for discipline and direction under leadership. They have made me the present instrument of their wishes. In the spirit of the gift I take it. In this dedication of a Nation we humbly ask the blessing of God. May He protect each and everyone of us. May He guide me in the days to come."

The new president had not exaggerated the nation's economic prostration. In the forty months since the Wall Street Crash of 1929, national income had declined $40 billion, 85,000 businesses had failed, and over 5,000 banks had suspended operations. The Dow-Jones average had dropped from a high of $125 to less than $27, and many issues had disappeared from the market altogether. Industry was operating at 48 percent of capacity, wages had been cut 60 per cent, and unemployment was estimated at 13 million—an incredible 25 percent of the work force. Agricultural income had plummeted from $12 billion to $5 billion, and thousands of farmers had lost their homes and moved further west, into an equally uncertain and dismal future. No one was spared. "Hooverville" shanties had sprung up on the outskirts of most major cities, "Okies" on the move became a national symbol, and white-collar workers stood dejectedly in breadlines or sold apples on street corners.[2]

"This Nation asks for action, and action now," the president had declared, and he moved immediately to meet the crisis. Within hours of his inaugural address, he ordered all banks across the country closed and he summoned Congress into special session for March 9. Shortly before noon that morning, while many legislators were hurrying back to Washington, he sent Congress an Emergency Banking bill which would formally approve his Bank Proclamation of March 5 and empower the Treasury Department to permit the reopening of stable banks and supervise the reorganization of others. The House of Representatives, with only the Speaker's copy of the bill at hand, passed the legislation by a voice vote in less than forty minutes, and the Senate concurred a few hours later. The president signed it into law that same evening. On Sunday, March 12, Roosevelt explained its provisions to an anxious nation in his first "fireside chat," and on the following morning, when banks in the twelve Federal Reserve cities across the country opened their doors for business, more persons came to deposit money than to withdraw it. The financial panic was over.[3]

The president admitted that he had no master plan for curing the Depression but he was determined to take advantage of the cooperation of Congress to attack the economic debacle on a variety of fronts. Within a week, Congress passed the Economy Act, to reduce veterans' pensions and curb government spending; it legalized light beer and wine on March 22; and it established the Civilian Conservation Corps to provide work for two million unemployed youths on public highways and in national parks and forests. Eager to halt the downward trend in prices and attract foreign markets, the president abandoned the gold standard in April and permitted the dollar to float. In May, Congress approved the president's request for regulation of the stock market, appropriated $500 million for emergency relief, authorized wide-ranging development of the Tennessee Valley, and, in the Agricultural Adjustment Act, agreed to subsidize farmers who limited production in order to eliminate crop surpluses and raise prices. By mid-June, the legislators had passed a second banking act, created the position of coordinator of transportation to oversee reorganization of railway lines, established the Home Owners' Loan Corporation, and, after much debate, approved the National Industrial Recovery Act in an effort to check the downward spiral of industrial productivity, increase prices, and raise wages. When Congress adjourned on June 16, at the end of the first "One Hundred Days," more fundamental and far-reaching legislation had been passed than in any comparable period in our history. Although recovery was still several years away, the new president had taken firm control, Washington was alive with activity, monthly business indicators moved upward, and the American people were confident that the economic turnaround had finally begun.

Perhaps the most far-reaching and controversial of the acts passed by Congress during this emergency session was the National Industrial Recovery Act.[4] The United States was an industrial nation, the greatest industrial power in the world, and permanent economic recovery was impossible without a revitalization of industry. The National Industrial Recovery Act, founded on the theory that prices were kept at an unprofitably low level through excessive competition for dwindling markets, encouraged leaders in each industry to band together and adopt mutually agreeable regulations, formulated in codes of fair competition, which, if obeyed by all members of the industry, could halt the downward trend in prices, make manufacturing more profitable, and stimulate production. These codes might prohibit sale of goods below cost, payment of rebates, marketing materials from inventory, or reduction of prices without prior public notice. Section 7(a) of the law declared that all workers in industries governed by these codes had the right to organize freely and bargain collectively, could not be required to join an "inside" or company union as a condition of employment, and were to be protected by minimum wage and maximum hour provisions, specified in each code. When formally approved and signed by the president, the codes were given the force of law; convicted violators could be fined and imprisoned, and activities sanctioned by the codes were exempt from anti-trust prosecution. Consumers were encouraged to patronize only businesses that had adopted such codes and exhibited the official NRA symbol, the "Blue Eagle," over the phrase "We Do Our Part."

The signing of the NIRA on June 16 inaugurated several months of circuslike activity in Washington under the direction (and general showmanship) of NRA Administrator Hugh Johnson. Industry representatives, consumer advocates, labor officials, and scores of legal assistants hurried to Washington to draft, revise, sponsor, or oppose codes of fair competition that, somehow, were to inject new life into the nation's stagnant industrial economy. A sprawling bureaucracy of interrelated and even overlapping NRA agencies emerged immediately—Legal Division, Code Analysis Division, State Recovery Councils, Local Compliance Boards, and so on—and thousands of workers were recruited to staff new offices, take part in code deliberations and reviews, and assist General Johnson in his massive effort to restore jobs to 13 million workers and increase industrial output by $20 billion. One of the officials drawn almost immediately into this busy, sometimes disappointing, but always exciting whirl of activity during that summer was Father Haas, since 1931 the director of Washington's National Catholic School of Social Service.

Father Haas's public service began, ironically, through a misunderstanding. Less than three weeks after President Roosevelt took his oath of office, the new secretary of labor, Frances Perkins, invited a group of labor leaders and other public figures to confer with her later that month on the problems of unemployment and relief. On March 27, four days before the conference was to take place, Monsignor Robert F. Keegan of New York, president of the National Conference of Catholic Charities, asked Father Haas to represent Catholic Charities in place of Monsignor John O'Grady, who could not attend. Haas wired his acceptance immediately, only to discover that a mistake had been made. Miss Perkins by that time had also invited Monsignor John Ryan,

presuming that he could represent Catholic Charities, and she
hesitated to add a second Catholic representative. Since both Ryan
and Haas had been unwittingly invited, however, she accepted the
predicament with her usual good grace, and on March 28 she sent
Father Haas a formal invitation.[5]

The conference proved most successful. The secretary of
labor had traditionally been appointed from the ranks of organized labor, and President William Green had earlier declared that
the AFL "would never be reconciled" to Miss Perkins's appointment. Her background had been in social work and she had
served as a member of the New York State Industrial Commission,
under Governor Al Smith, and as industrial commissioner under
Governor Franklin Roosevelt. The discussions on March 31,
however, revealed little disagreement. The secretary accepted
labor's proposals for a $3 billion public works program, another
$1 billion for relief, and for legislation outlawing child labor.
Although Green preferred slum clearance projects to reforestation,
labor agreed to support the administration's plan for a Civilian
Conservation Corps. Government and labor officials further
agreed that public works projects should not compete with private
industry and that organized labor should be represented on all
public works labor boards. The following day the *New York Times*
commented: "With a unanimity and complete freedom of expression characterized by the labor leaders as 'remarkable,' by technical experts present as 'unique,' and by Secretary Perkins as
'significant and impressive,' labor wrote its own program."[6]

At the close of this conference (March 31), Secretary Perkins
asked each participant to submit a memorandum to her on the
unemployment crisis and the feasibility of a federal public works
program. Father Haas replied the following day:

> The public works program which seems likely to be
> agreed to by Congress can have either a definitely good or
> a definitely bad effect. To secure the good and to avoid the
> bad there should be set up an airtight Public Works Labor
> Board on which union labor would have a representative
> with one out of three votes (one for Government, one for
> employers, and one for workers) on all policies.... The
> Public Works Labor Board would have power to classify
> workers by trades, fix minimum wages for each class, and
> set maximum hour standards.
>
> Before going into the question of labor standards which
> the Public Works Labor Board should set up let me say

something about the larger question of the wisdom or un-
wisdom of a public works program. A public works program
will have a beneficial effect only if it will increase purchasing
power, not only among workers immediately engaged in
public construction, but in all other industries. In fact, this
is its only justification.

Increasing purchasing power outside of the construction
groups is even more important than increasing purchasing
power within them. This can be done if the Public Works
Labor Board will enforce on all its projects high wages and
ruthlessly limit the working week to thirty hours. On the
contrary if the Labor Board refuses to do this or, what is the
same thing, if there is no Labor Board, a public works program can do a tremendous amount of harm. If public works
are carried on without labor standards, that is if wages as
low as two or three dollars a day are allowed to be paid and
a fifty or sixty hour week allowed to be worked, these
conditions will tend to be copied by the private industries
of the country and the result of the public works program
will be the very opposite of that intended.

All this is merely intended to emphasize the necessity of
a national Labor Board for public construction with regional
sub-boards as required, on all of which organized workers
have one of three votes. With an agency of this kind a three
to six billion dollar public works plan can undoutedly achieve
the purpose of increasing consuming power. Without it,
public works will unquestionably reduce buying power and
intensify the present evil.[7]

This letter clearly set forth two of Father Haas's deepest
concerns—the level of wages and industry-labor-government
cooperation. He believed firmly in the underconsumption theory
of the Depression: the Depression had been caused by the inability
of the American economy to consume all that industry was
producing and it could be remedied only by increasing purchasing
power through a substantial rise in wages. Since wages, hours,
prices, and levels of production affected the economic stability
of the whole nation, Father Haas felt that these factors should
be determined jointly by labor, management, and government.
Such cooperation, in the form of a Public Works Labor Board, he
hoped might be a first step toward implementing the Occupational
Group System of Pope Pius XI. It was appropriate that two
themes so basic to his social and economic philosophy should

appear so explicitly in his first official communication with the New Deal administration.[8]

The National Industrial Recovery Act, drafted by legislative assistants throughout the succeeding weeks of April and May and signed into law by President Roosevelt on June 16, seemed to fulfill several of Father Haas's social and economic goals. It was an example of wide-ranging but legitimate government intervention, since the private sector, after four years of depression, seemed incapable of spurring recovery. Section 7(a) attempted to raise wages, reduce hours, and guarantee to each worker the right to organize. Title II of the act appropriated $3.3 billion for public works, almost the exact amount that Secretary Perkins's labor conference in late March had recommended. Most important of all, with the establishment of industrial, labor, and consumer advisory boards to assist in the code-drafting process, the NRA seemed to encourage the industry, labor, and government cooperation which Father Haas saw as basic to the reorganization of society advocated in *Quadragesimo Anno*.

The powers and authority of these three advisory boards, however, remained vague. The Recovery Act made no mention of a Labor Advisory Board, and on June 16 the president announced only that "a Labor Advisory Board appointed by the Secretary of Labor will be responsible that every affected group, whether organized or unorganized, is fully represented in an advisory capacity and any interested labor group will be entitled to be heard through representatives of its own choosing."[9] The precise powers and jurisdiction of this board were to be a source of controversy during the twenty-three months of the NRA's existence.

General Johnson announced the membership of the Labor Advisory Board at a news conference on June 20. Leo Wolman, professor of economics at Columbia University and general counsel for the Amalgamated Clothing Workers of America, was appointed chairman, and the other members were drawn chiefly from organized labor: William Green, president of the American Federation of Labor; Rose Schneiderman, secretary of the Women's Trade Union League; Joseph Franklin, president of the International Brotherhood of Boilermakers; John P. Frey, secretary-treasurer of the AFL's Metal Trades Department; Sidney Hillman, president of the Amalgamated Clothing Workers; George Berry, president of the International Printing Pressmen's Union; John L. Lewis, president of the United Mine Workers of America;

and Father Haas, director of the National Catholic School of Social Service.[10]

The reasons for Father Haas's appointment can only be surmised. Some observers emphasized his friendship with leaders of the American labor movement. "Beyond his rhythmic understanding of Catholic teaching and economic realities," the *Milwaukee Catholic Citizen* declared, "we believe that his capital asset is and has been contacts. For many years Father Haas has been in vital communication with the men and women locally, nationally and internationally, who have counted most for intelligent and sympathetic work in his specialty."[11] Father Haas's contacts were undoubtedly important. He had been a friend of Sidney Hillman since his research for *Shop Collective Bargaining* in 1921; he had corresponded occasionally with labor spokesmen John Frey, Harry Millis, Matthew Woll, Sumner Slichter, and William Leiserson; and he had met several union presidents at Secretary Perkins's unemployment conference on March 31. Any of them might have recommended him to the Roosevelt administration.

Father Haas's religion must also have been a consideration, if only because his Roman collar could not be ignored. As recent historians have pointed out, President Roosevelt frequently used federal patronage to give public recognition to ethnic and religious minority groups.[12] With a large percentage of the American labor force Catholic in the 1930s and with many Catholics openly suspicious of the social philosophies of several union leaders, the presence of a Catholic on the Labor Advisory Board, with high-ranking union officials, was politically advantageous; and in the public eye, no one was more Catholic than a priest.

The fact that Father Haas was *not* a union executive might also have contributed to his selection. With approximately 85 percent of American labor unorganized in 1933, a nonunion official like Father Haas might give unorganized workers at least nominal representation. John L. Lewis, however, emphatically rejected this view. "No one who knew Father Haas," he once remarked, "could ever have considered him a non-union man."[13]

The most important factor in Haas's appointment to the Labor Advisory Board was the fact that by June 1933 he had won the respect and confidence of Secretary Perkins, and it was she who made the appointment. There is no evidence that Father Haas and the secretary were acquainted before the Department of Labor conference on March 31, and a letter Haas received from his niece in April suggests that this was their first meeting. "I see by the newspapers," she wrote, "that you are hobnobbing with Secretaries of Labor now."[14] Haas of course knew of the secretary's work before she had come to Washington. When she was first mentioned as a possible choice for the Labor Department, Haas wrote to a friend: "Permit me to say that I fully agree with you regarding Miss Perkins' outstanding fitness for the position. . . . In my opinion, none of the persons mentioned so far for the Secretaryship of Labor is nearly so well qualified to handle the work intelligently and in a social minded way as is Miss Perkins."[15] The secretary was apparently impressed with Father Haas also. A deeply religious woman, she had at one time given serious thought to joining the Catholic Church, and she was undoubtedly attracted to Father Haas's religious view of human dignity and of social and economic rights. Soon after the March conference on unemployment and relief, she accepted his invitation to speak at the commencement exercises of the School of Social Service on June 13, and one week later she appointed him to the Labor Advisory Board of NRA.[16]

The members of the Labor Advisory Board met for the first time on June 22, just two days after their appointment, and at this first meeting, perhaps significantly, took a stand in direct opposition to the policies of NRA Administrator Hugh Johnson. Outlining the NRA's code-making process on June 16, President Roosevelt had stated: "Every affected labor group . . . [will be] fully and adequately represented in an advisory capacity and any interested labor group will be entitled to be heard through representatives of its own choosing." The members of the Labor Advisory Board, with the Recovery Act's explicit guarantee of collective bargaining in mind, interpreted the president's statement to mean that codes would be drafted through employer–employee negotiations. General Johnson disagreed. In a bulletin issued on June 20, he announced that "basic codes containing provisions respecting maximum hours of labor, minimum rates of pay and other conditions of employment, which are in themselves satisfactory, will be subject to approval, although such conditions may not have been arrived at by collective bargaining." Johnson attended the Labor Advisory Board's meeting on June 22 and, according to the *New York Times*, promised that the NRA would at least "encourage" joint negotiations in the formulation of codes. Johnson recalled the meeting quite differently. In a radio address three days later, he declared that the union leaders on the

Labor Advisory Board "were told that there was no reason for them to demand collective bargaining in advance of the submission of a code." With the voice of the workers thus excluded from the councils of code drafting, the Labor Advisory Board announced that it would assume responsibility for safeguarding labor's interests at all NRA hearings, and this in fact soon became its principal work.[17]

Although feverishly active during the first month of its existence, the National Recovery Administration was singularly unproductive.[18] On June 20, four days after the act was signed, General Johnson urged the country's ten basic industries—steel, automobiles, textiles, coal, petroleum, lumber, garments, construction, and retail and wholesale trades—to submit codes of fair competition immediately; but only cotton textiles came forward. Smaller industries rushed their codes to Washington—fifty-two of them in the first three weeks—but no action was taken, since Johnson preferred to wait until the "Big Ten" industries and their millions of workers were corralled. The Big Ten, however, did not respond, and the result was near-disaster. From March to July 1933, industrial production increased, partly as a result of restored business confidence and partly from the efforts of many business leaders to anticipate the codes, but wages and purchasing power failed to keep pace. Production, consequently, pulled away from consumption, supply outran demand, and on July 19 the stock market crashed again.

The NRA by that time, however, seemed to be making progress. The Cotton Textile Code became effective on July 17; hearings on the Lumber, Electrical, and Shipbuilding codes were scheduled for July 19 and 20; the Coal, Petroleum, Wool, and Steel codes had been submitted to the NRA for approval; and the President's Re-employment Agreement had been drafted: a "blanket code" of fair competition containing minimum wage and maximum hour provisions which an industry might adopt until its own code was prepared and approved. By the end of July, six weeks after the National Industrial Recovery Act was signed, codes of fair competition were beginning to take effect and wages were slowly on the rise.

Although the NRA could claim few accomplishments in late June and early July, the Labor Advisory Board was overwhelmed with work. The board met frequently during its first week to debate General Johnson's decision to exclude collective bargaining and the voice of labor from the early code-making process.

Throughout June, scores of industries had organized company unions, and the Labor Advisory Board frequently protested to NRA officials against this circumvention of Section 7(a)'s guarantee of unrestricted unionization. Hearings on the proposed Cotton Textile Code were held from June 27 to 30, and the full Labor Advisory Board participated. The board then began a series of meetings with the Industrial Advisory Board to draft the "blanket code" President Roosevelt would announce in late July. On July 11, Father Haas confided to a friend in Milwaukee: "We have been holding meetings literally day and night for the last five days and from all appearances we have not yet got started." The lumber manufacturing industry submitted its code to the government that same week, Father Haas was appointed labor adviser, and the endless round of conferences, discussions, and public hearings began again.[19]

By mid-July, the pace of the Labor Advisory Board was almost frantic. A headline in the *New York Times* on July 14 announced "Rush of Industry Codes Swamps Recovery Board," the Cotton Textile Code became effective on July 17, the stock market collapsed on July 19, and Haas began hearings on the Lumber Code that same day. "The NIRA is in full swing," he wrote on July 24. "Codes are coming in. Men rushing from hotel to hotel for conferences. Trade associations fighting. Everybody in the Administration in a great stew. . . . We have been having hearings morning, afternoon, and night."[20] In a hurried interview at lunch in the Department of Commerce cafeteria eight days later, he described the excitement of these early weeks in greater detail:

> Time makes no difference in the work of these boards. The work on the Labor Advisory Board requires my attention every day. . . . When I am not here [in the Department of Commerce] people are coming to see me at the National Catholic School of Social Service.
>
> General Johnson called our committee together at two a.m. one Sunday morning, and he himself seems to work twenty-four hours a day. There are four or five meetings going on at one time. Everyone is working on reserve strength. The tragic fact is that twelve millions of people are out of employment and something has to be done to get them back to work, and done now.
>
> The hearings on the Cotton Code were the first business after the formation of the committee. The day after the

Cotton Code was promulgated by the President, the three Advisory Boards held a joint meeting. It lasted from 9:30 o'clock in the morning until 11:30 o'clock that night.

The public hearings for the Electrical Manufacturing Industry came next. ... Then came the Lumber Industry hearings. They began last Thursday, and are still going on. I was asked to be present and to make a statement on the labor section for the Lumber Code. I proposed that the provision calling for a continuing committee of employers be changed to provide for a continuing committee composed of both employers and employees. That code has not yet been approved.

Now the hearings on the Men's Clothing Industry code are being held, and this morning I had that last-minute call to serve as an emergency adviser.[21]

It was during these same weeks of hectic meetings, hearings, and interdepartmental squabbles that Father Haas was asked to accompany Secretary Perkins on her celebrated visit to the steel mills of Pittsburgh and Homestead, Pennsylvania. The purpose of the one-day trip was to provide the secretary with firsthand information about the industry in preparation for the critical Steel Code hearings, which were to open on July 31. In her book, *The Roosevelt I Knew*, Miss Perkins explained her choice of an associate: "I took Father Haas with me. I chose him because he was a friend of labor, because I needed at least one other individual to go along as aide and observer and helper. I did not want to go 'in state' with a battery of economic advisers, publicity men, minor public officials, and obsequious secretaries."[22]

The incident that gave the trip its publicity occurred that afternoon in Homestead. Father Haas and the secretary arrived in Pittsburgh early on July 28 and spent several hours touring steel mills in the area, meeting company officials, conferring privately with workers, visiting homes, and talking with the workers' families. At 5:00 that afternoon, Miss Perkins met with approximately three hundred workers in the Homestead borough hall to discuss local working conditions and proposals for the Steel Code. During this meeting, Miss Perkins received word that the local burgess, John Cavanaugh, had barred two or three workers from the meeting, allegedly because he considered them too radical. The secretary asked Father Haas to investigate, and as he stepped outside he saw a police officer restraining one of the workers from entering the building. Haas immediately informed the secretary and she notified the burgess that she intended to hold a second meeting in the hall for all workers who had been unable to crowd into the first meeting. The burgess replied that he would not allow "those radicals" to take part in any meeting in the borough hall. When Miss Perkins suggested that the meeting be held in the public park across the street, Cavanaugh answered that that too was borough property and that he would bar those workers from speaking even there.[23] Finally Miss Perkins walked to the nearby post office and, standing on a table, held her meeting on property outside the jurisdiction of the local burgess. "I am just beginning to appreciate Postmaster General Farley and his post offices," she remarked later. "He told me to use them any time I liked."

To permit the secretary to meet as many workers as possible, Father Haas had asked a Catholic pastor for permission to use his parish auditorium for a meeting that evening. Haas had spoken earlier with Bishop Hugh Boyle of Pittsburgh and the permission was readily granted. Hundreds of workers assembled that night in St. Anne's parish hall to discuss local working conditions with Father Haas and the secretary. After the meeting adjourned, about midnight, Miss Perkins, Father Haas, and several leaders of the local steel workers (including at least one of the "radicals") repaired to the church rectory and continued the discussion over cake and coffee. Although the secretary concealed her feelings at the time, she acknowledged on her return to Washington that she had been shocked at these "uncalled for" actions of "the nervous Burgess" of Homestead. "It was a perfectly unbelievable experience," she stated. "I've read about such things, but I never expected to have such a thing actually happen to the Secretary of Labor while on a peaceful mission."[24]

This Pittsburgh visit also had its lighter side. When Miss Perkins was later asked why the incident with the Homestead burgess had not been reported by newsmen at the time, she admitted that none were present. After fifteen years of Prohibition, she added with a smile, "I believe they were all over at the drug store getting a soft drink."[25] Monsignor Michael Ready of the NCWC (later bishop of Columbus), chided Haas good-naturedly about another incident reported in the press. Secretary Perkins had lunch in Homestead that day in a plant cafeteria with local steel executives and the reporters noted that she insisted on paying for her own meal. Recalling Haas's enjoyment of an evening of cards for modest stakes, Monsignor Ready wrote: "I was especially pleased to hear of the honor of your appointment to investigate the steel industry, but you were either very gallant or not too alert when you failed to suggest a hand of rummy to see who would pay the check in the cafeteria. Watching pennies is no part of our training on the old front porch." In a short reply, Haas admitted that "we had a great time in Homestead," but added that "the pennies story was a reporter's invention."[26]

On his return from Pittsburgh on July 29, Father Haas faced his two most active months on the Labor Advisory Board. He found time during those weeks to deliver addresses in Montreal, Racine, Cleveland, and Uniontown, Pennsylvania, and as director of the School of Social Service he had final responsibility for the new school year, but his chief preoccupation that August and September was the work of the Labor Advisory Board. His mail brought almost daily pleas for assistance in improving labor standards in fields ranging from social work and independent banking to the sugar beet and playing card industries.[27] As hundreds of proposed codes of fair competition poured into NRA offices and as General Johnson intensified his "Blue Eagle campaign" to enroll all American industries under the President's Re-employment Agreement before winter, the Labor Advisory Board worked almost around the clock in a futile effort to keep pace.

By the beginning of August, however, the work of the Labor Advisory Board was better organized. A competent staff was recruited under the direction of Gustav Peck, a young economist from Columbia University. Realizing the impracticality of all members' attending all code hearings, the board had adopted the policy of apportioning its work among the members. As General Johnson announced the date for public hearings on each proposed code, the Labor Advisory Board assigned one or more labor advisers to attend all sessions to guarantee that the voice of labor was heard. This labor representative might be a member of the Labor Advisory Board, a member of its staff, or—especially after the autumn of 1933—a high-ranking union official selected by the board because of his or her familiarity with the industry concerned. By the end of September, for example, Father Haas had been appointed labor adviser for at least a dozen codes: hosiery, fishing tackle, retail lumber, salt, boot and shoe, work clothing, retail jewelry, watch-case manufacturing, and liquified gas—among others.[28] The labor standards which the advisers attempted to incorporate into each code were similar to those

written into the President's Re-employment Agreement of July
27: abolition of child labor, a maximum work week of thirty-five
or forty hours, a minimum wage of thirty cents, elimination of
wage differentials based on race or sex, and prohibition of discrimination because of union membership. At the close of public
hearings, the Labor Advisory Board would send a formal memorandum of approval or disapproval to the NRA administrator. The
board was strictly an advisory panel, however, and its recommendations were often ignored by deputy administrators, by Hugh
Johnson, and even by President Roosevelt.

One of the first codes to which Father Haas was assigned as
labor adviser on his return from Homestead was the Salt Manufacturing Code. Public hearings on this code were held by Deputy
Administrator R. B. Paddock on August 14, and Father Haas raised
strong objections to several of its labor provisions. He insisted that
the industry could easily bear a minimum wage of forty cents an
hour since labor costs accounted for only 17 percent of the final
cost of production, and that a thirty-hour week would be necessary to further the recovery administration's goal of providing
work for thousands of the unemployed that fall. The industry,
however, would make only minor concessions: employment of
children under sixteen was forbidden, maximum work weeks of
from forty to forty-eight hours were established, and minimum
wages of twenty-five and thirty-two cents an hour were set for
different sections of the country. Although these provisions
represented a substantial increase in wages and reduction in hours,
Father Haas was not satisfied. On August 24, after discussing the
code with other members of the Labor Advisory Board, he sent
a formal letter of protest to the deputy administrator, but to no
avail. Despite these objections to the labor provisions, President
Roosevelt approved the code on September 7 and it became
effective ten days later.[29]

Father Haas's work on the Retail Lumber Code was similarly
less than satisfying. At public hearings before Deputy Administrator Malcolm Muir on August 16, just two days after hearings
on the Salt Code, Father Haas objected to the code's provisions
for a forty-hour week and twenty-five-cent minimum wage. He
presented a recent Department of Labor study which showed
steady gains for the lumber industry since the preceding February,
and he suggested that since labor costs never exceeded 11 percent
of total sales cost, the industry could support a substantial wage
increase. The industry, however, stood firm. Father Haas con-

ferred with industry representatives on August 17, 18, and 21 in an attempt to arrive at a satisfactory compromise, but by August 21 he realized that his case was lost. Two days earlier, President Roosevelt had approved a forty-hour week and twenty-three-cent minimum wage in the Lumber Manufacturing Code, and there was little hope that the president would reject similar provisions in this allied industry. On October 3, consequently, over the objections of the Labor Advisory Board, the president signed the Retail Lumber Code, with the labor provisions substantially unchanged.[30]

As labor adviser for the Boot and Shoe Code that summer and fall, Father Haas was more successful. In late July, the National Boot and Shoe Manufacturers' Association had submitted a code to the NRA and on July 30 Father Haas conferred in Washington with delegates of the several unions concerned. At a preliminary conference with Deputy Administrator C. C. Williams and representatives of the boot and shoe industry on August 17, Father Haas submitted his objections to several of the code's labor provisions. He disapproved designation of the executive committee of the manufacturers' association as the code authority or enforcement agency; he objected to the provision for a forty-hour week and a $12 minimum wage; and he insisted on elimination of the code's so-called "merit clause," which guaranteed the employer's "right to select, retain, or advance employees on the basis of individual merit, without regard to their membership or non-membership in any organization," but which could be used by management to discriminate against union members.[31]

By the time public hearings on the code opened on September 12, the merit clause had become a national issue. When President Roosevelt formally approved the merit clause in the Automobile Code on August 28, the Labor Advisory Board issued a strong protest. "No section or sentence contained therein," the board insisted, "modifies, qualifies or changes Section 7(a)... [or establishes] a precedent to be followed in the preparation or acceptance of any other code."[32] Three days later, in the absence of Leo Wolman, William Green, the board's acting chairman, declared:

> The Board opposed this clause in one code. Now it finds it in 29 other codes recently submitted. Codes are being revised on the eve of hearings to get this clause in.... As practical men with long experience with this very clause, we know the

misuse to which "efficiency" and "merit" are put. The terms
have served as a screen behind which employers opposed to
any organization by their employees have intimidated and
eliminated wage earners favoring organization. The terms as
applied have left the sole determination of what constitutes
efficiency or merit to the employers without adequate appeal
by the workmen who have been discriminated against.[33]

Although the Labor and Industrial Advisory Boards held
joint meetings in early September in an effort to work out a
compromise, the future of the merit clause was still in doubt
when public hearings on the Boot and Shoe Code began on September 12. Father Haas repeated his earlier objections to the
code's wage, hour, and child labor provisions and then directed his
attack against the merit clause:

> I submit, Mr. Deputy Administrator, that the reading of
> Article IV, Section 1, is either in harmony with Section 7
> of the National Industrial Recovery Act, or it is not in
> harmony. It must be one or the other. If it is in complete
> harmony with the Act of Congress, signed by the President of
> the United States on June 16, then Article IV, Section 1, is
> superfluous, unnecessary, and should have no place in the
> code. On the other hand, if it is not in complete harmony
> with Section 7(a) of the National Industrial Recovery Act,
> then it is illegal, and by the same token it has no place in the
> code.[34]

The day ended, however, without compromise. Deputy
Administrator Williams insisted that since General Johnson and
the president had already approved the merit clause in the Automobile Code, he had no authority to prohibit it in others. There
the matter rested.

Public hearings the following day were concerned chiefly
with wage differentials in different sections of the country. Since
the union leaders were more familiar with local conditions, Father
Haas let them present labor's case. He intervened personally,
however, to oppose lower wages for southern workers since here
he saw the specter of racial prejudice. When one southern industrialist attempted to justify this differential on the grounds that
the extreme heat of the South made workers less efficient, Father
Haas countered that lower efficiency might result from malnutri-

tion, due to low wages.[35] He had taken this same stand in an earlier code hearing. "The point is made in the code," he had stated one month before, "that the lower minimum wage and higher maximum hours be allowed in the South because of lower living costs. This ought not to be a reason for lower wages and longer hours. It may be very plausibly argued that lower living standards prevail in these areas because of these longer hours and lower wages."[36] In most codes, however, the Boot and Shoe Code included, sectional differentials remained.

When the Shoe Code hearings closed on September 13, there was still no agreement on wages, hours, and the merit clause. The merit clause was clearly the critical issue. The Labor Advisory Board discussed it again at its meeting on September 22 and Father Haas conferred with high NRA officials throughout the following week. In a speech prepared for delivery at the annual convention of the AFL a few days later, he stated his opinion:

> Organization must set its face against the so-called "merit clause" and every other subterfuge invented to avoid real collective bargaining. The "merit clause" proposed by some employers' associations leaves the decision on merit solely with the employer. Because it can be used as a hideout to break up unions, it must be known for the fraud that it is and fought to the last ditch. Organized workers are not opposed to payment for performance. They do want a guarantee that "merit" will not be used to destroy their only protection. That guarantee is organization.[37]

A compromise was finally reached on September 30. The code would be sent to the president with the merit clause intact (thus saving face for the industry), but after approving the code, the president would issue an executive order eliminating the controversial clause.[38] This the president did. After approving the code on October 3, he released the following statement: "Because it is evident that attempts by those submitting codes to interpret Section 7(a) of the NIRA have led to confusion and misunderstanding, such interpretation should not be incorporated in codes of fair competition. Therefore Article IV [the merit clause] must be eliminated." A letter from Deputy Administrator Williams to Stanley King of the Industrial Advisory Board suggested that the management representatives might have known of the president's action beforehand. "The President has signed the Boot and Shoe Manufacturers' Code," Williams wrote on October 7, "but by executive order he has eliminated Article IV which was the so-called 'merit clause.' I have heard from Mr. Selby, the President of the National Boot and Shoe Manufacturers Association and from Gentlemen associated with him on the Committee presenting the Boot and Shoe Code, and they seem to have acquiesced in the President's action." After a battle of over two months, victory belonged to labor.

Since the authority and duties of the Labor Advisory Board were never clearly defined by executive order, the members gradually assumed responsibility for a wide variety of tasks and projects. They represented labor at public hearings and private conferences as each industrial code was drafted, held weekly meetings to coordinate activities with other NRA agencies, advised General Johnson and other government officials on labor policies, counseled labor groups on their rights and duties under Section 7(a), listened to endless charges of code violations, recommended amendments to code labor provisions, and nominated labor representatives for appointment to code authorities and industrial relations boards. The board studied the effects of higher labor standards on industrial profits, employment, and production; investigated industries' compliance with code provisions; and collected statistics on the growth of company unions and employee representation plans under the NRA. Board members, furthermore, were in frequent demand as public speakers or participants at Department of Labor or other government conferences. "It will be a miracle," Father Haas stated in August 1933, "if out of this hurrying and twenty-four hours a day work something practical and worthwhile emerges."[39]

Since the Labor Advisory Board insisted on the right to appoint labor representatives to all code authorities (the agencies responsible for overseeing compliance with code provisions), it was not surprising that when General Johnson established a General Code Authority in the NRA in the summer of 1934, he chose as labor representative a member of the Labor Advisory Board—Father Haas. This General Code Authority was set up to administer codes of fair competition in industries which had never had code authorities of their own or whose code authorities (for whatever reason) had ceased to function. General Johnson announced the establishment of this panel on July 10 but its members were not appointed until two months later. Four small industries, unable to afford code authorities of their own, immediately subscribed to the President's Re-employment Agreement and entrusted its administration to the General Code Authority: the ring traveler manufacturing industry, the shuttle manufacturing industry, the horse hair dressing industry, and the brattice cloth manufacturing industry. Code enforcement in these industries was singularly routine, however, and was rarely discussed at Code Authority meetings.[40]

The chief work of this committee was serving as temporary code authority for the retail solid fuel industry, the cotton garment industry, and the hand-machine embroidery industry for several weeks in late 1934 and early 1935. In each case, the industry's own code authority had ceased to function—in the fuel industry, all the members had resigned; in the garment industry, several members had been removed by higher NRA officials; and in the embroidery industry, the code authority required reorganization. Administration of their codes was assumed by the General Code Authority until their own authorities could be satisfactorily reestablished. The General Code Authority followed the same procedure in all three industries: it assumed jurisdiction over all property and finances of the former code authority, it appointed an executive custodian to act in its name in all routine matters of code administration, it decided all major controversies arising under the code, and it returned jurisdiction to the industry's code authority as soon as it was reconstituted.[41]

For Father Haas, work on the General Code Authority was of secondary importance. The executive custodians were responsible for routine administration of the codes and very few questions were referred to the Code Authority. Father Haas and other members met each week to listen to a report of the custodians' activities, to appropriate funds for necessary expenditures, to approve decisions lower officials had made, and to determine when code administration might be returned to an industry's code authority. More urgent and consequential matters apparently did not arise. The General Code Authority undoubtedly contributed to the efficient operation of the NRA in these few industries, but in the hectic days of the mid-1930s Father Haas and other committee members could give it little time and attention.

In fact, although Father Haas remained a member of the Labor Advisory Board until the summer of 1935, his enthusiasm had begun to decline after the first few months. One reason for this was that by the fall of 1933 the major work of the Labor

Advisory Board was completed. By early November, almost 10 million workers were covered by codes of fair competition and as many more by the President's Re-employment Agreement. Over 2 million unemployed had been returned to work. After the fall of 1933, the NRA turned from code drafting to code administration, and in code administration the Labor Advisory Board had little jurisdiction.[42]

Another reason for Father Haas's declining interest was that, toward the end of 1933, the Labor Advisory Board was being ignored by higher officials. Labor policies were frequently decided without its consultation, public hearings were being held without its representation, and codes were approved over its opposition. As early as September 1933, William Green sent a letter of formal protest to General Johnson. Three months later, John Frey complained that "members of the Board have had little if any knowledge of the labor provisions contained in [recent] codes, and in most instances the members of the Board had not given their approval." A year later, Heaton Vorse of the Labor Advisory Board staff declared that the board "has had no part in the formation of either of the last two Telegraph Codes," and "when I asked for a conference I was told by the Deputy that he had heard all that he cared to hear from labor."[43] As General Johnson and his deputy administrators paid less and less attention to the work of the Labor Advisory Board, Father Haas and the other board members felt justified in devoting less and less time to it.

The most important reason for Father Haas's limited service for the Labor Advisory Board after the fall of 1933, however, was that on October 6, President Roosevelt appointed him to the National Labor Board.[44] Because of the wave of strikes across the country that summer and early fall, the new labor disputes board scheduled hearings morning, afternoon, and evening. Father Haas became one of the board's most active members, serving five or six days a week, eight or twelve hours a day, and, as a result, was forced to delegate most of his other government and ecclesiastical responsibilities, including his work for the Labor Advisory Board.

Despite frequent criticism of the president's industrial recovery program, Father Haas was not dissatisfied with his work for the Labor Advisory Board. The NRA, admittedly, was hurriedly organized and poorly administered; it promised too much to both labor and industry; and its top officials were rarely able to work together as a team. At a time when the nation urgently needed an expanding economy, many industries restricted production and thereby retarded recovery; the interests of small businessmen were not adequately represented in either the formulation or the administration of indutrial codes and NRA policies may have forced some of them into ruin; and the price fixing tolerated under NRA codes often reduced competition and aided the growth of monopolies. As one historian suggested: "It prevented things from getting worse, but it did little to speed recovery, and probably actually hindered it by its support of restrictionism and price raising."[45]

Labor, on the other hand, made significant advances under NRA. The right of workers to organize and bargain collectively was guaranteed, child labor was abolished in most industries, sweatshop conditions were greatly curtailed, and over two million unemployed returned to work in the summer and fall of 1933, most of them in NRA-codified industries. By October of that year, the average work week declined from forty-three hours to thirty-eight and hourly wages increased from forty-four cents to fifty-two. Union membership increased almost 40 percent during the NRA, and in 1935 the AFL was at its greatest strength since the early 1920s.[46]

For these very real contributions to the cause of labor—perhaps the NRA's most significant achievement—the Labor Advisory Board deserves at least part credit. Workers were excluded from code-making negotiations, NRA Administrator Hugh Johnson and most of his deputy administrators were chosen from the ranks of business, and the Industrial Advisory Board was established to safeguard the interests of management at all NRA conferences and hearings. In the whole code-making process—from the drafting of a code by industrial leaders to its final approval by General Johnson and the president—almost the only voices raised in behalf of the worker were those of organized labor and the Labor Advisory Board. A former NRA official has written:

Such progress as was made by the National Recovery Administration in reemployment, in increasing wage rates, in improving standards of labor, in creating in the minds and plans of business men a larger consciousness of their social responsibilities, was due as much to the activities of the Labor Advisory Board as to any other division of the

Administration. This group at least never forgot the purposes of the Act, and in general it pushed wisely and effectively in all directions to effect those purposes. They were ever the spearhead of the NRA and a constant thorn in the side of lazy or ineffectual deputy administrators.[47]

The members of the Labor Advisory Board may not have been "the spearhead of the NRA," but they were staunch defenders of labor's interests in NRA proceedings, and their successes, though limited, were real. Labor made genuine advances under the NRA—wages were increased, hours shortened, child labor curtailed, and union membership expanded—and at least part of the credit for these benefits was due to the watchfulness and concern of the Labor Advisory Board.

5

Mediator for the National Labor Board

On the day he signed the National Industrial Recovery Act into law, President Franklin Roosevelt insisted that it was "not a law to foment discord," but with almost universal confusion over the interpretation of several of its provisions, discord and conflict seemed inevitable. The act expressly prohibited monopolies but permitted price fixing and production control, which the courts had generally considered monopolistic. Business leaders saw in Section 7(a) the prohibition of the closed shop, while labor executives hailed it as "the second Magna Carta of Labor" and advertised that "President Roosevelt wants you to join a union." AFL officials hoped the act would put an end to minority collective bargaining, but President Roosevelt expressly sanctioned it in the automobile settlement in March 1934. "Management has just carved out of that Section 7(a) the interpretations that suit their point of view and published it all over their plants," General Johnson complained in the fall of 1933, "and, on the other hand, the labor people have carved out of the President's speeches or simple statements I have made, or Richberg had made, whatever they like until the whole thing is in confusion." Later historians have agreed. In the opinion of Sidney Fine, "Section 7(a) actually raised more questions than it answered."[1]

The result of this conflict and confusion could have been near-disaster for the president's recovery program. According to Department of Labor statistics, 131 strikes had broken out in June 1933, with the loss of 500,000 man-days of work. In July, the National Recovery Administration's first full month, the figure soared. Over 200 new strikes were reported, costing 1.4 million man-days of work. In the clothing industry alone, almost 70,000 workers walked off their jobs, more than the total number of strikers in all industries in June. The statistics for August continued to climb. An additional 85,000 workers struck the garment industry, joined by 22,000 miners, 9,000 tobacco hands, and 13,000 textile workers. Within two months of the passage of the NIRA, one New Deal authority has stated, "there was serious danger that the whole re-employment campaign would collapse under the growing pressure of labor disputes."[2]

To cope with this sudden outbreak of strikes under the NRA, President Roosevelt set up the National Labor Board on August 5. Father Haas had recommended creation of a Public Works Labor Board in his letter to Secretary Perkins on April 1, but his influence on the establishment of this new board is uncertain. One authority stated that "Father Haas of the Labor Advisory Board seems to have been the first to recognize the probable necessity for some such bi-partisan board, the creation of which he proposed at a meeting of the Labor Advisory Board on July 9." Since complete minutes of the Labor Advisory Board's meetings that summer have not been preserved, this statement is difficult to corroborate. The Labor and Industrial Advisory Boards met jointly throughout that month to discuss labor and trade practice provisions in the president's "blanket code," and toward the end of the month they unanimously recommended establishment of a labor disputes board. Higher New Deal officials, however, still could not agree. General Johnson wanted the board set up within the National Recovery Administration rather than in the Department of Labor, because, in his view, the Department of Labor was by definition partisan. Secretary Perkins, on the other hand, insisted that only her department had the necessary mediation machinery and experience. She was skeptical, furthermore, of the labor views General Johnson might have absorbed as a Wall Street associate of Bernard Baruch. "The trouble with Hugh," she once remarked, "is that he thinks a strike is something to settle."[3]

Perhaps because his close advisers could not agree, President Roosevelt at first left the powers and jurisdiction of the National Labor Board unclear and, as a consequence, open to almost continuous controversy. On August 5 he announced the appointment of a "distinguished tribunal to pass promptly on any case of hardship or dispute that may arise from interpretation or application of the President's Re-employment Agreement." The bulletin released by the National Recovery Administration was only slightly more precise: "The board will consider, adjust and settle differences and controversies that may arise through interpretations of the President's Re-employment Agreement and will act with all possible dispatch in making their findings."[4] The original jurisdiction of the board thus seemed to extend only to industries subscribing to the President's Re-employment Agreement and not to those signing individual codes of fair competition. No enforcement machinery was provided, the binding force of these NLB "findings" was left unclear, and the division of jurisdiction between the board and the NRA's Compliance Division was not specified. Furthermore, the president had neglected to issue an executive order giving the board legal foundation.

Only gradually was this confusion remedied. On December 16, more than four months after the board was established, the president issued an executive order empowering it "to settle by mediation, conciliation or arbitration all controversies between employers and employees which tend to impede the purpose of the NIRA." This order also gave the board authority to set up regional boards, hear appeals, and in general "make rules and regulations governing its procedures and the discharge of its functions." Six weeks later, on February 1, the NLB was authorized to order and supervise union elections whenever the workers' collective bargaining agent was challenged, and on February 23, faced with industry's growing refusal to accept NLB directives, the board was given authority to refer its decisions to other government agencies for enforcement: to the Department of Justice for prosecution when Section 7(a) of the Recovery Act was violated, and to the Compliance Division of NRA for removal of the Blue Eagle when the provisions of an industrial code were disobeyed.[5]

General Johnson called the new board "as distinguished a board as was ever set up" to pass upon labor disputes, and perhaps it was. The chairman and public representative was Senator Robert F. Wagner of New York, the Senate's leading spokesman on industrial problems and one of the principal authors of the NIRA. The original labor representatives were Leo Wolman, William Green, and John L. Lewis, all members of the Labor Advisory Board. The management representatives, all from the NRA's Industrial Advisory Board, were Louis Kerstein, Gerard Swope, and Walter Teagle. Kerstein, one of the most influential business executives in New England, was vice president of William Filene's Sons of Boston, chairman of the Boston Port Authority, and a member of the board of directors of both Abraham and Straus and Federated Department Stores. Swope, president of General Electric, was the author of the Swope Plan for the Stabilization of Industry, a proposal for industrial self-government through strengthened trade associations. Teagle, president of Standard Oil of New Jersey since 1917 and a member of President Harding's "poker cabinet" in the 1920s, had little sympathy for government economic activity. "Government should not write the rules," he liked to remark, "name the umpire, and then enter the field as one of the players in the business game." On October 6, President Roosevelt announced the appointment of four additional members: for labor, Major George Berry of the International Printing Pressmen's Union, and Father Haas; for industry, Thomas Austin Finch, North Carolina industrialist, and Edward Hurley, board chairman of the Hurley Machine Company of Chicago. When Hurley died, on November 14, 1933, and Swope and Finch subsequently resigned, President Roosevelt named as successors Pierre DuPont of E. I. DuPont and Company, Henry Dennison of Dennison Manufacturing Company of Massachusetts, and Ernest Draper, president of Hills Brothers Company and, later, assistant secretary of commerce.[6]

By October 6, 1933, when Father Haas received his appointment, the National Labor Board was overwhelmed with work. Over 3.5 million man-days of work had been lost because of walkouts in September, and in the first week of October, 160,000 workers were still on strike. The hurried notes Father Haas jotted down in a makeshift dairy over a two-week period that first month indicated the demands made by this new assignment[7] :

Oct. 16: A.M. Hearings on Ford disputes at Chester and Edgewater
P.M. Wierton Steel negotiations

Oct. 17: Meeting of NLB to discuss reply to Ford

Oct. 18: A.M. Board heard West Virginia miners' dispute
P.M. Arbitration hearings

Oct. 19: 11 a.m. Formal Hearings
2 p.m. Voting on yesterday's arbitration hearings
8 p.m. Adjournment

Oct. 20: Negotiations with Teagle all morning
Brooklyn Shoe hearings in afternoon
Agreement reached in morning's dispute at 7:30 p.m.

Oct. 23: A.M. Meeting with chairmen of regional boards
P.M. Heard charges of racketeering in New York unions

Oct. 24: 11 a.m. Formal hearings in Wagner's office
        2 p.m. Leather Workers' hearings
        4 p.m. Brooklyn Shoe hearings
        7 p.m. Adjournment

Oct. 25: 11 a.m. Brooklyn Shoe negotiations
        Dinner with Bishop James H. Ryan
        4 p.m. Lecture called by Secretary Perkins
        5 p.m. Presided at formal hearings
        8 p.m. Adjournment

Oct. 26: 9 a.m. Left for New York with Wagner
        2 P.M. Silk hearings begin in New York
        Hearings afternoon and evening
        Midnight: Left New York for Washington

Oct. 27   7 a.m. Arrived in Washington from New York
        9 a.m. Class
        Noon: Lunch with Dr. Ryan
        2 p.m. Negotiations for the NLB

Father Haas discontinued this diary at the end of October, but official releases of the National Labor Board suggest that succeeding months were little different. There were eleven new cases before the board from November 14 to 29 and Father Haas was assigned to all eleven. Of the fourteen cases pending on January 25, Father Haas was involved in twelve, four more than any other board member. A government memorandum lists him as the only member assigned to all twelve disputes pending before the NLB on February 5, and he was assigned to six of the nine cases submitted to the board on March 24. Soon after his NLB appointment, Father Haas was forced to delegate most of his work for the NRA's Labor Advisory Board to others, and by November he had adopted the policy of declining all speaking engagements outside Washington. "I am giving the entire day and frequently much of the night to the National Labor Board," he wrote hurriedly to Father Muench that November.[8]

One of the earliest controversies in which Haas intervened as a member of the NLB was a dispute between the Ward and Baur bakeries of Pittsburgh and their bakery workers and drivers.[9] On October 19, 1933, the business agent for the two unions—the Bakery and Confectionary Workers and the Bakery Wagon Drivers—protested to Secretary Perkins that the bakeries were discriminating against employees who refused to join company unions. At the secretary's request, the National Labor Board assumed jurisdiction over the case and requested the disputing parties to appear in Washington for public hearings on November 1. At these hearings, presided over by Senator Wagner and Father Haas, the companies announced their official policy: workers were free to join any union they wished and could select any bargaining agent, but the final contract had to be signed by the companies' employees, not by outside union officials. The companies insisted also that the open shop be maintained.

At the end of the formal hearings, Senator Wagner departed and Father Haas continued mediation efforts until close to midnight. He suggested that the parties agree to begin collective bargaining with a "gentlemen's agreement" that the closed shop not be a subject of negotiation. This would meet the companies' demand and still permit the union leaders to save face before their membership. The companies asked that the "gentlemen's agreement" also exclude discussion of union recognition and the union contract, but this the workers rejected. The meeting broke up without agreement and the workers in Pittsburgh walked off their jobs soon after.[10]

The negotiations resumed on November 3, with Wagner and Haas acting as mediators. At the request of Senator Wagner, the workers agreed to drop their demand for a union contract and the way was cleared for agreement on the proposal Father Haas had drafted two days before: the strike was to be called off at once, all workers were to be reinstated without discrimination, the companies were to begin collective bargaining with representatives of the company unions and the Bakery Wagon Drivers immediately, and all questions not settled by November 10 were to be submitted to the National Labor Board for arbitration. The negotiations began at once, but union and management representatives still could not agree. On November 27, arbitration hearings were held before Wolman, Haas, and Lewis, and on December 27 the board handed down its arbitration ruling. Debate continued for several weeks on the interpretation of this award and the case was not concluded until February 1934, but the final settlement was little different from the collective bargaining agreement proposed by Father Haas the previous November.[11]

During the fall and winter of 1933, Father Haas was also involved in efforts to settle the strike at Weirton Steel, one of the most difficult disputes the board encountered. Company officials that September had refused to meet with the leaders of the AFL's Iron, Steel, and Tin Workers' Union, and as a result several thousand workers walked off their jobs in West Virginia and southeastern Ohio. The National Labor Board assumed jurisdiction over the case on October 14 and formal hearings were scheduled for two days later. At the close of these hearings, union and company officials signed an agreement, proposed by Senator Wagner and Father Haas, providing for immediate termination of the strike, restoration of all workers to their jobs without discrimination, a union election in December—"the procedure and method of election to be prescribed by the Board"—and submission of issues not settled by collective bargaining to the final determination of the NLB. At the end of the day, Father Haas noted in his diary (all too optimistically): "Agreement signed. Steel is at stake. Important victory."[12]

Although an agreement had been signed, victory had not been won. The "war," in fact, was just beginning. On December 11, company president Ernest Weir notified Senator Wagner that the employee election would be held under company union procedures, that only plant employees would be eligible for office, but that the National Labor Board could send representatives to conduct the election according to this procedure, if it wished. The members of the board were deeply annoyed. "We are determined to have a fair election," Wagner declared. "The Board will see that the agreement will be carried out." On December 14 Johnson notified Weir: "In my opinion you are about to commit a deliberate violation of federal laws, and ... if you do, I shall request the Attorney General to proceed against you immediately."[13]

Despite the objections of General Johnson and the NLB, the election was held as planned on December 15. Over 9,000 workers voted (81 percent of the payroll), and company officials were elated. "The men themselves," Weir declared that evening, "by this action overwhelmingly demonstrated their preference for their own organization and the election of representatives under their own by-laws."[14] The National Labor Board discussed alternative courses of action for the next several weeks and, on March 1, referred the case to the attorney general for prosecution.

A few weeks later, Father Haas was called by the District Court of Delaware to testify under oath to the meaning of the agreement he and Senator Wagner had drafted on October 16. Haas insisted that the purpose of the agreement had been to give the workers a chance to choose between the Employee Representation Plan and the Amalgamated Union, since dissatisfaction with the company plan had allegedly been a cause of the strike. "The agreement settling the strike," he asserted, "was designed to permit the employees to determine whether or not they wanted this plan or some other... and to choose between any forms of self-organization they might desire. There obviously was no need for any special agreement permitting the striking employees to participate in the company union election as they already had that right independent of any agreement." Haas denied Weir's assertion that he and Wagner had agreed to the company union proposal. "My recollection of this conversation," he stated, "differs materially from the summaries contained in these affidavits.... To intimate that in conversation Senator Wagner and I made statements in such plain contradiction of the evident meaning and purpose of the agreement is to ascribe to us either duplicity and deceitfulness or a willingness to participate in a futile proceeding."[15]

This was Father Haas's last connection with the Weirton controversy. On May 29, Federal Judge John P. Nields of the Delaware District Court denied the board's request for an injunction against the company.[16] Nine months later he ruled further: Section 7(a) of the NIRA was unconstitutional; and before the Justice Department could appeal to the Supreme Court, NRA codes were invalidated in the Schechter decision of May 27, 1935. Almost a year previously, however, in July 1934, the National Labor Board had been dissolved by presidential order and the new National Labor Relations Board had been established, and Father Haas, consequently, was no longer involved in the Weirton Steel dispute.

Father Haas was much more successful in his efforts to settle a serious strike involving several Remington Rand plants in upstate New York that spring. The dispute had begun in late 1933 with a demand by the International Association of Machinists for higher wages, shorter hours, union recognition, and reinstatement of two dismissed workers. After several weeks of negotiations, company and union officials reached an agreement on all points except union recognition, and in an effort to prevent a walkout, the Buffalo Regional Labor Board assumed jurisdiction over the case in mid-February 1934. The regional board conducted public hearings in March, but, unable to solve the dispute over a union contract, referred the case to the National Labor Board on April 20.[17]

Hearings before the NLB were postponed until April 30 since Father Haas and other board members were scheduled to hear a similar dispute between the Machinists and the Underwood, Elliott-Fisher Company of Hartford that day. Father Haas met with Machinist and Underwood representatives throughout the day, and by seven o'clock had reached an agreement on most points in dispute.[18] Senator Wagner immediately requested him to intervene in the dispute at Remington Rand.

By early May, the situation at Remington Rand had greatly deteriorated. Seven thousand workers had walked off their jobs in four plants, and when the company inaugurated a "back to work" movement, violence had broken out in Syracuse. Father Haas met with both parties throughout May and early June and was able to announce a settlement on June 18. The wage-and-hour standards that had been agreed upon earlier were written into the settlement and the union contract was compromised: an open shop was guaranteed, but for the first time the company formally recognized the union as bargaining agent for its workers. According to the *New York Times*, both sides were satisfied.[19]

Father Haas's hectic pace of the preceding October and November continued throughout the spring of 1934. One historian has stated that Father Haas "served as acting chairman in the majority of cases coming before the National Labor Board from October, 1933, to June, 1934," and the statement is probably accurate. In the spring of 1934, Senator Wagner was frequently occupied with affairs in Congress, especially the progress of the Wagner-Lewis Social Security bill and his Labor Disputes bill, and the office of acting chairman of the NLB, as a result, often fell to Haas. Records of June 1934 indicate that Father Haas was still presiding at public hearings five mornings each week, and he usually spent the afternoons, evenings, and weekends attempting to mediate in informal conferences the points of disagreement revealed in public hearings. Father Haas, in fact, assumed such a prominent part in the board's activities that spring that one of Senator Wagner's secretaries in later years mistakenly thought he had been appointed chairman in the senator's place.[20]

Father Haas and the other members of the NLB were justly proud of the board's success during its first six months. The national board had resolved 69 percent of the cases brought before it, and its regional boards 64 percent. More significantly, together they settled close to 80 percent of the strikes submitted to their jurisdiction and averted close to two hundred others. In a letter to President Roosevelt that February, Senator Wagner made the further point that the official statistics might be low. "There is a marginal area of settlements," he noted, "through the influence of the mere existence of the Boards. Disputants have settled up because it was realized there was a tribunal to which the matters would ultimately have to go." More than 185 disputes had been brought before the national board in Washington and Father Haas had been involved in most.[21]

Soon after the new year opened, however, the board began to experience greater difficulty in reaching satisfactory agreements. In January 1934, Father Haas was unsuccessful in his efforts to mediate the Harriman Hosiery dispute and three months later the NRA was forced to remove the company's Blue Eagle. That same month, Haas presided at hearings in the National Lock controversy, but this company also rejected the board's recommendations. In February, he took part in discussions of the Denver Tramway dispute and on March 1 voted with the majority of the board to prohibit minority bargaining. This case was especially significant because Pierre DuPont publicly dissented from the majority decision and for the first time the unanimity of the board was broken. Father Haas also presided at hearings in the Houde Engineering Corporation case in February and May. The board again affirmed the principle of majority rule but the company rejected it and appealed to the federal courts.[22]

By the spring of 1934, consequently, a major weakness in the NLB's line of defense was exposed: it was unable to enforce its decisions and directives. Lacking enforcement machinery of its own, the board could only refer its disputes to the NRA's Compliance Division or to the Justice Department, and both procedures were unsatisfactory. The Compliance Division often disagreed with the board's interpretation of Section 7(a)—on the question of minority bargaining, for example—and was at times reluctant to remove a company's Blue Eagle at the NLB's request.[23] The Justice Department had well-founded fears about the constitutionality of the NRA and it hesitated to test it in the courts. Consequently, as several major industries—Weirton Steel, Harriman Hosiery, and Houde Engineering—successfully challenged the NLB's authority in the spring of 1934, the prestige of the board declined.

In late March, President Roosevelt delivered a final blow to the board's diminishing prestige when he intervened directly in the automobile controversy. A dispute over wages, seniority, and union recognition had broken out between the automobile industry and the AFL's United Automobile Workers, and armed with the increased authority of the president's executive orders of February 1 and 23, the National Labor Board had assumed jurisdiction and had held public hearings in mid-March. Before the board could release its recommendations, however, President Roosevelt unexpectedly announced his own settlement. This agreement of March 25 had not only been achieved without the board's assistance but in several of its provisions directly contradicted its policies. It did not provide for an employee election to determine the proper bargaining agent, it expressly permitted minority bargaining, and it established an Automobile Labor Board to function independently of the National Labor Board. Deprived of jurisdiction over this key industry and unable to ensure enforcement of its decisions and orders, the board lost even more of its effectiveness.[24]

Recognizing the board's weaknesses, Senator Wagner introduced into the Senate on March 1, 1934. a Labor Disputes bill to increase the authority of the National Labor Board and extend the rights of workers guaranteed by Section 7(a) of the NIRA. This new measure would make it a misdemeanor, punishable by fine, for an employer to interfere with the right to organize, to refuse to bargain in good faith with employee representatives, to establish a company union or support one financially, or to discriminate against a worker because of union affiliation.[25] The bill expressly approved the closed shop and would establish a seven-member National Labor Board to mediate industrial disputes, to act as a board of voluntary arbitration, and to issue cease-and-desist orders (enforceable in the courts) against industries engaging in unfair labor practices.

On March 15, the day on which the National Labor Board made its last attempt to settle the automobile dispute before the president's intervention, Father Haas was called before the Senate Labor Committee to testify in support of Senator Wagner's proposal. He defended the measure as an effort toward emergency, short-range relief. By forcing employers to recognize the rights of workers, without recourse to strikes and walkouts, he insisted, the bill would reduce the number of work stoppages, increase production, and stabilize employment. "But we dare not merely pull the car out of the ditch," he continued, "and run it for a year or two to go into the ditch again for another four or five years."[26] By guaranteeing the worker's right to unrestricted unionization, the new proposal would also help to raise wages and increase the nation's purchasing power. For Father Haas, this was the central issue:

This Bill seeks as its ultimate purpose to increase purchasing power. There is no recognized authority who does not hold that inadequate purchasing power caused the precipitous business decline from June, 1929 to June, 1933, and that increased purchasing power is essential both to recovery and permanent prosperity. With the aim of the proposed legislation, there is unanimous agreement.

To effect increased purchasing power, the Bill defines certain acts as unfair labor practices and sets up machinery to prevent or restrain them. There are, of course, persons who object, and strenuously, to the proposed machinery but, in my opinion, this machinery is the only possible method of increasing buying power now and of maintaining it, and thereby putting the country on a lasting basis of prosperity.

From his experience on the NLB, Father Haas was convinced of the need for a Labor Disputes Board with specific authority to order union elections:

The question of the identity of workers' representatives, who they are, and what authority they have, is full of complications and large with strife and controversy. The common sense expedient is to settle such questions through the medium of the secret ballot. The National Labor Board has in the brief period of its existence held more than 97 elections for such purposes. ... Moreover, in the course of time the Board will develop a body of precedents and these will act as guiding principles in effectuating mutual agreements. ... There parties to an industrial dispute can come to the Board, and with the advice and experience of trained conciliators, have their respective rights clarified and composed and thereby avoid what may result in costly industrial warfare. ... The National Labor Board as proposed is necessary to make collective bargaining an actuality. Only such a governmental agency can prevent unfair labor practices and maintain equality of bargaining power in the wage contract.[27]

Discussion of the new Labor Disputes bill continued for three months. Violent strikes that spring by Toledo electrical workers, Minneapolis truck drivers, and San Francisco longshoremen added to the seriousness of the debates. Opposition to the bill was formidable, and on May 26 the Senate Labor Committee, under Chairman David I. Walsh of Massachusetts, reported out a revised and weakened measure, the National Industrial Adjustment bill. This version—too strong for Senate conservatives but too weak for liberals—pleased almost no one and was never brought to a vote. Finally, on June 13, as Congress prepared to adjourn, President Roosevelt sent his own proposal to Congress, a measure empowering the president to establish new labor boards, at his discretion, in order to secure the goals of the National Industrial Recovery Act. This bill was rushed to a vote as Public Resolution 44 and was signed by the president on June 19. Armed with the authority of this public resolution, the president, on June 29, issued an executive order setting up a National Labor Relations Board to replace Senator Wagner's National Labor Board, effective July 9.[28]

On the same day that President Roosevelt issued the executive order under Public Resolution 44, June 29, Father Haas performed his last and probably most important service for the old National Labor Board. After passage of the public resolution authorizing the president to appoint new labor boards as he judged necessary, the National Labor Board simply bided time until its successor could be named, and since the National Catholic School of Social Service had closed its doors for the summer, Father Haas felt free to leave Washington for a few days in Racine. He had agreed to speak on July 1 at ceremonies commemorating the one hundredth anniversary of the founding of his native city, and he welcomed a few days of leisure to prepare his address.[29] Less than three days after his arrival in Racine, however, he was asked by the board to intervene in the serious dispute that had broken out in Milwaukee between the city's Electric Railway and Light Company and three AFL unions.

In many ways, this strike and the chain of events leading to it were typical of the numerous labor disputes that plagued these early months of the New Deal. Soon after the passage of the National Industrial Recovery Act in June 1933, the AFL had undertaken to organize the Milwaukee Railway and Light Company's electricians, engineers, and the streetcar men and had then demanded a new labor contract. The company refused, however, because it had a closed shop agreement with its company union since 1918, the Employees' Mutual Benefit Association, and it insisted that the Recovery Act explicitly honored prior agreements. When the company dismissed thirteen workers the following March, allegedly for AFL activities, the unions voted to strike, but, at the urging of Senator Wagner, postponed the walkout until the National Labor Board could attempt a settlement. The board held public hearings on March 13 and soon after set up a private tribunal to investigate the alleged anti-union discrimination. On May 23, after reviewing the findings of this panel, the board ordered eight of the thirteen reinstated. Five days later the company formally refused, and on June 6 the NRA's Compliance Division ordered its Blue Eagle removed. By this time the workers were also demanding union elections and an increase in wages—besides the rehiring of all the dismissed workers—and when the company remained adamant, they voted to strike on June 26.[30]

The strike began at 4:00 A.M., with only 300 of the company's more than 3,000 workers walking off their jobs. Transportation and power service remained normal throughout most of the day, but violence erupted that evening. Thousands of people swarmed through the streets, throwing rocks, breaking windows in power plants, and derailing streetcars. When police finally restored order, twelve persons had been injured, seventeen arrested, and forty-seven streetcars had been damaged. On the following day, the federal mediator in Milwaukee, Major John D. Moore, wired the Labor Board that, in spite of its closed shop agreement with the EMBA, the utility company was willing to hold an election if the board would order it. Moore recommended an immediate election. Fearing renewed violence, the company discontinued all trolley service that evening and, after operating a few cars the following morning, cancelled all service for the duration of the strike. Despite the explosiveness of the situation, the National Labor Board hesitated to order an employee election: with Public Resolution 44 signed into law, the NLB did not have time to conduct an election or to defend such an election in the courts, if challenged by the EMBA. A voluntary agreement among the parties seemed to be the only solution. Consequently, on June 28, the board assigned Father Haas to the case and asked him to assume direction of all mediation efforts.[31]

Haas arrived in Milwaukee from Racine that same evening and conferred immediately with Major Moore. The two mediators met with union leaders until midnight and then with company officials until 4:00 A.M. At the end of these sessions, the *Milwaukee Journal* reported cautiously that "negotiations were still not hopeless." Progress in fact had been made. "We were up all night," Father Haas informed the Labor Board later that morning, "and I think we're getting somewhere—in fact, I know we are."[32]

Time, however, was crucial. Rioting had broken out again the night before: company property throughout the city had been destroyed, scores of people were injured, and one person had been electrocuted in an attempt to break into the huge Lakeside power plant. On June 29, the newspapers announced that the city would be in total darkness that night, since the company could no longer guarantee the safety of its workers, and would close the power plant in late afternoon. Fearing a renewed outbreak of violence and looting, Father Haas insisted: "We must settle this strike before dark." The *Milwaukee Journal* called the negotiations "a race against darkness." At noon on June 29, the first break-through occurred when, for the first time, company officials agreed to meet with the AFL leaders. Father Haas presented each side with a compromise proposal, but the company rejected the clause designating the three AFL unions as bargaining agents for its workers. The mediators then suggested that the National Labor Board be authorized to determine these representatives, "not by an election but by some other suitable means."[33] This pro-posal, intended probably to satisfy the AFL leaders, who realized from the small strike turnout that they might not win an election, was also rejected by the company. By late afternoon, as workers began to leave their jobs at the power plant and as electric power was reduced in Milwaukee and surrounding cities, the strike was still not settled.

At about five o'clock, Father Haas returned with a third compromise. According to this proposal, the strike was to be called off, all strikers were to be reinstated, the thirteen dismissed workers were to be rehired, a committee of three was to "deter-mine by some suitable means" the proper employee representa-tion, collective bargaining was to begin as soon as these represen-tatives were chosen, and the NRA would be requested to restore the company's Blue Eagle. The only important changes in this draft were that a committee of three was to determine the em-ployees' representation, instead of the National Labor Board, and that the committee was free to order a union election or not, as it wished. Father Haas and the negotiators discussed this proposal for almost an hour, with the threat of another night of darkness and rioting looming larger. Finally, shortly before 6:00 P.M., Father Haas emerged from the conference room, weary but smiling, and nodded to the assembled newsmen: "It's all over."[34] The most violent strike in Milwaukee's history was settled.

Although Father Haas admitted at the end of the strike that he was "glad to have had a small share at least in the efforts to bring this victory to others," he declined major credit for the settlement. "It just happened," he wrote a friend a few days later, "that I came in twenty-four hours before the truce was signed. A good many of my friends were inclined to give me entire credit for working out the agreement. Of course I did nothing of the kind and for that reason felt that I was flying under false colors."[35]

Others, however, did not agree. The *Milwaukee Journal* gave special praise to "the smiling priest from Washington, D.C., the Rev. Francis J. Haas, who arrived at the psychological time. He soothed open wounds of bitterness." Other newspapers credited the settlement to this "chief Federal conciliator." In a telegram to the National Labor Board on July 2, Major Moore acknowledged that "Doctor Haas was largely responsible" for solving the representation problem. To the *Milwaukee Catholic Herald*, Haas was "the Man of the Hour."[36]

The settlement of the Milwaukee strike, almost the last act the National Labor Board performed, was in many ways representative of the board's career. When it attempted to impose terms of settlement on disputing parties—as in controversies at Weirton Steel, National Lock, Houde Engineering, and the Milwaukee utility company in May—it often failed. Employers felt free to ignore the board's directives, since it had no statutory basis for the first third of its life and its constitutionality—like the NRA itself—was always in doubt. The board, furthermore, had no enforcement machinery of its own and the assistance of the Department of Justice and the NRA's Compliance Division was inadequate. During the eleven months of the board's existence, the Justice Department prosecuted only one company for violating NLB directives—Weirton Steel—and the Compliance Division removed the Blue Eagle from only four: A. Roth and Company, Harriman Hosiery, National Lock, and Milwaukee Electric.[37] By the spring of 1934, consequently, major industries across the country were able to challenge the board's jurisdiction and ignore its decisions almost at will.

Because several large industries were successful in flouting the NLB's authority in the early months of 1934, the board has often been judged a failure. The judgment, however, seems harsh. The primary goal of the NLB was not to impose terms of settlement on disputing parties, or to litigate through the courts, but to reach voluntary agreements. "The function of the National Labor Board is that of mediation," one authority stated in 1934, and in a letter to President Roosevelt that same year Walter Teagle agreed: "I have felt that the Board's greatest usefulness was as an agency of mediation to clear the way for labor and industry to bargain collectively as provided in the NRA and arrive at their own understanding."[38] Since the president's recovery program was an emergency measure, requiring an immediate rise in employment and prompt settlement of all work stoppages, the board was not expected to become involved in lengthy enforcement proceedings. Coersion, in fact, was to have little part in the NRA. After describing the outrage and public scorn that would erupt if an American businessman dared to violate the National Industrial Recovery Act, General Johnson had assured the nation in 1933: "It will never happen. The threat of it [public opposition and scorn] transcends any puny penal provision in this law." The influence of men like Gerard Swope and Pierre DuPont with business executives and of William Green and John L. Lewis with labor leaders would be sufficient, New Deal officials were confident, to ensure compliance with NLB recommendations, without recourse to force or penalties. Although the few cases in which the National Labor Board turned to the Compliance Division or the Justice Department for assistance received wide publicity, the principal work of the board remained mediation.

In the field of mediation the National Labor Board compiled an impressive record. In the eleven months of its existence, from August 1933 to July 1934, it successfully mediated 123 of the 148 strikes brought before it and it averted 36 others. Its nineteen regional boards were only slightly less successful, settling 75 percent of the strikes they entered and averting 460 others. More than 1.2 million workers returned to work, or remained at work, through the mediation efforts of the national and regional boards.[39] In all these settlements, the board strove to guarantee to workers the rights listed in Section 7(a)—unrestricted unionization, collective bargaining, and the higher wages and reduced hours which would not only permit workers to live more comfortably but would further economic recovery by increasing purchasing power and reducing unemployment. The NLB, finally, was successful in establishing a kind of "common law" of labor relations, writing the principles of union elections, the secret ballot and majority rule into our national labor policy. Father Haas, consequently, never considered his work for the National Labor Board a failure. The board had entered more than 250 controversies, involving 500,000 workers, and it had settled close to 200. A permanent resident of Washington, he had presided at more public hearings than anyone except Senator Wagner and had intervened in so many disputes that he was called the federal government's "chief conciliator." The board's greatest success was in mediation and it was in this field, above all, that Father Haas made his most significant contributions.

6

The Minneapolis Truckers' Strike of 1934

Despite the violence and bloodshed of the Milwaukee Electric strike in late June, the upheaval that rocked the Midwest most deeply that summer—and most severely challenged Father Haas's mediation skills—was the clash between Teamster Local 574 and more than 150 trucking firms in Minneapolis, Minnesota. The spring and summer of 1934, in fact, were a time of unusual violence in American industrial relations. In March, striking drivers burned taxicabs in New York and other eastern cities in disputes over wages and union recognition. Workers struck the Electric Auto-Lite plant in Toledo in May and, led by leftists A. J. Muste and Louis Budenz, confronted tear gas, bayonets, and even rifle fire from the Ohio National Guard. The bitter Milwaukee conflict erupted in June. Longshoreman Harry Bridges called for a general strike in San Francisco in July, when two of his workers were shot in the violence that accompanied efforts of the Industrial Association to reopen the California port by force. In Minneapolis the upheaval was no less severe: four persons were killed, hundreds were injured, and property damage was estimated in the millions of dollars.[1]

According to most accounts, the Minneapolis conflict began with the strike call issued by Teamster officials on May 15. Actually, it had begun almost seventy years earlier. The immediate cause of the controversy may have been the employers' rejection of union demands for formal recognition, higher wages, and a closed shop, but the violence which suddenly erupted was the culmination of over half a century of social antagonism. During the preceding decades, there had developed side by side in Minneapolis one of the nation's most militant and radical labor organizations and one of its most powerful business associations, and they met in head-on clash in the summer of 1934. If the result was not open class warfare, as some have suggested, it was dangerously close.[2]

The history of Minneapolis from the close of the Civil War to the strike of 1934 is in part the story of two antagonistic social classes. In the 1870s and 1880s, Minnesota's rich resources in timber and fertile soil contributed to the vast personal fortunes of lumber magnates Thomas B. Walker and Frederick Weyerhaeuser and flour barons William D. Washburn and Charles A. Pillsbury, but they offered only hard work and a bare livelihood to thousands of farmers, lumberjacks, and mill hands. John D. Rockefeller and his associates built an iron empire on the newly discovered Mesabi Range in the 1890s, but the miners of Minnesota often found only hazardous working conditions, long hours, and short pay. Sinking deeper into debt to the bankers, industrialists, and railroad builders of Minneapolis and St. Paul after the Depression of 1873, the grasshopper plagues of the following years, and collapse of the land boom in 1887, the farmers and the factory workers of the Old Northwest turned to the Grange, the Anti-Monopoly Party, the Northern Alliance, and Populism for relief. Despite the agitation of Ignatius Donnelly and the occasional election of an Alliance or Populist congressman, the Pillsburys and Washburns and their associates continued to dominate Minnesota's political and economic life throughout the late nineteenth century. "Of all the Midwestern states," historian Russel Nye has written, "Minnesota was perhaps... most completely in the grip of organized business."[3]

The man who did most to shape the destiny of Minneapolis and the Northwest during these years was probably James J. Hill, builder of the Great Northern Railroad. Hill was one of the shrewdest and most ambitious industrialists the Gilded Age produced. Farmers of the time lamented: "First we had grasshoppers—then Jim Hill," and a St. Paul editor commented that Hill was "the most even-tempered man I ever saw—always bad."[4] But Hill was not courting the popularity of farmers or editors; he was building an empire in rails across half a country, and in this he had few equals. He realized that a permanent empire could not be founded on the timber lands of Minnesota, the wheat fields of the Dakotas, or the iron deposits along the Mesabi Range, since these in the time would fail or be exhausted. What Hill wanted and needed most was people. He sent his agents throughout Europe, with steamship tickets and glowing descriptions of the Northwest, and he resettled thousands of immigrants, chiefly

Germans and Scandinavians, in the cities of Minnesota and along the route of the Great Northern. These newcomers to the Northwest, often more familiar with the socialist regimes they had left in Europe than with the private-enterprise system they found in America, became steady customers for Hill's far-flung railroad and a ready source of labor for the lumber, flour, and iron mills of the Weyerhaeusers, the Pillsburys, and the Rockefellers.

Soon after the turn of the century, this "Golden Age of Economic Empire" in the Old Northwest came to a close.[5] By 1910, most of the Minnesota forests had been leveled and the lumber industry was in fatal decline. The Interstate Commerce Commission of 1887, the Northern Securities decision of 1904, and the Panama Canal in 1914 combined to check Hill's domination of the Northwest's transportation. Buffalo, New York, strategically located on the Great Lakes and only a short distance from the populous markets of the East, soon rivaled Minneapolis as the flour capital of America. "Minneapolis has outgrown the Northwest, from which it must live," *Fortune* magazine noted. By the time of America's entrance into the First World War, the city could compete nationally only by reducing its labor costs below those of its competitors, and this it consistently did. The result was not only a widening gulf between the upper and lower social classes, but a deepening of the bitter antagonism between them.

The farmers, mill hands, and railroad workers, native and immigrant, did not submit meekly. The discontent which had found expression in the Grange and Populism in the nineteenth century erupted into the agricultural unions of the Industrial Workers of the World, the Non-Partisan League, and the Farmer-Labor Party of the twentieth. Socialism seemed particularly attractive to the Scandinavian immigrants of the upper Middle West; the Finnish Federation was allied with the Socialist Party as early as 1904, and socialism seemed more radical in Minnesota than elsewhere. When the Socialist Party split after World War I, the Minnesota branch followed the Third International, and when communism itself split in 1928, the Minnesota party joined the Trotskyites on the left. When Floyd B. Olson of the Farmer-Labor Party won the governorship in the early 1930s, insisting "I am not a liberal, I am a radical," thousands of discontented farmers and industrial workers were determined to redress the wrongs of nearly half a century of social inequality and oppression.[6]

The embattled farm and factory workers of Minneapolis in the 1930s faced a worthy opponent. In 1903, a small group of bankers and businessmen had organized the Citizens' Alliance— "a mysterious organization with no known membership but immense power and resources," one observer called it—primarily to preserve freedom of individual bargaining and the open shop throughout the city. During the next thirty years the Alliance established its own employment agency, its own craft schools (to eliminate the need for union training), and its own corps of industrial spies. The organization's anti-union policies were remarkably successful. Although wages across the country rose 11 percent in the 1920s, they rose only 2 percent in Minneapolis; for a long time the Alliance was able to force the open shop even on the powerful AFL building trades; and in 1934 the Alliance could boast that it had defeated every major strike in the city since the end of the First World War. Minneapolis in the early 1930s was known across the nation as a "one hundred per cent open shop town" and "the worst scab town in the Midwest."[7]

The Twin Cities not only knew the extremes of rich and poor but were also familiar with bloodshed and violence. Charles Walker called St. Paul "the crime center of the nation" and *Fortune* noted that "most of the crime committed in the Midwest could be traced to plans made in St. Paul." "If you want someone killed," the magazine continued, "inquire along St. Peter Street." John Dillinger shot his way out of a St. Paul apartment in early 1934, and much to the annoyance of local police, "Baby Face" Nelson liked to spend a Sunday afternoon cruising along county highways in a chauffered limousine, "practicing with his machine gun against telegraph poles."[8]

The coming of the New Deal and passage of the NIRA drew the battle lines tighter. The Citizens' Alliance refused to relax its opposition to organized labor. The only difficulty with the president's Recovery Act, Charles Pillsbury suggested, was that "labor leaders have interpreted it to mean that collective bargaining can come only through belonging to a union." Alliance leader Albert W. Strong added: "I can conceive of dealing with a conservative and responsible labor leader, but certainly not with any of the A.F. of L. leaders in Minneapolis." But Section 7(a) and the economic upswing of late 1933 gave the workers greater confidence. In February 1934, the newly organized Local 574 of the General Drivers and Helpers Union called a strike against local coal dealers. Caught by surprise in the middle of a harsh Minnesota winter, the companies capitulated to the union's demands.[9] By April 1, the union numbered 2,000 members and felt strong enough to threaten all the city's trucking interests with a general strike. On April 30, the union leaders presented their demands to the employers' bargaining committee— union recognition, seniority rights, and higher wages—and when these were rejected, they called a strike for May 15.

The first citywide strike lasted eleven days and was both violent and successful. Pickets halted all commercial trucks and common carriers, except those carrying ice, milk, and coal. From large factories to corner groceries, all business was hurt. The city was closed "as tight as a bull's eye in fly time," the strikers boasted. "They had the town tied up tight," the sheriff later admitted; "not a truck could move in Minneapolis."[10] On May 19, a "citizens' army" was recruited and deputized by local officials to help convoy trucks through the city, and two days later they clashed with strikers in the "Battle of Deputies Run." Business executives with badges were no match for truck drivers with ball bats. Before police could intervene, two deputies were killed and hundreds from both sides were injured. The workers were further embittered when the Hennepin County chapter of the Minnesota Law and Order League offered a reward of $5,000 for information leading to the arrest and conviction of persons responsible for the deaths of these two deputies, while offering a reward of only $2,500 for John Dillinger. Class hatred in Minneapolis had boiled to the surface.

On May 21, the regional labor board in St. Paul assumed jurisdiction over the case and the following day a federal mediator arrived from Washington. After five days of almost around-the-clock negotiations, a compromise was reached on May 26. The agreement followed in general outline the usual NLB formula: the strike was to be called off at once, all strikers were to be reinstated without discrimination, hours of work were to be regulated by NRA code provisions, arbitration machinery was to be established to determine wage rates in case negotiations did not bring agreement, and Local 574 was recognized as bargaining agent wherever it commanded a majority of the workers.[11] Although the "war" was far from over, the union had won the first battle.

The compromise of May 26, however, had been possible only because one of the main points in dispute had been left unsettled. Leaders of Local 574 had claimed jurisdiction over all "inside workers" (warehouse employees primarily), besides their truck drivers and helpers, but the companies did not agree. The regional board's consent order of May 31 was intentionally vague: "The term 'employee' as used herein shall include truck drivers and helpers, and such other persons as are ordinarily engaged in trucking operations of the business of the individual employer." Union leaders immediately requested an official interpretation of this agreement, and on July 7 the regional board declared that although inside workers did not fall within the union's jurisdiction, the board "recommends that all workers of the firms involved who were on strike should be dealt with on the bases... provided in the consent order of May 31."[12] The industry chose to ignore this recommendation and the union voted to strike on July 16.

By mid-July, Father Haas was again in Washington. He had successfully mediated the Milwaukee Electric strike on June 29 and on July 1 had returned to Racine to speak at the centenary celebration of the founding of the city. This address, "The Church and Economics in Society," was a strong defense of the New Deal and a plea for full cooperation by all citizens in the president's recovery program. The following week, Father Haas was recalled to Washington to serve as technical adviser to the National Labor Relations Board, which had replaced Senator Wagner's National Labor Board on July 9.[13] Haas met with the new board members— Lloyd Garrison, Harry Millis, and Edwin Smith—from July 13 to 16, recommending appointments to the NLRB staff, suggesting procedures for reducing industrial disputes, and pointing out dangers that had plagued the Wagner board. Another important topic of discussion became evident on July 17, when Father Haas suddenly left Washington by plane—perhaps for the first time in his life—to take charge of mediation efforts in the Minneapolis truckers' dispute.

The leftist leadership of Local 574 had by this time become a major point of controversy. Union president William Brown, a political activist in the Farmer-Labor Party, was openly sympathetic to the class-conflict theories of Minnesota socialists, and his chief assistants and most effective organizers in Local 574—Carl Skoglund, Farrell Dobbs, and Vincent, Grant, and Miles Dunne—were supporters of the Trotskyite Communist League of America. Vince Dunne and Carl Skoglund were reported to be members of the League's national committee.[14] A Minneapolis business executive informed President Roosevelt that the strike was a Communist plot "to create one big union in Minneapolis and compel all industry to become part of that union." The *Minneapolis Journal* charged that "the real objective of the Communists is to enlist Minnesota in the revolution they hope to start in this country for the overthrow of the constitution and the laws of the land." Even Daniel Tobin, international president of the Teamsters, repudiated the strike and eventually suspended the Minneapolis local, presumably because of its Communist leadership, although the local's preference for "vertical" unionism may have been a factor.[15]

Father Haas was severely criticized throughout the strike for his association with these radical officials. One Chicago businessman wrote to the rector of Catholic University to inquire whether it was true that Father Haas "has been thrown out of several Catholic schools in which he taught because of strong Socialistic and Communistic tendencies, etc., and that he is not in good standing with the Ecclesiastics of the Church." Father Maurice Sheehy, assistant to the rector and a close friend of Haas, immediately replied that Father Haas was "one of America's most respected educators" and that "Catholic University would appreciate favor if you would deny calumny mentioned in letter." Father Sheehy then sent copies of the correspondence to Father Haas in Minneapolis with the wry comment: "I called up Comrade McGowan [Father Raymond McGowan, Ryan's assistant at the NCWC] who is the only good Communist I know and he assured me that you were not a Communist in good standing, that he hadn't been able to collect any dues for months from you." Toward the end of the strike, even Local President William Brown jokingly noted that he was "practically convinced that the rumor that Father Haas is a paid Communist agent is greatly exaggerated." Leftist domination of Local 574 seriously affected negotiations, however; it marshaled much public opinion in Minneapolis and across the nation on the side of the employers, but it had little effect on Haas. He saw no real threat of Communist domination of organized labor in the 1930's and he considered such accusations more often a ploy on the part of industry.[16]

Father Haas arrived in Minneapolis early on July 18, two days after the strike began, and spent the rest of that morning conferring with federal conciliator E. H. Dunnigan, who had been assigned to the dispute since the end of June. He met with the union leadership at 1:30 and with the employers' committee at 3:30, but the employers seemed cold to the suggestion of a union election to settle the jurisdictional dispute. On the following day, Haas submitted the first of many compromise proposals to each side. According to this plan, the strike would be called off immediately, all strikers would be reinstated, and minimum wages of fifty-five cents an hour for drivers and forty-five cents for helpers and inside workers would be established for one year. The strategy behind this suggestion was obvious. He realized that the employers' committee and the union bargainers were hopelessly deadlocked on the question of union jurisdiction over the inside workers and he therefore wanted to bypass that central issue. If the parties could agree on temporary wage rates, collective bargaining could be delayed a full year and, with it, determination of the proper representation of inside workers. The employers, however, rejected the proposal, insisting that it implied union jurisdiction over the inside workers. Representation was clearly the crucial issue. "Father Haas and I believe," Dunnigan wrote that evening, "that just as soon as we have the question of representation smoothed out, we won't experience difficulty in bringing both sides into agreement."[17]

By Friday morning, July 20, Father Haas was confident of early agreement. "I am sanguine that we are going to settle this strike without much more delay," he remarked after Thursday's conferences, and negotiations the following morning progressed well. The mood of optimism, however, was suddenly shattered when violence broke out that afternoon. A crowd of pickets and bystanders had been milling around the center of town when, shortly after noon, a delivery truck, convoyed by approximately twenty police cars, began to make its way toward a retail store. The strikers had earlier permitted a truck carrying hospital supplies to pass unmolested, but this second truck, transferring fresh vegetables, was not directed toward the hospital. As the truck approached Third Street, ten pickets in an open truck moved to intercept it, followed by other strikers on foot and a crowd of onlookers. After a brief scuffle, more than fifty policemen opened fire on the unarmed pickets. In the unequal battle, which lasted only a few minutes, two strikers were killed and sixty-eight were wounded. The workers insisted that this "Battle of Bloody Friday" had been a deliberate trap and that the police had opened fire without provocation. Others blamed the union leadership, because union headquarters had been informed of the armed convoy and, perhaps, had ordered the unsuspecting workers into the area in a deliberate effort to provoke the shooting. Whatever the explanation, the police assertion that its men had fired only in self-defense was largely discredited when it was revealed that forty-eight of the wounded had been shot in the back.[18]

To Father Haas, the incident was disheartening and inexcusable. On the day after his arrival in Minneapolis he had asked Chief of Police Michael Johannes to maintain a truce and not convoy trucks during the early stages of the negotiations, and Haas insisted that this assurance had been given. Haas noted in his diary, however, that the employers had met with Johannes that same evening and, by emphasizing "liberty of the streets," had persuaded him to furnish the convoy on Friday. "We were progressing nicely," Father Haas recalled later. "It was because of these negotiations that we asked the chief not to convoy any trucks. He promised us he would not. We got an awfully bad setback as a result of Friday's violence. Aside from the tragedy, developments definitely have postponed any attempts for immediate settlement." Governor Floyd Olson concurred: "I dislike to become involved in a dispute with a public official, but there is no question but that Mr. Johannes, the Chief of Police, promised Father Haas and me that he would not convoy any trucks until Saturday evening." After this outbreak of violence, Commissioner Dunnigan urged a declaration of martial law, but Governor Olson and Father Haas felt that negotiations could continue more calmly under a voluntary truce.[19]

The negotiations had undoubtedly suffered "an awfully bad setback." Union officials were discredited in the eyes of those who believed that the incident had been deliberately provoked in order to precipitate class warfare. The employers, confident of the sympathies of Mayor A. G. Bainbridge and Police Chief Johannes, renewed their determination to break the strike and, if possible, Local 574. But the workers were no less determined. Soup kitchens were opened for the pickets, farmers donated produce to feed strikers and their families, and "women's auxiliaries" were set up to care for the wounded. On the night of the shooting, union leaders organized a march on city hall and many embittered workers threatened to lynch both the mayor and the chief of police. Negotiators' tempers were not soothed when a scorching heat wave descended on the city, with the temperature reaching 104 degrees during afternoon discussions. Citizens across the country feared that Minneapolis was on the brink of civil war.[20]

Although the atmosphere was not conducive to calm negotiations, Haas met with the employer representatives on the day after the shooting. The companies indicated a willingness to

reinstate some of the strikers and to recognize the union's jurisdiction over inside workers in twenty-two of the more than one
hundred and fifty firms involved. On the other issues, however,
they would not compromise: they refused to admit the union's
jurisdiction over the other companies' warehouse employees and
they insisted that the wage dispute be submitted to the regional
labor board for arbitration. The workers by this time had repudiated intervention by the regional board in St. Paul because its
official interpretation of the earlier agreement of July 7 had taken
the side of the employers. On July 23, Haas and Dunnigan suggested a compromise settlement, calling for arbitration of wages
and secret elections to determine employee representation, but the
union rejected the first provision and the employers the second.
Negotiations were thus deadlocked. The two mediators, consequently, broke off discussions and, with the aid of Governor
Olson, Mayor Bainbridge, and other local officials, began to draft
a new proposal which the governor promised to support with the
full authority of his office.[21]

This "Haas-Dunnigan plan," approved by Lloyd Garrison,
chairman of the National Labor Relations Board in a telephone
conversation that morning, was submitted to each party at noon
on July 25. According to its provisions, the strike was to be called
off at once, all workers were to be reinstated, union elections
were to be conducted by the regional labor board, negotiations
on wages and hours were to be undertaken as soon as employee
representation was determined, and, if no agreement could be
reached, wage levels were to be established by a five-man board of
arbitration. Wages, however, could not be set below 52½ cents
an hour for drivers and 42½ cents for other workers. Lloyd
Garrison had at first opposed this minimum wage provision,
but Governor Olson had insisted and Garrison finally agreed.
Olson accompanied the release of this Haas-Dunnigan plan with
the announcement that unless both sides accepted the proposal
by noon the following day, he would declare martial law and
permit trucks to move only with special military licenses.[22]

The governor hoped that this threat of martial law would
force the employers to accept the Haas-Dunnigan proposal, since
trucks could no longer be convoyed by local police sympathetic
to the companies. As expected, President William Brown of Local
574 notified the mediators that "by overwhelming majority in a
secret ballot Local Union 574 accepts your proposal of July 25,
1934, to settle the strike." The governor's strategy failed, how-

ever, when the employers' committee accepted the plan only with modifications—elimination of the minimum wage clause and the provision to rehire all strikers. These modifications, Haas insisted, "nullified their acceptance." He continued to meet with the employers, however, to urge acceptance without reservations, but to no avail. The Haas-Dunnigan plan, the employers insisted, would leave "the issues and the methods of the present strike wide open for repetition in the future."[23] On July 26, consequently, in keeping with his earlier announcement, Governor Olson placed the city under martial law.

Very little progress was made during the next ten days. On July 30, the two mediators submitted an amended version of the Haas-Dunnigan plan to the disputing parties, but once again the employers rejected it. On August 1, the National Guard raided union headquarters just before dawn, allegedly because pickets were assembling there in violation of martial law, and fifty-five union members, including leaders William Brown and Vincent and Miles Dunne, were imprisoned in a temporary stockade. On the following day, the employers' committee submitted its terms to Father Haas and Commissioner Dunnigan: minimum wages of fifty cents for drivers and forty cents for helpers, reinstatement of strikers not involved in the violence of July 20, and secret elections to determine jurisdiction over the inside workers. Father Haas suggested certain revisions more favorable to the workers, and when they were declined by the committee, the union rejected the whole proposal. On August 4, under severe criticism for the recent attack on union headquarters, the National Guard raided the offices of the Citizens' Alliance. The Alliance, however, had been warned beforehand and no incriminating evidence was found.[24]

On Sunday, August 5, Governor Olson played his final card, announcing that, effective that midnight, no trucks would be permitted on city streets except those owned or operated by employers who subscribed to the Haas-Dunnigan plan of July 25. The governor took this step in an effort to recapture the waning support of the workers. Under military permits issued since July 26, especially blanket permits issued to almost all meat trucks and restaurant and hotel suppliers, city trucking had returned to 65 percent of prestrike volume and union leaders vehemently accused the governor of using the National Guard to aid the employers. The Farmer-Labor administration, William Brown declared, was "the best strike-breaking force our union has ever been up against." Neither Haas nor Dunnigan had recommended this further step by the governor. "Olson intended putting his order into effect midnight last Friday," Dunnigan wrote on Monday, "but Haas and I persuaded him not to do so. We made the same effort Sunday night but he declined to yield." The mediators were not discouraged, however. "Haas and I worked on case from nine o'clock Sunday morning until three o'clock Monday morning," Dunnigan continued on August 6, "and it now begins to look as though our efforts to bring about a settlement is [sic] in sight."[25] After eighteen hours of meetings, the commissioner's meaning was clearer than his syntax.

The following ten days were undoubtedly the most difficult of all for Father Haas. In an attempt to nullify Olson's directive of August 5, the employers' committee petitioned the U.S. District Court the following day for an injunction to force the governor to suspend martial law. Father Haas feared the worst. "If it is granted," he wrote a friend in Washington, "I dread to think of the violence and bloodshed that will follow." Governor Olson argued the case personally on August 9, insisting that the employers' rights had not been abridged and warning the judges of the violence that would be unleashed if the troops were removed. After five days of uncertainty and almost no progress in strike negotiations, the court, on August 11, decided in favor of the governor.[26]

On August 13, two days after the federal injunction was denied, Father Haas took the controversial step of bypassing the union negotiators and presenting an employer proposal directly to a rank-and-file Strike Committee of One Hundred. The workers not only rejected the companies' plan, chiefly for its clause denying union jurisdiction over all inside workers, but bitterly criticized Haas's conduct. "All my life I have been a follower of the Church," one worker declared, "and I say it's a crying shame when a man wearing the cloth of the Church as you do stands up before his brother workers and attempts to swindle them into acceptance of such a sell-out as you are giving us." The strikers' bulletin, *The Northwest Organizer*, declared that the mediators "thought they could put over the rotten settlement if they got a chance at the rank-and-file." Herbert Solow, in a letter to *The Nation* six weeks later, stated that Haas had first tried "to put something over on the strikers," and then ". . . a moral and almost physical wreck, withdrew his endorsement of the scheme he had urged the strikers to adopt."[27]

Such criticism seems unjustified. Even after four weeks of negotiations, the employers' committee refused to meet with the union leaders and, consequently, all communication between them was carried on through the federal mediators. Father Haas frequently presented the proposals of one side to the other, regardless of his personal views, and the *Northwest Organizer*, although critical of Haas's appeal to the rank and file, was careful to note that Father Haas had not given the employers' plan his endorsement. From Father Haas's diary, furthermore, it seems clear that he agreed to appeal to the rank and file only at the urging of John W. Barton, local Reconstruction Finance Corporation official for industrial loans, who recommended either submission of the plan over the heads of the union leaders or an agreement signed by the Minneapolis employers and the NLRB in Washington. Father Haas was apparently attempting one controversial step, supported by the employers, before adopting a second, favorable to the truckers. From this time on, officials of the RFC began to play a decisive role in the strike negotiations.[28]

The federal mediators had been in contact with the RFC since late July. On July 26, Father Haas had notified Washington that "the Citizens' Alliance dominates the employers by the threat of cutting off bank credit." Many of the Alliance leaders were bank executives who had little personal interest in the trucking dispute but were determined to see the union defeated and the open shop preserved in Minneapolis. "I have been told that banks in Minneapolis are threatening some of the merchants over in Mpls," Vince Day, secretary to the governor, confided in a memo. "The pressure is on the merchants who are figuring on signing up. The bankers say that if the merchants sign up they will give them no more credit."[29] But these same bank executives, Benedict Wolf of the NLRB staff reported to Father Haas on July 28, were indebted to the RFC for more than $25 million, and the mediators immediately sought ways to bring the influence of the RFC into the negotiations. On August 8, President Roosevelt visited Rochester to take part in ceremonies honoring Doctors William and Charles Mayo, and Governor Olson discussed the Minneapolis situation with him there. Apparently at the urging of Olson, the president immediately contacted Jesse Jones of the RFC and Jones then telephoned Haas. According to Governor Olson, the RFC could legitimately recall at least a portion of the $25 million loan since the collateral on which it was based was shrinking in value because of financial losses caused by the strike. On July 23, in fact, the executive committee of the RFC in Washington had written to Northwest Bancorporation in Minneapolis to request information on assessed values, gross incomes, and current appraisals on "properties covered by mortgages pledged to us." At Jones's suggestion, Father Haas met on August 8 with Clive Jaffray of the First National Bank and Theodore Wold of the North West Bank Corporation, and he reported back to Jones that afternoon. Haas knew that the negotiations could now turn unpleasant and he advocated secrecy. "Suggest no news release giving details in present status of controversy," he wired the NLRB as talks with the RFC began.[30]

In the week following President Roosevelt's visit to Minnesota, Father Haas kept in daily telephone contact with Jesse Jones in Washington and with RFC officials in Minneapolis. All this time, the employers' position was becoming more and more difficult. On August 11, the District Court in St. Paul denied their request for an injunction, and two days later the rank-and-file strike committee angrily rejected the settlement proposal they offered through Father Haas. With this rejection, Father Haas on August 13 asked for and received NLRB approval for Barton's alternative recommendation, an agreement signed by the employers with the NLRB itself. As leading Minneapolis bankers, the chief financiers of the employers' resistance, became concerned over the safety of their government loans, the employers' committee began searching for an acceptable compromise. On August 15, it notified Father Haas that the companies were willing to permit employee elections in all 166 firms if the National Labor Relations Board in Washington would suggest them. Union leaders immediately agreed to this proposal and Haas requested the NLRB that evening to send a special representative to Minneapolis to supervise the balloting.[31]

Almost simultaneously with this first apparent breakthrough, however, a further controversy erupted. The employers' committee, or a member of it, had sent a letter to individual employers with instructions on how to influence workers to vote for representatives in their plants, rather than for the union leadership. An employer who was sympathetic to the union permitted the workers to make a copy of the letter and the strikers' newspaper published it on August 16. Union leaders characterized the letter as an unjustifiable interference in an employee election and announced their opposition to any election under these conditions.[32]

Father Haas continued to work behind the scenes with Jesse Jones to reach a full settlement. On August 16, the day P. A. Donoghue of the NLRB left Washington to oversee the Minneapolis elections, Haas had a particularly stormy session with several leading bankers of the Citizens' Alliance. Jones had suggested that he "knock their heads together," and apparently he did. One bank executive, according to Father Haas's notes, was "furious": he denounced the "politics in this thing," threatened to call a mass meeting of citizens to demand the recall of "you two," and then slammed the receiver with a "Damn!" Disagreeable as such sessions were, they were bringing the controversy closer to a settlement. At 6:00 p.m. on August 18, Jones again called Father Haas from Washington and Haas advised him that the union was still insisting on removal of the "violence clause" from the agreement (the clause permitting employers to rehire only workers not involved in violence during the strike) and inclusion of specific minimum rates as a starting point for arbitration. Jones immediately contacted Albert W. Strong, the "prime force in the Citizens' Alliance," according to *Fortune* magazine. At 9:00 p.m., Strong phoned the NLRB's Donoghue and asked for a conference the following day. When Donoghue met with Strong and the employers' committee on August 19, the employers agreed to rehire all strikers, without discrimination, and to accept arbitration of wages above basic minimums demanded by the union. That evening, Donoghue and Father Haas worked until long after midnight, drafting the final agreement, and on August 20 the union accepted it by an overwhelming vote. The companies agreed to the proposal by a vote of 155 to 3 the following day.[33] After thirty-six days of violence and controversy, peace was restored.

The final agreement, in the words of Governor Olson, was "practically an acceptance of the Haas-Dunnigan proposal."[34] The strike was to be called off immediately, all strikers were to be reinstated in order of seniority, elections were to be conducted in all firms by the regional labor board, and collective bargaining was to begin as soon as representatives were chosen. The agreement differed from the Haas-Dunnigan plan only on wages. Both plans provided for arbitration of wages if no agreement could be reached through collective bargaining, but the final settlement established minimum wages of fifty cents an hour for drivers and forty cents for others, while the Haas-Dunnigan plan had provided minimums two and one-half cents higher.

The part played by the Reconstruction Finance Corporation in the final settlement was crucial. Father Haas later apologized to his Rochester friend, Dr. Andrew Rivers, for bypassing the president's visit on August 8, the day of Jesse Jones's entrance into the case. "By a strange coincidence," Haas confided, "if I had left Minneapolis on that day, I should have missed a very important call from Washington, which was the beginning of the settlement of the strike." Indicative of the role he had played, Jones took the liberty of notifying Roosevelt of the final agreement on August 22: "Glad to report Minneapolis strike settled. Men at work this morning.... All happy. Employers have made substantial concessions in the general interest." Three months later the executive committee of the RFC in Washington approved a request from the Northwest Bancorporation in Minneapolis to undertake a financial reorganization of some of its banking subsidiaries.[35]

Reaction to the strike settlement was generally favorable. The *Northwest Organizer* on August 22 printed a one-word headline: "VICTORY!" Union leader Vincent Dunne considered the settlement "substantially what we have fought for and bled for since the beginning of the strike." His brother Grant agreed: "We did not get all we ought to have, but the union is recognized, it is now well established, and—what is better—the machinery of arbitration is established whereby disputes ought to be settled without trouble." Although the employers declined to comment, the conservative *Minneapolis Journal* called the agreement "a fair compromise." "There is, in fact," the paper added, "little difference between the final settlement and the employers' proposal of July 25, nine days after the strike began."[36] The feelings of the rank and file were indicated by a twelve-hour celebration that broke out as soon as the final agreement was announced.

Father Haas was justly proud of his part in settling this Minneapolis controversy. The strike had lasted thirty-six days and had cost the city an estimated $50 million. Bank clearings during the strike were down $3 million a day, approximately $5 million was lost in wages, and maintenance of the National Guard had cost taxpayers over $300,000. Violence left four persons dead, hundreds injured, and a city very close to civil war. For his part in the settlement, Father Haas was hailed as the "ace of federal peacemakers" by the diocesan newspaper.[37] George Lawson of the Minnesota State Federation of Labor wrote to Secretary Perkins in late August:

I am taking the liberty of writing to you to express my high regard for the untiring work done in Minneapolis during the Teamsters' Strike by Rev. Father Haas and Mr. Dunnigan. I had occasion from time to time to confer with them and I know full well the many difficulties that confronted them, and the unfair and unkind things that were said about them, and the many obstacles that were placed in their path. In spite of these things, they labored night and day to bring about a fair and equitable adjustment of the controversy, and it seemed to me that it was only fair to give you these expressions of my high regard for them and the work they did under extremely difficult circumstances.

But Father Haas had done more than settle a strike and restore peace to a city after five weeks of industrial upheaval. In fact, Father Haas did not consider a strike as evil or simply as something to settle. He had stated his views in a speech in New York the year before:

At the biennial convention of the American Federation of Labor held in Cincinnati in November, 1932, Secretary of Labor Doak expressed gratification at the fact that during the preceding three and one-half years there had been no labor outbursts or uprisings. Let it be said in all seriousness that the absence of organized strikes during these three and one-half years should not be viewed with satisfaction by American employers or for that matter by the officials of the American labor movement. The nonoccurrence of strikes is of course not a matter for regret, nevertheless their non-occurrence is proof positive of the debasement, and degradation of the American wage population. It is mute but unmistakable evidence of deep-seated disease in the social body.[38]

Father Haas returned to this analogy of disease frequently throughout the 1930s, and nowhere did it apply more aptly than in the Minneapolis strike of 1934. "A strike is like an operation," he liked to remark. "Of course it is not a good thing in itself. But when there is a diseased condition in an industry a strike may be necessary. The refusal of an employer to deal with a union, low wages and long hours are diseases in an industry. Very often the strike is the only way to remove these evils, and under these conditions it is wholly justified."[39]

Minneapolis in 1934 was undoubtedly afflicted by "serious disease." For more than fifty years the city's economy had been dominated by a small aristocracy of bankers and industrialists, the rights of workers had been restricted, collective bargaining had been a sham, wage-and-hour standards were among the lowest in the country, and the city was torn with class antagonism. In the violent strike of 1934, the city's "deep-seated disease" was brought into the open and in the settlement of August 20 the first steps toward relief were provided. Reasonable standards of wages and hours were established, grievance machinery was set up, and the right of collective bargaining was explicitly recognized. Even more important, the power of the Citizens' Alliance was broken, the non-union shop was overthrown, and the right of workers to organize unions of their choice was guaranteed. Minneapolis never again had a strike as violent as the Teamsters' strike of 1934, nor did it need one. The strike settlement that August left the city healthier than it had been for decades, and much credit for this agreement was undoubtedly due to the patience, persistence, and mediation skill of Father Haas.

7

Return to Milwaukee, 1935-1937

Father Haas's first two years in government service had been crowded but exciting. With little government experience before 1933, he had been projected suddenly into the New Deal maelstrom and had worked closely with such prominent government and labor officials as Secretary Perkins, Senator Wagner, John L. Lewis, and William Green. His duties as federal mediator and as a member of the Labor Advisory Board and the National Labor Board often occupied, he admitted, "the entire day and frequently much of the night," but it was very satisfying. "The tragic fact is," he noted, "that twelve millions of people are out of employment, and something has to be done to get them back to work, and done now."[1]

By midsummer of 1935, Father Haas was especially optimistic. The financial difficulties of the National Catholic School of Social Service continued, but most economic indicators showed progress since 1933 and the worst of the disaster seemed over. The Supreme Court struck down the National Industrial Recovery Act in May of 1935, but that seemed to spur the president to greater efforts, and Father Haas was pleased with the legislative results. The Emergency Relief Appropriations Act had been passed in April and one month later a nationwide public works program, the Works Progress Administration, was established under presidential adviser Harry Hopkins. The National Labor Relations Act, sponsored in the Senate by Robert Wagner of New York, was signed into law July 5; a stringent Wealth Tax Act was passed the following month; and the long-debated Social Security Act, embracing both unemployment compensation and old age pensions, was signed a week later. Rural electrification through federal aid, a bill to curb the pyramiding of holding companies in public utilities, and the Guffey-Snyder Act to raise wages and limit production in the coal industry followed. When Congress ad-

journed in late August, Father Haas and other New Deal supporters looked forward confidently to a renewed campaign of
economic recovery and social reform.[2]

Early that fall, however, Father Haas's direct participation
in this campaign was suddenly curtailed. On August 12, Monsignor Aloysius Muench of St. Francis Seminary had been appointed bishop of Fargo, North Dakota, and three months later
Father Haas was named his successor as seminary rector.[3] For
the next two years he again made Milwaukee his home. He continued his work for the federal government, when seminary
obligations permitted, accepted government assignments for the
state administration in Madison occasionally, and continued his
writing and public speaking; but his primary responsibility from
1935 to 1937 had to be the direction and supervision of St.
Francis Seminary.

It is uncertain how Father Haas viewed this new assignment.
He realized, of course, that it was one of the most prestigious
positions Archbishop Stritch could bestow on a priest of his
diocese—for Father Muench, it had led directly to the bishopric—
and Father Haas must have felt honored by this expression of
confidence. He had spent nine years as a student at St. Francis
Seminary and thirteen on the faculty, and thus the assignment
was in many ways a return home. He had deep respect for both
the priesthood and the academic life, and in this new position
he could exert unique influence over both. The seminary assignment would also bring him closer to his family in Racine, and as
legal guardian for Arthur's children, this would be beneficial for
them and satisfying for him.

The transfer to Milwaukee, however, brought disappointments too. For over two years he had collaborated with high
government officials and had contributed, in his limited way, to
the successes of the early New Deal and he realized that he would
miss this satisfying work. "I deeply regret," he admitted that
November, "that my new duties will make it impossible for me
to continue actively in the administration of the splendid labor
legislation enacted since 1933.... It is hard for me to leave."
He also regretted taking leave of his close friends, Fathers John
Burke, William Kerby, Raymond McGowan, and especially John
Ryan. The rectorship of St. Francis Seminary would entail long
hours of administration—responsibilities for finances, personnel
decisions, and curriculum—and Father Haas was never comfortable
behind an administrative desk. Despite these very real difficulties,

he apparently never suggested that the assignment be withdrawn nor complained of the transfer, even to his closest friends. He concluded his work as rapidly as possible at the National Catholic School of Social Service and returned to Milwaukee on November 14.[4]

St. Francis Seminary at that time had an enrollment of approximately three hundred students in its high school, college, and theology programs and a full-time faculty of almost twenty. Although Church regulations recommended separation of minor from major seminaries, so that high school and early college students might be housed apart from those in philosophy and theology, this was not feasible (for financial reasons) in Milwaukee. All seminarians resided in the main seminary building, younger students in the north wing and philosophers and theologians in the south. The broad outline of seminary life had been set forth in the revised Code of Canon Law of 1918: religious exercises, like morning and evening prayer, and daily Mass were required; younger students were to receive a basic education in the liberal arts; all philosophy and theology courses were to be taught according to the principles and method of St. Thomas Aquinas; and the rector was to be particularly watchful over the religious and moral development of his seminarians. Under the archbishop of Milwaukee, the rector held final responsibility for the whole of seminary life—regular discipline, religious training, academic procedures, and finances—although in daily administration he was assisted by the vice rector, spiritual director, procurator, and deans of the collegiate and theology programs.[5]

Supervision of the seminary's finances in the midst of the Depression was one of Father Haas's heaviest responsibilities. Gross annual expenses were in the neighborhood of $130,000 and students' tuition ($350 per year) was almost the sole source of income. The archdiocese paid full tuition for students in theology and half-tuition for those in philosophy, although in the first years after ordination each priest was asked to reimburse the archdiocese a part of this sum. Many high school and college students found it impossible to pay the tuition fees and therefore an Educational Foundation had been established in 1932 to extend loans to students at between 2 and 5 percent interest. These deferred tuition loans for college students averaged about $8,500 a year throughout the 1930s. Since 1931 the seminary farm no longer produced its own meat and dairy products, and even with the generous loan arrangements expenses during these

Depression years were generally higher than income. This was not unexpected but it added to the rector's heavy responsibility.[6]

When Father Haas returned to St. Francis Seminary in the fall of 1935, the school's academic program had for several years been strong and well respected. The seminary had been chartered by the state of Wisconsin to confer both bachelor and master of arts degrees and, through affiliation with Catholic University in Washington, qualified students could be awarded a bachelor's degree in sacred theology from that university for work completed at the seminary. Major emphasis in the high school and early college curricula was on Latin, English, Greek, mathematics, history, and science; philosophy courses predominated during the final two years of college; and the theology curriculum was composed almost exclusively of standard courses in dogmatic and moral theology, Sacred Scripture, and Church history. During his two years as rector, Father Haas resumed his courses in homiletics or elocution to students in theology, courses which he had taught in the 1920s.[7]

One innovation by Father Haas in the seminary curriculum, not unexpectedly, was increased emphasis on the social sciences. Soon after his arrival, the seminary bulletin announced a new course, "Social Science Surveys," to be taught by the rector himself. A brief description followed: "This course surveys current problems of production and distribution in the light of Catholic social teaching. The Social Encyclicals from Pope Leo XIII to Pope Pius XI form the basis of exposition and study. The method followed is lecture and discussion, and the course is open to students of Theology and Philosophy." No time was listed, but the class usually met on Saturday evening so that it would suffer less interference from any government work Father Haas might be called on to perform. Haas also found time to deliver periodic addresses to the student body on social justice, labor relations, and the goals and policies of the New Deal. St. Francis Seminary from 1935 to 1937 was probably the only Catholic seminary in the country that offered lectures by the rector on "Legislative Trends since N.R.A.," "The President's Message to Congress," and "The Guffey Coal Bill."[8]

In his two years as rector, Father Haas probably exerted little lasting influence on St. Francis Seminary. Although these were difficult Depression years, the seminary suffered no major financial setbacks and Father Haas deserves at least some credit for that. There were apparently no major crises in the academic, disciplinary, or personnel areas, and thus Father Haas's administrative abilities were not seriously tested. He made few changes in either the curriculum or seminary discipline, except for expansion of the social science offerings, but Church regulations encouraged little experimentation. Since he was never wholly at ease with the details of seminary administration—overseeing the physical plant, arranging class schedules, and supervising the daily routine of seminary life—he usually delegated them to others. Because of his distaste for administrative detail and his frequent absences from Milwaukee for government work, he probably devoted less time to his seminary responsibilities than any of his predecessors, but he insisted that it was not necessary that the rector do everything personally. But Father Haas had too strong a sense of duty to let administration grow lax or drift out of hand, and seminary discipline remained steady. His term was only two years, however, and this was probably not long enough to permit any permanent impact on seminary training, even had he desired to exert it.[9]

But Father Haas *did* influence the seminarians he guided. They could not but admire his industry, conscientiousness, and sense of duty. He was a recognized scholar, familiar with the world of higher education, both private and public, and he demanded high standards of scholarship in his future priests. He gave them an example of manly piety, of devotion to the Mass and the rosary, and an unostentatious charity (he frequently sent checks to needy causes and dropped loose change or dollar bills in parish poor boxes). He had deep respect for the dignity of the priesthood and was uncompromising in his efforts to prepare others to fulfill their priestly responsibilities. His special influence, however, was undoubtedly in social justice. He urged his seminarians to become familiar with the social encyclicals, to understand the problems and hardships workingmen and their families faced, and especially to be zealous in championing the cause of the poor and the needy in their priestly ministry.

Father Haas was not only responsible for the direction of St. Francis Seminary during these years, but he was also forced to assume increasing responsibility for his family in Racine. After almost a year of steadily declining health, his father passed away in October 1934, at the age of seventy-four. Doctors had discovered the previous December that he was suffering from hardening of the arteries and moderate hypertension and they speculated that, some time in the past, he had suffered a stroke. His condition deteriorated and by the spring of 1934 someone had to be with him most of the time. "He can't be left alone," Margaret wrote to her brother, "as he doesn't seem to know what he's doing at times. Sun. A.M. Pete went in the kitchen to see what he was doing and he had the gas turned on, thinking it was the water to get a drink." Al seemed especially concerned. "Just a few lines to let you know how Pa is," he wrote that same month. "Marge and Pete don't seem to realize how bad he is but I think he is worse than they think. One of his hands is stiff and if you ask me I think it is a slight stroke of paralysis. They see him every day and don't know how bad it is." Eventually, someone had to be with him even at night, but relatives were generous and they were able to care for him without outside assistance. Margaret, who had several years' experience as a private nurse, supervised his care until he died peacefully at home on October 4. A comment of Amy a month later was a fitting tribute to their father. "Surely he must be in Heaven," she wrote her brother. "I just wish I could be just one-half as good as he was, so quiet and always just enduring something in his quiet way. Just to show you how the children will always remember him, the other day Judith said, 'Say, mother, don't you remember how swell Grandpa always wiggled his ears when he played with Petie and me?' The youngsters will always remember him in that way, 'sort of happy and smily.'"[10]

With the death of Peter Haas, Father Frank assumed greater family responsibility. He was still the executor of the will of his brother and sister-in-law, Arthur and Liz, and trustee of the estate they left for the care of their children, and he was now executor of his father's estate also, including the family home on Barker Street, the pickle factory, the old grocery store, and an additional property on North Main. Peter Haas had left this estate in six equal shares, with each of the five surviving children receiving one share and Arthur's three children dividing the last. At least one property was rented and another was mortgaged, and Father Haas spent much time at St. Francis Seminary (1935 to 1937) attempting to dispose of the estate. Negotiations with lawyers and real estate agents continued, however, until the final disposition in 1948.[11]

Father Haas received a steady income from St. Francis Seminary during these years, augmented at times by his government work and public speaking, and thus was able to help members of his family in financial emergencies. He continued to send money home each year to cover property taxes and he was usually able to assist in times of serious illness. Amy's daughter, Jayne, was an invalid for almost eight months after injuring her leg in November 1934; Al had to be hospitalized with a serious nervous disorder; his wife had major surgery in late 1934; and in 1935 Margaret had a large tumor removed, which the family feared might be malignant. At one point, when everyone seemed to be sick at the same time, Margaret facetiously suggested that they investigate the possibility of hiring a doctor by the week. A pathetic account was confided in a letter from Amy: "Talk about a pitiful condition in Milwaukee," she wrote in 1935, "they won't bury Joe's aunt (and she's down at the morgue) because none of them have any money. Tomorrow Joe and I are going to take Grandma down to Milwaukee and see what we can do about it, see if we can't suggest some thing or some way. Joe says its getting pretty bad when they won't even bury the people any more but those are the facts."[12] In almost every emergency, the family turned instinctively to "Father Frank," confident that he would not only provide the necessary advice and financial assistance but would ease the burden by accepting much of the responsibility.

His most serious family responsibility during these years, however, was the guardianship of his brother Arthur's children. The two youngest, Billy and Dick, were finishing high school. Father Haas had not only arranged for their board and lodging but provided them with spending money, supervised their class work, approved their recreation and vacation plans, and was called to intervene in their youthful pranks and run-ins with authority. The boys lived with Margaret on Barker Street for a while after their grandfather's death; Dick probably lived with Amy in Kenosha for a time in 1936, and Billy enrolled in St. Charles boarding school in Milwaukee as a candidate for the religious life in the fall of 1937. Billy's early poor health, however, continued to decline. He had spent several weeks in Wisconsin General Hospital in Madison in 1934, probably with St. Vitus's Dance, had a recurrence or similar ailment in 1936, and his health never improved. Despite almost constant medical attention, his condition steadily worsened, and he died on April 25, 1939, at the age of twenty-three.[13]

Father Haas's relations with his niece, the eldest of the three, were relaxed and open. "Just between you and me, I do get awfully lonesome out here," she admitted after her first few weeks as a boarding student at Mount Mary College in Milwaukee, "but don't tell anyone, will you? Because a girl eighteen years old is supposed to be over that baby stage." She wrote to her uncle at least twice a month, sending whatever news she had of Dick and Billy, describing the college classes that she particularly liked or disliked, requesting money for new clothes or other needs, and sharing her personal thoughts and feelings. "I'm afraid in my last letter that I didn't appear very appreciative of all the nice things you sent me," she wrote in 1934, "but I really was, and still am. You know, it isn't at all pleasant having to watch girls get cakes on their birthdays, and never getting one yourself. That's why I particularly appreciated the cake.... You see, I haven't had a birthday cake for so long—not since mother died. And it meant just that much more coming from you." Despite the loss of her parents, frequent financial difficulties, and other family disappointments, she retained her sense of humor. She could jokingly complain how difficult it was to live up to such "an internationally famous uncle," she informed him immediately when someone predicted that he would eventually be made a bishop, and she could even make light of her financial difficulties. "Last night," she wrote in 1932, "the dean says in her most cultured voice that 'starting this Thursday and every Thursday thereafter, there will be a formal dinner, and the young ladies will dress accordingly,' which means the young ladies will dress according to everything but their means."[14]

On her graduation from college in 1935, Father Haas arranged a scholarship for her at the National Catholic School of Social Service, but she decided to decline and take a position in a government office outside Milwaukee. "I have thought this out very thoroughly and as impartially as possible," she wrote that September. "There is only one thing in this world that I want, and that is a family and home of my own.... I appreciate all you have done for me, you know that, and I am gratified, too, for the scholarship you succeeded in getting for me. But, I just can't come. It wouldn't be fair, to myself, or Tony, or you, or anyone." She had met Anthony Charnon in college several years before and she had not concealed her feelings from her uncle. "I know that you have never fully approved of my going with Tony," she wrote later that fall. "But I know, too, that you trust my judge-ment enough, and give me enough credit for a little mature judge-ment to know that I am not making a mistake."[15]

When she and Tony decided to marry the following year, she requested her uncle's permission and asked him to perform the ceremony. Her financial indebtedness was her one source of anxiety:

> I may as well say it frankly; Tony and I want to be married this June. But we don't want to be married without your blessing and consent, and so I am writing for just that.
>
> If it were not for the fact that I owe you so very much I would feel that I was about the happiest girl in the world. But knowing that I owe you so much, I could not pursue my own happiness without coming to some sort of definite conclusion about my responsibilities to you and the boys. Frankly, Father Frank, I am asking you to take care of my brothers for me. That is selfish of me, I know, and it is also imposing on your ever-present generosity, and still I am asking you.[16]

Father Haas's reply revealed his affection and concern, and his respect for tradition:

> Your coming marriage, dear child, is much too intimate a matter, and much too sacred, to be discussed in a letter. Of course, you have my blessing and consent. May God bless you and Tony, and give you every happiness and all good things.
>
> There is one procedure that should be observed before anything else is done. I refer to the old and honored practice, its wisdom proved by the centuries, according to which the prospective groom privately at least asks for the hand of his future bride. I am not standing on ceremony, but have only your own future in mind. Tony should ask my permission to marry you, as I stand in relation to you in loco patris. Heaven knows that I have done my best in that respect both toward you and Bill and Dick.
>
> The money I loaned you is, and I would not be frank with you if I did not say so, a matter of concern to me. I am not thinking of myself but of others I had planned to

help.... But I do not wish to and will not place the loans
I made you in the way of your marriage this summer. We can
discuss the matter together and arrive at some kind of understanding.[17]

Mary's wedding was one of the joyous occasions, as Billy's
death a few years later was the saddest, in this unusual relationship of Arthur's three children with their priest-guardian. Father
Haas remarked "I have done my best," and the children knew
it had not been easy. Mary chided her uncle, on one occasion,
that in a recent autobiographical sketch he had forgotten to
mention that he was also the guardian of three awful children.[18]

Writing of Father Haas during his two years at St. Francis
Seminary, his classmate, Monsignor Peter Leo Johnson, stated that
his "tie-up with special work in economics in Washington for the
federal government created a barrier to any lasting application of
his talent and ripe experience as an educator while rector." There
can be no question that Father Haas never lost his enthusiasm
for the New Deal policies of Franklin Roosevelt during those
years. "I do not find it easy to suggest how your Administration
could have done more than it did in the field of social legislation,"
he wrote the president in October 1935. "Your Administration
has made history by making government serve the people, and it
is my firm conviction, and, I need not add, my hope, that a
grateful people will demand your continued service."[19] Milwaukee
was 800 miles from Washington, however, and the federal government called on him less frequently—and for much less important
assignments—and his public service during those years, consequently, was often unsatisfying.

It is not difficult to fix a precise date for one of the major
disappointments in Father Haas's life as a public official. On
May 27, 1935, by unanimous decision in *Schechter Brothers
Poultry Corp.* vs. *the United States*, the Supreme Court invalidated
the NRA codes of fair competition as improper delegation of
congressional legislative authority and thereby shattered the
foundation on which the president's industrial recovery program
was built. As a member of the Labor Advisory Board and the
National Labor Board, Father Haas had consistently defended
the NRA in numerous articles and public addresses, had devoted
hundreds of hours to further its success, and the Schechter deci-

sion was understandably frustrating. He had called the NRA in 1933 "the most momentous experiment our country has yet made in the field of industry and business," and less than one month before the Schechter decision was announced he had addressed a mass meeting of the Amalgamated Clothing Workers in Troy, New York:

> Twenty-two months ago, NRA set its face to do something. Under the direction of President Roosevelt, it fixed minimum wages and maximum hours. It set out to make every industry conform to a minimum of industrial decency.
>
> NRA has made administrative mistakes. Mention one and I will mention ten. But its basic principles and purposes are right. Who can question the essential soundness of enforcing a minimum wage below which no worker may be paid? Who can deny the simple arithmetic of reducing working hours in order to reemploy the unemployed? And yet that is the essence of NRA. Under the profit system there is no other procedure but the one NRA has adopted.[20]

The Schechter decision was a particularly heavy blow for Father Haas because he had viewed the NRA not only as a temporary recovery measure but as a first step toward permanent social reform. "As a member of the Labor Advisory Board of the NRA from the first day to the last," he stated that October, "I can say its basic principles were right and that it was a beginning of an application of the social programs of Popes Leo XIII and Pius XI."[21] He was of the same opinion three years later: "Let it be said that the basic principles of the NRA were sound. Employers were to organize. Employees were to organize. The Government was to be the impartial third party.... The theory of the experiment was right and just, and I do not hesitate to say that if labor had been admitted to an equal place with management in NRA in fixing wages, prices, and output, with the Government acting as chairman to represent the public, NRA would still be here teaching us year by year how to evolve a sane social order, and even a Christian social order."[22] Father Haas continued to urge reestablishment of the NRA, or at least a similar implementation of Pope Pius XI's Occupational Group System, throughout the 1930s, but much to his disappointment, the federal government never again attempted such a fundamental reform of the American economy.

Within one month of the Schechter decision, Father Haas was appointed to a government committee to investigate a possible decline in business and labor standards following the invalidation of the NRA codes. In early June the AFL had charged that "at least a million wage-earners have been affected by lengthening of hours of work and wage-cutting in a short space of six business days following the Supreme Court's decision." The acting NRA administrator, James L. O'Neill, agreed: "We have received reports through our Compliance Division that a good deal of chiseling is going on." Since these reports had been compiled hurriedly and haphazardly from information submitted by state NRA officials, industrial code authorities, and the staff of the Labor Advisory Board, they were in no way complete or definitive. President Roosevelt decided that a more detailed study should be undertaken, and on June 17 he forwarded the following directive to O'Neill: "In line with our recent discussion, I am requesting you to set up in the Division of Business Cooperation a section devoted to accumulating, checking and reporting accurate information concerning the extent to which changes occur in the maintenance of labor standards or fair practice provisions of codes of fair competition, following the abolition of such codes." This new board, the Committee to Report on Changes in Business and Labor Standards, was set up on June 24. Retired Major General Amos A. Fries was named chairman, assisted by John Dickinson of the Department of Commerce, Isador Lubin of the Department of Labor, John W. Upp, representing industry, and Father Haas, representing labor.[23]

The main work of the committee did not begin until late July, after Captain W. P. Robert had replaced General Fries as chairman and Colonel J. M. Johnson had replaced Dickinson as representative of the Department of Commerce. Since the president had requested the committee to submit its report by the end of the year, the members decided in mid-August to limit their survey to approximately fifty representative industries. Congress, on June 14, had extended the life of the National Recovery Administration until April 1, 1936, and this enabled O'Neill to authorize the Robert Committee to call on NRA field examiners to conduct its survey in each state. The committee drew up a detailed questionnaire to guide the examiners in their study but the examiners were free to consult public and private records and to interview workers and employers at their discretion. The committee emphasized, however, that it was strictly a fact-finding body and the examiners were to make no effort to persuade employers to return to former NRA code provisions, nor were they to offer opinions whether deviations from former code standards were justified in particular industries.[24] All information, finally, was to remain confidential until released by the committee in Washington or by the secretary of commerce.

While the survey was conducted by NRA field examiners in approximately two hundred cities across the country that summer and fall, the committee held biweekly meetings in Washington to review the data forwarded by NRA regional offices, to examine similar studies undertaken by the Bureau of Labor Statistics, and to determine what form the final report should take. The last two weeks of December were the committee's busiest and Father Haas returned to Washington for the whole period. By that time, all the reports of the NRA examiners had been submitted, the data had been collated with other government studies, and a preliminary report had been drafted by the Washington staff. The committee members then reviewed the report line by line, revising paragraphs, changing the report's emphasis in several places, and adding summaries of findings for each industry. The committee held to its target date of January 1, and Father Haas later told a friend that he had attended meetings of the Robert Committee every day from December 18 to 31, except the two Sundays and Christmas.[25]

The tone of the completed report was surprisingly moderate and its findings were generally favorable to industry. The committee found that the child labor standards in the codes were retained by most industries and that there were apparently few significant deviations from the codes' trade practice provisions. Departure from minimum wage standards, however, were more numerous. In nine of the forty-four industries surveyed, over 40 percent of the workers received less than the minimum wages formerly stipulated in the codes, and in another nine industries over 25 percent of the workers received less than the minimum. The committee found disregard of maximum hour standards even more common. Although exact figures for each industry were not available, the report affirmed that "the data show clearly that in general a larger number of establishments have disregarded hour provisions of the codes than have disregarded minimum wage standards." Despite such evidence, the report concluded on a note of praise for industry: "The data received indicate that in nearly all the industries surveyed large numbers of establishments adhere substantially to the former code standards as to labor provisions. Taking all the industries surveyed, the majority of members thereof and those carrying by far the largest number of employees adhere substantially to the Code labor standards; similar comments apply in regard to those adhering to trade practice standards."[26]

Committee discussions had at times been heated and Father Haas felt that the final report should indict industry more severely. In meetings during the last two weeks of December, he proposed numerous revisions and amendments which would emphasize the worsening of labor conditions since the abolition of NRA codes.[27] In the report on the retail drug industry, he wanted to change "minor reductions in hourly earnings" to "wide-spread reductions" in order to emphasize the large numbers of workers affected. The section on the retail trade industry acknowledged "a general tendency to increase hours," but Father Haas wanted to make explicit that fully half of the industry's employees were affected by this increase. Where the report on the dress manufacturing industry noted that "departures in various respects exist in this industry," Father Haas would add "to a serious degree." Haas had similar objections to almost every section. He also wanted to emphasize the contributions of organized labor in maintaining high labor standards in various industries, but the committee decided that such observations fell outside the scope of the report. Although many of Father Haas's suggestions were rejected by the committee, they contributed to whatever indictment of industry the final report contained.

By the end of December, Father Haas was confident that the committee report had at last won the approval of all five members and was ready for publication. Such was not the case, however. By that time, Ernest Draper had replaced Colonel Johnson as representative of the Department of Commerce, and because of a unique set of circumstances he hesitated to sign the final report. On December 21, President Roosevelt had issued an executive order abolishing the National Recovery Administration, as of January 1, and transferring the NRA's Division of Business Cooperation, of which the Robert Committee was part, to the Department of Commerce. Draper at that time was assistant secretary of commerce and he feared that since the report would be released (after January 1) by an agency of the Department of Commerce, his signature would give the document an official status that might later prove embarrassing to the department.

Father Haas first suggested that Draper's alternate sign in the assistant secretary's place, but Chairman Robert felt that this would weaken the report in the public's eye. Several times in early January the chairman discussed the matter by phone with Father Haas at St. Francis Seminary and Father Haas was understandably disturbed. "It had three signatures then [December 31]," he insisted, "and was ready for yours, and I don't think it's fair. I don't want to disparage the Secretary, but we made concessions in the report to get it through."[28] Father Haas and Isador Lubin, in fact, had reluctantly agreed to several changes suggested by the management representatives, and it was disconcerting to learn that, even after these compromises, the report might not have the unanimous approval of all five members.

Assistant Secretary Draper eventually signed the report but the committee's troubles were not at an end. On June 17, 1935, President Roosevelt had told Acting NRA Administrator O'Neill that "the purpose of this work is the gathering and publication of reliable information and to counteract any propaganda from private sources which may be designed to promote special interests." Anxious to have industry's deviations from the former wage and hour standards made public, Haas looked forward to the release of the report by the middle of January, but by that time he had begun to fear the worst. "Confidentially, our report on changes in Business and Labor Standards has been signed and submitted," he wrote to a friend on January 20. "My only fear is that it will be kept in hiding too long to accomplish the good we expect." On January 27 he informed Jacob Baker, assistant administrator of the Works Progress Administration, that the secretary of commerce was apparently still holding the report, and he suggested that if it was not released within a few days the WPA might try to exert pressure on the Commerce Department. As late as March 2, Father Haas was informed that even some cabinet members had no idea of the report's "contents and whereabouts." By that time, however, the report had probably reached the White House, because on March 17 Secretary of Commerce Daniel Roper finally released it to the press with the president's approval. The three-month delay, however, had been critical. By mid-March, the committee was almost forgotten, the report received little notice in the press, and its influence on public policy was minimal.[29]

For Father Haas, consequently, the Robert Committee was a frustrating assignment. The committee may have been established in the summer of 1935 in part to collect data to support the president's legislative proposals that summer and fall, but when Congress speedily enacted the president's program during that "Second New Deal," even liberal government officials may have lost interest in the new committee.[30] The president, however, reluctant to dismiss subordinates, allowed the committee to complete its work but did nothing to guarantee its effectiveness. The committee's findings, furthermore, were open to divergent interpretations and its conclusions were ambiguous. Haas and Lubin emphasized the number of industries that deviated from former code provisions while industrial representatives publicized those firms in which high labor standards had been maintained. Secretary of Commerce Roper, fearful perhaps that the report would be harmful to business, withheld it from publication for almost three months. In an effort to accommodate both labor and management, consequently, the committee accomplished very little. It was "broker politics" at its worst.

Equally frustrating—and time consuming—during his two years as rector of St. Francis Seminary was Father Haas's service as a member of the three-man Labor Policies Board of the Works Progress Administration. On April 8, 1935, President Roosevelt had signed into law the Emergency Relief Appropriations Act, releasing $5 billion for federal public works projects, and one month later he issued an executive order establishing the Works Progress Administration under Administrator Harry Hopkins. Labor leaders immediately objected that the security wage, contemplated by the WPA, would tend to lower wages in all industries and that increased public employment would hinder the growth of organized labor. On July 24, consequently, Harry Hopkins set up a Labor Policies Board within the WPA to advise the administrator on labor policies and to hear appeals and complaints of WPA employees.[31] Arthur O. Wharton, president of the International Association of Machinists and a vice president of the AFL was named chairman, assisted by Father Haas and James Wilson, former president of the Pattern Makers' League of North America and also a vice president of the AFL (1924 to 1934).

The authority and jurisdiction of the new board were never clearly defined (which was common for many New Deal agencies) and they soon became a source of conflict. The press release of July 25 stated vaguely: "In addition to advising Mr. Hopkins on policies of labor relations, the board will receive reports from the

Labor Relations and Administrative executives of the Works Progress Administration.'' A WPA bulletin three months later declared that ''at all times workers have the right of appeal from the decision of local or District WPA officials to state WPA officials, and from state officials to the Works Progress Administration at Washington and the Labor Policies Board.'' In May 1937 the board's executive assistant, Margaret Stabler, stated her opinion:

> The Labor Policies Board is an appeals board. I do not think of it as a division of the Works Progress Administration but as an agency created by the Administration to determine whether the rights of the workers have been observed in the administration of the program. Individual workers, or groups of workers, and the several state administrations come before it in appeals cases as parties to disputes. It is the Board's function to examine the arguments of each party and make a decision as to which is valid under WPA regulations.[32]

As a labor disputes agency, however, the Labor Policies Board had several drawbacks. The board was not given exclusive jurisdiction over industrial disputes. Deputy Administrator Aubrey Williams, the several assistant administrators, and even Harry Hopkins himself could and did hear labor complaints, if either disputing party preferred to bypass the Labor Policies Board. The AFL-CIO split at Atlantic City in 1935 further reduced the board's effectiveness. CIO leaders seldom appealed to the new agency since both Wharton and Wilson were affiliated with the AFL. Most importantly, however, the Labor Policies Board lacked genuine authority. It was empowered to hear appeals, review the rulings of state administrators, and conduct investigations, but it could do no more than submit recommendations to higher WPA officials. In August 1935, Daniel Tracy, of the Brotherhood of Electrical Workers, complained: ''Organized labor is dissatisfied with the lack of machinery to handle labor disputes arising under the Works Progress Administration program, and they will not be satisfied to bring their complaints to the Labor Policies Board if it merely has authority to make recommendations which might or might not be given consideration.'' The board, in fact, was not even authorized to submit its recommendations directly to Administrator Hopkins. In the early weeks it reported to Assistant Administrator Jacob Baker and after February 1, 1936, to Assistant Administrator Thad Holt of the Division of Employment.[33]

Deprived of real authority, the board members soon became disheartened. In February 1936, Wilson resigned to accept a position with the International Labor Organization in Geneva. About the same time, one staff member confided to Father Haas: "I actually hate this place and I am beginning to feel lower and lower in the biological scale as the realization grows upon me that I am a face-saving device for a face-saving Board." The board was ignored so frequently by higher WPA officials in its early months that Father Haas wrote to Miss Stabler in March 1936, with perhaps a touch of cynicism: "If there is to be anything like a meeting of the Labor Policies Board in the near future, will you be so good as to provide me ahead of time with transportation so that I can leave at once for Washington as soon as the call comes, if and when it does."[34]

Labor disturbances generally increase during the warm months of spring and summer, however, and after the early weeks of inactivity the pace of the Labor Policies Board accelerated. From April to November 1936, the board held perhaps a dozen meetings and Father Haas made the long train trip from Milwaukee to Washington to attend each one. The activities of the board were varied and irregular. In early May, Haas and Nels Anderson, of the WPA's Labor Relations Section, investigated working conditions in Harrisburg, Pennsylvania, and in an official report, issued at the close of the hearings, Father Haas recommended establishment of higher minimum wages, appointment of state labor adjusters to handle industrial complaints, and the fullest guarantee of the workers' right to organize. In late July, Haas was in Malone, New York, to investigate complaints that the WPA was competing with the private pulpwood industry for skilled labor. In September, he made an extensive tour of Georgia, Alabama, Louisiana, and Texas to report on the success of revitalized southern industries in reducing the number of workers on WPA relief rolls. Twice during that period he delivered major addresses before WPA gatherings, in Washington on May 20 and in Cleveland on October 31.[35] During the spring and summer of 1936, these duties for the Labor Policies Board had taken Father Haas away from Milwaukee for an average of ten days every month, a further reason why he found it necessary to delegate many of his seminary responsibilities to others.

The most common complaint brought before the Labor Policies Board was the charge of discrimination against workers because of race, religion, or union activity. Few wage disputes were submitted to the board since it was primarily a tribunal of appeal from the rulings of state and local officials, who generally had no voice in setting wage rates. Charges of racial or religious prejudice or anti-union discrimination were usually investigated first on the state or local level, and perhaps later by a representative of the WPA's Washington office. The Labor Policies Board entered cases only after these other agencies had failed to reach a satisfactory settlement.[36] The most serious and most publicized controversies which Father Haas was called upon to resolve were the strike against the Detroit Public Health Service, in March 1937, and the dispute over the dismissal of Bernard Greenberg from a WPA project in Washington eight months later.

On March 1, 1937, seventy-five WPA workers staged a sitdown strike in two Detroit offices of the U.S. Public Health Service to protest the dismissal of sixty workers found eligible for social security benefits and therefore, by directive of Harry Hopkins, unqualified for WPA employment.[37] Nels Anderson, director of the WPA's Labor Relations Section, asked Father Haas to intervene, and on his arrival in Detroit, on March 6, he discovered that the strikers had added to their complaints. Besides the reinstatement of the sixty discharged workers, the strikers now demanded a 20 percent wage increase, removal of a Public Health foreman, and recognition of the American Federation of Government Employees as their sole bargaining agent. Father Haas saw no hope of settling these issues unless the workers could be temporarily reinstated, and he urged Harry Hopkins that same night to rescind his recent directive that all mothers eligible for social security benefits be dismissed from WPA employment. On Sunday, March 7, Hopkins withdrew the order and Father Haas began negotiations with the strikers' committee on the other grievances. The situation had become critical, since the workers were threatening to stage a sitdown strike at the WPA's central offices in Detroit, hampering all relief projects throughout the city. At noon on Monday, however, the disputing parties agreed to a compromise settlement suggested by Father Haas and the strike at the WPA central offices was averted. According to this agreement, the Public Health Service strike was to be called off, the dismissed workers were to be reinstated, all Public Health officials were to retain their positions, hours of work were reduced slightly, and all company unions were forbidden on the Detroit project. Neither side won a complete victory but peace had been restored.

The dispute over the dismissal of Bernard Greenberg, several months later, was perhaps more typical of the complaints that came before the Labor Policies Board.[38] Greenberg had been transferred from one WPA project to another within the Division of Social Research in Washington on June 15, and was dismissed outright four months later. Charging that a WPA foreman was prejudiced against Greenberg's Jewish religion and that several other officials had objected to his union activities, leaders of Local 1 of the United Federal Workers of America appealed the dismissal to higher WPA officials. Dean Brimhall, administrative assistant in the Division of Labor Management, conducted an investigation and recommended that Greenberg be reinstated. The project director in Washington, however, refused to follow this recommendation, Brimhall declined to insist on reinstatement, and Greenberg appealed to Acting Administrator Aubrey Williams. Williams upheld the earlier ruling of Brimhall, recommending but not demanding the reinstatement of Greenberg. When Greenberg and union officials threatened to appeal to the National Labor Relations Board, WPA officials, unwilling to test NLRB jurisdiction over federal works projects, agreed to submit the dispute to Father Haas for final arbitration.

Haas conducted formal hearings into the case in late February and early March 1938, and found the evidence far from convincing. Religious prejudice and anti-union discrimination were difficult to substantiate in public hearings and Father Haas pleaded for concrete proof. "Feelings won't do," he declared. "Did you hear somebody say on the part of the Administration that the Administration was opposed to organization or discouraged organization? It is evidence we want. We want definite statements made that somebody here heard, not what was told him or some impression somebody had. . . . We can't put feelings in the record. A feeling is a rational thing if it has a basis, if you can put something in the record, some act, some conversation, some notice, but obviously without that we can't proceed. If a feeling is there, there has to be a foundation."[39]

After hearing long hours of testimony, studying transcripts of conflicting evidence for several days, and weighing alternative solutions, Father Haas released his decision on March 12:

No good purpose can be served by reciting all the charges and countercharges made at the hearings. Two conclusions however seem to be warranted by the evidence. First, as to the transfer of June 15, the record establishes that a discriminatory policy pursued by one supervisor in particular, rather than low efficiency ratings, was the basic reason for the action taken. Second, as to the termination of October 18, the evidence does not conclusively sustain the charge of discrimination. Nevertheless the proof adduced to substantiate the charge of discrimination with respect to the termination carries sufficient weight to create a reasonable doubt as to the controlling purpose of the termination. This conclusion, when taken in conjunction with the almost certain conclusion that discrimination motivated the transfer of June 15, justifies the union's claim that Bernard Greenberg was dismissed on October 18 "without proper cause."[40]

Greenberg was eventually reinstated, union leaders praised Haas for his decision, and Father Haas gained valuable insight into the complex question of racial and religious discrimination—a question of even greater concern after his selection as chairman of the President's Fair Employment Practices Committee in 1943.

By the spring of 1938, however, when the Greenberg decision was announced, the Labor Policies Board was rapidly losing whatever influence it had within the WPA. That February, Deputy Administrator Aubrey Williams announced that all controversies involving WPA workers in New York City, which had the largest WPA program in the country, would hereafter be reviewed by his own office rather than by the Labor Policies Board. The board complained that its recommendations were repeatedly ignored by higher WPA officials and that, on some occasions, it was not even permitted to make the investigations it considered essential for reviewing specific disputes. In a letter to David K. Niles, assistant WPA administrator, Father Haas repeated his complaint that the AFL-CIO split seriously blocked the board's effectiveness, since the board's AFL majority had never won the confidence of the CIO unions. In late spring of 1938, Harry Hopkins decided to terminate the board's activities, and he announced that on June 30 the work of the Labor Policies Board would be taken over by other WPA agencies.[41]

Father Haas's work for the WPA, however, might not have been finished. On August 2, 1938, Margaret Stabler informed him that government officials were considering establishment of new labor disputes machinery within the WPA and that his name was prominently mentioned. Harry Hopkins, Assistant Administrator Niles, and Father Haas met frequently during the next few weeks in Washington and on September 22 Hopkins released the following statement: "Francis J. Haas has been appointed as Labor Consultant to the Division of Employment. The Assistant Administrator and/or Labor Consultant, Division of Employment, Works Progress Administration, Washington, D.C., are authorized to review labor complaints appealed from the decisions of the State Administrator or of any other WPA representative exercising final authority in a state upon such complaints."[42]

This position was even more frustrating than his membership on the Labor Policies Board. At the time of his appointment, one labor spokesman wrote: "Now Father Haas has the unenviable job of serving as one-man court for the more than three million WPA workers of this far-flung country. Well, if any man can do the job, Father Haas is the man. But how can even such a good man and fair man as Father Haas possibly wade through and act on the hundreds of cases inevitably arising on such a vast program." The task, as this observer suggested, was impossible. Haas was not given exclusive jurisdiction over WPA disputes nor was he given authority to enforce his decisions, and as a result labor complaints were usually submitted directly to one of the assistant WPA administrators. Disillusioned with this new appointment after only four months, Father Haas resigned on January 20, 1939, and severed all connections with the WPA. As labor consultant for the Division of Employment, he apparently never heard an appeal.[43]

A further disappointment and source of embarrassment for Father Haas during these years were the activities of Father Charles Coughlin of Detroit, especially his anti-Roosevelt speeches and his support of William Lemke in the election of 1936. Father Coughlin was vehemently opposed to much that Father Haas held in high esteem—the World Court, the labor leadership of John L. Lewis and Sidney Hillman, the NRA and other New Deal legislative programs—and his demagogic tactics, in Haas's opinion, had lowered the Church and the Catholic priesthood in the eyes of many Americans. Because of his respect for the dignity of the priesthood, however, Haas refused to criticize Father Coughlin in public. When Forrest Davis, in an article in the *Atlantic Monthly*, attempted to link what he considered Coughlin's fascist beliefs to *Quadragesimo Anno*, Father Haas wrote a vigorous reply in defense of Pope Pius XI. He attacked Davis's "misstatements, omissions and suppressions of fact regarding the Encyclicals" and his "serious mutilation of the text"—but he said not one word to defend or exonerate Coughlin.[44] In a private letter to William Gorham Rice, Jr., in February 1935, he lamented Father Coughlin's attack on the World Court, and he admitted to a priest-friend two years later that he had little respect for anything appearing in *Social Justice*. Without mentioning names, but without disguising his meaning, Haas declared in an interview a few months before the 1936 election that "the business of the Church is to build up standards of public morals and ethics, but a priest has no place in partisan politics." In October 1937, at the time of Archbishop Mooney's first confrontation with the Detroit priest, Father Haas wrote the archbishop: "I hear nothing but commendations for the way you are handling the Detroit situation. More power to you."[45] Beyond these scattered comments, Haas was silent. He felt that the spectacle of two priests embroiled in a public quarrel over questions of politics could bring only further embarrassment to the Church and thus he chose to remain aloof in public from the whole sorry episode.

Despite these disappointments, Father Haas's activities beyond the walls of St. Francis Seminary during these two years in Milwaukee were not without satisfactions. As one of the American Church's foremost authorities on social justice, he was in wide demand as a public speaker; he contributed significant articles to Catholic periodicals; and he presided at Summer Schools of Social Action for Priests in Toledo and Milwaukee. In 1937 he published *The American Labor Movement* and *The Wages and Hours of American Labor*, pamphlets that summarized the growth and accomplishments of organized labor in the United States and reviewed the teachings of the papal encyclicals on social justice and social welfare. He retained keen interest in the National Catholic School of Social Service, and on the death of Monsignor William Kerby in 1936 he was appointed vice president of the school's board of trustees. He continued to serve as confidential adviser to members of the American hierarchy—Archbishops Stritch of Milwaukee and Mooney of Rochester and Detroit, most notably—and he assisted John Ryan and Raymond McGowan with NCWC publications in Washington.[46]

Beyond this service to his Church, Father Haas retained the respect and esteem of government, labor, and education leaders.

In September 1935 he was asked by Secretary Perkins to intervene in a labor dispute in the Florida cigar industry. Although one Tampa newspaper asked "what a Ph.D. and President of a Catholic Seminary knows about the cigar industry," Father Haas brought the controversy to a satisfactory conclusion. He was a visiting lecturer at Temple University in November 1935, addressed the Amalgamated Clothing Workers' biennial convention in Cleveland the following June, and attended the annual AFL convention in Tampa that November. In December 1935, the Milwaukee Federation of Labor honored him with a public dinner. "In the history of organized labor," the Federation declared, "we have had no greater champion of our cause than Father Haas, and it is only fitting that we acknowledge our esteem with a public demonstration in his honor."[47]

One of the proudest moments of Father Haas's two years in Milwaukee—and probably of his life—occurred on June 21, 1936, when the University of Wisconsin awarded him an honorary degree, the first priest ever so honored in Madison. Father Haas had great respect for the state university: he had been a student there in the summers of 1916 and 1917, had long admired the work of Wisconsin social economists John Commons and Richard Ely, and was proud of the university's record of public service to governors and state legislatures for over three decades. He was deeply honored, consequently, to be singled out that June (with Katherine Cornell, Grant Wood, and Douglas Freeman) for this special recognition, and he was particularly moved by President Glenn Frank's citation:

> As stimulating teacher in Marquette University and in your alma mater and latterly as productive administrator of the Seminary of St. Francis, which was the mother of your mind in earlier years, you, a native son of Wisconsin, have made and are making significant contributions to the purpose and process of education in this commonwealth.
>
> As priest, in this age of incredible confusion of mind and distraction of spirit, you have travelled an ancient highway in your quest of spiritual satisfaction and, on that highway, have, for yourself, found faith reasonable and God real.
>
> As sociologist, you have made your secular service an organic part of your spiritual priesthood, toiling without stint to effect in the minds of men and the practice of groups that infusion of economic enterprise with ethical purpose which is one of the fairest flowers of vital religion.

As distinguished public servant, actively concerned with problems of security for the aged, effective justice in criminal administration, protection of public service from the mucker and the spoilsman through the safeguards and standards of an impartial civil service, and the maintenance of peace and equity alike in the workshop and in the world, you have served the state and nation with magnanimity, sympathy, and fidelity, and have brought to the troubled economy of our time high qualities of mind and heart.[48]

The two years in Milwaukee, 1935 to 1937, were in many ways unsatisfying and even frustrating for Father Haas, both as seminary administrator and as government official, but this occasion of public tribute from his native state in 1936 was one of his proudest moments.

8

The Wisconsin Labor Relations Board, 1937-1939

As might be expected of a successful government mediator and leading labor spokesman, Father Haas was a strong defender of the National Labor Relations Act of 1935 and of the National Labor Relations Board, which it established. He was confident that such government intervention would contribute to industrial peace, protect the worker's right to a living wage and improved working conditions, and even increase business, labor, and government cooperation as envisioned by Pope Pius XI in *Quadragesimo Anno*. Father Haas had recommended the establishment of "an air-tight Public Works Labor Board" in his letter to Secretary Perkins in April 1933, had served as a member of the National Labor Board for nine months, and had testified in favor of the stronger Labor Disputes bill before a congressional committee in 1934.[1] While the National Labor Relations Act was debated in Congress in the spring of 1935, Father Haas gave it full support in a major address before the Amalgamated Clothing Workers, and when the act was finally upheld by the Supreme Court two years later, he wired Senator Wagner immediately: "The Wagner Act is the law of the land. Accept my heartiest congratulations. Your victory is the people's victory and your name will live in their hearts with gratitude and affection." "The law is designed to protect the natural right to organize," he wrote two years later. "Catholics in particular should rise to the defense of the law as a necessary use of government power."[2]

Within months of the passage of the Wagner Act, Father Haas was appointed rector of St. Francis Seminary and for the next two years he had few opportunities to serve the National Labor Relations Board in Washington. In the spring of 1937, however, Wis-

150

consin passed a "Little Wagner Act" of its own and Father Haas was immediately selected as a member of the state's Labor Relations Board. Preoccupied with administrative duties at St. Francis Seminary and with his WPA work in Washington, he agreed to serve only until the board was firmly established and a permanent appointment could be made. Governor Philip La Follette refused to accept his repeated letters of resignation over the next twenty months, however, and Father Haas remained a member of the Wisconsin Labor Relations Board until it was abolished in the spring of 1939.

The Wisconsin Labor Relations Act of 1937 closely followed the main provisions of the national act. Their primary goals were the same: to protect the worker's right to organize and to preserve industrial peace. "It is hereby declared to be the policy of the United States," the Wagner Act declared, "to eliminate the causes of certain substantial obstructions to the free flow of commerce... by encouraging the practice and procedure of collective bargaining and by protecting the exercise by workers of full freedom of association, self-organization, and designation of representatives of their own choosing." "The purpose of this act," the Wisconsin statute repeated, "is to diminish the causes of labor disputes, to assure workers the privilege of joining labor organizations of their own choice, and to guarantee collective bargaining." To accomplish this purpose, each law declared five "unfair labor practices" illegal: establishment of company unions, interference by employers with the worker's right to organize, discrimination against workers because of union membership, refusal of employers to bargain collectively with worker representatives, and discrimination against employees for filing charges under the statute. The state law forbade the blacklisting of employees and use of industrial spies, and the national law was generally interpreted to prohibit these also. Under each law, a three-man Labor Relations Board was established to investigate industrial complaints and institute proceedings against employers found guilty of the enumerated unfair practices. Both acts, finally, exempted agricultural workers, domestic servants, and public employees from their provisions.[3]

The national and the Wisconsin Labor Relations Acts differed, however, in several provisions. The jurisdiction of the state law, for example, was more comprehensive. While the Wagner Act affected only industries engaged in interstate commerce, the Wisconsin law covered both interstate and intrastate business.

"It makes no distinction between interstate and intrastate commerce," the state Labor Relations Board noted, "the theory of the act being that this state is vitally interested in any disputes which occur within the boundaries of Wisconsin. . . . The Wisconsin law thus applies to some employers in certain situations where the national law may also be applicable."[4] This overlapping jurisdiction could have been a serious obstacle to the efficient operation of both labor boards, but a division of jurisdiction was agreed upon soon after the state law was passed and serious conflicts were avoided.

The Wisconsin Act was also unique in providing for the listing or registering of bona fide labor unions with the state Labor Relations Board. Although such listing was not mandatory, only unions thus listed and approved could be included on an employee election ballot, could legally sign a closed shop agreement, or were entitled to the protection of the state Labor Relations Act. No union was listed until the board, after a careful investigation, was satisfied that the organization was in no way company dominated. Under this provision of the Wisconsin statute, to which the national law offered nothing comparable, the state Labor Board drew up and published a complete list of legitimate labor organizations in the state which all workers could freely join and with which employers could confidently sign collective bargaining agreements, under the full protection of the state law.

The most important difference between the two laws, however, was the provision in the Wisconsin act that authorized the state Labor Relations Board to serve as an agency of mediation and voluntary arbitration. The National Labor Relations Board had been set up exclusively to enforce the provisions of the Labor Relations Act and was expressly forbidden to serve as an agency of mediation. "It is important," President Roosevelt had declared in 1935, "that the judicial function and the mediation function should not be confused. Compromise, the essence of mediation, has no place in the interpretation or enforcement of the law."[5] The mediation clause of the Wisconsin act, according to the state Labor Board, was the chief difference between the two:

> The Wisconsin board has the same duties in relation to unfair labor practices as has the national board, but in addition is specifically charged with responsibility for trying to prevent and settle labor disputes. It also has authority,

with the consent of both parties, to act as a board of arbitration or to name arbitrators to pass upon the merits of disputes.... These provisions relating to investigation, arbitration, and mediation occupy but little space in the Wisconsin law but mark the major difference between the national and the state acts. The Wisconsin law very plainly is designed not merely for the protection of the rights of employees but also for the protection of the public, the preservation of industrial peace, and the development of improved labor relations.[6]

"Our law differs from the federal law in that we are charged also with the duty of mediation," added one board member. "It is our hope that this will prove our principal duty. We believe that the intent of our law is the peaceful adjustment of difficulties between employers and employees much more than the determination of whether there have been any violations of the statute. It is in this work that we intend to discharge our duties."[7]

In a speech before the annual convention of the International Association of Governmental Labor Officials in 1937, Father Haas admitted that there were advantages and disadvantages in charging the same board with law enforcement and mediation functions. On the positive side were government expense and time. One board could be financed more cheaply than two, and could eliminate serious delays: if mediation efforts failed, the board could immediately begin its judicial process without a new investigation. But the negative side seemed equally compelling. "Against these advantages," Father Haas noted, "is the very real objection that a quasi-judicial body, any one of whose members has acted as a mediator, and unsuccessfully, in a given labor controversy, may well be less than judicial when called upon to discharge the duties of an impartial judge in issuing a complaint against an employer and in passing upon the lawfulness of his conduct." "It is too early," he admitted, "to say which of the two arrangements is better."[8]

The Wisconsin Labor Relations Act was passed by both houses of the legislature in the first week of April 1937 and was signed into law by Governor La Follette on April 14. Nine days later, the governor announced the appointment of the three-man state Labor Relations Board. For chairman, he selected Voyta Wrabetz, chairman of the state Industrial Commission since 1933. The second member of the board was Edwin E. Witte, professor of economics at the University of Wisconsin, formerly chief reference librarian for the state legislature and by 1937 one of the nation's foremost authorities on social security. The third member was Father Haas.[9]

The reaction of the press to these appointments was most favorable. "If Governor La Follette had searched the entire state," declared the *Sheboygan Press*, "he could not have picked three men better-informed and better able to function as members of the new Wisconsin Labor Relations Board." *Labor*, the national weekly, announced that "Wisconsin's 'Little Wagner Act' got off to a flying start this week, manned by three nationally known labor relations experts." According to Madison's *Capital Times*, "the members of the board are outstanding, experienced, capable men whose integrity is freely recognized by all industrial groups." The *Wisconsin State Journal* stated that "probably no three men could have been chosen for the positions in whom labor has larger confidence. The appointees are also men who have shown in participation of the settlement of labor disputes that they are reasonable and are aware that concessions must be made by both sides to gain harmony in labor difficulties." "Governor La Follette's appointments to the newly created Wisconsin Labor Board," the *Racine Day* commented, "may well be called the most statesmanlike act of his three administrations."[10]

Despite this newspaper acclaim and the senate's speedy and unanimous confirmation of the new board members, Governor La Follette was the target of adverse criticism in the state legislature. The Labor Relations Act had stipulated that the first appointments to the board were to serve terms of two, four, and six years, and that no member could hold any other office during tenure on the board. Since no funds were appropriated for the board's use until the start of the new fiscal year (July 1), it was presumed that the members would not be appointed until then. The sudden increase in strikes throughout the country that spring, however, convinced the governor that a Labor Disputes Board was needed immediately. Father Haas and Professor Witte accepted appointment to the board on the condition that they could retain their other positions and that they would serve for only a few weeks. "My original understanding with the Governor," Father Haas wrote to Margaret Stabler of the Labor Policies Board in May, "was that I remain only until the Board gets organized and its policies [are] more or less definitely laid out." Highly critical of the governor's action, the state legislature eventually amended the law to allow the first board members to serve on a temporary, part-time basis. At the same time, the legislature appropriated $5,000 for the board's immediate use, part of which was to serve as remuneration for Father Haas, since he was the only member of the board not already on the state payroll.[11]

At the time of their appointment to the state Labor Board, Professor Witte and Father Haas were in Washington, attending an unemployment conference called by the Department of Labor. Father Haas immediately telephoned Archbishop Stritch in Milwaukee to secure his permission before notifying Governor La Follette of his acceptance. Witte also wired his acceptance from Washington, although he later insisted that he would have declined to serve if he had been in Madison and able to confer with the governor personally. Haas and Witte then took advantage of being in Washington to work out an agreement with the members of the NLRB on the overlapping jurisdiction of the state and national acts. "At that time," Witte recalled, "the Federal Board urged us to take jurisdiction in all cases which might arise within Wisconsin, regardless of whether the industries involved were engaged in interstate or intrastate commerce." This practice was generally followed. Although there were a few cases in the early days of the board when, unknown to each other, both the state Labor Board and the Milwaukee regional branch of the national Labor Board assumed jurisdiction over the same dispute, relations between the two boards were excellent. Major credit for this harmony probably belongs to Father Haas. While Chairman Wrabetz and Professor Witte remained in Madison, Haas assumed direction of the state board's Milwaukee office, where the NLRB's regional board was also located. From his earlier years in Washington, Father Haas enjoyed the confidence of the national Labor Board and its branch offices.[12]

Father Haas left Washington to return to Milwaukee on April 23, the day on which the state legislature in Madison unanimously confirmed his appointment to the state Labor Board. During the following week, he met several times with Wrabetz, Witte, and Governor La Follette in Madison to discuss the organization of the board's staff and its basic rules and procedures. Since no money had yet been appropriated for the board's use, they decided that the governor's secretary, Jack Kyle, could serve temporarily as executive officer and that the offices and administrative personnel of the state Industrial Commission could be put at the board's disposal. The governor and the board members met that same week with leaders of the state AFL and CIO to urge full cooperation from all Wisconsin locals and to solicit labor's views on the maintenance of industrial peace.[13] Similar meetings were planned with state business and industrial leaders, but since the board was immediately confronted with several serious labor disputes it is doubtful that these meetings took place.

On April 28, even before the members had taken their oath of office, the board received its first industrial complaint. Earlier that month, local leaders of the CIO United Automobile Workers had attempted to organize the Creamery Package Manufacturing Company and the James Manufacturing Company at Fort Atkinson, and two weeks later each company had established an employee representation or company union plan. The CIO had demanded union recognition, an increase in wages, and reduction of the work week, but these requests were rejected by officials in both plants. Fearing violence, the sheriff had deputized sixty men in the James plant and sixteen in the Package plant—several of them officers of the employee unions but none from the CIO. Leaders of the CIO submitted their complaints to the new state Labor Board on April 28 and, that afternoon, the three board members drove to Fort Atkinson to speak with company officials. The board assumed jurisdiction over the two disputes and won from the CIO the promise to postpone its strike call until the mediators could investigate the controversy more thoroughly.[14]

The board took no further action in the case, however, for over a week. On the day following this visit to Fort Atkinson, Father Haas left Wisconsin for Washington again to participate in the Department of Labor's Conference on the Stabilization of Industrial Relations, a continuation of the conference he and Witte had attended a few days earlier. Secretary Perkins had invited William Green, John L. Lewis, Gerard Swope, Walter Teagle, and approximately twenty-five other representatives of industry, labor, and government to take part in what she later called "a free and frank discussion" of this critical issue. Although the conference adopted no resolutions and released no declarations, the participants agreed on the importance of state and federal conciliation agencies in maintaining industrial peace and they explored different ways of making collective bargaining more effective. While in Washington, Father Haas also attended a meeting of the Labor Policies Board of the WPA, and returned to Wisconsin and the Fort Atkinson disputes on May 7.[15]

Haas and Witte met with officials of the two companies and the CIO leaders that same afternoon. In an effort to compromise the differences, Father Haas suggested that "the management recognize the C.I.O. with the provision that any dispute which could not be adjusted through collective bargaining should during the life of the agreement be arbitrated," but both parties rejected this proposal. The discussion continued well into the night. At 2:00 A.M., after more than eight hours of negotiations, the officials reluctantly agreed to open company payrolls and union records to the two mediators in order to determine which organization—the CIO or the company union—represented the majority of the workers. After examining the records for three days, the board announced that the CIO held the majority of workers in the Package company but that neither union represented a majority in the James plant. Eventually, an election in the James plant gave the victory to the independent union, and after a brief strike in the Package plant over recognition of the CIO both companies agreed to bargain with the victorious unions in late May.[16]

While the Wisconsin Labor Board was occupied with these long negotiations at Fort Atkinson, Father Haas had intervened in a dispute between the Milwaukee Automotive Truck Drivers and the Milwaukee Produce and Fruit Exchange. A strike had been called during the first week of May, after the Exchange had rejected the union's demand for higher wages and a closed shop. Haas returned from Secretary Perkins's Washington conference on May 7, spent three days on the Fort Atkinson disputes, then turned his attention to the truck drivers' strike. On May 11, he drew up a compromise agreement which both sides, after long hours of discussion, accepted. By the terms of this settlement, the drivers were given a small increase in wages, a forty-eight-hour work week was established, and a modified version of the closed shop was accepted whereby all workers not hired through Local 200 of the Automotive Truck Drivers were obliged to join the union within thirty days. The *Wisconsin State Journal* congratulated the board on this first settlement. "The Wisconsin Labor Relations Board," it declared, "has been successful in settling the first major labor trouble upon which its decision was requested. Settlement of the strike indicates that the board is functioning and that it is likely to prove as valuable an agency as its friends have predicted."[17]

During the next six weeks, the Wisconsin Labor Board was particularly active. On May 15, less than three weeks after the board was established, Chairman Wrabetz announced that the members had already settled ten strikes, involving over 1,000

workers, and adjusted twenty complaints of unfair labor practices. During the last two weeks of May, the board was occupied
with hearings in the state legislature on a proposed amendment
to permit the three original appointees to serve on a part-time
basis, and with meetings to draft the "Rules and Regulations,"
which the board published later that month. Strikes, labor disputes, and mediation efforts continued as usual. "The Wisconsin
Labor Relations Board is taking far more of my time than I had
anticipated," Haas wrote on May 22. "The night before last we
held hearings for six consecutive hours running into the morning.
This is the third all night session, two of them cross country in an
auto within a short time. Company unions are springing up like
weeds. On top of all this, there is the C.I.O.-A.F. of L. fight, and
not always according to the rules of the game."[18]

Although the number of strikes in Wisconsin declined from
May to June, the pace of the state Labor Board did not slacken.
On June 2, the board investigated working conditions in one of
Milwaukee's largest restaurants and conducted an employee
election which resulted in an overwhelming victory of the CIO
over the AFL.[19] A few days later, the board heard a complaint of
unfair labor practices against the Fred Rueping Leather Company
of Fond du Lac (the case in which the state Supreme Court later
upheld the board's jurisdiction over industries engaged in interstate commerce). On the following day, the board intervened in
a dispute between the United Catering Workers Union and the
Milwaukee Athletic Club. On June 9 and 10, Wrabetz and Haas
conducted hearings on the application for listing by the Union of
Public Utility Employees Mutual Benefit Association, earlier
involved in the Milwaukee Electric Strike of 1934. On June 11,
the mediators settled a five-week strike at the Robert A. Johnson
Candy and Biscuit Company of Milwaukee and a few days later
intervened in a twenty-one-day strike at the Yahr-Lange Wholesale Drug Company. Later that month, after several days in Washington for a meeting of the WPA's Labor Policies Board, Father
Haas entered the controversy between the International Brotherhood of Carpenters and four large furniture plants in Oshkosh.
After more than two weeks of bargaining, in Oshkosh and Madison, an agreement was signed and 1,300 strikers returned to their
jobs in early July.

Most of these disputes in the spring and early summer of 1937
were small and unpublicized outside the localities immediately

affected, but they revealed how active and how successful the board could be. The success of the state Labor Board during those months was, in fact, extraordinary. By late July, 197 complaints had been submitted to the board's jurisdiction.[20] The board had settled sixty-five strikes through mediation, had averted seventeen others, had resolved thirty-three charges of unfair labor practices, and had conducted fifteen union elections. Of the remaining cases, several complaints had been dismissed as unfounded, others had been withdrawn voluntarily, and a few had been handed over to the jurisdiction of the National Labor Relations Board in Washington. The Wisconsin board's report noted that since the establishment of the state Labor Board in late April, the number of work stoppages in Wisconsin had steadily declined, and that on July 31 only seven strikes, with less than five hundred workers involved, were still pending settlement. Such a record seemed to vindicate Governor La Follette's decision to establish the Labor Board before July 1, the date apparently envisioned by the state Labor Relations Act.

It was fortunate that the number of Wisconsin strikes diminished during the spring and summer of 1937, because the Labor Board could not have handled more. On June 10, Professor Witte left Wisconsin for a previously scheduled summer teaching assignment at the University of Washington, and Father Haas was increasingly occupied with other government and ecclesiastical responsibilities. Throughout July he lectured at the newly organized Summer Schools of Social Action for Priests in Milwaukee and Toledo; mediated a textile strike in New York and Philadelphia at the request of Secretary Perkins that August; and in September left St. Francis Seminary to become dean of the School of Social Science at Catholic University in Washington.[21] For several months after July 1, Father Haas had very little time to devote to the Wisconsin Labor Board.

The first Summer Schools of Social Action for Priests were established that year in San Francisco, Milwaukee, Toledo, and Los Angeles through the efforts and urging of Father Raymond McGowan and other officials of the Social Action Department of the NCWC. At the annual meeting of the American hierarchy, held in Washington the preceding November, the bishops had given their official approval for a series of "Priests' Social Action Schools" but had left implementation of the proposal to Bishop Edwin O'Hara, episcopal chairman of the Social Action Department, and his NCWC associates.[22] Two months later, Father Haas confided further details in a letter to Bishop Robert Lucey of Amarillo:

> Last Saturday Bishop O'Hara met with Dr. Ryan, Father McGowan and myself in Washington, laying out plans for the Social Science Schools for Priests to be held next summer. I do not think I am anticipating announcements that should be made by Bishop O'Hara as chairman when I tell you that curriculum, length of institute, and dioceses sponsoring institutes are pretty well formulated. The plan as it stands now is to have eight schools, four in the East and four in the West. Each is to run for four weeks and is to be in no way an outing but an honest to goodness school with written reports and examinations. Bishop O'Hara is chairman, and perhaps that says enough.
>
> There will be in each school an enrollment of twenty to thirty priests assigned to the school by the Ordinary. It is also understood that the Ordinary will appoint a resident director. A traveling faculty will cover all the schools so that at least one guest lecturer will remain one week in each school. According to this arrangement there will be an outsider in each school throughout the four week period. There is a multitude of details to work out but the whole plan looks extremely promising.

This was the format that prevailed, although a few changes had to be made: the schools were established in four, rather than eight, dioceses—San Francisco in June, Milwaukee and Toledo in July, and Los Angeles in August—and the "traveling faculty" found it impossible to participate in all four programs. "The purpose of these month-long Summer Schools of Social Action is three-fold," Father McGowan stated that summer: "to study the great social encyclicals; to investigate the facts of industrial and labor conditions; and to review the principles and methods of the priests' participation in economic questions."[23] Since he had been so intimately involved in the early planning, it was not surprising that Father Haas was selected by Archbishop Stritch to serve as director of the Summer School in Milwaukee.

More than 120 priests from eleven dioceses and ten religious orders enrolled in the Milwaukee program, from July 6 to 30. Because of their restricted educational backgrounds, their limited contact with factory conditions, and their crowded schedule in parochial ministry, many of these priests had only a superficial acquaintance with current labor and industrial problems and with the Church's social teachings concerning them. One of the priests who participated in the Milwaukee Summer School later commented:

> One of the objectives of the summer school was to help the parish priest in both of these difficulties. For the first difficulty—how to learn the truth about labor conditions—it showed him where to get the really abundant factual material published by the United States Department of Labor and other government agencies. It acquainted him with the sources, such as the Brookings Institution, Senate investigation hearings, etc., from which he may learn the factual background of the labor problem. Not that a complete mastery of this factual background could possibly be obtained in four short weeks—far from it; but at least, the highways to the truth have been indicated and marked, which is something. For the second difficulty—where to find an up-to-the-minute presentation of the application of the principles of Catholic moral theology to these industrial problems, the summer school introduced him to a rich pamphlet literature edited by the N.C.W.C. and other Catholic publishers, and also to a number of splendid books such as Nell-Bruening's *Reorganization of Social Economy*. These source materials are the armories from which the busy parish priest may equip himself with the proper weapons for carrying on the battle of the Church for truth.[24]

As Father Haas had indicated in his letter to Bishop Lucey, each week of the session was to be under the direction of a recognized expert in the social justice field. Monsignor John A. Ryan presided over the week devoted to "Economic Morality"; Father Wilfred Parsons, S.J., of Georgetown University, over the week on "The New Social Order"; Bishop Lucey over the week on "Legislation"; and Father Haas, in addition to his duties as coordinator of the total program, directed the week on "Economic Organization." The four-week program included individual presentations and comments by Father Peter Dietz, Voyta Wrabetz of the state Labor Board, Harold Story, vice president of Allis-Chalmers in Milwaukee, and James Carey of the CIO. After delivering their prepared addresses, the speakers opened the session to questions and comments, and one participant noted that "it happened not infrequently that more real knowledge was gleaned from this 'third degree' than from the formal talk."[25] There were usually three of these sessions each day, with a formal presentation or panel discussion each morning, afternoon, and evening, and additional time set aside for seminars and less structured discussions among the participants and with the visiting faculty.

During the second week of July, while Father Parsons directed the study on the "New Social Order" in Milwaukee, Father Haas presided over discussions on "Economic Organization" at a similar institute sponsored by Bishop Karl Alter in Toledo. The subjects of Father Haas's lectures in both Toledo and Milwaukee were topics he had written and spoken on repeatedly for more than fifteen years: "The Right and Necessity of Organization," "Wages and Hours in the United States," "Processes of Organizing and Bargaining," "Strikes," "Women in Industry," and "Mediation and Arbitration." As always, Father Haas's lectures were popular and well attended. He not only possessed a scholar's detailed grasp of the subject at hand but could support his theories from firsthand experiences in government mediation and public service.

Catholic theologians at that time were divided on the morality of the sitdown strike, and Father Haas made his position clear in these Summer Schools of Social Action. "From the standpoint of effect and purpose," he stated in his Toledo lectures, "there is no important difference between the sitdown and the outside strike." The purpose of both strikes was to withhold property temporarily from an employer's use, and he saw no difference in doing this from the outside or the inside. "When the conditions necessary for any strike to be morally justified are met, the sitdown is as moral as the ordinary outside strike."[26]

Father Haas always advised caution, however. In an address before the Chicago Summer School for Priests the following year, he declared:

> Maintaining that there are cases in which the sit-down can be morally justified is quite another matter from saying that it should be used more generally than it is. The latter I do not hold. In fact I believe its use should be restricted to the narrowest possible compass. It should be discouraged not because it cannot be used in conscience under any circumstances but for an entirely different reason. The sit-down makes control by union officials over the rank and file difficult if not impossible. Inasmuch as union officials are the negotiating

body with the employer consummating a collective contract, it is essential that they have proper control over their members in order to execute the contract in all its provisions. The sit-down undermines the authority of union officials and cannot but have the effect of making collective bargaining impossible. For this very weighty reason I should say that the sit-down should be discouraged in every legitimate way.[27]

From Milwaukee, Toledo, San Francisco, and Los Angeles in 1937, the Summer Schools of Social Action expanded into New York, Chicago, Buffalo, Pittsburgh, Brooklyn, Richmond, and Washington over the next two years. Through them, hundreds of priests throughout the country gained clearer understanding of the social teachings of the Church and deeper concern for the problems of the farmer, the industrial worker, and other underprivileged groups; and through these priests this understanding and concern were transmitted to parochial classrooms, parish societies, and even into local welfare and reform programs. Many of these institutes were modeled on the successful Milwaukee experiment and thus owed much to the guidance and planning of Father Haas and other members of the NCWC Social Action Department in the spring and early summer of 1937.[28]

The decline in strikes, which the Wisconsin Labor Relations Board had noted in its report of August 1, continued throughout the rest of 1937 and into 1938. Figures released by the Bureau of Labor Statistics listed fifteen strikes in Wisconsin in September, nine in October, four in November, and two in December.[29] In early January 1938 an official informed Father Haas (then in Washington) that "in the Milwaukee office, we have found that strikes have practically disappeared."[30] Labor statistics for 1938, however, can be deceiving. Although only half as many strikes broke out in Wisconsin in 1938 as in 1937, they involved almost twice as many workers, and labor unrest throughout the state, consequently, was much greater than in the year before. Several of these 1938 disputes, in fact, were among the most serious and most threatening the state experienced throughout the New Deal period, and in three of them—at Allis-Chalmers, Nash-Kelvinator, and Harnischfeger Manufacturing Corporation—Father Haas served as the board's chief mediator.

Father Haas's settlement of the Allis-Chalmers dispute that spring was probably his greatest personal success as a mediator for the state board. On April 27, Harold Christoffel, president of

UAW Local 248 in Milwaukee, notified Governor La Follette that his 8,000 members had voted to walk off their jobs unless company officials acceded to union demands for a closed shop and for adherence to strict seniority in the discharge of workers. Members of the Labor Board's mediation staff met with company and union officials from April 28 to 30, but neither side would compromise. Company officials insisted on including a "merit clause" in the contract, allowing them to dismiss workers according to merit or efficiency, regardless of seniority or union affiliation. Union leaders, on the other hand, demanded a closed shop. The plant had been organized as an AFL union but President Christoffel had later swung the union to the CIO. By 1938, the CIO represented an overwhelming majority of the workers, but company officials and the remaining AFL employees opposed a closed shop agreement. At the end of fruitless discussions on April 30, the state mediators could only win assurances from Christoffel that he would delay the strike call for forty-eight hours. Chairman Wrabetz immediately called Father Haas in Washington and asked him to take charge of all mediation efforts at Allis-Chalmers.[31]

On May 2, Father Haas returned to Milwaukee and conferred with Wrabetz, company vice president Harold Story, and union president Christoffel. The discussions continued for two days but little progress was made. Neither party would compromise on the closed shop or the merit clause. At the close of negotiations on the second day, Christoffel agreed to extend the truce a further forty-eight hours. "The bargaining committee reported it does not want to call a strike," he announced, "as long as there is any hope of working out a basis for peaceful settlement in mediation conferences. We want no such move until all efforts have failed."[32]

Negotiations began on May 4 under very difficult conditions. Despite Christoffel's repeated assurances, workers that morning had staged a series of unauthorized sitdown strikes throughout the plant, at one time interrupting work simultaneously in all departments. Company officials accused union leaders of bad faith in breaking the truce and Christoffel worried that he was losing control of his workers. A local newspaper insisted that "relationships apparently were straining nearly to the breaking point," but Father Haas was not discouraged. "The patient is still breathing," he remarked. "There is some hope."[33] Father Haas was scheduled to address a WPA luncheon that day in Boston, but at the request of Chairman Wrabetz he agreed to remain in

Milwaukee. His efforts were successful; after a day of unauthorized strikes and charges and countercharges of bad faith, the negotiators accepted his proposed settlement that evening. A staff member's report summarized the final session with calm detachment:

> At about 3:30 p.m. the mediation conference was resumed with Msgr. Haas presiding, and after running through the entire contract and noting the differences between the parties, Msgr. Haas made a proposal for settlement of the case. At about 8 p.m. the parties agreed on the terms of the settlement and authorized Msgr. Haas to issue a release to the newspapers advising that the settlement would be submitted to the union membership on Saturday, May 7, with the recommendation of the bargaining committee that it be ratified. Msgr. Haas released this news item to the *Milwaukee Sentinel* reporter who was present, and authorized me to release it to all other newspapers in Milwaukee.[34]

This final agreement was a victory for compromise and a tribute to Father Haas's mediation skill. The union dropped its demand for a closed shop but received the company's promise to cooperate with its organization efforts. The union likewise withdrew its demand for a blanket agreement covering Allis-Chalmers plants in Boston and Pittsburgh, but the company agreed to include the basic provisions of the Milwaukee agreement in its other contracts. Seniority was to be followed in hiring and dismissing workers, as the union wanted, but the company was permitted to make exceptions in cases of workers with special talents or training. All workers with ten years' employment were awarded ten days' annual vacation, instead of six.[35]

Father Haas's part in the final settlement was hailed on all sides. Union president Christoffel declared: "Our committee comes out of the conciliation with the highest regard for Father Haas. We appreciate his service and attribute successful conclusion of the discussions in large measure to his efforts." Company vice president Story agreed. "This is my first experience with outside mediators," he admitted, "and I cannot speak too highly of mediation as conducted by men of standing." Lloyd Garrison, former chairman of the National Labor Relations Board, wrote: "Just a line to congratulate you on the wonderful job you did at Allis-Chalmers. I know enough about the situation, first from Story and later from [Nathan] Feinsinger after he had attended the first mediation session, to believe that the strike could not be averted.

You did the seemingly impossible and avoided what could have been an exceedingly ugly situation. You have earned the gratitude of all of us." Governor La Follette, of course, was most gratified. "As you know," he wrote Haas a week after the settlement, "the Wisconsin Labor Relations Board has most amply fulfilled my every expectation. Your mediation of the Allis-Chalmers dispute was, in my judgment, the outstanding accomplishment of the Board up to this time. I am especially grateful to you for your efforts in that case because you averted what would have been the largest strike in the history of Wisconsin."[36]

A few weeks after this Allis-Chalmers settlement, an almost equally serious controversy broke out in the Nash-Kelvinator plants of Racine and Kenosha. Company executives notified workers that summer that they were closing the Racine plant and transferring all operations to the Kenosha factory in an effort to recover financial losses. On August 22, the workers who were dismantling the Racine plant went out on strike and the United Automobile Workers in Racine announced that they would prevent the transfer, by force if necessary. "The company will build Lafayette cars in Racine or not at all," the president of the Racine local declared.[37] Haas attempted to mediate the dispute in the early weeks of September but without success, and was then forced to return to Washington for the opening of the new school year at Catholic University. On October 3, he returned to the controversy and, after ten hours of negotiations, the disputing parties agreed to his compromise proposal. According to the terms of this agreement, the Racine plant would continue to operate for at least sixty days as a parts plant, the main operations of the Racine factory would then be transferred to Kenosha, the seniority lists of the Kenosha and Racine locals would be combined, all new hiring in the enlarged Kenosha plant would be taken from this combined list, and an appeals board would be set up to decide all cases of disputed seniority.[38]

On October 5, the Racine local and company officials accepted the agreement, but two days later the workers in Kenosha voted it down. Father Haas then telephoned UAW President Homer Martin in Detroit, and on October 8 Vice President Richard Frankensteen arrived in Kenosha to participate in the discussions. The influence of Frankensteen was crucial. Near midnight the following day, after several minor changes had been made in the provision for combining the two unions' seniority lists, the agreement was accepted by the Kenosha workers.[39] Since Father Haas

had returned to Washington by that time, his part in the negotiations could easily be overlooked. Those closest to the discussions, however, appreciated his contributions. "Your agreement of
October 3," acknowledged one board mediator, "constituted the
basis for settlement."

The dispute at the Harnischfeger Manufacturing Company
in Milwaukee later that fall was probably even more difficult
to mediate than the controversies at Allis-Chalmers or Nash-
Kelvinator. The controversy began on August 22, when company
officials notified the workers that, due to the 1938 business
slump, all wages would be reduced 10 to 15 percent, effective
August 29.[40] Local 1114 of the Amalgamated Association of Iron,
Steel and Tin Workers of America countered immediately, with
demands for a wage cut of only 5 percent, reinstatement of
several workers recently discharged, and a written contract to
replace the "statement of policy" then governing labor relations.
Father Haas met with both sides during the last week of August
but no agreement could be reached. In early September, Haas
left Milwaukee to prepare for the opening of the school year in
Washington and, on September 6, several hundred Harnischfeger
employees walked off their jobs.

As the negotiations continued throughout September and
October, difficulties mounted. Father Haas was seldom able to
leave Washington during that time and he could keep informed
of developments in Milwaukee only by telephone. Besides the
Wisconsin board, the National Labor Relations Board and the
U.S. Conciliation Service had also entered the case and much
of Father Haas's time in Washington was spent coordinating
the efforts of these three government agencies. In mid-September,
company executives challenged the validity of the union's strike
vote since the balloting had not been secret—as the union by-laws
required—and many outside union members had been present at
the meeting and perhaps had voted. Prejudice and personality
conflicts complicated the discussions. The chief company nego-
tiator, Haas noted at the time, "is an 18 carat Prussian, and Myer
Adelman of SWOC is Jewish, and that isn't helping the situation."[41]

After more than ten weeks of negotiations, an agreement was
signed on November 19. The settlement granted the union's request for a written contract and reinstatement of four of the
seven dismissed workers, but it also provided for the 10 percent
wage reduction which the company had demanded from the beginning.[42] Chief credit for the agreement belonged to Father Haas

and the Wisconsin Labor Board. The U.S. Conciliation Service had
withdrawn from the dispute in early November, and the National
Labor Relations Board was concerned primarily whether the
Wagner Act had been violated in the dismissal of the seven workers.
During the final days of the negotiations, the dispute was in the
hands of Father Haas and the mediation staff of the state Labor
Board. As soon as the settlement was announced, Governor
La Follette sent Haas a telegram of warmest congratulations.

Father Haas's assistance in this Harnischfeger settlement was
probably his last major service for the Wisconsin Labor Relations
Board. He had submitted his resignation repeatedly to Governor
La Follette throughout 1937 and 1938 but the governor had just
as frequently rejected it. In the 1938 elections, however, Governor
La Follette was defeated by Republican Julius Heil, a conservative
Milwaukee industrialist and millionaire.[43] Realizing that the Labor
Board could not function effectively under the new administration,
Haas and Witte notified the governor-elect of their intention to
resign. On January 1, 1939, Haas again tendered his resignation:
"In accordance with our conversation in Madison on December 20,
I herewith submit my resignation as a member of the Wisconsin
Labor Relations Board. Although I have tendered my resignation
on different occasions since October, 1937, it has never been
accepted. I beg you to accept it at this time."[44]

The governor, however, had other plans. Soon after his
inauguration in the first week of January, a new Employment
Peace bill was introduced into the state legislature to repeal the
Labor Relations Act of 1937. This new measure provided for a
Labor Disputes Board with greatly reduced powers and outlawed
several unfair practices on the part of employees, and since the
governor was confident that this new act would pass, he saw no
need to alter the membership of a board he hoped would never
again function. On February 28, Father Haas, becoming impatient, again submitted his resignation, this time in a sworn and
certified affidavit. On March 29, finally, the day before the new
Employment Peace Act was signed into law and three months
after Father Haas had formally submitted his resignation, the
new governor found time to reply. "It has slipped my mind,"
he wrote, "since I last met you in Madison that you informed
me that you wished to resign from the Wisconsin Labor Relations Board. I want to take this opportunity of saying to you,
Sir, that I am sure the citizens of Wisconsin appreciated your

services while you were on the Board, but in order to clarify my records I am accepting your resignation at this time and will appoint someone to succeed you."[45] With this letter from Governor Heil, Father Haas's work as an official of the Wisconsin state government came to an end.[46]

During the twenty months of its existence, the Wisconsin Labor Relations Board compiled a commendable record. In its official report to the governor in December 1938, the Board noted that it had heard and closed 847 cases. It had successfully mediated 588 controversies, settling 175 strikes and averting 80 others. The board had also settled 38 disputes by arbitration, investigated over 350 charges of unfair labor practices, heard 105 applications for union listing, and determined the proper collective bargaining agent in approximately 100 cases. The report noted also that industrial disputes had declined steadily since the establishment of the board in April 1937, that no deaths had resulted from industrial violence during its existence, and that the National Guard had never been called to maintain peace. "During this period," the report concluded, "Wisconsin has made a record in labor relations of which it can be justly proud."[47]

Although Father Haas's resignation from the state Labor Board in the spring of 1939 had occasioned few public expressions of gratitude from the new Republican administration, his months of dedicated service had not gone unnoted. Religious leaders, union officials, business executives, and private citizens throughout the state had sent him frequent letters of appreciation and commendation. In August 1937 the *Wisconsin State Journal* had stated: "No one has shown himself more a man of judgment and he has the confidence of both the laboring classes and employers. His work even before his appointment to the state labor board as an arbitrator of labor disputes brought about many results of great value to both labor and employers." The *Capital Times* of Madison echoed the same sentiments: "For a number of years labor and government officials have counted upon you to step in when various crises brought about the need of one whose clear thinking on social questions made him an invaluable mediator and counselor. You never failed them in this regard." Two days before leaving office, Governor La Follette sent the following note in longhand: "This note very inadequately expresses the deep appreciation the State of Wisconsin owes to you for your outstanding service as a member of the Wisconsin Labor

Relations Board. In a difficult period in industrial relations the Wisconsin Board made a record of fair and impartial administration, and achieved results not equalled anywhere in this country. In large measure this was due to your understanding, experience, and great spirit."[48]

It was unfortunate that Governor Heil chose not to write a similar letter in the spring of 1939. Haas's long experience as a government official in Washington and his wide reputation as a champion of social justice had contributed much to the prestige and success of the Wisconsin Labor Board. He was largely responsible for maintaining harmonious relations with the NLRB in Washington and with its regional board in Milwaukee, he had the respect of AFL and CIO leaders throughout the state, and he had successfully mediated several of the board's most difficult disputes. The wording of the governor's letter—"I want to take this opportunity of saying to you, Sir, that I am sure the citizens of Wisconsin appreciated your services while you were on that Board"—was less than gracious. It was one of the very few discordant letters which Father Haas received during his twenty months of service.

Bishop Francis J. Haas

Peter Haas and children Allen, Arthur, and Margaret in family grocery.

Young Frank Haas

Minnesota Historical Society and Minneapolis Tribune

Gov. Floyd Olson, Father Haas, and E. H. Dunnigan at conclusion of Minneapolis truckers' strike, 1934.

Department of Archives and Manuscripts, Catholic University of America

U.S. delegation to American States Conference of ILO in Havana, 1939. Msgr. Haas is at far right. Also standing are James Carey (3rd from left), Arthur Altmeyer (6th from left), George Harrison (3rd from right), and Kathryn Lewis (between Altmeyer and Harrison).

Western Michigan Catholic *photo by Robinson Studio, Grand Rapids*

Serving the elderly at Home for the Aged, Little Sisters of the Poor, Grand Rapids, 1949.

9

The Church's Monsignor and Labor's Troubleshooter: Washington, 1937-1943

In late August 1937, after a summer crowded with hearings of the Wisconsin Labor Relations Board, WPA meetings, and lectures at Summer Schools of Social Action for Priests, Father Haas returned to St. Francis Seminary to be invested with the purple robes of a monsignor by Archbishop Samuel Stritch.[1] Elevation to the rank of domestic prelate, with the title Right Reverend Monsignor, is an honor bestowed by the Holy Father on select diocesan priests— usually pastors of large parishes and officials of diocesan departments and tribunals—in recognition of distinguished service to the Church and to the local diocese. Father Haas had served his Church for more than twenty years as seminary professor and rector, director of the National Catholic School of Social Service, author, lecturer, and adviser to members of the American hierarchy and officials of the National Catholic Welfare Conference. Because of his well-publicized work for the NRA and the Wisconsin Labor Relations Board and his success in settling numerous thorny disputes for the Department of Labor, he was also recognized across the country as an outstanding government servant. Few priests in 1937 seemed more deserving of this honor and public recognition.

August 24 was selected for the investiture because it coincided with the biennial meeting of the St. Francis Seminary Alumni Association and more than three hundred priests would be present to honor their classmate, former professor and rector, and long-time editor of the association's publication, *The Salesianum*. Archbishop Stritch officiated at the investiture ceremony in the seminary chapel that morning, surrounded by members of the alumni association and numerous friends and relatives. Following this solemn investiture, Bishop Aloysius Muench of Fargo,

171

a classmate of the new monsignor and his predecessor as rector of St. Francis Seminary, offered a pontifical High Mass of thanksgiving, with Archbishop Stritch delivering the sermon. An official meeting of the alumni association was held that afternoon in the seminary gymnasium, and the day concluded with a formal banquet in the dining hall that evening.[2]

Father Haas received numerous congratulatory messages and tributes throughout the day. In his brief address during the investiture ceremony, Archbishop Stritch suggested that the honor had been bestowed primarily "because of his exceptional labor in enunciating, interpreting and executing the principles laid down in the social Encyclicals of the Holy Father." "The honor comes not only as a reward for effective work in the field of sociology," the *Milwaukee Catholic Herald-Citizen* added, "but also as a seal of papal approval." In the official notice of appointment, Pope Pius XI commended Haas for "the exemplary character of your life" and "the expertness and energy which you bring to social questions in conformity with the Pontifical Letters on these subjects." The presence at the investiture ceremonies of Monsignor Joseph Corrigan, rector of Catholic University of America, might have suggested a further reason for this honor. At the formal dinner that evening, the new monsignor revealed that he was leaving St. Francis Seminary on September 1 to accept the position of first dean of the newly established School of Social Science at Catholic University in Washington.[3]

Erection of the new School of Social Science had been a subject of discussion for several years. Some reorganization of the university seemed necessary, first of all, from recent directives from Rome. In May 1931, Pope Pius XI had issued an apostolic constitution, *Deus Scientiarum Dominus*, on the education of the clergy and the structuring of pontifical universities—those, like Catholic University, under the direct supervision of the Holy See. This constitution emphasized the importance of philosophy in the education of the clergy and insisted that philosophy be given the same academic status as theology and canon law. Since the revision of the university's statutes in 1930, however, theology and canon law formed separate schools at Catholic University, while philosophy was only a department within the Graduate School of Arts and Sciences. Rome, consequently, seemed to demand at least this revision.[4]

Reorganization of the social sciences seemed appropriate also. Not only had Pope Pius XI urged universities to give Catholic social teachings a more prominent place in their curricula, but the social sciences at Catholic University seemed in special need of coordination. The university's departments of sociology, politics, and economics belonged to the Graduate School of Arts and Sciences and offered degrees of master of arts and doctor of philosophy; the School of Social Work had been established in 1934, independently of the Graduate School of Arts and Sciences, and offered its graduates a degree of master of science; and the nearby National Catholic School of Social Service was separate from the School of Social Work and offered degrees of master of arts through its affiliation with the Graduate School of Arts and Sciences. Only lay and religious women could be admitted to the National Catholic School of Social Service, while the School of Social Work admitted men, clerical and lay, and religious women. By 1937, such overlapping seemed to have little academic, administrative, or financial justification.[5]

Bishop James H. Ryan, rector of the university, Monsignor John O'Grady, dean of the School of Social Work, and Father Haas, director of the National Catholic School of Social Service, had discussed restructuring these departments on several occasions in 1934 and 1935, but no definite steps were taken.[6] When Monsignor Joseph M. Corrigan of St. Charles Seminary, Overbrook, Pennsylvania, was appointed rector in April 1936, however, he immediately reopened the negotiations. He had originally hoped to include the two professional schools, Social Work and Social Service, and at least the three graduate departments of sociology, politics, and economics in the reorganization, but serious obstacles again arose. First, there was the university's promise in 1934 not to admit lay women into the new School of Social Work, and this seemed to block any formal merger or union. Second, many university officials objected to the removal of Monsignor O'Grady as the dean of the School of Social Work, which this reorganization would probably demand. Third, it seemed difficult to reorganize the social sciences distinct from philosophy and theology since ethics and moral theology are the basis of Catholic teachings on social justice. Furthermore, the revised statutes of 1930 stipulated that all graduate degrees (except those in the professional schools) would be under the jurisdiction of the Graduate School of Arts and Sciences, and university officials saw establishment of a second graduate school, exclusively for the social sciences, as a needless violation of this principle. Finally, the American Association of Schools of Social Work threatened to withdraw professional approval of the School of Social Work if such a change were made; it notified Monsignor O'Grady of the view of the executive committee: "Any change in the present status of the School of Social Work as an independent educational unit within the Catholic University would automatically cancel provisional membership in the Association of Schools."[7]

After much confusion and controversy, it was therefore decided to leave the two professional schools unchanged and to form the new School of Social Science from the three departments of the graduate school. Father Haas was pleased with this minimal reorganization but it is uncertain how influential he was in its adoption.[8] In a letter to Monsignor Corrigan in the fall of 1936, he had urged increased emphasis on the social sciences. Social service was excellent, he suggested, because it was concerned with the care of the already needy and distressed, but social science sought to remove the causes of this poverty and insecurity. Social justice, he noted, was an essential part of Catholic doctrine, and thus, of all places, the Catholic University of America should give it proper emphasis in its curriculum and administrative structure. In the encyclical *Quadragesimo Anno*, Pope Pius XI had singled out, as the two great needs of the time, "reform of the social order and the correction of morals," and Father Haas noted that these evils could not be remedied without a clergy and laity competently trained in both the social sciences and moral philosophy. He further suggested that the needs of the nation demanded increased understanding of the social sciences since unequal distribution of wealth and inability (thus far) to uplift the socially and economically underprivileged might be the greatest problem the country faced in the 1930s. Less than two weeks later, he sent a second memorandum to the rector, recommending that the new School of Social Science include the departments of anthropology, sociology, history, economics, political science, international affairs, and statistics, but there is no evidence of serious disappointment when this proposal was rejected.[9]

The official news release from the university noted this was not strictly a "new" School of Social Science but reestablishment of a school that had existed as early as 1895 and was later discontinued. It was hoped that the school would be able to make classes in the social sciences and moral philosophy available to the increasing number of employees who staffed new government social agencies, and also offer a demanding graduate program to men and women preparing "for careers as professors in colleges and high schools, as consultants and research specialists in government and private agencies, as editors of social science publications, and for allied activities in business, labor, farm, and international organizations." For anyone who believed that these were purely secular subjects, with little or no place in a religiously oriented university, the publicity noted that the new school would adhere "strictly to Catholic philosophy, practice and tradition in its interpretation of basic economic, political and sociological facts."[10]

When Monsignor Haas returned to Washington in the fall of 1937, he had no doubts about the demanding and even controversial post he was assuming. University officials who had opposed his appointment to the Faculty of Theology in 1929 were not enthusiastic over his return to the university as dean, and other officials considered the new school unnecessary. "As a layman, I offer you no advice," one professor wrote him. "It would be fine for this institution to have you. As for yourself, you are an idol now. Can you really make this inchoate thing go? If not, it might hurt your future advancement." Despite the difficulties his new assignment entailed, Haas was eager to return to Washington. "In leaving the labor board and rectorship of St. Francis Seminary," he declared that August, "I am going back to where I belong—in the classroom."[11]

During the next six years in Washington, however, the classroom occupied only a small portion of his time. He held the rank of professor of economics but he taught only one course each semester, and his major influence on students resulted more from the popular seminar he conducted each Sunday morning. This seminar, open to all interested students (and the public), was an informal discussion of current problems of social justice—labor legislation before Congress, recent NLRB decisions, and (most often) labor disputes in which he had been recently involved. Even after a lapse of thirty-five years, former students could recall the fascination of these "Sunday morning seminars." But Haas was not primarily a teacher, and his classroom influence was limited. Tied down to administrative responsibilities as dean, he was able to teach few courses and he directed fewer dissertations. Although numerous students of John A. Ryan, John O'Grady, Edward Pace, and Peter Guilday staffed Catholic universities and social agencies across the country in the decades after their graduation, there were, surprisingly, few "students of Francis Haas."[12]

Monsignor Haas devoted most of his time at Catholic University to duties outside the classroom. As dean of the School of

Social Science, he was responsible for a graduate enrollment of approximately 175 students and a faculty of sixteen. He held final jurisdiction over the admission of students, the granting of scholarships, approval of curricula, the granting of degrees, and the hiring of faculty. He read all master's and doctor's dissertations before final approval (which at one time numbered seventy-three in progress). In his annual report to the rector in 1942, he estimated that this work alone required twenty-five hours each month, noting that one dissertation "required about 50 hours of my time to put it in presentable form," and others required even more time. His correspondence reveals daily concern about scholarship assistance, salary increases, shortage of funds for book purchases, inadequate faculty office space, and—after 1941— leaves of absence for faculty members called into the armed services. Monsignor Haas served not only as dean of the School of Social Science but also as head of the Department of Economics, and thus his executive duties could be doubled. He was never attracted to administrative work, and he found it even less congenial during his two terms as dean, from 1937 to 1943, four years of economic depression and two years of world war.[13]

In 1938, Monsignor Haas was also appointed chairman of Catholic University's Commission on American Citizenship. This commission had been established by the American hierarchy, at the initiative of Pope Pius XI, to encourage deeper understanding of the obligations of responsible citizenship among American Catholics through the publication of grade and high school textbooks and through the organization of parish study groups and summer workshops. During its first year, Haas noted in an early report, "the Commission is supplying materials on citizenship to *The Young Catholic Messenger*, *The Junior Catholic Messenger*, and *Our Little Messenger*, which reach over 700,000 school children weekly, and preparations are under way for the writing and distribution of text-books and other materials to effectuate the principles of Christian Democracy."[14]

The "text-books and other materials" under preparation comprised a comprehensive, three-volume elementary school curriculum, titled *Guiding Growth in Christian Social Living*, and a series of readers emphasizing the citizen's obligations toward the state, toward fellow citizens, and toward the world beyond national borders. The purpose of the curriculum, according to the project's director, was to help organize the child's education toward goals of physical fitness, economic competency, social virtue, appreciation of culture, and moral and spiritual perfection. Rejecting a suggestion to publish only supplementary materials to be used in conjunction with basic texts, the commission decided to produce a Faith and Freedom series of basic readers, one volume for each grade: *This Is Our Family, This Is Our Town, This Is Our Heritage*, and so on. Haas estimated that he spent an average of forty hours each month in conferences with authors and publishers, and he was obliged, as ecclesiastical censor, to read and approve all volumes before they were submitted to the printer. An associate later remembered him as a "kindly, exacting scholar,... insistent (but not in a domineering way) upon meticulous scholarship," and she credited him with much of the work's emphasis on "labor...racial, human rights and international peace and brotherhood."[15]

The commission's efforts bore almost immediate fruit. Despite wartime restrictions on publishing, the first two volumes of the curriculum were ready for publication by early 1944 and eight volumes of the readers were in use in more than 5,000 of the 8,000 Catholic elementary schools in the United States. "It has been the hope of the Commission, from the beginning," Haas wrote in late 1943, his final year in Washington, "that its work would help to make social education a living moral force and would take Catholic education far toward the goal set for it by the Bishops of the United States. It is now our belief that we have already accomplished a large part of the work."[16]

During these six years in Washington, Monsignor Haas also cooperated with Father Raymond McGowan in publishing a new translation of *Rerum Novarum* and *Quadragesimo Anno*. Haas had complained that papal encyclicals were too often translated by Latin scholars quite unfamiliar with both the social teachings of the Church and contemporary economic problems, and as a result the Pope's meaning was distorted. "Of course the great need is a true translation of the official text," he wrote Bishop Henry Althoff of Belleville in 1936. "It is a pity that the mind of the Holy See as contained in *Quadragesimo Anno* is so shabbily presented and even distorted in the English, French, and German translations."[17] Haas and McGowan had begun their translations in early 1935, and in January 1936 Haas wrote optimistically to a friend: "I hope that we can bring them out in Latin-English form in the near future." The work of translation, however, was tedious and slow: Haas by that time had been transferred to Milwaukee as rector of St. Francis Seminary, McGowan remained in

Washington with the NCWC, and both were preoccupied with numerous other duties. The translations, consequently, were not completed until 1939.

Publication was then delayed a further four years. Monsignor Haas had sent the translations to the Vatican for approval in October 1939, and seven months later he confided to a friend: "With regard to the publication of the translations of *Rerum Novarum* and *Quadragesimo Anno*, I anticipate no more obstacles standing in the way of going ahead with the publication. We have authorization from Vatican City for the publication of the translations but this authorization is so general that it amounts to little or nothing. What we want, you know, is something in the way of a letter from Vatican City that will make this translation something more than just another translation." It was not until two years later that this additional authorization was granted. On March 19, 1942, the apostolic delegate in Washington notified Bishop Corrigan: "I am pleased to state, under authority committed to me by the Secretariate of State of His Holiness, that the present translations of the Encyclicals *Rerum Novarum* and *Quadragesimo Anno* have been duly examined and found faithful to their original Latin texts. They are to be regarded as English translations authorized by the Holy See." This was still not the official commendation Haas and McGown desired, but they could delay no longer. "We have been at this job for approximately eight years," Haas wrote Bishop Muench in March 1942, "not, to be sure, full time. We have, however, run the translations through as many as eleven revisions, and by revisions I do not mean eleven sets of changes made here and there. Actually, the documents have been re-typed that many times."[18] The translated encyclicals finally appeared in 1943.

Even more important than his work in translating the social encyclicals was his contribution to the influential statement of the NCWC's Administrative Board of Bishops in 1940, *The Church and Social Order*. John A. Ryan called the document "the most important pronouncement made by the Catholic Church in the United States on labor and economic issues," and Dr. Charles Bruehl commended "the sane realism with which it approaches the problem and deals with the issues involved." Pope Pius XII praised it as "a contribution to the social health of the nation" and predicted that it would "exert a historic influence on the course of events in a period of change and crisis."[19]

The Church and Social Order was issued over the signatures of the fifteen bishops on the NCWC's administrative board, but its true authorship was not revealed. One historian has suggested that the principal author may have been Ryan, assisted by Haas and McGowan, but Bishop Karl Alter of Toledo, a member of the administrative board at that time, later stated that the document was primarily his. All four probably had a part in drafting the statement but the influence of Haas deserves special mention. Two years earlier, in the spring of 1938, he had drafted a statement, "The Church and Social Justice," to be issued as a pastoral letter by Cardinal Patrick Hayes of New York, but because of the cardinal's failing health that summer and his death in September, the statement was never released. This statement, however, was almost certainly one of the basic documents used in preparing the bishops' pronouncement of 1940. Their titles are almost identical; they are divided into the same six sections; and ten of the paragraphs have identical wording. Bishop Alter almost certainly wrote the final draft of the bishops' statement, but just as certainly he had Haas's earlier document before him and relied heavily upon it.[20]

The bishops' pronouncement was essentially a restatement of the principles of *Quadragesimo Anno*. The document stressed, as did Haas's social and economic philosophy, the inherent, God-given dignity of every human being. "Man cannot be treated as a mere chattel," the statement declared, "but rather with dignity and respect as a child of God. His labor is not a thing to be ashamed of, but an honorable calling, whereby he achieves a necessary livelihood and fulfills the divine plan of an earthly economy."[21] The statement admitted the right of owners to a just return on their investments but insisted that the right of workers to an adequate wage was even more basic. "The first claim of labor," the bishops declared, "which takes priority over any claim of the owners to profits, respects the right to a living wage." The means to guarantee this wage were the means Haas advocated repeatedly: organization and legislation. "The remedy," the bishops said, "lies first in the adequate organization of both employers and employees in their own proper associations and in their joint action; secondly, the adequate regulation and supervision by the state through proper legislative enactment." The bishops' statement accepted the underconsumption theory of the Depression. "Unless working-men as a class," it asserted, "have sufficient income to purchase their share of the goods which our economic system is capable of producing, the markets will automatically be closed to the sale of goods, and idle factories and unemployment are the disastrous result." The document concluded with a plea for the Christian reconstruction of the social order:

> Our economic life then must be reorganized not on the disintegrating principles of individualism but on the constructive principle of social and moral unity among the members of human society. In conformity with Christian principles, economic power must be subordinated to human welfare, both individual and social; social incoherence and class conflict must be replaced by corporate unity and organic function; ruthless competition must give way to just and reasonable state regulations; sordid selfishness must be superseded by social justice and charity. Then only can there be a true and rational social order; then only can we eliminate the twin evils of insufficiency and insecurity, and establish the divine plan of a brotherhood of men under the fatherhood of God.

After *The Bishops' Program of Social Reconstruction* of 1919, *The Church and Social Order* was probably the most important statement ever issued by the American hierarchy on the social question, and Monsignor Haas's contribution to it was undoubtedly one of the prouder achievements of his ecclesiastical career.

Although Monsignor Haas's responsibilities at Catholic University and on the Commission on American Citizenship absorbed most of his time and attention during these years in Washington, they were not his only, or perhaps even his primary, interests. He believed that every citizen has an obligation to contribute to the common good of society, and after his long months on the Labor Advisory Board, the National Labor Board, and the Wisconsin Labor Relations Board he was convinced that his own contribution would be chiefly in the field of government service. If his two years at St. Francis Seminary had been in some ways disappointing, it was primarily because they had removed him further from public life, and it was not surprising, consequently, that he was eager to resume his government work as soon as he returned to Washington in the fall of 1937.

The Washington to which Monsignor Haas returned, however, was vastly different from the city he had left only two years earlier. The wheels of New Deal reform had ground to a halt.

During Haas's final year as director of the National Catholic School of Social Service in 1935, the Roosevelt administration had enacted a program of social legislation matched only by the First Hundred Days in 1933, but by the fall of 1937 this "Roosevelt Revolution" had run its course and the New Deal was nearing completion. The failure of Roosevelt's efforts to enlarge the membership of the Supreme Court earlier that year; the outbreak of violent strikes in Chicago, Detroit, and Akron; the sudden drop in the economy and the resulting recession that fall; and threatening communiques from the foreign offices of Berlin, Tokyo, and Rome combined to divert popular interest and support from the president's program of domestic reform. Only two important pieces of social legislation were enacted in 1938, the Fair Labor Standards Act and the second Agricultural Adjustment Act; in 1939, perhaps there were none. Monsignor Haas resumed his work for the federal government on his return to Washington in 1937, but the times had changed and so had the nature of his public service. He was rarely appointed to official commissions or agencies, like the NRA or the WPA, but he was used chiefly as a Department of Labor "trouble-shooter" wherever Secretary Perkins felt his special talents might prove successful.

In February 1936, Father Haas had written from Milwaukee to Margaret Stabler of the WPA: "I have been following the Green-Lewis controversy with deepest interest and only hope that the factions can be brought together for continuous conferences so that a split will be avoided." During the next three years, however, Monsignor Haas was able to do much more than hope. The rift between William Green and John L. Lewis had broken out in the AFL annual conventions of 1934 and 1935 over the unionization of mass-production or unskilled workers. John L. Lewis and several of his associates insisted upon a modification of the Federation's traditional policy of unionization by craft and urged an intensive campaign to recruit the millions of unskilled workers into the ranks of organized labor. As a successful labor mediator and close friend of both Green and Lewis from NRA days, Haas was asked to intervene in the controversy on several occasions by Secretary Perkins and other government officials. The *Racine Journal-Times* in March 1939 asserted that "if C.I.O. and A.F. of L. chieftains finally establish a permanent peace, historians of the future may regard termination of the conflict between the two labor organizations as the crowning achievement in the career of a Racine man, Monsignor Francis J. Haas."[22] The reunion of the

AFL and the CIO did not take place until 1955, two years after Haas's death, but the records of the "peace negotiations" of the 1930s suggest that the tribute of the Racine paper was not unfounded.

Monsignor Haas had been involved in the controversy from its beginning. At the request of President William Green, Haas had addressed the stormy AFL convention in Atlantic City in October 1935. He took the occasion to praise the Federation and its leaders for their cooperation with the president's recovery program in the days of NRA and he urged even greater cooperation with industry and government in the months and years ahead. But he spoke near the end of the convention and he could not overlook the momentous events of that week—the rejection of the convention's minority report urging industrial unionism; the bitter words exchanged between high-ranking labor officials; and the widely publicized slugfest between John L. Lewis and William Hutcheson:

> For the last two days, the American Press has been carrying stories about what has been taking place in this convention. It is not necessary to tell you that the stories are that there have been in this convention very decided differences of opinion. It has been said that there was sharp conflict.
>
> To me, delegates of the convention, the report of what has been taking place here is not something to regret, but it is something to rejoice about. It is proof that the American Federation of Labor is for freedom of speech, freedom of expression, that it is prepared to openly, frankly and courageously come to grips with the great problems that are facing the American working people.
>
> The American Federation of Labor is growing, and with its growth there goes pain and suffering and some bruises. I sympathize with those who have suffered during these days, but I know that you, officers and delegates, are not unacquainted with suffering and bruises, and that if the American labor movement requires your suffering, you are ready and willing to take it, because that is the cause that you as labor representatives have chosen for yourselves.[23]

The seriousness of this breach within the Federation—which Father Haas either underestimated or attempted to play down in public—was made evident during the following month. On November 9 eleven dissident labor leaders, including John L. Lewis of the Mine Workers, Charles Howard of the Typographers, Sidney Hillman of the Amalgamated Clothing Workers, and David Dubinsky of the International Ladies Garment Workers, met in Washington and formally organized the Committee for Industrial Organization. Two weeks later, Lewis signaled the opening of hostilities with his curt note to Green: "Dear Sir and Brother: Effective this date I resign as vice president of the American Federation of Labor." As each side undertook extensive organization campaigns, often accompanied by violence, to lure millions of the unorganized into their ranks, the split within the Federation widened into open civil war.[24]

Father Haas followed the negotiations closely throughout 1936. In July, the AFL's executive council met in Washington to consider suspension of the dissident unions, and the *Washington Daily News* the following day found it "most encouraging" that Father Haas and three others "who enjoy the confidence of the workers of the nation are negotiating for a settlement of the C.I.O.-A.F. of L. controversy." The discussions were fruitless, however, and the decision on suspension was left to the Federation's annual convention, scheduled for Tampa that fall.[25] "This afternoon I leave for Tampa," Haas wrote from Milwaukee on November 21. "In all likelihood the Convention will get down to real business next week. According to reports in the *New York Times* the break between the A.F. of L. and the C.I.O. is widening. Nevertheless I cannot think that the Convention will let a complete break come." Although the convention voted to uphold the suspensions, Haas refused to lose heart. "There is still some hope," he insisted in December, "slight though it be."[26]

Soon after the Tampa convention adjourned, Father Haas attempted to clarify labor's basic differences in an article for the *Milwaukee Catholic Herald-Citizen*. "It is of course utter nonsense," he asserted, "to speak of a personal feud between President Green of the Federation and President John L. Lewis of the United Mine Workers." The dispute was basically one of craft unionism versus industrial unionism.

On the one side are the equities of hundreds of thousands of middleaged and elder craft unionists who have invested money in building up their organization and in numerous cases four or five years of their lives in preparation for their trade. The most elementary kind of justice requires that these equities be protected and safeguarded to the fullest.

On the other side is the right of the more than twenty
million unorganized to organize, enjoy the benefits of collective bargaining, and be given freest opportunity to be
part of the labor movement.[27]

There were undoubtedly difficult conflicts to resolve. Haas
strongly supported the organization of unskilled workers. "I assure
you," he had written to Lewis in March 1936, "that I am following the work of the Committee for Industrial Organization with
greatest interest, watching for every scrap of information about it.
Please accept my best wishes for success in bringing the benefits
of organization to the millions who are deprived of it." But Haas
just as strongly opposed dual unionism. "Union war like all war is
wasteful," he wrote a few years later. "Workers themselves are the
worst sufferers ... without arguing the point that there might have
been greater gains if there had been no split, no one will deny that
there should be unity here and now."[28]

Monsignor Haas returned to the controversy again soon
after his arrival in Washington in the fall of 1937. On October 11,
Secretary Perkins telephoned to ask his advice on calling a conference of influential businessmen, politicians, and educators to
discuss methods of marshaling public opinion behind efforts to
reopen peace negotiations.[29] Monsignor Haas and the secretary
met in her office the following day and drew up a list of approximately thirty national leaders to participate in such a gathering,
but the conference apparently was never called. On October 14,
AFL and CIO executives agreed to meet in Washington later that
month and Secretary Perkins decided to await the outcome.

These negotiations between AFL and CIO committees
under Matthew Woll and Philip Murray opened on October 25.
Herbert Harris has written that "Philip Murray ... opened discussion with a proposal devised by Father Haas, of Catholic University, and the Roosevelt Administration's chief nuncio in its attempt
to close the A.F.L.-C.I.O. gap."[30] This plan, to create a CIO
Department within the Federation, was discussed by the rival
leaders for several weeks but eventually was rejected. The AFL
leaders would accept it only if jurisdictional agreements were first
reached with the Federation's Building Trades, Metal Trades, and
other departments, while the CIO leaders demanded full autonomy.
After two months of deadlock, negotiations broke off on December 22, amid charges of bad faith and broken trust on both sides.

Within a few weeks, however, Monsignor Haas returned to
the conflict. At the suggestion of David K. Niles, close adviser to

President Roosevelt, Haas met separately with Green, Murray, and Thomas Kennedy of the United Mine Workers to ask their opinion of a proposal that Green and Lewis formally request the president to intervene.[31] Green and Murray apparently felt that the plan had merit, but when Haas discussed it with Secretary Perkins, she voiced strong opposition. The president, she insisted, must not become involved until he had a specific settlement to offer, and since at that time the administration had none, the project was carried no further.

Monsignor Haas was scheduled to address the annual convention of the United Mine Workers Union in Washington later that month and he could not ignore the deepening controversy. John L. Lewis and other CIO leaders had received chief blame for the failure of the peace negotiations in December and Haas took advantage of this January address, before Lewis's union, to plead for resumption of the talks:

> First, [let] both sides give up discussing which side on what issue caused the negotiations on December 20 to end in deadlock; second, [let] each side draw up a list of concessions constituting its best offer and stating in writing what its procedure for ratification is to be; third, [let] both sides agree at once on a day, hour, and place for conferences, with the understanding that the conferees continue negotiations without interruption and in no event to discontinue them until they have evolved a fair and workable settlement.[32]

"Mr. President and delegates," he pleaded, "labor knows how to be generous. It may have to tax itself to the limit of generosity in the great task before it. Let it not forget that there are even greater problems ahead, and greater stakes to be won. It is on trial and it may not fail."

Haas's plea, however, was in vain. John L. Lewis was not on the platform during Haas's address and on the following day he refused to comment—or to return to the conference table.[33] Green was even less diplomatic. "We have a high regard and respect for Father Haas," he declared, "but his proposals are impractical. It is not a question of blaming the C.I.O. for the collapse of the peace negotiations.... The A.F. of L. does not blame the C.I.O. It blames John L. Lewis alone." The refusal of the two labor chieftains to reopen negotiations must have seemed ironic to Father Haas when he recalled the many occasions, only three years before, when he, Green, and Lewis, as members of the National

Labor Board, had pleaded with disputing parties to sit down and talk over their differences. Times indeed had changed.

Monsignor Haas's final involvement in the controversy did not begin until almost a year later. Increasing unemployment throughout 1938 weakened both organizations, CIO leaders were preoccupied with preparations for their first "constitutional convention" in November, and the formal requests of David Dubinsky in May and Daniel Tobin in October that the negotiations be reopened fell on deaf ears. On December 3, finally, Monsignor Haas, Sidney Hillman, and the AFL's George Harrison met in New York "to discover if possible what preliminary steps might be taken to initiate conferences to heal the unfortunate breach in the labor movement."[34] At this December meeting, Monsignor Haas wrote later, Harrison "voiced the opinion that the A.F. of L. would recognize industrial unionism in the basic industries such as steel, automobiles, rubber, and others, with the possible exception that building construction should be handled by the building trades." Hillman, for his part, indicated that CIO leaders were willing to reopen formal reunification negotiations without any prior commitment by the AFL respecting the chartering of the CIO unions. The meeting thus closed on an optimistic note and Haas wrote to Hillman: "I hope I need not add that I sincerely trust that conferences will soon be initiated to work out a genuine and effective peace and build up a labor movement worthy of all our people."

When Haas met with Murray and Woll one month later to probe these channels, however, Murray admitted that Lewis now refused to reopen peace talks until the AFL was willing to charter all CIO unions. AFL leaders rejected this condition because Federation unions already claimed jurisdiction over many of these same workers. Monsignor Haas then proposed that the AFL charter the CIO unions en bloc for a year or two while negotiations were continued to work out the details. After further discussion, the conferees agreed on the following: (1) the CIO might be chartered en bloc as a division within the AFL for not more than two years; (2) all union warfare would cease during this period and negotiations would continue in an effort to settle all differences; (3) if these differences were not settled within two years, each party would be free to go its own way; and (4) if the differences were adjusted, the controversy would be considered terminated. The memorandum concluded: "Messers Woll and Murray regard the above as a truce rather than a settlement, but believe under existing circumstances, it is the wisest procedure. Both agreed to urge it on their associates."[35]

Before Monsignor Haas could return to the peace negotia-tions, however, President Roosevelt decided to intervene person-ally. Prospects for a peaceful settlement had improved and the increased harmony evident in the recent negotiations may have convinced him that the time was now right. He conferred separ-ately with Green and Hillman that same January and on February 23 invited Green and Lewis to appoint representatives to meet with him at the White House on March 7. These White House meetings, unfortunately, were no more successful than the talks of the preceding three years, and before long the outbreak of war in Europe and the increased threat to national security diverted public attention from labor's internal squabbles. With the presi-dent's personal intervention in the controversy that March, Mon-signor Haas withdrew from further negotiations. Haas may well have been, as Herbert Harris declared, "the Roosevelt Adminis-tration's chief nuncio in its attempts to close the A.F.L.-C.I.O. gap," but the points of disagreement were too fundamental and the personal animosities too pronounced for even this "ace of federal peace-makers" and close friend of both Green and Lewis to succeed.[36]

Monsignor Haas's success as a labor mediator, his understand-ing of the complexities of industrial problems, and his close acquaintance with leaders of both the AFL and the CIO also made him a leading candidate for appointment to the National Labor Relations Board on several occasions in the late 1930s and early 1940s. In the summer of 1936, when John M. Carmody resigned from the board to accept a position with the Rural Electrification Administration, Secretary Perkins sent the president a list of six possible appointees, with Haas as her first choice.[37] When an opening occurred in 1939, Drew Pearson called Haas the "leading possibility" for appointment, and the *Washington Daily News* added that "Administration leaders feel that the appointment of a man of Msgr. Haas' ability and reputation would tend to restore confidence in the board and reduce chances of a drastic curb of the board's powers." When the term of Chairman Warren Madden expired in August 1940, the *New York Times* noted that Haas and Dr. Harry A. Millis were the leading candidates. They were also first on the list of nominees recommended to the president by Secretary Perkins: "I have also thought of Carter Goodrich as a possibility..., but since you indicated an offhand preference for Father Haas I worked hardest on him." When the term of Edwin Smith expired the following year, Monsignor Haas noted in his diary: "Attorney General Francis Biddle telephoned today asking me to allow him to present my name to the President for appointment to the vacancy."[38] On the following day, James Carey of the CIO visited Haas to urge his acceptance.

Monsignor Haas's view of appointment to the board was revealed in a letter he wrote to Archbishop Stritch, his ecclesiastical superior in Milwaukee, in March 1939, at the time he was mentioned as a possible successor to Donald Wakefield Smith:

> Today I saw the Secretary of Labor and she said that the President does wish me to serve. I told her in unmistakable language that I have no inclination to do so, but she asked me "to think it over."
>
> My own feeling runs something like this. My personal preference is to keep on doing the work at the University—uphill but most important work. At the same time I am satisfied that membership, if only for a year or so, on what is in effect the supreme court of labor relations in the country, cannot but redound to the credit and prestige of Religion. There is, too, the further consideration that the N.L.R.B. is a practical application of *Rerum Novarum* with respect to the right of association prescribing "the State must protect natural rights, not destroy them." Notwithstanding all this, I believe that I should not ask for a year's leave of absence from the University to serve on the Labor Board. This I made very clear to the Secretary of Labor today.
>
> It may be that the matter will die there. But in case it does not and if I am pressed to "reconsider," and especially if this pressing comes from the White House, I may be in a tight corner. If the President insists, I may have practially no choice but to accept.[39]

It is difficult to know with certainty why Father Haas was never offered the appointment. The eventual appointees—Donald Wakefield Smith in 1936, William Leiserson in 1939, Harry Millis in 1940, and Gerald Reilly in 1941—were well-known lawyers or economists and had strong support among President Roosevelt's advisers. In 1936, Father Haas had been rector of St. Francis Seminary for less than nine months and immediate reassignment back to Washington would have been particularly difficult. Also, by the late 1930s, Monsignor Haas's acceptance of the CIO may have antagonized supporters of the AFL. Father Haas, furthermore, had proved himself a very successful and valuable labor mediator, and since members of the NLRB were excluded by law from engaging in mediation, President Roosevelt may have preferred to retain his availability as a "labor trouble-shooter."

Whatever President Roosevelt's reasons, it is certain that Haas himself was most reluctant to serve. This reluctance was personal, since both the apostolic delegate in Washington and his own archbishops in Milwaukee—Stritch in the 1930s and Moses Kiley after 1940—offered no objections. As his letter to Archbishop Stritch in 1939 suggested, he was anxious to continue his work at Catholic University. As first dean of the new School of Social Science, he was eager to remain until the school was firmly established and a proven success. Monsignor Haas also found his work in labor mediation most satisfying and he was hesitant to resign from this work in order to accept an appointment to labor's "supreme court." It is possible, finally, that Monsignor Haas had doubts about the future effectiveness of the board. With the increase of labor violence in 1937 and 1938 and the rising conservative influence in Congress, there was increasing support across the country for amending the Wagner Act and altering the powers of the National Labor Relations Board. Haas might have been reluctant to accept an appointment to a board that might soon be stripped of its powers.[40] Appointment to the NLRB might have been an additional mark of confidence and public recognition, but when President Roosevelt, for whatever reasons, decided to appoint others, Monsignor Haas was not disappointed.

The year 1939 was particularly active for Monsignor Haas in government service. He resigned from the WPA's Division of Employment in January and from the Wisconsin Labor Relations Board two months later, but new assignments followed immediately. In August, he was requested by the Department of Commerce to investigate labor conditions in the Inland Waterways Corporation, an enterprise set up a few years previously to operate barges for the federal government on large inland lakes and rivers. For three weeks he visited the corporation's terminals in Minneapolis, St. Louis, Memphis, New Orleans, Vicksburg, and Birmingham, studying labor conditions and interviewing employees, and on his return, in early September, he submitted a sixty-one page report of his findings to Commerce Secretary Harry Hopkins. He criticized the corporation's wage-and-hour standards and interference by several foremen with the workers' right to organize. As a result of his report, Secretary Hopkins ordered important personnel changes in the corporation that fall.[41]

In November, Monsignor Haas was appointed by President Roosevelt as an "expert adviser" to the United States Labor delegation at the American States Conference of the International Labor Organization in Havana. Since he was only an adviser to labor delegates George Harrison and James Carey, he took little part in the formal deliberations and did not vote. The conference adopted several important resolutions, however, and Monsignor Haas strongly supported its recommendations for more widespread minimum wage legislation, establishment of tripartite labor-industry-public boards in each country to advise governments on economic problems, and promotion of world peace through economic cooperation. At a time when many American Catholics viewed the ILO as an unnecessary foreign entanglement and a world platform for Communist revolutionaries, Monsignor Haas's participation was significant.[42]

Much more influential, however, was Monsignor Haas's appointment, earlier that fall, to the National Resources Planning Board's Committee on Long Range Work and Relief Policies. The National Resources Planning Board, successor to the National Resources Committee of 1935, was established July 1, 1939, "to collect, prepare, and make available to the President such plans, data, and information as may be helpful to a planned development and use of national resources, and related subjects referred to it by the President," chiefly in the fields of agriculture, employment, industrialization, urbanization, and foreign and domestic trade. Later that fall, the board established a Committee on Long Range Work and Relief Policies to draft a comprehensive report on the present effectiveness and future needs of federal programs of public aid. William Haber, of the University of Michigan, was named chairman and Monsignor Haas a member of the nine-man committee.[43]

The committee held eighteen meetings from November 1939 to October 1941, with Monsignor Haas attending all but five. Haas was chiefly concerned with the committee's discussion of wages, hours, and working conditions on federal relief projects, but he voiced alarm over the danger of excessive encroachment by the federal government into social and economic affairs. He insisted, for example, that a ceiling on hours be recommended, just as strongly as a floor on wages; that wages on federal relief projects be sufficiently high to raise wage levels in related private industries; and that government and industry accept joint responsibility for guaranteeing an adequate family wage for every worker.[44]

But he opposed inclusion in the final report of a discussion of the importance of public works programs in preparing young people for future private employment and, by inculcating a sense of industry and public service, for more responsible citizenship. The first of these goals, he asserted, could be performed far better by industry and unions and the second by homes, schools, and churches. In neither of them, he insisted, did the federal government have any primary responsibility.

After two years of research and discussion, the final report was submitted to the president by the National Resources Planning Board in early December 1941, and was published the following spring under the title *Security, Work, and Relief Policies*.[45] After surveying past and present public relief projects, the report recommended that work relief be continued and expanded, but only to complement private employment; that the government give particular encouragement to programs of unemployment compensation, old age pensions, disability benefits, and other forms of social insurance to which industry and the workers contributed; that the government increase its aid to public service programs such as employment agencies, school lunches, and public health centers; and that it give special attention to persons unable to take advantage of public works, chiefly the aged, the blind, and minors. The report also recommended several fundamental administrative changes in order to make government welfare agencies more efficient and effective.

This strong plea for increased social legislation met with Monsignor Haas's full approval. He had been an outspoken champion of unemployment compensation, social insurance, public works, and old age pensions since the 1920s and he termed the committee's study "excellent," "comprehensive and scholarly," and "a splendid piece of work." "Needless to say," he wrote Chairman Haber in January 1941, "I am in complete agreement with its whole philosophy."[46] Although the report received little publicity at the time—it was submitted to the president on the weekend of Pearl Harbor and was published during the economic upswing of early 1942—it was not without influence. Many of its recommendations for expanded welfare facilities and increased social security benefits were adopted in the postwar years and the 1950s. "In the course of time," one member of the National Resources Planning Board has stated, "the general principles of the security reports were accepted without much regard for political parties."[47]

In 1939 Monsignor Haas also received the first of several appointments to chair industry committees established to recommend higher minimum wages after passage of the Fair Labor Standards Act of 1938. This act stipulated that workers in interstate commerce were to receive a minimum wage of twenty-five cents an hour, effective October 1, 1938, and that this minimum was to be increased gradually, until a mandatory forty cents an hour was reached on October 1, 1945. The act also authorized the wage-and-hour administrator to appoint committees, representing labor, industry, and government, to study conditions in each industry and to recommend higher minimum wages, up to forty cents, even before 1945, if conditions warranted. From 1939 to 1942, Monsignor Haas was appointed chairman of several such committees: leather, boot and shoe, canned goods, and three Puerto Rican industries committees. These committees operated in similar ways, and Haas's work for the Boot and Shoe Committee was typical.[48]

On March 17, 1939, Wage and Hour Administrator Elmer F. Andrews announced the appointment of the twenty-seven-man committee for the boot and shoe industry, under the chairmanship of Monsignor Haas, one of the nine public representatives. The committee met in executive session in early April, held three days of public hearings one month later, and met again in executive session in August to discuss its findings and to prepare its recommendations for the administrator. At that time the minimum wage of twenty-five cents was in effect for the 215,000 shoe workers across the country, and Monsignor Haas's committee unanimously recommended that this be raised immediately to thirty-five cents.[49] The wage and hour administrator then conducted a second hearing on this recommendation and on March 23, 1940, ordered adoption of this thirty-five-cent minimum. Eighteen months later, the committee reconvened, again with Monsignor Haas as chairman, and recommended that since conditions in the industry had improved, the minimum wage should be raised to forty cents an hour, the maximum permitted under the Fair Labor Standards Act. This recommendation the administrator likewise accepted, and the minimum wage of forty cents went into effect in the shoe industry four years before the mandatory date of October 1, 1945.

Monsignor Haas's work as chairman of this and other committees met with almost universal commendation. Wage and Hour Administrator Philip B. Fleming sent word of his appreciation, and labor officials across the country were pleased with the committee's recommendations.[50] Even the industrial members seemed satisfied. George Noland, president of General Shoe Corporation, declared at the public hearing on May 27: "I believe I express the sentiments of the committee that we have the finest chairman of any industry committee, and the speed with which we have worked and everything has been due to his patience, and I don't think any witness who has appeared here can go away and say that he hasn't had a very fair hearing and been very complimentary of the way our chairman has conducted the hearing. I think that belongs in the record." Mr. H. O. Rondeau, a shoe executive from New England, agreed. "I think your handling of the difficult committee, of which I was a member," he wrote in May 1940, "was masterful, so I take this means of showing my appreciation." "Masterful" was the right word. Monsignor Haas had brought together a committee of several conflicting opinions, presided at harmonious public hearings on the always explosive issue of wage increases, almost invariably succeeded in presenting a unanimous recommendation to the wage-and-hour administrator and, in doing so, won the praise of both labor and industry representatives.

Monsignor Haas's most important government work during these years, however, and the work which earned him national fame as "labor's trouble-shooter," was in the field of mediation. According to *Time*, he was "surpassed only by Edward McGrady as a mediator of strikes." Newspapers called him "the ace of federal peace-makers" and "one of the Government's most able trouble-shooters." In 1937, Secretary Perkins reportedly named him "one of the ten outstanding mediators in the country." Drew Pearson wrote that when WPA Administrator Harry Hopkins had a difficult strike on his hands, he called in Father Haas, "a stalwart, blue-eyed, black-garbed Catholic clergyman who is a doctor of philosophy and president of a Catholic Seminary,...an old hand at arbitration." Monsignor Haas himself once remarked: "I've been at it so long that I can sense the trouble in a labor dispute just like an old family doctor who comes into the sick room, sniffs the air, and says 'measles.' "[51]

From 1935 to 1943 Monsignor Haas was undoubtedly one of the Department of Labor's most active and successful mediators.[52] Besides his conciliation work for the WPA's Labor Policies Board and the Wisconsin Labor Relations Board, he mediated disputes for the National Labor Relations Board, the U.S. Conciliation

Service, the National Defense Mediation Board, and the National War Labor Board. In February 1943, he was appointed to an Emergency Railway Labor Panel under the National Mediation Board. Many of the controversies he entered were of national importance—Tampa Cigar in 1935, Minneapolis Electric in 1937, Chicago and North Shore in 1938, Marathon Rubber and General Tire in 1940, and Marshall Field and Montgomery Ward in 1942—but the majority probably went unnoticed beyond their local communities.[53] Of the disputes that attained national prominence during these years, the two most important were probably strikes in the silk industry in 1937 and at Allis-Chalmers in 1941.

The textile strike in New York, New Jersey, and eastern Pennsylvania in August 1937 was one of the most significant and most unusual strikes of that turbulent year. The walkout was unusual because a large number of employers actually welcomed it and cooperated with it. The silk industry in the 1930s was composed of hundreds of small manufacturing firms and was unscrupulously competitive: the average plant numbered only sixty-nine workers, work was often sublet to outside jobsters in cut-throat competition, and a sixty-hour week often earned as little as six or eight dollars. Many employers welcomed the strike as a means of achieving a uniform contract for the industry, eliminating chislers, and restoring respectable competition. For all this, however, the strike was no less bitter. Repeated attempts to unionize the industry had failed in the past, and the hundreds of manufacturers who profited from low wages and long hours were determined that they would fail again. But Sidney Hillman, leader of the CIO's Textile Workers Organizing Committee, was equally determined. Asked how long he would carry on the fight, he replied: "Just one day longer than the last employer will fight us."[54]

Hillmen met with silk executives throughout July and early August but could win contracts for only one-fourth of the industry's more than 50,000 workers. On August 9, consequently, he ordered his men off their jobs. Within a week, sixty manufacturers of the Silk and Rayon Manufacturers' Association agreed to Hillman's terms, but several larger manufacturers still held out. On August 13, after state and federal mediators had failed to win an agreement, Secretary Perkins telephoned Father Haas in Milwaukee. "We have a difficult situation in silk here in the East," the secretary declared. Trying on his Monsignor's robes for the first time, in preparation for his investiture ceremony later that month, Haas reportedly answered: "We have a difficult situation in silk here in Milwaukee, too, but I will come."[55]

Haas left St. Francis Seminary that night and spent the next five days in New York, Paterson, and Philadelphia, conferring with labor, management, and government officials. Although his first proposals were rejected by company executives, an agreement was finally signed on August 20. Minimum wages of $14 for hand workers and $18 for machine operators were established throughout the industry, a forty hour week was agreed upon, employee elections were arranged, and grievance machinery was provided to settle future disputes.[56] The agreement was significant not only for returning 40,000 striking textile workers to their jobs but also for assuring the success of Hillman's organizing campaign and for eliminating some of the industry's more serious labor abuses. On August 21, after notifying Secretary Perkins of the settlement, Haas returned to Milwaukee and hurried preparations for his investiture ceremony three days later.

The strike at Milwaukee's Allis-Chalmers plant in 1941 was one of the longest and most serious of the year—"the granddaddy of all defense strikes," *Business Week* called it. The company held government defense contracts estimated at $45 million, chiefly in turbines, generators, and other electrical equipment, and business leaders insisted that the ten-week strike hampered work in thirty defense plants across the country and wholly or partially blocked production on one-third of all government defense contracts. DuPont munitions factories, Bendix Aviation, the power plants at Boulder Dam, and twenty-five destroyers, earmarked for Great Britain, awaited equipment from Allis-Chalmers. In March, administration officials discussed the need for a government takeover.[57]

The dispute was further complicated by bitter controversy over the leftist leadership of the local UAW union. Harold Christoffel, the youthful president of Local 248, had been threatened with expulsion from the Socialist Party in 1938 because of his Communist leanings. "Local 248," a Communist official later testified, "has long been the pride of the Communist Party."[58] "Not wages or hours or working conditions were back of the Allis-Chalmers stoppage," Stanley High insisted. "It was a Communist-concocted scheme—prepared through five years—to give the country a preview of the revolution." Even the *Milwaukee Catholic Herald-Citizen*, a strong champion of organized labor, criticized the union leadership relentlessly. As a member of the Wisconsin Labor Relations Board, Haas had settled a similar dispute at Allis-Chalmers in 1938 and had averted what Governor La Follette affirmed would have been "the largest strike in the history of Wisconsin." Unfortunately, the strike broke out in all its fury three years later.

Events of the weeks and months before the strike call of January 22, 1941, indicated the seriousness of the situation. Management and union representatives had been unable to reach an agreement on the closed shop and as a result, the plant had operated without a written contract since May 1940. Throughout that year, the plant had suffered seventeen work stoppages, chiefly as a result of CIO opposition to the employment of a small number of AFL workers. In late December, violence had erupted between rival AFL and CIO workers, and company vice president Harold Story immediately telephoned Monsignor Haas in Washington for assistance. Haas conferred with CIO director John Brophy and Conciliation Chief John Steelman, and then hurried to Milwaukee before the end of the month. The union by that time had presented formal demands for a written contract, a substantial wage increase, dismissal of the two AFL workers involved in the December 22 violence, and a closed shop agreement. Monsignor Haas remained in Milwaukee until January 4, and returned for several days one week later, but on each occasion his mediation efforts were unsuccessful. The situation grew more threatening each day. The UAW local requested the assistance of leftist CIO General Counsel Lee Pressman—"a very serious turn of affairs," in Monsignor Haas's opinion—and company president Max Babb, a member of the conservative America First Committee, hired Leo Mann as company attorney, a nationally known opponent of organized labor. The battle lines were thus drawn when, despite contrary assurances from high UAW officials, Christoffel unexpectedly called a strike for January 22.[59]

Monsignor Haas was taken by surprise and returned to Milwaukee at once.[60] He spent the first several days, at the request of John Steelman and other government officials, attempting to win union approval for the removal of needed defense materials, but union officials refused. On January 25, Haas, Regional Conciliator James Holmes, and Thomas F. Burns of the Office of Production Management drafted an arbitration proposal, but company executives rejected it immediately. Negotiations continued, but by the end of the month the only success Haas and his fellow mediators had achieved was that the parties had finally agreed to come together for joint discussions. Union officials, however, continued to insist upon a union shop and company executives rejected even a "maintenance of membership" clause. At Haas's suggestion, UAW President R. J. Thomas arrived from Detroit on January 31, but his presence had little effect on the negotiations. On February 3, after more than a week of daily reports of "nothing accomplished," Monsignor Haas returned to Washington to confer with Department of Labor and OPM officials.

Monsignor Haas spent the next week in top-level conferences with John Steelman of the Conciliation Service, Edward McGrady of the War Department, and William Knudsen and Sidney Hillman of OPM. On February 11, company and union executives were summoned from Milwaukee for further conferences in Washington. These negotiations continued four days, with Haas and Hillman meeting with union officials and Knudsen and Steelman with company spokesmen. At the end of discussions on February 15, the Office of Production Management announced that an agreement had been reached. By the terms of the settlement, the strike was to be called off at once, all strikers were to be reinstated, negotiations for a wage increase and a written contract were to begin within two days, and—in a deliberately vague clause—the company agreed to "maintain employee discipline." In case of disagreement over the interpretation of "employee discipline," the matter was to be decided by a referee selected by OPM. The company accepted this proposal only after Hillman released a statement to the effect that the "maintenance of employee discipline" clause was "not to be considered or used as a device to promote a closed or all-union shop or to make a man's job dependent upon union membership." When contract negotiations began in Milwaukee on February 17, however, union officials asserted that "maintenance of employee discipline" meant "maintenance of union membership"—an interpretation which Monsignor Haas privately declared unfounded—and when this position was rejected by the company, union leaders repudiated the whole agreement of February 15.[61]

Negotiations resumed again in Washington with R. J. Thomas and other UAW officials on February 28. Since the major controversy by that time concerned Hillman's statement of February 15, Haas and other government mediators urged him to issue a retraction.[62] Hillman agreed and then suggested a new course of action. A mass meeting of workers was to be called in Milwaukee on March 3, Monsignor Haas was to read Hillman's retraction, and then Thomas and UAW vice president Richard Frankensteen were to urge the workers to accept the February 15 agreement without any assurances on union security. After Haas read Hillman's statement, Thomas was loudly jeered for recommending acceptance of the agreement, but the workers eventually voted to return to work. That same evening, however, the mood of optimism was shattered when company officials notified the mediators that the agreement of February 15, which the union had just approved, was no longer acceptable to them. There were charges that the union strike vote of January 19 and 21 had been fraudulent, and the company hoped that, if the charges were correct, it might win without any concessions of its own.[63]

Voting irregularities, in fact, were discovered, and on March 26, a few hours after Sidney Hillman left Washington for a much-needed rest in Florida, William Knudsen of OPM and Frank Knox, secretary of the navy, sent company officials a formal request to reopen the Milwaukee plant.[64] Knudsen notified Philip Murray that "the final decision to ask the plant to open came after the fact was established that the original strike vote was obtained by fraudulent means. To continue the strike in view of this and subject critical defense material to further indefinite delay would seem entirely unreasonable." Reaction to this directive was generally unfavorable. "This isn't an order," one New Deal official declared; "it's a coup d'etat." Labor leaders across the country were outspokenly critical; Milwaukee workers on March 29 voted to disregard it; and when company executives opened the plant despite union protests, violence erupted. On April 1, forty-eight persons were injured in clashes at the factory gates, Governor Heil's car was stoned when he arrived to plead for harmony, and that night he notified President Roosevelt that the situation "is absolutely out of control of all the peace officers available." The plant was closed that same day.

On April 6, however, the strike suddenly ended. The National Defense Mediation Board assumed jurisdiction over the dispute on April 5 and all that afternoon and evening company and union officials met with William H. Davis, vice chairman of the board, Monsignor Haas, and other government mediators. On the following day, Chairman Clarence Dykstra announced a settlement. By the terms of this agreement, the strike was to be called off, negotiations on a new contract and wage increase were to begin as soon as work resumed, maintenance of union membership was to be recommended to all workers, the company was to maintain "employee discipline," and disputes over "discipline" were to be submitted to an impartial referee. Except for the additional recommendation that union membership be maintained, the agreement was similar to the one Hillman and Haas had proposed on February 15. On April 7, a grateful Monsignor Haas was able to write to a friend in Milwaukee: "Last night we finally succeeded in getting an agreement between the management and the union in the Allis-Chalmers strike, and the plant will reopen tomorrow. All I can say is that this was a long, tedious process, the conference on Sunday running continuously for sixteen hours."[65] Of all the disputes which Monsignor Haas mediated as "labor's trouble-shooter," this was unquestionably one of the most difficult.

After two years in Milwaukee as seminary rector and member of the Robert Committee and the Labor Policies Board of the WPA, Monsignor Haas found the years 1937-1943 in Washington much more satisfying. His elevation to the rank of domestic prelate, his selection as first dean of the School of Social Science at Catholic University, his appointment as chairman of the university's Commission on American Citizenship, and his contribution to the NCWC's declaration, *The Church and Social Order*, attested to the high esteem in which he was held by leaders of the Church, both in America and in Rome. His selection as chairman of several industry committees under the Fair Labor Standards Act, his appointment to the National Resources Planning Board's Committee on Long Range Work and Relief Policies, his work as mediator in the AFL-CIO split, and especially his services as labor conciliator and "strike doctor" for several government agencies indicated the prestige he had attained in public service. When President Roosevelt in the spring of 1943 needed a highly respected champion of social justice to head the reconstituted Fair Employment Practices Committee, he called on Monsignor Haas. When Pope Pius XII a few months later sought an outstanding American churchman for the vacant See of Grand Rapids, he likewise selected Monsignor Haas. By 1943, Monsignor Haas's life as both priest and public servant was approaching its zenith.

10

Chairman of the FEPC, 1943

When President Roosevelt appointed Monsignor Haas chairman of the Fair Employment Practices Committee in May 1943, he chose a public servant long concerned with religious bigotry and racial discrimination. In 1930, commenting on the words of Thomas Jefferson, "We hold these truths to be self-evident, that all men are created equal," Father Haas had written:

In other words, although individuals differ as to sex, age, color, and physical and mental ability, they all possess an identical human nature, and the dignity and inviolability inherent in it. Thus an individual Indian living on one of the government reservations is in the most accurate sense of the term a human being, possessing the same innate worth and inviolability as the most cultured man or woman in the university district of New York or Chicago. The same holds true of the most illiterate Negro on a Southern plantation, of any one of the teeming millions in the Canton district of China, or of the numerous barbarian tribes of Bushmen in South Africa. Young and old, men and women, sick and healthy, the normal and the handicapped, all possess the same essential human dignity.[1]

Monsignor Haas admitted, however, that this "same essential human dignity" was not everywhere recognized, even in the United States:

Charity obliges the people of one race to treat those of other races, at least, as human beings possessing human dignity with all its prerogatives. Unfortunately, this minimum of charity is not generally observed by the white population in the United States toward the non-Caucasoid races, especially Negroes and Indians. The attitude of the American white population toward the Negroes and Indians too often has been characterized by a lack of common fellow-feeling and charity. Until this attitude is changed, the race problem in the United States will remain unsolved. The solution can be permanent and adequate to all concerned only when it proceeds on the principle that the Negro and the Indian, like their white fellow citizens, are human beings possessed of an immortal destiny, and fully entitled to be dealt with on a basis of justice and charity.[2]

"So far as Catholic principles are concerned," Haas had stated in 1933, "there can be no discrimination just because of the color of a man's skin. [All] human beings are in possession of a human soul."[3]

But economic recovery, not racial equality, was the major concern of the 1930s and Haas's efforts in the area of minority rights were limited. As a member of the NRA's Labor Advisory Board, he had recommended the appointment of more minority representatives to the Labor Advisory Board staff and to other NRA departments. In public hearings on both the Salt and the Boot and Shoe codes, he had objected to wage differentials for southern workers, a large proportion of whom were Black. During his three years on the WPA's Labor Policies Board, he had heard numerous complaints of discrimination against Black relief workers by WPA officials, and his extensive tour of five southern states in the fall of 1936 gave him firsthand knowledge of working conditions in the construction industry, in the cotton fields, and on various WPA projects, all employing large numbers of minority workers.[4] As a special commissioner of conciliation for the Department of Labor and as a mediator for other government agencies in the 1940s, he had intervened in numerous controversies which were seriously aggravated by racial prejudice and religious bigotry.

Monsignor Haas's closest familiarity with the economic plight of Black Americans probably resulted from his work as a member of the National Resources Planning Board's Committee on Long Range Work and Relief Policies in 1939. Black Americans, the committee report noted, earned less than other Americans; they were the first discharged when unemployment struck; few had sufficient savings to protect them against the ravages of depression, and as a result they appeared on federal relief roles with much greater frequency than their fellow workers. The report continued:

> The need for public aid is especially likely to be felt by Negroes, Mexicans, and other minority groups character-ized by relatively limited economic opportunity. Repre-senting principally unskilled labor, these groups have also faced racial discrimination as reflected in lower wage rates and lay-offs. They are also in general the marginal groups when employment improves.... A higher incidence of ill health, higher death rates, and greater instability of family life due to this relatively less favorable economic position, coupled with an increasing degree of urbanization, have accounted for a higher rate of dependency.
>
> It is therefore obvious that a higher percentage of Ne-groes than whites are apt to experience need for public aid.... In October, 1933, Negroes formed about eighteen percent of the relief population, as against ten percent of the total population in 1930.
>
> In interpreting these data, it is important to note that the Negro population is concentrated in the Southeast and Southwest regions, where access to minimum security is known to be highly restricted.... It is thus evident that the majority of Negroes are at a marked disadvantage in access to public aid.[5]

Racial discrimination, however, was not the only form of prejudice which concerned Monsignor Haas. He was equally familiar with religious bigotry, especially anti-Catholic sentiment in the 1920s and anti-Semitism a decade later. As an Irish Catholic, he had listened to firsthand accounts of the influence of the American Protective Association in the Midwest near the turn of the century, had witnessed an outbreak of anti-Catholic feeling in Wisconsin elections from 1914 to 1920, and had noted with anxiety the resurgence of the Ku Klux Klan in the 1920s. Through-out the 1920s and 1930s, he had lamented the attacks of anti-Semitism his close friends Sidney Hillman, David Dubinsky, and Jacob Potofsky were forced to suffer, even from his fellow Catholics. His work as a "trouble-shooter" for the WPA and the Department of Labor had brought him into direct contact with anti-Semitism in the Bernard Greenberg arbitration case and the Harnischfeger strike in 1938.[6] He added his name to public pro-tests of Nazi persecution of the Jews and pleaded for religious tolerance and understanding before numerous interfaith gatherings. "The man or woman," he declared in 1932, "whether Catholic, Protestant, or Jew, who raises the voice of bigotry, is a traitor to his country and a criminal before his God." If the new chairman of the FEPC needed deep understanding of industrial relations, the temperament of a successful mediator, and strong aversion to racial and religious discrimination, Monsignor Haas seemed well qualified.

President Roosevelt had established the Fair Employment Practices Committee in 1941, after much wavering and hesitation. Although the New Deal had brought higher wages, steadier employment, and a minimum of relief work to thousands of minority workers in the 1930s, the social and economic status of many Black Americans at the end of the decade was still dismal. Sectional differentials in the codes of fair competition had deprived southern Blacks of the full benefit of NRA wage increases; the Agricultural Adjustment Act had driven minority tenant farmers off their land; subsistence homesteads had been established for whites only; and many major industries and labor unions still conspired to deny Black workers employment opportunities. When Mrs. Roosevelt asked the president why he had not supported anti-lynching and anti-poll tax legislation more strongly, he had replied: "First things come first, and I can't alienate certain votes I need for measures that are more important at the moment by pushing any measure that would entail a fight." During these same years, however, scores of civic and religious organizations—among them the CIO, the National Negro Congress, the American Civil Liberties Union, and the Council against Intolerance in America—continued to protest against racial discrimination in government employment and in defense industries, and as these protests became more insistent, the Roosevelt administration decided to act—but cautiously.[7]

In July 1940, the National Defense Advisory Commission appointed Robert C. Weaver administrative assistant in its Labor Division, to facilitate the employment of Black Americans in defense industries, and one month later it announced its official policy of nondiscrimination in all defense production. In a letter to Congress on September 13, President Roosevelt confirmed the commission's recommendation that defense workers "should not be discriminated against because of age, sex, race, or color."[8] All this had little effect, however. In late January the *Chicago Defender* asserted that "all efforts toward elimination of racial bias in the industries that are receiving defense contracts have so far met with a stone wall." In some defense industries, Black employment actually declined from October 1940 to April 1941. Even a strongly worded directive of Sidney Hillman, co-director of the Office of Production Management, was largely ignored. "Mr. Hillman has spoken boldly," one Black newspaper complained, "but unless he follows through with something more punitive than a mere plea, his words are going to fall on deaf ears." "The masses of Negroes are getting fed up on these frauds," warned Black journalist George S. Schuyler. When President Roosevelt still declined to issue an executive order eliminating racial discrimination from government employment and defense industries, Black leaders in the spring of 1941 decided to take a more drastic step.

In the early weeks of 1941, A. Philip Randolph, president of the Brotherhood of Sleeping Car Porters, suggested that Black Americans stage a "March on Washington," a petition-in-boots reminiscent of "Coxey's Army" half a century earlier, "to exact their rights in National Defense employment and the armed forces of the country." President Roosevelt and his advisers immediately attempted to discourage the demonstration, insisting that the march would be "notice to foreign critics of our domestic disunity at a time when a semblance of unity was most essential to national prestige." Former NRA administrator Hugh Johnson and Secretary of the Navy Frank Knox both sent appeals to Randolph. Even Mrs. Roosevelt, a firm champion of civil rights, opposed the march. "I feel very strongly," she wrote Randolph in June, "that your group is making a very grave mistake at the present time to allow this march to take place. I am afraid it will set back the progress which is being made, in the Army at least, towards better opportunities and less segregation." Randolph and his March-on-Washington committee stood firm, however. "The Administration leaders in Washington will never give the Negro justice," they insisted, "until they see masses—ten, twenty, fifty thousand Negroes on the White House lawn." The march, Randolph added, "represents a technique and method of action that is the hope and salvation of the Negro people," and he promised to make it "the greatest demonstration of Negro mass power for our economic liberation ever conceived."[9]

The march had been scheduled for July 1, but in mid-June Roosevelt capitulated. He met with Randolph, Walter White, and other Black leaders at the White House on June 18, other conferences followed with William Knudsen, Hillman, and Civil Defense Chairman Fiorello LaGuardia, and an agreement was finally reached on June 24. On the following day, the president issued Executive Order 8802, demanding equal employment opportunities "without discrimination because of race, creed, color, or national origin" in all government departments and in defense industries. Government defense contracts were to contain a provision "obligating the contractor not to discriminate against any worker," and a Fair Employment Practices Committee would be established to "receive complaints" and "redress valid grievances." In the opinion of one authority, it was "that most important effort in the history of this country to eliminate discrimination in employment by use of governmental authority."[10] Randolph immediately cancelled his "March-on-Washington."

On July 18, President Roosevelt announced the appointment of this first Fair Employment Practices Committee. Mark Ethridge, publisher of the *Louisville Courier-Journal*, was named chairman, assisted by David Sarnoff, president of Radio Corporation of America; Milton Webster, vice president of the Brotherhood of Sleeping Car Porters; Earl Dickerson, city councilman from Chicago; and William Green of the AFL and Philip Murray of the CIO.[11] Despite its meager budget of $80,000, the committee set to work immediately. In well-publicized hearings in Los Angeles, Chicago, New York, and Birmingham, the committee uncovered shocking instances of employment discrimination. Boeing Aircraft of Seattle employed no Blacks among its 41,000 workers, Douglas employed 10, Lockheed-Vega 54. Three of Milwaukee's largest industries—A. O. Smith, the Heil Company, and Allis-Chalmers—averaged one Black worker each, and several large New York firms refused to hire either Black or Jewish Americans. The president of North American Aviation stated boldly that "regardless of their training as aircraft workers, we will not employ Negroes in the North American plant. It is against company policy." Officials at Standard Steel Corporation in Kansas City declared: "We have never had a Negro worker in twenty-five years and do not intend to start now." Several AFL unions and railroad brotherhoods likewise refused to accept Black members. One committee member remarked disgustedly after the Los Angeles hearings: "Here company after company admitted that it did not employ Negroes, or persons of Oriental background, regardless of their fitness for the job. Here, in the midst of around-the-clock appeals for national unity and for an all-out effort to build our instruments of defense, we found unfair employment practices only slightly removed from the Hitler pattern."[12]

Despite serious administrative and financial difficulties, the committee achieved considerable success during its first twelve months. The number of Black workers employed by the Heil Company of Milwaukee rose from 1 to 1,440, and in the aviation industry from fewer than 300 to 3,500. Black employment in the nation's shipyards increased over 300 percent. A survey of select government departments in early 1942 showed that the percentage of Black workers had risen from 6 to 17 percent since 1938 and the proportion of those engaged in custodial work had declined from 90 to 50 percent during the same period. Reflecting on the committee's small appropriation, one authority stated that the "FEPC traveled further on less than any other agency in New Deal history."[13] This was probably true. At the close of the Birmingham hearings in June 1942, the chairman received a letter of commendation from the White House, a budget of $1 million was under discussion, and preparations were progressing for establishment of twelve regional offices across the country.

The first FEPC had reached the peak of its power and influence that summer, however, and its decline soon after was rapid. Conservative southern congressmen had become alarmed at the Birmingham hearings, influential AFL leaders were determined to maintain their lily-white unions, and powerful industrialists, North and South, insisted that unrest and violence would accompany integration of their plants. On July 30 the president yielded to their demands and announced the transfer of the FEPC from the War Production Board to the War Manpower Commission, where Congress could exert more direct control over its budget.[14] President Roosevelt insisted that it was his purpose "to strengthen, not to submerge, the Committee, and to reinvigorate, not to repeal, Executive Order 8802," but the fact that he failed to discuss the transfer with committee members beforehand raised serious doubts about his true intentions.

Although the committee continued to hold hearings and issue directives during the succeeding months, they were the final gasps of a dying body. For three months the FEPC and the War Manpower Commission struggled to reach agreement on the scope of the committee's work, and the committee's budget was not approved for several weeks more. Appointments to the FEPC staff seldom received the commission's confirmation. Hearings in El Paso into charges of discrimination against Spanish-speaking Americans were cancelled because the State Department feared that such revelations might tarnish the country's image in Mexico and South America. On January 11, 1943, finally, Chairman Paul McNutt of the War Manpower Commission personally delivered the death blow, announcing that the much-publicized railroad hearings, scheduled for later that month, were "indefinitely postponed." Although the president at that time was attending the Casablanca Conference with Winston Churchill, the directive almost certainly had White House approval. McNutt gave no explanation. "I felt it [the hearing] unwise," he stated, "and therefore decided they should not be held at this time. I do not care to go further." The members of the FEPC had not been consulted, four were critical of the postponement, and Mark Ethridge, David Sarnoff, and Chairman Malcolm MacLean submitted their resignations soon after. Committee member Earl Dickerson assumed the acting chairmanship and attempted to carry on some of the committee's work—often contrary to the wishes of the War Manpower Commission—but the committee's influence was minimal.[15] By the late spring of 1943, the first FEPC was dead.

McNutt's directive of January 11 proved a serious political blunder and President Roosevelt recognized it immediately. "To put it bluntly," wrote James Wechsler in *The Nation*, "the hopes of Negroes have been raised and their disillusionment now will be far more disastrous than if the President had never shown a willingness to wage this battle." *Commonweal*, a Catholic weekly, editorialized: "So now we find that Southern pressure has made the Administration go back on what is one of the fundamental policies capable of justifying anyone's hope that we are fighting for the Four Freedoms at home as well as abroad." National unity, in fact, was even more necessary in 1943 than in 1941 and thousands of Americans, formerly indifferent, were increasingly embarrassed that Black servicemen, who were dying with their fellow citizens in Tunisia and New Guinea, could not work with them in Birmingham and Seattle. On his return from Casablanca, the president requested McNutt to call a top-level conference of Black, Jewish, and other minority leaders in mid-February, and these leaders unanimously recommended that the FEPC be reconstituted independently of the War Manpower Commission.[16] Similar requests poured into Washington from all sections of the country. By the end of March the president had decided to re-establish the committee, but his first and perhaps most difficult task was to find a public servant willing to accept the chairmanship.

"It is no exaggeration to say," the *New Republic* wrote that spring, "that the post has been offered to literally scores of men. Every last one has refused. The joke around the Manpower Commission last week was that the chairmanship should be smuggled into Horace Heidt's 'Treasure Chest' and palmed off on some unsuspecting winner in that telephone-radio lottery." Will Alexander told Samuel Rosenman and Marvin McIntyre: "I'm as loyal to the President as either of you, and neither one of you would do this if he told you because you know you couldn't. I can't do it. You tell him if he wants me to go over and let the Germans and Japs shoot at me, I'll do that. But I won't try that FEPC thing. I can't make it work." Washington buzzed with rumors that the post had been declined by former Governors Charles Poletti of New York and James Price of Virginia, industrialist Paul G. Hoffman, Senator George Norris, Howard W. Odum, and several others.[17] On April 23, finally, Attorney General Francis Biddle wrote the president:

> There has been no appointment of the Fair Employment Practices Committee and the matter has now been dragging for three months since you made the announcement that it would be promptly reorganized. As you know, Paul McNutt has tried to get Frank Graham, Oscar Chapman, and several others without success.
>
> I have suggested to Paul that he recommend Monsignor Francis Joseph Haas, who in my opinion would do the job better than anybody now available. He had great success on the old N.L.R.B., is an outstanding Roman Catholic, a strong liberal, entirely loyal to you, and a great admirer of the New Deal. . . . I talked to him recently and believe that he would accept the appointment if he could get an adequate appropriation and a free hand under the Executive Order. I am afraid that we might lose him, however, if the appointment is delayed.

On May 19, three weeks after this memorandum was sent, the White House announced the appointment of Monsignor Haas. "I have not sought this position," Haas declared. "I was much opposed to taking it. But we are in a war and I have accepted." To his friend Archbishop Lucey he wrote: "You probably have seen by the press that I have accepted chairmanship of the Fair Employment Practice Committee. Of course, no one in his sound mind would accept such a job, but nevertheless I did." Haas had solid reason, however, to believe that the new committee could succeed. He confided to Archbishop Stritch a few days later that he had accepted the position "only on the personal request of the President and his oral assurance that he would back up the Committee in whatever it would do within the Executive Order."[18]

Press reaction to the appointment was favorable. "The President's selection of Father Haas to head the new FEPC augurs well for its success," commented the *Washington Post.* "Father Haas has an excellent record as a liberal," the *New Republic* added, "and is to be congratulated on his courage in accepting a post which previous candidates had rejected as though it were a hot potato." The Jesuit weekly, *America,* stated that "Monsignor Haas' record of firmness and competence in adjudicating matters of social justice, and his familiarity with this particular situation, are a guarantee that the FEPC will now do the work it was originally created for." The *Christian Century* lamented the political maneuvering that had rendered the earlier committee ineffective, and added: "Father Haas therefore takes up an almost lost cause. But this Catholic priest, with his intimate knowledge of the labor world, is also no tyro in politics. It is certain that he would never undertake a task he believed hopeless; neither would he shoulder such responsibility without a clear understanding as to his freedom of action and the extent of his White House support. The fact that Father Haas now takes over direction of the FEPC is to be regarded, therefore, as notice that that much abused but sadly needed body is to be given a real chance to render the national service for which it was designated." Associate Justice Felix Frankfurter of the Supreme Court added his congratulations. "I am very happy that you were free to accept the appointment as chairman of the President's Committee on Fair Employment Practice," he wrote Monsignor Haas in late May. "Intrinsically I know of no one better fitted for the guidance of this Committee. But, in addition, as a symbol you represent things that these days should be emphasized and not subordinated."[19]

Immediately after accepting the chairmanship, Monsignor Haas was called upon to assist the president and the attorney general in drafting the new executive order and in selecting the other committee members. He met with the attorney general and other government officials throughout the week following his appointment on May 19, and Executive Order 9346 was ready for release on May 27. It differed only slightly from the original order of 1941: it stated that both employers and unions have the "duty" to eliminate discrimination in employment and in "union membership"; it set up the FEPC in the executive office of the president, thus giving it greater autonomy; it empowered the committee to "conduct hearings and issue findings of fact"; and instead of being limited to redressing grievances, the committee was directed to "take appropriate steps to obtain the elimination" of racial and religious discrimination. The committee, however, was still denied explicit enforcement machinery.[20]

Selecting the other six members of the committee proved to be a more trying task. Haas immediately chose Sara Southall, supervisor of employment at International Harvester Company, and three members of the first FEPC: Milton Webster of the Brotherhood of Sleeping Car Porters, Boris Shishkin of the AFL, and John Brophy of the CIO.[21] He also hoped to appoint a Spanish-speaking member to represent the thousands of Latin American immigrants and their descendents in the Southwest, and as early as May 20 he had written to Archbishop Lucey of San Antonio for suggestions. The archbishop, however, feared that a southwestern representative would be unable to attend regular meetings in Washington and suggested that someone be selected from New York's Spanish-speaking population. But Haas preferred a Southerner and eventually decided upon Samuel Zemurray, a Jewish immigrant from Poland and millionaire president of United Fruit Company in New Orleans. The retention or dismissal of Earl Dickerson was especially difficult. Dickerson, the former committee's most militant member, had an extensive following among Black Americans and eagerly desired reappointment. Two of Haas's closest friends in Chicago, Monsignor Reynold Hillenbrand and Dr. John Lapp, urged his retention. Dickerson had alienated government officials, however, by releasing statements to the press in the spring of 1943 against the wishes of War Manpower Commission chairman Paul McNutt, and Haas himself was suspicious of Dickerson's leftist affiliations. After a month of deliberation and discussion, Haas recommended that Dickerson be replaced by P. B. Young, publisher of the *Norfolk Journal and Guide*. When President Roosevelt announced appointment of the new membership on July 2, the six persons named—Southall, Webster, Shishkin, Brophy, Zemurray, and Young—were all Monsignor Haas's nominees.[22]

Even before the full membership of the FEPC could be announced, however, Monsignor Haas had found it necessary to intervene in the new committee's first major dispute—an explosive situation in the Mobile, Alabama, shipbuilding industry. The Mobile metropolitan area at the time was a rapidly growing urban center of 200,000, approximately one-third of whom were Black. Wartime shipbuilding was the city's leading industry, with the Alabama Drydock and Shipbuilding Company employing approximately 25,000 and Gulf Shipbuilding Company another 10,000. Despite full employment and resultant prosperity, the waterfront industry was beset by serious problems: new, migrant, and at times unstable workers were drawn constantly into the industry; employee absenteeism was estimated at a disconcerting 12 percent; Black workers were restricted to low-salary jobs; and the CIO local that had been certified in an NLRB election in the Alabama Drydock and Shipbuilding Company in early 1942 had since had its charter suspended by international union leadership.[23]

FEPC hearings in Birmingham the preceding June had revealed that three-fourths of the 7,000 Black workers employed by the Alabama Drydock Company held unskilled jobs and the rest only semiskilled; and in November, as the first FEPC was rapidly losing influence, it issued a directive ordering the company to halt all discriminatory practices and to begin the immediate upgrading and promoting of Black workers. Although the company acknowledged its need for additional welders to fulfill its government contracts for ship construction and repair, little action was taken on the directive through the early months of 1943. Finally, on May 22, company officials announced that they were upgrading twelve Black workers to the position of welder and were assigning them immediately to the third or midnight shift.[24]

Work continued without incident for three days, but violence suddenly erupted between Black and white workers on the daylight shift on May 25. Approximately a dozen workers were injured in the rock-throwing and pipe-wielding melee—all of them Black, except one white employee who, according to one account, was attempting to assist Black workers. Contrary to early rumors, no one was killed. Production in the yards immediately stopped as Black workers left their jobs or were ordered home by company or union officials. City police were placed on overtime; approximately 350 State Guards were dispatched to Mobile by the governor; and 150 federal troops patrolled the yard each shift, with an additional 1,000 troops in nearby reserve. By June 1, three men had been arrested and charged with assault and with threats leading to disorder.[25]

Representatives of the War Manpower Commission, the Maritime Commission, and the FEPC met with company and union leaders in Mobile on May 27 and 28 in an effort to arrive at a formula which might maintain full production in this vital wartime industry, and also reduce racial tension and violence. After long hours of discussion, they agreed on a plan to assign four shipways or departments exclusively to Black employees and to reserve the rest for white workers, thus providing for the upgrading and promotion of Black workers in four departments but also establishing segregation as the company's policy. Company executives suggested calling a mass meeting to present this plan to the workers and urge its acceptance. The situation was so explosive that company officials felt that neither they nor the union leadership would be able to persuade the workers to accept the plan and return to work unless military leaders, especially from Washington, were present to emphasize the wartime importance of the industry and the patriotic duty of each worker to give full cooperation to the nation's soldiers and sailors overseas.[26]

On May 28 this proposal, still a closely guarded secret, was sent to Monsignor Haas in Washington for approval. This was one day after the release of Executive Order 9346, reestablishing the FEPC, and a month before the other committee members were appointed. Alone on the FEPC, Monsignor Haas asked the advice of other Washington officials and, on June 3, formally approved the company's proposal. His official telegram to company officials suggested both the difficulty of the decision and his own reservations:

> The President's Committee on Fair Employment Practices approves as a practical settlement of the existing situation the proposed solution for settlement of difficulties at shipyards of Alabama Drydock and Shipbuilding Company drawn up by a conference committee on May twenty-eighth in which this Committee was represented by E. G. Trimble and Clarence Mitchell, under which settlement all employees used on bare hull erection on ways one through four will be Negroes. You will readily understand that the Committee on Fair Employment Practices cannot approve restrictions for the future with respect to the upgrading of Negroes into the outfitting

crafts such as electricians, pipe fitters, etc., which restrictions would conflict with the provisions of the Executive Order and we feel sure that you would not expect the Committee to do so.[27]

The War Manpower Commission was optimistic. "The present basis of agreement that separate shipways should be maintained for colored workers, thus enabling them to participate at all grades of skills," an official release stated, "seems to solve at one and the same time both the difficulty of upgrading negro workers adequately and that of providing them with adequate protection while at work in designated shipways apart from the whites."[28] The uneasy situation was still so explosive, however, that the mass meeting of workers, recommended on May 28, was never held because of the danger of renewed violence between Black and white workers, and the FEPC renewed its insistence, despite contrary wishes of local officials, that federal troops remain on duty for the protection of Black workers in all shipyards.

This decision on June 2 was undoubtedly difficult. In the summer of 1942, Mark Ethridge of the FEPC had aroused a storm of protest by suggesting that "there is no power in the world ... which could now force the Southern White people to the abandonment of the principle of social segregation." Earl Dickerson immediately countered that "Mr. Ethridge's statement, in support of segregation in the South, in my opinion violates both the letter and the spirit of the President's Executive Order 8802. ...Because of the very nature of its creation, the Committee on Fair Employment Practice must be opposed to segregation and discrimination.... There should be 'no pussy-footing' on segregation by members of the Committee." This was twelve years before the Supreme Court, in *Brown v. Board of Education*, rejected the "separate but equal" doctrine and the FEPC, in 1942, had adopted the position that segregation could, but did not necessarily, constitute discrimination.[29]

It was later revealed that the War Manpower Commission in early May had first recommended such a solution to the Mobile controversy. After five months of little or no progress in implementing the FEPC directive of the previous November, the commission on May 3, more than two weeks before Monsignor Haas was appointed to the FEPC, explicitly recommended that, as a start, at least one company shipway be reserved exclusively to Black workers, skilled and unskilled. If the War Manpower Com-

mission did not oppose the company's plan for immediate integration of the workers on May 22, it at least made it known that
it was not enthusiastic and that it preferred segregated shipways.[30]
The compromise plan of May 28 had accepted and extended the
recommendation of the War Manpower Commission three weeks
earlier, and thus Monsignor Haas's approval seemed to conform
to the policy of the first FEPC and other wartime government
agencies. Rejection of the plan would have been a direct repud-
iation of the War Manpower Commission's recommendation of
May 3, a difficult decision for a government official only two
weeks in office. In these circumstances, Monsignor Haas saw the
proposal as an imperfect first step toward full equality and elimination of discrimination in employment.

Monsignor Haas seemed far from satisfied with this decision,
however. At the first meeting of the reconstituted FEPC in July,
he presented the decision to the other members and voted with
them in their declaration that "the Committee accepts the accomplished fact of the settlement made in Mobile to end a crisis in
war production, except that the Committee cannot give its approval to the complete segregation of Negroes on the four ways and
does not consider this as a precedent."[31] In an interview shortly
thereafter, Haas explained that the FEPC resolution did not constitute "either an antisegregation or a prosegregation stand"; the
FEPC simply refused to accept the compromise as a precedent
"one way or the other." He followed this decision, however, with
a formal directive to his twelve regional offices, ordering all public
facilities in buildings leased by the FEPC immediately desegre-
gated.[32]

Ten months later, after he had left Washington for his episcopal duties in Grand Rapids, the new bishop happened to be
visiting in the South, and in a personal letter to his successor as
chairman of the FEPC, Malcolm Ross, he made one final—and
favorable—comment on this controversial Alabama settlement:

> While I was in Mobile I went out to the Alabama ship-
> building yards, in fact, I went out there twice. In addition
> I was waited upon a whole evening by a Negro committee
> consisting of Messrs. Jackson, LeFlore and Williams. The
> first is a national representative of the shipbuilding union,
> the second a local representative to the N.A.A.C.P., and the
> third a personnel man for management on racial problems.
> Of course, I was concerned about the working out of the

settlement of last July. Here is what each of the three men said. Jackson said progress is 'very good,' Williams said the situation is 'beautiful' and LeFlore smiled and shook his head. . . .

My own impressions from going through the yards and from private conferences with Daly, Greiser [for the company] and the Negro committee are that the July settlement is not working out too badly. Actually on the Four Jim Crow Ways, Negroes are advanced without any restriction. On the other ways Negroes and whites are working together and a considerable number of Negroes are doing skilled work along side of whites on the white ways. Please do not think that I regard the situation as ideal. On the other hand, I would be much less than honest if I did not say that tremendous progress has been made.[33]

A second controversy, the Capital Transit dispute in Washington, was also inherited from the earlier FEPC. Black leaders had charged the company with discrimination in the hiring of bus and streetcar drivers, and after a careful investigation in December 1942 the FEPC had ordered the company to remove all barriers to Black employment. When the company had failed to comply with this directive to the satisfaction of the committee, Acting Chairman Earl Dickerson prepared to hold public hearings into the controversy in early 1943. At the suggestion of the White House, however, the hearings were postponed until a new FEPC chairman could be named. By that time, the case was further complicated by an announcement of a high War Manpower Commission official that the FEPC had no jurisdiction over the controversy since the Transit Company was not a defense industry. Immediately after his appointment, Monsignor Haas took up the challenge. The FEPC had no intention of withdrawing from the case, he insisted. "What powers there are in that executive order, the new committee will consider and use." The FEPC, he added, "is not going to dodge anything. Our country is too big for discrimination."[34]

Monsignor Haas once again turned his attention to the dispute even before the other committee members were appointed. By mid-June the company had been ordered to conform its policies to FEPC directives; in response, company officials announced that they were considering establishment of a separate corporation to take over some services of the Capital Transit Company and to be staffed entirely by Black laborers. The Office of Defense Transportation advised against this but suggested that "some form of segregation might be worked out similar to that approved in the Mobile Shipyard case." FEPC officials urged the company to seek a nondiscrimination clause in its union contract, since this policy now had the support of the federal government, but company officials insisted that such a controversial issue would stalemate forthcoming negotiations and essential services would be disrupted.[35]

The case was discussed in detail by the full committee at its first two meetings in July. Company officials wanted to reserve particular lines for Black workers, undoubtedly after the precedent set at the Alabama Shipbuilding and Drydock Company a month earlier, but they realized that this might be in conflict with the seniority clause in their union contract and would thus meet with opposition. With the approval and assistance of the FEPC, the company agreed to hire a personnel officer for minority employment, and the committee notified company officials that it expected a progress report within two or three weeks. When company officials reported on August 7 that they were hiring a personnel officer to study and investigate the situation, Haas immediately replied that this officer was not only to investigate and study but to begin implementing the program of hiring Black workers without discrimination.[36]

By the end of August, Monsignor Haas was able to announce that progress had been made. Although he had been unsuccessful in his efforts to persuade union leaders to notify company officials in writing that they did not oppose the hiring of Black workers, Black leaders in the controversy expressed satisfaction with the progress thus far. About that same time, however, the company's personnel officer announced that, in his opinion, the majority of the white workers would strike if more Black workers were hired, and as a result the company began to relax its efforts toward wider minority employment. Monsignor Haas scheduled public hearings into the controversy for early October, but he remained optimistic. "The Capital Transit hearing is reaching a satisfactory conclusion," he told a reporter in September. "You can't set a definite time limit but I should say it is a matter of weeks."[37]

Within that "matter of weeks," Monsignor Haas had been appointed bishop of Grand Rapids and had found it necessary to resign his position on the FEPC.[38] The Transit hearings of October 5 were again postponed. In fact, the hearings were not held until January 1945, and even then they brought the dispute no closer to settlement. When a violent strike erupted the following November, the government assumed control of the company and the FEPC took the opportunity to issue a directive ordering an end to all racial discrimination. On November 24, however, President Truman intervened and insisted that since the law under which he had assumed control of the company stipulated that "existing terms and conditions of employment" must be maintained, the FEPC could not order changes in hiring procedures.[39] When the committee, abandoned apparently by both Congress and the president, passed out of existence six months later, the Capital Transit controversy was still unsettled.

Racial tensions erupted into violence all across the country in the summer of 1943—from Los Angeles to Harlem and from Hartford, Connecticut, to Beaumont, Texas—but nowhere with greater fury than in Detroit on the night of June 20. Detroit had been a smoldering volcano for several years.[40] In an article, "Detroit Is Dynamite," *Life* magazine had asserted ten months earlier that "Detroit can either blow up Hitler or it can blow up the U.S." At a church dedication on June 3, Walter White of the NAACP declared: "Let us drag out into the open what has been whispered throughout Detroit for months—that a race riot may break out here at any time." The county prosecuting attorney admitted later: "We felt the riot coming. Race tensions have been growing here for three years." From 1940 to 1943, 450,000 southern whites and 50,000 Blacks had moved into Detroit, seeking employment in the city's prosperous defense industries and straining its uneasy racial truce. Most of Detroit's 200,000 Black residents, one-tenth of the population, were concentrated in overcrowded and deteriorating housing projects in five main districts. Paradise Valley, the largest, consisted mostly of inadequate, near-slum dwellings and white and Black commercial establishments along Hastings Street, with approximately 65,000 Black residents in an area one-half mile wide and about three miles long. Parks and beaches were segregated throughout the city and Black and white workers often competed for the same jobs. Only one-tenth of city teachers were Black, and 3 percent of the women in defense industries—but over 50 percent of the citizens on relief.[41]

Despite the increasing racial and economic tensions, municipal security was precarious. Many members of the police department had been drafted into the armed forces, others had transferred into essential war industries (where wages were higher and draft deferments more accessible), and the number of city policemen, despite an increase of approximately 500,000 in the city's population since 1940, had declined, leaving 280 positions unfilled. Racial disorders during the same period had accelerated ominously. In February 1942 a riot had broken out over discrimination in housing projects, and white employees held wildcat strikes in several automobile and munitions industries in the first months of 1943 to protest the upgrading of Black workers. On May 27, the day Executive Order 9346 was released, 20,000 workers walked off their jobs in the Packard motor plant to protest the promotion of three Black welders. Only the firm stand of UAW president R. J. Thomas prevented the incident from escalating into open warfare.[42]

On the hot Sunday evening of June 20, this smoldering volcano of racial antagonism erupted. The riot began apparently with a fist fight between youths, either at the Belle Isle amusement park pavilion or on one of the streets or bridges leading to the park—although other racial scuffles that evening might also have triggered the violence. Before police reinforcements could arrive, two hundred white recruits from the nearby Brodhead Naval Armory and scores of Black youths, already at the park, joined in the melee. Rumors spread rapidly—of the attempted assault of a white woman on a public bus and of an attack on a public bridge, in which a Black woman and her baby had reportedly been thrown into the Detroit River—and they excited both sides to greater violence. White hoodlums invaded the housing settlements of Paradise Valley, beating, burning, and looting at will. Bands of Black youths pillaged and burned stores on Hastings Street and attacked white workers as they emerged from defense plants as far as three miles from Belle Isle. Black store owners along Hastings Street immediately placed signs on their doors or windows, and it was noted ominously that Jewish shops and businesses were looted with particular vehemence.[43]

The violence continued throughout Monday. Gangs of white and Black teenagers, armed with knives and crowbars, roamed the streets in search of victims; Blacks were pulled off streetcars and beaten by white mobs; a white doctor was killed on his way to attend a patient in the riot area; and one Black, waiting for a bus, was murdered by four white youths because, they later explained, "other people were fighting and killing and we felt like it too."[44] Police poured 1,000 rounds of ammunition into one apartment before Black snipers were silenced. Classes in many elementary schools were cancelled at noon, the Michigan State Fair Grounds were closed, the Cleveland-Detroit baseball game was postponed, and a ten o'clock curfew was imposed that evening throughout the city. "The week ending June 28," commented the *New Republic*, "was in many ways the blackest for Americans since Pearl Harbor."

Unfortunate delays occurred in the calling of the National Guard. In an emergency meeting of city officials early Monday morning, police department officials apparently concluded that federal troops would not be needed, and only later that morning was this decision reversed. Governor Harry Kelly was attending a Governors' Conference in Ohio when he received urgent notice that the rioting in Detroit was out of control. He immediately ordered Michigan state police and state troops on alert, telephoned National Guard headquarters in Chicago, and boarded a plane for Detroit. Unfortunately, General Henry Aurand of the Sixth Service Command in Chicago interpreted the governor's call as a notice of *possible* deployment of troops and maintained that such deployment would have to await an explicit presidential proclamation of martial law. Governor Kelly and Mayor Edward Jeffries had not realized that this was necessary, they hesitated to call the president and indicate to voters their helplessness in the emergency, and thus federal troops did not arrive until eleven o'clock that evening. In the day and a half of rioting before their arrival, 34 persons were killed, almost 1,000 injured, 1,800 arrested, and an estimated $1.5 million in property have been damaged. Of the thirty-four killed, according to police records, seven of the nine whites were killed by Blacks during the rioting while seventeen of the twenty-five Blacks were shot by police, most during looting. "All these words of anguish which swirl and flow through the press and out upon the air waves in the wake of the Detroit race riot are useless," wrote one observer. "The thing is done. We have lost a battle in Detroit. It was a clean defeat. Nothing was salvaged."[45]

Several days before the other FEPC members were appointed, Monsignor Haas was forced to act. He hurried to Detroit on June 29 and for three days visited the riot area and interviewed civic and religious leaders in an effort to uncover the causes of the sudden outbreak; and on his return to Washington in early July he submitted a detailed report to the attorney general. He discounted, first of all, charges of outside interference. Despite frequently voiced suspicions of sabotage, he insisted there was no evidence of Axis instigation.[46] A four-man state investigating committee later charged Detroit's militant Black leadership with inciting the riot, while Black leaders blamed white extremists like Gerald L. K. Smith and officials of the Ku Klux Klan. Monsignor Haas rejected both conclusions. The chief causes of the riot, in his opinion, were much less sinister. Black Americans in Detroit were bitterly and justifiably discontented with overcrowded housing, insufficient recreational facilities, and inadequate transportation, and the city's white population, swelled by almost half a million recent immigrants from the South, often resented the efforts of Black residents to gain full social and economic equality.[47] Sparked by the incident at Belle Isle, this latent discontent and prejudice had flared into open warfare. Although Haas refrained from criticizing local law enforcement agencies, he noted that many officers called into the armed forces had not been replaced and that the city's police seemed insufficient for a city of over 2 million inhabitants. The chief rioters, white and Black, he emphasized, were youths in their late teens and early twenties, many of whom were unemployed while awaiting their draft calls. Haas strongly urged city officials and industrial leaders to find ways of furnishing these youths with temporary, constructive employment. Attorney General Francis Biddle was impressed with Haas's memorandum, and when he sent his official report on the Detroit riot to President Roosevelt ten days later, he included, in the same order, the principal findings of Monsignor Haas after his three-day visit.[48]

As chairman of the Fair Employment Practices Committee, Monsignor Haas had paid special attention to conditions in Detroit's defense industries. Although the rioting that Monday had spread throughout the city, almost all war plants were spared. "I learned last week in Detroit, where mixed races make tanks and airplanes side by side, that the workers in war plants did not lose their heads at the time when hoodlums were rioting in the streets of Detroit."[49] He pointed out that during the height of violence and bloodshed, white and Black workers continued to labor side by side in aircraft and munitions industries, and he cited several incidents in which white and Black workers protected each other from gangs of rioters as they left the plants. Most of the more than twenty civic, business, and religious leaders Haas interviewed during his three-day visit acknowledged that conditions in the war plants had remained calm, due at least in part to UAW leadership. Haas discussed this view a few months later:

Actually a man-to-man feeling is established between Negroes and non-Negroes when they are thrown together and work side by side. It is highly significant that at the very time that the June, 1943, race riots were going on in the streets of Detroit, Negroes and Whites were working together in the city's war plants, going about their business.... For this fine achievement, the U.A.W.–C.I.O., and especially its top officials, deserve a great deal of credit. National officers of the Union "stuck their necks out" in the face of membership opposition which here and there was as deep and bitter as it was selfish and unjust. These officers set an example of courage and decency which cannot but enhance the prestige and strength of the International Union.[50]

The experience of the Detroit war plants made a permanent impression on Haas. Equal employment, he insisted, was the essential first step toward full racial equality. "I am convinced," he stated in 1946, "that, as a matter of practical strategy, we should concentrate our available resources on getting decent, Christian, brother-to-brother relationships between Negroes and Whites established in industry, and that we will thereby hasten progress in getting like standards established in social and political life." "It is axiomatic," he said in 1947, "that when people learn to work together, they also learn to live together."[51]

Although race riots in Harlem, Detroit, Mobile, Washington, Beaumont, and Los Angeles captured more newspaper headlines in the summer of 1943, the long-delayed railroad investigations were a more serious challenge to Monsignor Haas and the FEPC. Racial discrimination in railroad employment—usually through mutual agreements of carriers and the railroad brotherhoods—was probably the most complete of any major American industry. Of the thirteen unions which excluded Black membership by formal constitutional provision in 1943, ten were involved in rails.[52] Three of the industry's "Big Four" brotherhoods—engineers, firemen, and trainmen—excluded Black workers by statute, and the railway clerks and carmen admitted them only to segregated "auxiliaries." The railroad hearings were equally important for the FEPC. The hearings had been postponed three times in eighteen months, and the postponement of January 1943 had been fatal to the first FEPC. Haas understood, as Randolph had insisted, that the railroad investigations would be "the showdown test." "The key to saving the Fair Employment Practice Committee," Randolph warned, "is to save the Railroad hearings."

At the FEPC's first meeting, July 6, 1943, the committee members voted to proceed with the railroad investigation as quickly as possible and they authorized the chairman to make necessary preparations. Haas selected A. Bartley Crum of San Francisco as chief counsel, devoted much of July and August to preparing the committee's case against the carriers and the rail brotherhoods, and on September 5 issued his long-awaited announcement: "Exhaustive investigation by the F.E.P.C. has resulted in the compilation of a lengthy list of allegations involving agreements between railroads and unions whereby the effective utilization of available qualified manpower has been hampered because of discriminatory employment practices based on race."[53] These discriminatory practices, the announcement continued, included consistent refusals to hire, upgrade, or promote Black workers; violations of their seniority rights; maintenance of unfair wage differentials for Black workers; and their exclusion from work on diesel-powered locomotives. Haas then listed twenty-three railroads and fourteen unions accused of violating Executive Orders 8802 and 9346, most of them operating in the South. The hearings were scheduled for Washington, September 15–18, and all carriers and unions were requested to send representatives and witnesses.

The testimony taken during these four days of public hearings was damning to both carriers and unions. By an agreement of February 22, 1941, the Brotherhood of Locomotive Firemen and Enginemen and the twenty-six railroads of the Southeastern Carriers Conference Committee declared that "the proportion of non-promotable firemen, and helpers on other than steam power, shall not exceed fifty percent in each class of service established as such on each individual carrier."[54] Since all Black workers were "non-promotable," this clause not only discriminated against Black employment but relegated Black workers to a minority voice in all union deliberations. An agreement with Atlanta Joint Terminals that month gave "promotable" men preference in retaining jobs in slow seasons, even though other workers had seniority. On many lines Black workers were declared ineligible for employment as trainmen, and since conductors were chosen from the ranks of trainmen, they were excluded from both positions. Other companies agreed to hire only white engineers on diesel locomotives. Even when the FEPC could discover no explicit restriction on Black employment in the labor agreements, the committee's report noted repeatedly: "No Negroes hired in 1941"; "No Negroes employed as trainmen, brakemen, or engineers"; "No

Negroes promoted over eight months period." Possibly because the evidence was so irrefutable, the rail brotherhoods declined to send representatives to the Washington hearings.[55]

Monsignor Haas and the other members of the FEPC met on October 2 and 18 to determine what action should be taken to halt such blatant discrimination.[56] After long deliberation, the committee decided to issue cease-and-desist orders to all offending parties, allowing them seven days to initiate improvements before these directives and the FEPC's findings would be made public. If the carriers and the unions failed to comply even after publication of the findings, the cases would be submitted to the president for more decisive action.

The committee's plan soon went awry, however, when, on October 1—even before the committee's first meeting to discuss the results of the rail hearings—the Vatican announced the appointment of Monsignor Haas as bishop of Grand Rapids.[57] Monsignor Haas, well aware of the importance of the rail investigations to the ultimate success of the FEPC, decided to remain with the committee until after its meeting on October 18, but the loss of its chairman undoubtedly lessened the committee's prestige. The FEPC staff spent four weeks drawing up the necessary cease-and-desist orders and these were sent to the offending carriers and unions on November 18, one month after Monsignor Haas's formal departure from the committee. Unfortunately, these orders were leaked to the press that same day and made public.[58] Fourteen of the companies and all seven unions, although found guilty, accused the FEPC of broken trust and rejected the directives, and in late December the new FEPC chairman, Malcolm Ross, had no alternative but to certify the cases to President Roosevelt. The president subsequently appointed a committee under Chief Justice Walter Stacey of the North Carolina Supreme Court to meet with railroad and union representatives in an effort to implement the FEPC's order, but no agreement could be reached.

The FEPC's battle to abolish discrimination in the rail industry was finally lost in the early months of 1944. In March, a congressional committee, under Representative Howard W. Smith of Virginia, began an investigation of the FEPC and openly disputed the committee's authority to issue cease-and-desist orders. Senator Richard Russell of Georgia stated that he was "glad the Railroad Brotherhoods and the Southern railroads defied this organization and told it to go ahead and do its worst." Confronted by the failure of the Stacey Committee and the united opposition of the

                                                          A Priest in Public Service

railroad industry, the rail brotherhoods, and influential southern congressmen, the president took no further action.[59] Although the FEPC, under Monsignor Haas, received credit for conducting the railroad hearings, despite concerted opposition, and for issuing stringent cease-and-desist orders, the rail investigations proved a failure. The FEPC was no stronger than its presidential support, and at the critical moment the president withheld his backing. Had Monsignor Haas remained longer with the FEPC, the outcome could have been little different.

The Alabama Shipbuilding controversy, the Capital Transit dispute, the Detroit riot, and the rail investigations were only four of hundreds of controversies demanding Monsignor Haas's attention during his short term as FEPC chairman. His responsibilities, in fact, were so absorbing that he found it necessary to request a leave of absence from his duties at Catholic University that August. The cases brought before the committee during those four months ranged from complaints against the Boilermakers' all-Black auxiliary unions on the West Coast to segregated welders' classes in Maryland, and from refusal to hire Black telephone operators in Baltimore to discrimination against Jewish postal workers in Detroit and attacks on Japanese-Americans throughout the country during that summer of bitter fighting in the Pacific. The exact number of cases is difficult to determine. According to a memorandum of Will Maslow, director of the FEPC's field operations, the committee received 220 complaints during July 1943, Monsignor Haas's first month as chairman. An FEPC report, published in 1945, revealed that the committee heard approximately 250 cases a month from July 1943 to December 1944. Eighty-one percent of these complaints were submitted by Black Americans, 69 percent against private industry and 25 percent against the federal government.[60] As chairman and the only full-time, salaried member of the committee, Monsignor Haas held primary responsibility for the investigation and adjustment of these disputes and he found little time, consequently, to devote to other government or ecclesiastical commitments during the summer of 1943.

There can be no doubt about the sincerity with which Monsignor Haas attacked the problem of racial discrimination in employment during his four months on the FEPC. "Let men be just and charitable to their brothers," he declared at a news conference that fall, "and the rights of the individual will be assured. Let men be just and charitable to their fellow men, whoever they may be in the world, of whatever race, of whatever people, and international institutions can function with a minimum of hardship and friction. Let men be just and charitable toward those close to them at home, their next door neighbors, if you please, and a just social order will prevail within the nation."[61]

Monsignor Haas had little patience with those who insisted that full racial equality should not be attempted until the people were better educated. When two reporters asked him, earlier that summer, "if it wasn't going to take a lot of education on both sides—possibly several generations of it—to bring the white and colored races into a truly harmonious relationship," Haas replied:

> Of course it is. But all too often that word "education" is just a subterfuge behind which hide a lot of would-be liberals who talk mighty loud about racial equality—but secretly, or subconsciously, hope it won't come to pass in their generation. Actually, one of the most important parts of education is experiment. You can't learn chemistry merely from text books; you've got to go into a laboratory, mix the chemicals yourself and see what happens. In a racial field, experiment is even more important. If we can go into a plant and persuade the management just to "try" hiring a few negroes, we know the battle there is practically won. Because, in ninety-nine cases out of a hundred, the "experiment" works: the chemicals mix without an explosion, and the management accepts the formula. That's my idea of real "education."[62]

Despite Monsignor Haas's high ideals and conscientious service to the FEPC, however, his success as committee chairman was limited. Since the FEPC was created by executive order rather than by congressional statute, its effectiveness depended on the support it received from the president, and Roosevelt refused to stand firm on civil rights. He had established the committee in 1941 under the threat of Randolph's march on Washington; he was ever sensitive to the political opposition of the FEPC's critics in Congress; and on occasion (in the postponement of the rail hearings, for example) he aligned himself with the committee's opponents. The FEPC was also hampered by lack of enforcement machinery. The committee was authorized by executive order to direct private industries to cease discriminatory employment practices, but if they refused the FEPC could only recommend to other government agencies that they cancel the industries' defense contracts. Without the firm support of the president, however, these directives to industry and the recommendations to government departments were often ignored. In the whole history of the FEPC, apparently no government contract was cancelled because of discriminatory employment practices.[63] The FEPC was at a further disadvantage in dealing with organized labor. Labor unions were not parties to defense contracts and therefore were not subject to the FEPC's sanctions. The railroad brotherhoods, for example, decided to boycott the FEPC's rail hearings in September of 1943. Lacking the full support of the president and Congress, hampered by limited appropriations, and denied adequate machinery to enforce its directives, the FEPC was often ineffective in its efforts to abolish racial and religious discrimination from American economic life.

Despite these limitations, Monsignor Haas's four months as FEPC chairman were not a failure.[64] He assisted Attorney General Biddle in drafting the new FEPC order of May 25—a stronger directive than the 1941 order—and helped reestablish the committee after its disastrous decline in the spring of 1943. Labor disputes caused by the hiring of Black workers diminished steadily throughout 1943 and the number of Blacks employed in defense industries almost doubled. Black employment in government offices showed similar advances. "The FEPC," one authority has noted, "as the sole agency devoted entirely to the elimination of discrimination, acted in a sense as a gadfly to others and made certain that they were carrying out their obligations as set forth in the agreements and the President's executive orders." Despite well-publicized failures in the rail investigations and the Capital Transit dispute, the FEPC was successful in adjusting most of the 250 complaints it received each month. "In the vast majority of instances in which it intervened," one historian has written, "the FEPC did succeed in altering discriminating employment practices and helped to increase employment opportunities of Negroes and members of other minority groups." "The contrary impression," the committee's final report added, "that FEPC normally met with unyielding opposition, was created by the comparatively few difficult cases which received emphasis through public hearings and public expression of defiance by some recalcitrant employers and unions." Monsignor Haas was undoubtedly sincere, consequently, when he stated at the time of his resignation that the FEPC had been "one of the most satisfying associations of my life."[65] As chairman of the FEPC he had assisted in the crusade against injustice, discrimination, and bigotry, which he found incompatible with his social and religious convictions, and he did it in the field of labor relations, the area of his special competence. His success, though limited, was probably as wide as a vacillating president, an often hostile Congress, and the national mores in 1943 would allow.

11
Bishop of Grand Rapids, 1943-1953

Established in 1882, the Diocese of Grand Rapids in 1943 was only seven years older than its new bishop. Catholic missionaries first visited the area east of Lake Michigan in the 1640s, and Jesuit Fathers from Mackinac Island, Sault Sainte Marie, and Detroit preached Christianity to the Indians throughout the seventeenth and eighteenth centuries. In 1833, Father Frederick Baraga, a missionary from Austria and later first bishop of Sault Sainte Marie-Marquette, arrived at the present site of Grand Rapids, at that time a small bartering post on the Grand River, founded only seven years earlier by an Indian trader. Baraga immediately converted a log cabin into a primitive church and school, and from this early foundation Catholicism gradually spread north, east, and west through mission stations in Grand Haven, Manistee, Muskegon, Traverse City, and Cheboygan. Also in 1833, the Diocese of Detroit, the first in Michigan, was formed from the Archdiocese of Cincinnati, and twenty-four years later the Diocese of Sault Sainte Marie, in the Upper Peninsula, was separated from Detroit. In 1882, Rome announced formation of a third diocese from the northern and western counties of the Lower Peninsula, and selected Grand Rapids as its episcopal residence.[1]

The diocese at that time comprised an area of more than 22,000 square miles and included a Catholic population of approximately 45,000. Henry Joseph Richter of Cincinnati was named its first bishop, and during the thirty-three years of his tenure the growth of the diocese was extraordinary. The Catholic population, swelled by immigration from Southern and Eastern Europe, numbered approximately 145,000 by 1916. National parishes were erected for Germans, Poles, Dutch, Lithuanians, and Italians. The number of priests in the diocese increased from 34 to 162, seventy new churches were constructed, and almost that same number of schools to accommodate a student population that had burgeoned to 18,000. At the death of Bishop Richter in late 1916, Grand Rapids had a Catholic population greater than seventy of the nation's one hundred dioceses.[2]

The diocese continued to grow in the postwar years, but at a slower rate. Under Bishops Michael Gallagher (1916-1918) and Edward Kelly (1919-1926) a new chancery and cathedral rectory were constructed, fifteen new parishes were erected, and an enlarged St. Joseph's Seminary was built on seventeen acres of land in the residential, southeast section of the city. Deeply committed to Catholic education, Bishop Kelly expanded parochial school facilities to admit an additional 5,000 students and he campaigned vigorously in the 1920s against a constitutional amendment that would have obliged all Michigan pupils to attend public grade schools. Grand Rapids experienced Ku Klux Klan activity in the 1920s, but the Klan's influence on public life in Michigan was not great. By 1926, the year of Bishop Kelly's death, Catholics of the diocese still numbered approximately 145,000, comprising slightly less than 15 percent of the total population. By that year, too, industry was rapidly overtaking agriculture as the principal occupation of many in western Michigan, and Grand Rapids was becoming known as "the Furniture Capital of America."[3]

Bishop Joseph Pinten succeeded Bishop Kelly and served for fourteen years, 1926 to 1940, a tenure characterized by one historian as "a period of retrenchment." The preceding decades had witnessed extensive building and Bishop Pinten determined that time was now needed to reduce the diocesan debt and take stock of present needs and resources before further expansion. But three years after his installation came the Wall Street Crash and very little expansion was undertaken in the Depression that followed. In 1937 the new diocese of Lansing was formed out of the southwestern counties of the Archdiocese of Detroit, and in the following year the Diocese of Saginaw was created from the northern and eastern sections of Grand Rapids, leaving the Diocese of Grand Rapids a Catholic population of less than 70,000. In November 1940, after almost a year of ill health, Bishop Pinten resigned and was succeeded by Bishop Joseph Plagens of Marquette. The new bishop suffered a heart attack only four months after his installation and, because of periodic relapses over the next two years, was forced to retire into semiseclusion. When Bishop Plagens died in late March 1943, the diocese was healthy and vibrant—the Catholic population was over 90,000, the proportion of priests to laity was high, and the faith seemed firmly rooted in the daily lives of the French, Irish, German, Polish, and Italian Catholic families—but the diocese had also been left without a strong and effective central administration for four years: two years of receding depression and two years of World War II.[4]

As the apostolic delegate in Washington and Church officials in Rome began to search for a successor to Bishop Plagens, Monsignor Haas seemed well qualified. According to the Vatican decree of 1916 on the selection of American bishops, the candidate should be "mature, but not too old; of good judgment, tried in actual service; well-educated, devoted to the Holy See, and especially noted for rectitude and piety."[5] Thirty years a priest and in excellent health, Monsignor Haas had gained wide experience as a parish assistant, author, university professor, and ecclesiastical administrator. He was one of the country's foremost authorities on the social teachings of the Church and a loyal, uncompromising defender of the Holy See. Although many Catholics took issue with his views on labor and civil rights, no one seriously questioned his sincerity, good will, or the orthodoxy of his religious beliefs. The frequency with which ecclesiastical and governmental officials sought his advice attested to his prudence and good judgment. He had been born and raised in southeast Wisconsin, among immigrant Catholic families not unlike those of Grand Rapids, and thus the people of western Michigan might find him congenial, supportive, and understanding. When the death of Bishop Plagens in early 1943 created a vacancy in Grand Rapids, consequently, Monsignor Haas seemed to possess the qualities Rome was seeking in a successor.

Despite Haas's obvious talents, however, his elevation to the bishopric aroused suspicions in many quarters that he was being removed by Church officials from his controversial work in Washington and his close association with the Roosevelt administration. Rumors were so prevalent that, two weeks after his resignation from the FEPC, the bishop-elect begged newsmen: "Please do not say that the Catholic Church took me out of this job." Many influential prelates were undoubtedly opposed to Haas's government work. Some, mindful perhaps of the embarrassment brought on the Church by the political activities of Father Edward McGlynn in the 1880s and by Father Charles Coughlin more recently, felt that official representatives of the Church should not be part of any government regime and preferred to reserve public and political life to the laity. Conservative churchmen who had opposed the social justice philosophy of John

A. Ryan and who had brought about his retirement from Catholic University in 1939 did not look favorably upon the well-publicized government work of Ryan's close associate and his continued affiliation with the university. Others had taken issue with Haas's insistence on the obligation of Catholic workers to join a union, his support of the CIO, and his defense of the sitdown strikes of 1937-1938. Conservative Catholics, north and south, could be uncomfortable with his efforts to end racial discrimination in government and industrial employment. Whatever their objections, influential Catholics who had become disenchanted with President Roosevelt throughout the 1930s also increased their opposition to Monsignor Haas's collaboration with the president's New Deal administration.[6]

Many important changes had taken place within the ruling hierarchy of the Church, furthermore, since the triumphal days of 1937 when Haas and Ryan were named monsignors and Haas was appointed dean at Catholic University. Pope Pius XI, author of *Quadragesimo Anno* and a great champion of social justice, had died in 1938 and was succeeded by the more aristocratic Pope Pius XII. Monsignor Haas's close friend and ecclesiastical superior in Milwaukee, Archbishop Stritch, had been transferred to Chicago on the death of Cardinal George Mundelein in 1939 and had been replaced in Milwaukee by Archbishop Moses Kiley. The death of Bishop Joseph Corrigan in 1942 had brought Monsignor Patrick McCormick to the rectorship of Catholic University. Cardinal Patrick Hayes of New York, for whom Haas had prepared a pastoral letter on social justice in 1938, had died after a long illness and had been succeeded in 1939 by Archbishop Francis Spellman. A protégé of the conservative Cardinal William O'Connell of Boston, Spellman did not share the liberal social philosophy of Ryan and Haas, and, as a close personal friend of Pope Pius XII since the 1920s, his influence with the new Pope in the selection of American bishops after 1939 was often decisive. By the summer of 1943, consequently, prelates less sympathetic to Haas's liberal views, and possibly to his government work also, had succeeded to the important sees of Milwaukee and New York and to the rectorship of Catholic University, and with the deaths of Pope Pius XI, Cardinal Hayes, Bishop Corrigan, and the transfer of Archbishop Stritch from Milwaukee, Haas's support among the Church hierarchy may have altered.[7]

The evidence that Monsignor Haas was elevated to the bishopric primarily to remove him from government service in Washington, however, is far from convincing. Opposition to his

membership on the FEPC may not have been a major consideration since the committee did not begin its work until early July
and Haas was probably under consideration for Grand Rapids
before then. The *Amsterdam News* on October 9 stated: "Although announcement of Father Haas' church appointment gave
rise immediately to rumors that the move had been taken to shift
him from a 'hot spot' in view of the forthcoming railroad hearings
decision, revelation almost immediately that the first moves
toward his elevation to the bishopric could be traced back to last
March—before he had any contact with the FEPC—has served to
halt much of the speculation."[8] Although this might be overstat-
ed, since Haas's predecessor in Grand Rapids did not die until
March 31, the "first moves" might be traced back even further.
His selection as rector of St. Francis Seminary in 1935 was clearly
a recognition of his unusual qualities. Both his predecessor and
successor at the seminary, Aloysius Muench and Albert Meyer,
were appointed bishops at the close of their terms of office, and
Haas was probably considered "episcopal material" even at the
time of his appointment to the seminary in 1935.

Three prelates whose advice the Vatican would certainly have
sought before appointing Monsignor Haas to the bishopric were
Archbishops Stritch and Kiley of Milwaukee and the apostolic
delegate in Washington, and none of these had apparently expressed opposition to his government activities. Stritch had not
interfered with Haas's work for the NRA or the National Labor
Board in the early 1930s, nor even with his work for the WPA and
the Wisconsin Labor Relations Board during his term as seminary
rector, and both Stritch in 1939 and Kiley in 1941 had given him
permission to accept appointment to the National Labor Relations
Board. Archbishop Kiley had also approved his appointment to
the FEPC in May 1943. At the time of his selection as rector of
the Milwaukee seminary, Haas had confided to a friend that "the
Apostolic Delegate not only favored my continuation in government service but urged it with considerable emphasis."[9] Both
Archbishop Stritch and the apostolic delegate frequently called on
Haas for advice in matters of social justice and for assistance in
preparing speeches. There is no evidence that either Stritch, Kiley,
or Cicognani were ever embarrassed by Haas's government work in
Washington or in Madison, and all three were in a position to
terminate it at any time if they had so desired.

The major influence on Haas's elevation, however, was
probably Archbishop Mooney of Detroit. Although it is un-

certain when Haas and Mooney first became acquainted, by 1943 they were confidential friends and had sought each other's advice on numerous occasions.[10] Since his appointment to Detroit in 1937, Mooney had had to contend with Father Coughlin's return to the radio, the sitdown strikes of 1937 and 1938, and increasing labor and racial unrest in the early years of the war; and with these explosive situations ever at hand, a man of Haas's stature and experience in a nearby suffragan diocese was a valued advantage. As a matter of fact, Haas and Mooney were in frequent and at times daily telephone contact throughout Haas's ten years in Michigan, and as a close associate of Haas remarked: "No one who saw Cardinal Mooney cry so unashamedly at Haas's funeral could ever doubt what Haas had meant to him during those years." The influence of Archbishop Mooney could have been decisive in the selection of a Michigan bishop, and apparently Mooney wanted Haas.

Since the Vatican guards the choice of its bishops in strictest secrecy, the details of Haas's elevation may never be known. Haas certainly had not sought the appointment, nor was he enthusiastic after it was announced. "There is the letter," he told a reporter in early October. "In the organization to which I have devoted my life, we are good soldiers. We do what we are told."[11] Haas was aware of the opposition of many members of the American hierarchy to his government work but he was convinced that this opposition had little influence on his nomination for Grand Rapids. Several of the bishop's closest friends in Racine, Milwaukee, and Grand Rapids believed that the opposition of some prelates to Haas's government work was a major factor in his appointment, but all admitted that Haas did not share this view. As a confidant of numerous bishops and as a Church official familiar with ecclesiastical politics, his own opinion should not be ignored.

The announcement of Monsignor Haas's elevation occasioned numerous expressions of tribute. "I have received with regret," President Roosevelt wrote on October 15, "your letter of resignation as Chairman of the Fair Employment Practice Committee. With your other friends I rejoice in your advancement to the position of Bishop of the Diocese of Grand Rapids. I am not surprised that His Holiness Pope Pius XII has called you to this high position. In all the posts of responsibility in which you have served your government, you have shown a humanity and skill which both church and country greatly need in these difficult days.... We shall miss you in your post in Washington." Secretary Perkins, Senator Wagner, Congresswoman Mary Norton of New Jersey, William Green, and John L. Lewis expressed similar sentiments. Dr. Joseph Mayne of the National Council of Christians and Jews noted that "in Bishop Haas one of the truly great Christian gentlemen of this era has come to Grand Rapids." Catholics in Wisconsin were particularly enthusiastic. "In the hearts of millions of workers there is joy," the *Milwaukee Catholic Herald-Citizen* declared, "because their friend, Father Haas, has received the highest honor the Church can give."[12]

Although Bishop Haas found the ordination ceremonies on November 18 much too elaborate for his simple tastes and the reception too formal, he was gratified by the marks of esteem and honor he received. More than thirty bishops attended the ordination—almost one-third of the American hierarchy—along with hundreds of priests and sisters and over a thousand of the laity, including Governor Harry F. Kelly and Mayor George W. Welsh. Archbishop Amleto Cicognani, the apostolic delegate in Washington, agreed to be principal consecrator, assisted by Archbishops Mooney of Detroit and Kiley of Milwaukee. The ceremony of ordination was indeed impressive. It began with a solemn procession of priests and bishops down the long center aisle of St. Andrew's Cathedral and the recitation of the opening prayers of the Mass in the sanctuary. After a ceremonial examination of the bishop-elect's belief in the fundamental truths of the Catholic faith and his loyalty to the Holy See, Haas was invested with the robes of his new office. Then, at the most solemn moment of the rite, the sacrament of episcopal ordination was conferred through the prayers and imposition of hands of Archbishop Cicognani and the two consecrating bishops, and the new bishop's head and hands were annointed with chrism. Haas then received his episcopal ring, pectoral cross, crosier, and other symbols of his office, and joined Archbishop Cicognani in concelebrating the Solemn Pontifical Mass. Liturgical music throughout the ceremony was provided by St. Joseph's Seminary choir. At the close of the Mass, the archbishop formally installed Haas as bishop of Grand Rapids and the two-hour ceremony was terminated with the new bishop's first pontifical blessing on those present and on all his people in the Diocese of Grand Rapids.[13]

Archbishop Samuel Stritch of Chicago, Haas's former superior in Milwaukee, had been chosen to preach the ordination sermon. He lamented the growing secularism of American culture, "the fallacy, widely propagated in our time, which asserts that religious truth has no bearing on the social conduct of man."[14] This secularization increased the responsibilities of every bishop. "Christian culture," the archbishop declared, "is the reflection of the ministry of the bishops. As his work widens among men, they reflect it in their social, economic, and political living." The new bishop seemed equal to this responsibility. "Bishop Haas takes up his work as a bishop in the Church of God with a rare richness of knowledge and experience. With zeal and intelligence he has labored for a wholeness of Christian living, and resolutely and indefatigably he has opposed the miasmic secularism of our times.... He loves men, and among men he has a particular love for the weak and the helpless, because the Savior in loving all lavishes His love on the weak and the helpless." "To the clergy and laity of the Diocese of Grand Rapids today," the archbishop concluded, "we offer our sincere congratulations. We have known your Bishop as only a bishop can know one of his trusted, exemplary, able priests. To you we say that were we asked to mention the outstanding characteristic of Bishop Haas, unhesitatingly we would say it is his priestliness. He has other qualities which will evoke your love and admiration—his gentleness, his understanding, his fine gifts of mind, and others—but above everything else, you will find in him a pervading priestliness."

Other speakers at formal dinners and receptions honoring the new bishop echoed similar sentiments. Archbishop Cicognani called him "an outstanding authority for settling conflicts and restoring order to troubled circles" and pointed out that his life "has always been illuminated by his great love of his fellow men." At a special civic reception he was formally welcomed to the city and the state by Mayor Welsh and Governor Kelly. Representatives of the Catholic clergy and laity of his new diocese pledged their support and cooperation. Of all the tributes he received, however, the one he cherished most, by his own admission, was that of Monsignor Ryan. For over twenty years Ryan had been a friend, an associate, and an inspiring example. Now, at the age of seventy-four and nearing the end of his illustrious career, he had made the long trip to Grand Rapids to honor his former student. In his few remarks at the ordination luncheon, he recalled the progress the American Church had made in its social justice crusade over the past twenty-five years, and with wry humor alluded solemnly to "that great episcopal pronouncement of 1940, entitled 'The Church and Social Order,'" which he and Haas had helped to write. He praised the new bishop for his life of service to his fellow man, his defense of the rights of workers, and especially his "courageous and prudent efforts...to abolish the cruel and unchristian discrimination practiced against job-seeking Negroes." "Your Excellency," Ryan concluded that afternoon, "those who have been associated with you in Washington for almost a quarter of a century, cannot bid you good-bye without deep and poignant regret."[15]

The new bishop's response was evidence of his easy humor, his abiding interest in social justice, and his deep respect for his new responsibilities. "I hardly know how to begin," he noted with a smile. "Actually this is the first time I have ever been a bishop, and everything is so new to me." He expressed his gratitude and appreciation to those who were present and to many who were absent, and then continued solemnly:

> In all essentials the bishop's duties are not different from those of the Savior who taught as one having authority. Assuredly the bishop must teach the moral law, and in its entirety. He and the clergy may not limit their teaching activity to those concerning the relations of spouse to spouse, or parent to children, or of child to parents, but must embrace the entire field of relations of man to man, in industry, in business, in race, in international affairs, because wherever a man lives there the moral law has jurisdiction.
>
> *Funiculus triplex non facile rumpitus.* (Eccl. 4, 14). A threefold cord is not easily broken. The three strands of the Church are the Bishop, the clergy and the laity. When they cooperate cordially and are fully confident they can depend on one another they are not only not easily broken, but they cannot be broken at all. They unite to the benefit of one another and to that of the entire body. This was the spectacle that called forth the wonder of the early pagans, "See how these Christians love one another."[16]

As bishop of Grand Rapids, Haas changed little from what he was before. He was most comfortable, first of all, with traditional beliefs. He had never publicly questioned the theological teachings of the Church, he had been conscientious in his obedience to papal encyclicals and in his loyalty to the Holy See, and he expected other Catholics to be the same. He insisted, in conformity to canon law, that only officially approved theology be taught in the seminary, and he wanted his diocese characterized by acceptance of the Church's teachings on Sunday Mass, regular confession, abstinence on Friday, opposition to divorce, and adherence to a strict moral code.[17] When a young man, divorced from his Catholic wife, wrote to ask if it were possible for him to marry a second time, the bishop's answer was firm:

> These being the facts in your case, I wish to say it as plain as I can that although you have a civil divorce from your first wife, in the eyes of the Catholic Church she is still your wife. Consequently, no other Catholic woman can in conscience marry you either inside or outside the Catholic Church. If you and another Catholic woman were to present yourselves for marriage before either a civil magistrate, a non-Catholic clergyman, or any one else, there would be simply no marriage at all as far as the Catholic party is concerned.
>
> Indeed, in this case the Catholic woman, according to the teachings of the Church, would be entering into a relationship that would be nothing more or less than adultery. This judgment may sound harsh to you, but it is exactly what the Catholic party knows to be the truth as taught her by Almighty God speaking through His Church.
>
> Accordingly, I make but one request of you. Stop seeing the Catholic young woman in question who has been so weak and so unthinking as to receive your attentions. Do not outrage her conscience and ruin her whole future by talking her into a marriage which as she knows only too well is only a "make believe" marriage. I beg of you to do the honorable thing—honorable to yourself and honorable to the young woman—and "break up" with her at once.

Haas also had deep respect for authority. He willingly sought advice from close friends and associates, but once a decision was reached he expected acceptance and obedience. He presumed parishioners would follow their parish priests and that the clergy and laity would follow him, just as he followed and was obedient to Rome. His various assignments and changing ministries in the thirty years of his priesthood, including his appointment to Grand Rapids, confirmed his sense of obedience, even at times at the cost of personal sacrifice and departure from work he loved. He had little tolerance for public criticism of Church leaders and he refused to take issue with his fellow priests or bishops in public. He continued, as bishop, to receive requests for comments on the opinions and activities of Father Coughlin, but in his respect for the priesthood he always found an excuse to decline.[18]

The bishop's daily schedule soon became routine, and in broad outline it was not unlike the seminary regime he had lived in Milwaukee twenty years before. His episcopal residence was on Lake Drive, in southeast Grand Rapids. He arose about seven o'clock, spent a half hour at prayer, then offered Mass in the chapel with the sisters who cooked and kept house for him. After a substantial breakfast, alone or with a guest, he spent a few minutes with the morning papers, then returned to his first floor office to review the mail and begin his daily appointments. On most weekdays he drove late in the morning to the Chancery Office, next to the cathedral, to meet with diocesan officials and to be available for appointments from noon to one o'clock. If no appointments were scheduled, he often spent the time at prayer in a quite corner of the church. After a light lunch with the priests at St. Andrew's rectory or at his episcopal residence, he retired to his room to relax for forty-five minutes before returning to his office for his afternoon appointments. Supper was served at six o'clock, preceded usually by a half hour of prayer in the chapel. He retired to his office or room about eight o'clock, to continue work he had not completed during the day or to read some recent work in economics or history or one of his favorite literary classics. Many of his days, of course, did not fit this routine but were interrupted by formal luncheons or dinners to mark civic or religious occasions. He was often uncomfortable at these formal affairs, especially during his first years in Grand Rapids, and occasionally asked one of his assistants to represent him, but he understood that many commitments could not be delegated and that such public appearances could be an excellent means of familiarizing himself with his diocese. But he seemed more comfortable with a well-ordered schedule and he preferred a minimum of interruptions and outside commitments.

If the new bishop felt more secure with traditional beliefs and uninterrupted schedules, he also remained friendly, approachable, and understanding. He kept in close touch with his family, returned to Racine as commitments permitted each year, and always encouraged nieces, nephews, and cousins to visit whenever they were in Michigan. Never a loner, he visited the elderly in the Catholic nursing homes of the diocese, enjoyed meeting informally with the students and faculty at St. Joseph's Seminary, and looked forward to relaxing evenings over drinks and a cigar with his fellow priests in a parish rectory. By 1943 he had given up tennis as too strenuous, but continued to enjoy an occasional round of golf, though more for relaxation and exercise than for skill or expertise. During his first year in Grand Rapids he established close friendship with several priests of the diocese—Thomas Noa, Edmund Falicki, Anthony Arszulowicz, Joseph Walen, Charles Salatka, and a few others—and it was to them that he turned frequently for advice and in whose company he could relax most comfortably.[19]

Haas was not unmindful of his own idiosyncrasies and foibles. Somewhat overweight and uncoordinated, he could be uncomfortable and even ungraceful presiding at religious ceremonies. "If he did not look like an unmade bed when he came to the altar," a priest-friend remarked, "he was close." He was frequently forgetful, and on his return from trips would often have to write back for pills, a hat, or book that he had left behind. He returned with hotel keys from Puerto Rico on two occasions. He sometimes drove through Grand Rapids apparently oblivious of traffic lights, and neglected to shift out of first or second gear. Conscious of his own imperfections, he was understanding and forgiving with others. When the seminary faculty voted to expel a student because he did not seem qualified for the priesthood, despite several years of training, Haas was disturbed by the possible injustice in retaining the young man in the seminary that long and then denying him his goal. On another occasion, the seminary rector informed Haas that a student, basically good but difficult to control, had "broken every rule in the book." The bishop retorted with a smile: "Then write some more." When he made mistakes or lost his patience or showed displeasure in public, he was not above telephoning an hour or two later to apologize and give assurance that no hurt was intended.[20]

Even the bishop's closest friends, however, admit that his administration was unimaginative. He was a scholar and an intellectual but his personal studies were always within the guidelines of Church teachings and he rarely struggled with new discoveries or innovative theories. His administration was safe rather than experimental. His goal was to make current structures work more effectively rather than test new ones. The local parish remained the basic ecclesiastical unit, diocesan organizations and activities were to have the support of all, the seminary curriculum and order of the day admitted little variation, channels of authority were to be respected, and centralization of diocesan control in the bishop, the chancellor, and the appointed consultors was unchanged. More liberal ideas which were being discussed elsewhere and which would be accepted by the Church in the late 1950s and throughout the 1960s—increased participation of the laity in parish administration, ecumenical cooperation, modernization of the religious life, a more collegial approach to Church governing—received little public discussion in Grand Rapids during Haas's administration. The diocese, under Haas, continued the past—efficiently and with genuine benefit to many—rather than embarking upon the new. This was clearly the direction that Haas desired for his diocese and the direction with which he felt most comfortable, and it was probably the one preferred by Rome and by the majority of French, Italian, Irish, Polish and German Catholic families in his diocese.

Despite these limited and even conservative goals of the new bishop and the difficulties of wartime and postwar economic conditions, genuine advances were made during Haas's ten years as bishop. It is not surprising that one of the first concerns of this former director of the National Catholic School of Social Service was the care of the dependent and neglected of his diocese, especially children and the aged. Soon after his arrival in Grand Rapids, he initiated discussions with the Carmelite Sisters of the Divine Heart of Jesus to urge them to open and staff a home for the aged. Bishop Haas had long been familiar with their work, since their motherhouse was in Milwaukee and they operated ten similar homes across the country, one in nearby Detroit. The diocese agreed to undertake a loan of $300,000, which the sisters would repay, to purchase suitable property at the corner of Wealthy Street and Madison Avenue in Grand Rapids and to remodel the structure there, and on August 21, 1944, less than a year after his consecration, the bishop announced plans to open the home as soon as the wartime restrictions on construction materials were removed. Due to long delays caused by postwar inflation and other diocesan needs, it was not until August 1950, that the property was purchased, and St. Ann's Home for the Aged opened for approximately fifty residents two years later. Civic officials admitted that care of the elderly lagged behind other social services in western Michigan, and they were grateful for the bishop's initiative in founding St. Ann's Home.[21]

During these same months in which he first approached the Carmelite sisters about a home for the aged, he also took preliminary steps to expand the diocese's care for needy and neglected children. In March 1944 he transferred Father Joseph Walen from the faculty of St. Joseph's Seminary and asked him to pursue graduate studies in social work at Loyola University in Chicago. Father Walen received his master's degree in June 1946 and was immediately appointed diocesan director of Catholic Charities and superintendent of St. John's Home, an orphanage operated by the diocese since 1890. In May of the following year, Bishop Haas announced erection of a new diocesan agency, the Catholic Service Bureau, whose purpose, according to its constitution, was "to rehabilitate individuals and families who are, or who are liable to become, dependent; to undertake directly or indirectly the removal of preventable causes of dependency or delinquency in children and families; to centralize, coordinate and standardize diocesan social services; [and] to provide foster care for dependent or neglected children in free, boarding, wage or adoptive homes." Father Walen was appointed director of this new agency also.[22]

With the establishment of the Catholic Service Bureau, care of needy children improved markedly. Conscious of the need for trained professionals in welfare work, the bishop insisted that only fully qualified personnel be employed in the child welfare programs of the diocese. To assure an adequate professional staff, he inaugurated a scholarship program under which students who received educational assistance from the diocese would agree to serve the Bureau for two years after receiving their master's degrees. Altering the emphasis in the agency's work, in keeping with recent social theory, the Bureau reduced by half the number of children cared for at St. John's Home but tripled the number of children placed in foster homes. To aid the professional staffs in their liaison work with the public, Bishop Haas named prominent laymen and women of the diocese to a board of advisors for the Bureau in its central office in Grand Rapids and in its branch office in Muskegon. In 1948 the Catholic Service Bureau was admitted to membership in the Community Chest of both Grand Rapids and Muskegon, and by 1953, the year of Haas's death, the Bureau was caring for approximately 140 children annually, two-thirds in foster homes and one-third at St. John's Home; was offering assistance and counsel to more than fifty unmarried mothers annually; and had placed 150 children for permanent adoption during the past five years. In no way averse to relying on public assistance, Bishop Haas financed approximately half of the Bureau's work through funds from the Community Chest and the other half through diocesan collections and other activities. Of the latter, the most important was the annual Orphans' Supper, which always had the bishop's generous support and was one of the major social events of the year for Catholics of Grand Rapids.[23]

A third minority which absorbed the bishop's pastoral concern during these years was the Mexican American community which sought work on the beet farms and peach orchards of western Michigan each spring and summer. In the fall of 1947, Bishop Haas approved a proposal to build a mission church in Grant, near the center of the Mexican American population, and this church, dedicated to Our Lady of Guadalupe, was completed the following summer. On at least two occasions the bishop sent his own checks, for $200 and $300, to assist with the building. To emphasize the importance of the ministry to this traditionally Catholic minority, the bishop also appointed Father Aloysius Ulanowicz of nearby Newaygo as his diocesan representative in this apostolate. To provide religious services closer to Grand Rapids, the bishop two years later inaugurated a special Mass for Mexican Americans in the basement chapel of the cathedral, and this modest beginning soon gave rise to a Mexican American benevolent society which provided various services for those in need. By 1952 the mission at Grant was serving a Mexican American summer population of approximately 600. It remained open year round for services for its English-speaking congregation, and it received generous contributions from the bishop's special collection for the needs of the diocese.[24]

Although Bishop Haas was able to continue his civil rights work for the government in a limited way, he inaugurated few new programs specifically for Black Americans residing in his diocese. With a shortage of priests to minister to such a wide area, the bishop was forced to assign his clergy almost exclusively to areas of highest Catholic concentration—and frequently lamented that his resources were inadequate even for this—but only a small minority of Black Americans at this time were Catholic. The bishop made use of whatever opportunities became available, however. When nineteen Black converts were prepared for baptism at St. Ann's Church in Baldwin in 1946, the bishop made the trip to baptize them personally (along with seven white converts), in an impressive ceremony witnessed by approximately 300 friends and neighbors, most of whom were also Black. Such occasions, however, were rare. He accepted appointments to state and municipal civil rights agencies, urged his priests not to neglect the Black Americans within their jurisdiction, and forbade all discrimination in his diocesan institutions; but with a large proportion of

Catholics neglected because of the limited number of priests, ministry to Black residents of the diocese, most of whom were not Catholic, was not given priority.[25]

If Bishop Haas's ten years in government service had made him sensitive to the needs of minorities, his twenty-five years on college and seminary faculties had deepened his appreciation of Catholic education. While making plans for the building of St. Ann's Home for the Aged and for the establishment of the Catholic Service Bureau in the spring and summer of 1944, he inaugurated two fund-raising campaigns, of $750,000 each, to expand the facilities of the Catholic high schools of Grand Rapids and Muskegon. These campaigns were planned to coincide with the government's Sixth War Loan Drive that fall, and Catholics of the diocese were urged to purchase government bonds, which would then be turned over to the high school building fund, aiding both the national war effort and the educational needs of the diocese. The bishop estimated that over 1,500 students in Grand Rapids and 600 in Muskegon were excluded from Catholic education because of lack of facilities, and thus a massive campaign seemed essential.[26]

In his formal address that opened the high school campaign, the bishop summarized his high estimation of Catholic education:

> First, for whom are Catholic schools maintained? To be sure, they are maintained primarily for children. Others, as I shall indicate, have a stake in these schools, but the children benefit before all others. We say in the campaign slogan simply that the campaign is "For *Their* Tomorrow."
>
> We want them to be fully equipped in the cultural arts, in language, in mathematics, in history, in laboratory science and the rest, so that they can make an honorable living in the professions and industries, and play a respected part in community activities....
>
> But a child has right to even more than this. He has a conscience as well as a mind. True, he must be taught about things outside himself. But he must be taught about himself no less. In fact, unless the school can answer the questions which the youth is constantly turning over in his mind, "Where did I come from?" "What am I here for?" "Why should I restrain my passions?" "Why should I live an upright life?" the school is deluding the youth and is deluding itself.
>
> These are questions of religion, and religion alone can answer them. They are of such basic importance that Catho-

lics are willing to make any sacrifice to have them properly answered and to have the answers grained into the lives of their children. . . .

Justice in its original sense of righteousness is the goal. Justice to God to pay Him the debts of homage and love, justice to one's parents to repay them so far as it can be done for their care and sacrifice, justice to the community whereby each person contributes to public well-being in proportion to his wealth and natural gifts—this is the noble virtue which the Catholic school seeks to make the dominant passion of every child committed to its care. Do America and Grand Rapids and Greater Muskegon need such citizens? Here, I submit, they are and I make bold to say that the youths who follow through on the training they received in the Catholic school are essential to our public life, its honor and its bulwark. Indeed, our whole country and our city have a stake in the child in the Catholic school.[27]

The planning and organization of the High School Development Fund had been careful and thorough. The drive was to continue four weeks, from November 20 to December 17, and 2,500 workers had been selected to make a door-to-door canvass of Catholics in the city's sixteen parishes. The bishop insisted that the drive was more than financial. "Its purpose is basically religious," he stated in a pastoral letter. "It aims to enable the Church better to carry out the command given it by Christ: 'Go, teach all nations.' In this sense the drive should be regarded as a vast city-wide religious crusade." Response to the bishop's plea was enthusiastic. By early December, five parishes had met or exceeded their goal, and nine others were close. The drive was the largest financial undertaking in the history of the diocese, and it was a jubilant Bishop Haas who announced at its close that, with $835,000 either pledged or donated, the campaign had exceeded its goal by 11 percent. "The spirit of Grand Rapids was in the campaign," the bishop declared, "and that spirit triumphed. Catholics worked and gave because it was primarily their project. But our non-Catholic neighbors helped and encouraged us because they recognized in the enterprise something of far-reaching benefit to all."[28]

Almost immediately after the close of this campaign, the bishop began the necessary renovations. In January 1945, with the war continuing and construction materials still restricted, he purchased an apartment complex on La Grave Avenue to provide for expansion. Confident that there would be no immediate postwar recession and that campaign pledges were being fulfilled, the bishop approved construction in 1946. Accommodations for an additional 330 students were provided in West Side Catholic High School and for a further 270 at Catholic Central, about half of them in the high school itself and the others in the renovated St. Andrew's school building across the street. Amid some controversy, the sisters' convent at West Side Catholic was expanded and a new convent was erected on La Grave Avenue for the sisters who taught in both the boys' and girls' high schools on Sheldon Avenue. By the fall of 1947, over $600,000 had been collected from the 1944 pledges, approximately $500,000 of it had been spent, and the city's high school enrollment had increased from 1,175 in 1944 to over 1,780.[29]

This, however, was only a start. In January 1947, while major renovations at Grand Rapids Catholic Central were nearing completion, the bishop launched a campaign in Cheboygan to raise $200,000 to establish a Catholic Central High School there also. One month later he announced that the pledges were $25,000 beyond the projected quota. In the spring of 1951 he broke ground for a further expansion of Catholic Central High School in Grand Rapids: a five-story corner addition for classrooms and laboratories and a new power plant and student cafeteria. In 1952 a second $750,000 campaign was undertaken to complete the renovations which had been begun at Muskegon Catholic Central seven years earlier, and this drive was also a success. In January 1953, only eight months before his death, the bishop announced the opening of a Catholic Central High School Completion Fund campaign for Grand Rapids, with a goal of $1 million, and his people exceeded this figure again, this time by almost a third. The bishop's fund-raising campaigns were so successful, in fact, that he received inquiries from dioceses and institutions as far away as the West Coast.[30]

Despite the success of his high school expansion campaigns, Bishop Haas was concerned about the thousands of children, of grade and high school age, unable to attend Catholic schools. In June 1947 the bishop had met Father George Daly, C.SS.R., founder of the Sisters of Service in Toronto, who had developed a successful program for teaching catechism to the young by correspondence. The bishop was fascinated by the program and soon asked the Dominican Sisters of Marywood Academy to inaugurate a similar program in Grand Rapids. Fifty children from five rural parishes were enrolled in the first year. The program was an immediate success and Haas urged all his pastors to take full advantage of it. The pastors were asked to submit the names of all pupils in their parishes, fourth grade age or above, who were unable to attend Catholic schools, and the sisters then wrote a personal letter to invite each one to join the program. More than half of those contacted enrolled. The sisters sent study outlines, reading materials, magazine articles, and assignments and periodic tests for the students to complete and return for grading. There was no charge to students or parishes since the sisters volunteered their services and the diocese covered all other expenses. By 1952, over 1,300 children were enrolled in this Religion Correspondence Course ("Religion via RFD," some called it), several had been prepared for First Communion or confirmation, and at least two older children had been prepared for baptism. But the children were not the only beneficiaries. The program proved to be "a practical means in numerous instances," the bishop noted, "of bringing religious education not only to the children enrolled in the course, but to entire families." He thus saw it as a further fulfillment of his responsibility to "Go, teach all nations."[31]

Care of the aged and orphans and expansion of the diocesan education program may have been the major interests of Bishop Haas's first years in Grand Rapids, but they were not his only ones. He was also concerned with problems of postwar reconstruction, and gave his full support to national war relief drives, the fund-raising efforts of the St. Vincent de Paul Society, Red Cross campaigns, and Community Chest efforts in each county of his diocese. An outspoken champion of organized labor for over twenty-five years, he could rarely decline invitations to deliver the invocation or say a few words to delegates at labor conventions in Grand Rapids. Ever interested in the education of the clergy, he participated in a Social Action School sponsored by his close friend, Bishop Michael Ready of Columbus, for approximately thirty priests of his own and neighboring dioceses in the summer of 1946. As busy as his years were before his episcopal ordination, his first three years in Grand Rapids were no less crowded and occupied.[32]

With satisfactory progress being made in his high school expansion program and in the care of the dependent through the newly established Catholic Service Bureau, Bishop Haas in 1947 and 1948 turned his attention to other projects. One of these was establishment of the Catholic Information Center by the Paulist Fathers in downtown Grand Rapids. The Paulist Fathers— or the Society of Missionary Priests of St. Paul the Apostle, as it is officially known—was founded in 1858 by Father Isaac Hecker to conduct parish missions and retreats and especially to engage in convert work through preaching, writing, and personal instruction. Its work was well known to Bishop Haas through his close association with Paulist Father John J. Burke at the National Catholic School of Social Service and other Paulists at St. Paul's Seminary near Catholic University in Washington. The Society had recently opened information centers in New York, Boston, Baltimore, San Francisco, and Chicago, when, in early 1947, Bishop Haas invited them to Grand Rapids. In February of that year the bishop agreed to provide a building, the necessary equipment, and salaries for two priests, and the Society agreed to provide two of its members to staff the center, take charge of the half-hour Sunday evening radio broadcast the bishop had purchased the preceding fall, lecture (as requested) in parochial and diocesan schools, assist with parish missions and retreats, and supervise convert instruction throughout the diocese.[33]

The first two priests arrived later that year, property was purchased and remodeled at 329 Monroe Avenue, and the center was blessed by the bishop on June 4, 1948. The first floor contained a small chapel for Mass and confession, a reading room, lecture room, and two consultation offices; the second floor had a small meeting room and diocesan offices; and the priests' living quarters were on the third floor. "The reading room on the first floor," the diocesan newspaper remarked, "has comfortable chairs and bookcases well stocked with books and pamphlets on apologetics. It's a quiet atmosphere that gently calls to 'come in and browse around.' " The Paulist Fathers assisted the local clergy with their regular parochial ministry as needed, were available for counseling and advice in their downtown office, and explained the principal tenets of Catholicism to anyone who inquired, Catholic and non-Catholic alike. In the first three years, more than 200 persons were baptized at the center and approximately 800 Catholics and non-Catholics were given instruction. In the spring of 1953 Bishop Haas transferred the center to larger quarters on Ionia Avenue, equally close to the center of town, and there it remained.[34]

One of the most successful innovations of the bishop's ten years in Grand Rapids was the inauguration of the annual Diocesan Congress. The first, a Tri-State Congress involving Catholic leaders of Michigan, Indiana, and Ohio in 1947, was the joint undertaking of Bishop Haas and the Social Action Department of the NCWC in Washington. Haas called the congress a "vast project for adult education," a means of informing Catholic lay leaders of the Church's social teachings and of emphasizing the need for laymen, women, and young people to become more involved in the Church's ministry in hospitals, educational institutions, social and economic life, international affairs, and other areas of concern. The congress was scheduled for September 12 through 16, with prepared addresses, panel discussions, and informal sharing of ideas among recognized experts, bishops, clergy, and laymen and women. The outside speakers included Archbishop Lucey of San Antonio, Jane Hoey of New York, Clem Lane, city news editor of the *Chicago Daily News*, CIO President Philip Murray, Catholic educator George Shuster, and Archbishop Edward Mooney of Detroit. The 1947 Tri-State Congress, the first of its kind in the United States, was a remarkable success—6,000 attended the Solemn Pontifical Mass on the 14th and between 3,000 and 4,000 attended the other sessions—and Haas immediately decided to continue the program each year, exclusively for the Diocese of Grand Rapids.[35]

The bishop's invitation to the 1948 congress, scheduled for October 15–17, stated its goals well. "The purpose of the coming congress," Haas wrote, "is to promote better understanding of Catholic teaching on such vital matters as education, the Confraternity of Christian Doctrine, industrial and rural life, hospitals and charities, and youth."[36] "All the meetings will be open to the public," he noted. "In fact, the public is warmly invited to attend." Sixty addresses and panel discussions were scheduled during the three-day session. Youth delegates heard discussions of careers and vocations in service to others—nursing, law, education, social work, organized labor, journalism, the priesthood and religious life—and they were given an opportunity to discuss their views with recognized authorities. Women learned about volunteer services in the diocese that would not interfere with either their careers or their home responsibilities. Other sessions treated the problems of rural life, labor–management relations, the basis of good citizenship, and the reception of displaced persons. Bishop Haas presided at a Pontifical Mass on Sunday morning, with Auxiliary Bishop Allen Babcock of Detroit preaching, and Haas closed the congress with a final word of appreciation after Benediction that evening.

The 1949 congress provided similar topics—"Religion and Citizenship," "The Catholic Woman in the Community," "Problems of Unemployment," "Young Adults," and "Rural Life"—and it was estimated that approximately five thousand attended each day's session. The 1950 congress again discussed the traditional areas of Church concern—rural life, education, social action, family life—and provided information on diocesan agencies through which Catholics could become further involved in the Church's social ministry: Confraternity of Christian Doctrine, St. Vincent de Paul Society, and the diocesan Councils of Catholic Men and Women. The theme of the 1951 congress was the family, with sessions on "Women in Family Life," "A Living Wage for Decent Family Living," "Recreation in Family Life," and "Helps for Family Life on the Farm." Bishop Haas delivered the sermon at the final Pontifical Mass, on Christian marriage: "Christ in the Family."[37]

These congresses gave expression to the bishop's interest in education and his dedication to social justice, and he gave them his full support, taking an active part in their preparation and appointing one of his closest associates, Monsignor Edmund Falicki, as general chairman. He knew from personal experience (as few others could know) how little an individual priest or bishop could accomplish in labor relations and civil rights and how necessary it was to have the participation of well-educated and highly motivated laymen and women. The congresses provided excellent educational opportunities and gave the clergy and laity a chance to share ideas on areas of mutual interest. The bishop was understandably gratified that the participants each year numbered in the thousands.

The year 1948 was probably the busiest and most satisfying of Bishop Haas's ten years in Grand Rapids. His Catholic Service Bureau assumed responsibility for the care of neglected and dependent children, and for the first time received funds from the Community Chest campaigns of both Grand Rapids and Muskegon. The Catholic Information Center opened that summer, and the bishop's Religion Correspondence Course was successfully inaugurated. The First Diocesan Congress was held that fall, and in April the Grand Rapids chapter of Serra International had been established with the bishop's support. The twofold purpose of this organization was (and is) to foster vocations to the priesthood and provide a structure to encourage participation by Catholic men in the work of the diocese. Later that fall, again at the request of Bishop Haas, the Grand Rapids chapter of Te Deum International was founded to sponsor reliable Catholic speakers throughout the diocese to counteract inaccurate or misleading statements heard occasionally on local platforms.[38]

Two other interests that occupied much of Bishop Haas's time that year and bore fruit in its final months were the establishment in September of the local diocesan newspaper, the *Western Michigan Catholic*, and the convoking of a diocesan synod three months later. Until this time, the Detroit diocesan weekly, the *Michigan Catholic*, also served the Grand Rapids community, carrying international, national, and local Michigan news, with a page or half page each week devoted to events in western Michigan. By 1948, however, Bishop Haas had decided to begin his own paper. "The diocesan newspaper will make it possible," he stated, "for our people to obtain complete reports of international, national, and especially diocesan news. It will also enable our many families in rural areas without Catholic schools to obtain doctrinal information to supplement the catechetical work of the pastors. The paper will serve to strengthen Catholic life in all of our parishes by assisting the efforts of the priests in having a well-informed laity."[39] National and international news stories still came from the *Michigan Catholic* office in Detroit, but diocesan news would be entirely in the hands of the Grand Rapids office. The first issue of the paper appeared September 16, with Father Joseph Walen, the bishop's close collaborator and director of the Catholic Service Bureau, as its editor. The bishop, however, did not intend the paper to be an independent voice. "Frankly," he stated in the opening editorial, *"The Western Michigan Catholic* will be first, last, and all the time a Catholic paper. It will seek to make God's truth, revealed to mankind through the Catholic Church, better known and better loved." The paper was in many ways similar to other diocesan weeklies—especially the Detroit paper, on which it depended for much of its news—but, reflecting the views of its editor and bishop, it was more liberal and outspoken than most on issues of social justice, labor relations, and civil rights.

On December 28 of that same year, Bishop Haas presided at only the second diocesan synod in the history of Grand Rapids. (A synod is a consultative convocation of the clergy of a diocese to discuss disciplinary and liturgical regulations, although only acceptance, approval, and promulgation by the bishop gives them official sanction.) Bishop Haas and a committee of his close associates had drawn up a list of tentative regulations earlier that year and had sent copies to every priest in the diocese. Local meetings were then organized in each deanery to discuss this draft and suggest revisions. The synod of December 28, consequently, was a three-hour meeting of all the clergy of the diocese to hear the official promulgation of the ninety-six regulations the bishop had accepted and approved. Most of them concerned the care of church facilities, administration of the sacraments, clerical salaries, and minor disciplinary regulations. Any priest who wished to deliver a public discourse in the diocese, for example, or any Grand Rapids priest desiring to speak in another diocese, was required to submit a draft of the address for the bishop's "previous examination." The bishop's permission was also required before publication of "writings or discourses in newspapers, pamphlets, or periodicals concerning social or political questions or concerning civil or ecclesiastical policy." Statute 16 was of particular interest: "Unless approved by Us for this purpose, clergy and religious are not permitted in Our territory to be arbitrators in controversies or disagreements of workers, either among themselves or with their employers, nor are they in general to become publicly involved in settling controversies of this kind."[40] The bishop knew from personal experience the intricacies of this work and he insisted that any priest who intervened in such controversies have the necessary scholarly understanding and negotiating expertise.

After five and a half years as bishop of Grand Rapids, Haas was scheduled to make his first *ad limina* visit to Rome in 1949. According to the Code of Canon Law, each residential bishop, throughout the world, was to make an official visit to Rome every five or ten years (depending on distance), and after the six-year disruption of World War II, 1949 was decided upon for the visits of the American bishops. Each bishop, first of all, was to visit and pray at the tombs of the apostles Peter and Paul *(ad limina apostolorum* means "to the threshold of the apostles"), meet personally with the Holy Father, and present an official report on the state of his diocese to the Consistorial Congregation, the Vatican department directly concerned with diocesan administration.[41] Haas also took advantage of this visit to make short trips to Germany and Ireland, both to visit the homelands of his parents and to seek information of special concern to his diocese.

The bishop left Grand Rapids on April 25 and sailed from New York on the *Queen Elizabeth* two days later. After spending a few days in England, he crossed the Channel into West Germany

and devoted several days to visiting displaced person camps near
Frankfurt, Fulda, and Munich. During the preceding June, he had
received a letter from a relative he had met in Germany at the time
of an international peace conference in 1929:

> It has been almost nineteen years since you visited us on
> the occasion of the Catholic Congress in Freiburg. Since
> then we have often talked about that visit, but we do not
> even know, whether you are still alive. However we hope so.
> ... Our beautiful village was spared by the war, but the
> poverty is now worse than during the war.
> There are only three families left by the name of Haas, the
> Hug family is extinct. We do not exactly suffer starva-
> tion. However, we are in extreme need of shoes and working
> clothes for men and women. All would be bearable, except
> this shortage and the lack of underwear.
> Dear Professor Haas, it takes a whole lot of self-effacement
> to beg. Moreover, you mentioned on the occasion of your
> visit that our relatives in America are mostly poor people,
> who have to work hard. We find it, therefore, rather difficult
> to beg.
> But, maybe it will be possible for you to secure some of
> the above mentioned articles. We should be happy to pay
> for them, but our money is without value.[42]

Haas had replied immediately. He sent them information
about his episcopal consecration and three CARE packages,
and now, one year later, he had an opportunity to examine
conditions in Germany firsthand. He had long been interested in
the problems of postwar reconstruction and he was bishop of a
diocese with many German and Eastern European immigrant
families. He was especially interested in displaced persons. After
his brief visit to Germany, he wrote to his people in Grand Rapids:

> The families and unmarried adults in the camps in the
> American Zone, which are usually former German Army
> training barracks, are living from day to day on the charity of
> the United States Government, and on other charities, not
> the least of which are the free-will offerings of our own
> Catholic people. The persons in these camps are suffering far
> less than they did in the homes which they were forced to
> leave. Actually, they have enough to eat and wear, although
> their living quarters are far from adequate. In many cases two

or more families are crowded into a single room. But they suffer far deeper hardship than improper shelter. They are, for the most part, without any hope for the future. I sincerely trust our Michigan people will ask for them and pledge for them in far greater numbers than they have done in the past.

All in all, the civilian population looks fairly healthy and prosperous, both in France and Germany. The Marshall Plan is having the desired result. While business is not booming, there appears everywhere new activity, and the faces of people do not bear the look of strain and emaciation. There is, of course, a vast amount of poverty, not all of it is the product of the last war, nor even that of 1914. Here indeed is the challenge for social minded Christians, both individuals and government officials.[43]

From Germany, Haas proceeded to Rome, offered Mass at the tomb of St. Peter in the crypt of the Vatican basilica, visited other shrines throughout the city, and discussed affairs of his diocese with members of the Vatican Curia and their staffs. Although his official report to the Vatican on the state of his diocese was confidential, Haas could describe at least moderate growth and expansion since 1943. But a key statistic must have been that the number of priests in the diocese had increased from 190 to only 195, and growth in the number of parishes, missions, and other ministries was necessarily restricted to the number of priests available. The Catholic population had increased from 93,000 to more than 110,000, seven new parishes had been erected, and the number of children attending Catholic schools had risen from 13,500 to 16,000. New diocesan agencies had been inaugurated—the Catholic Service Bureau, the Diocesan Information Center, the *Western Michigan Catholic*, and the annual Diocesan Congress—and after five years of wartime scarcity the bishop had enlarged and renovated several diocesan facilities and had built twelve new churches, six elementary schools, eight new convents, and perhaps the same number of parish rectories, in addition to the largest high school building program in the history of the diocese.[44]

At the end of his Roman visit, the bishop had his long-awaited audience with Pope Pius XII. They discussed the status of the Church in the United States and especially in Grand Rapids, and probably the conditions of displaced persons in Germany, a problem of deep interest to both, since the Holy Father had been papal nuncio to Germany for several years before his election to the papacy. Haas pledged the continued loyalty of his diocese to the Holy Father and received an apostolic blessing for all the clergy and laity of Grand Rapids in return. Although the visit was brief and probably less than spontaneous because of the difference in languages, for someone of Haas's devotion to the Holy See his private audience was an impressive and memorable experience. At its conclusion, Haas quickly completed his other business and left Rome immediately for France, Ireland, and the return voyage home.[45]

The bishop was concerned that the Catholic population of his diocese had increased approximately 20 percent during the past six years while the number of priests had increased less than 3 percent, and he hoped to take steps on his trip to Europe to remedy this situation. The principal purpose of his trip to Ireland, besides a sentimental visit to the homeland of his mother's family, was to discuss with Irish seminarians the possibility of working as priests in Grand Rapids. "After I left Rome," Haas wrote Ireland's ambassador to the Vatican, "I spent some five days in Ireland. His Excellency, the Most Reverend Archbishop of Dublin, was exceedingly kind to me. He arranged for me to visit All Hallows, and the Seminarians at Kilkenny and Carlow. I did not accomplish what I went to Ireland for, that is, to get some seminarians. Nevertheless, the journey was profitable, and I am sure will, as we Americans say, 'pay off.' " He was more specific in a letter to an acquaintance in Mayo:

> Regarding seminarians, here is the information that the students in the Diocesan College may want: I should like to have a half a dozen or so young men who have completed their philosophy course. That is they ought to be ready to enter upon the study of Theology in our own theological seminary in Detroit, to complete their work for the priesthood in four years. The students need not be the pick of the class, but on the other hand, I do not want those who are just 'getting by.' I think any young man will understand what I mean.[46]

Although his efforts to recruit seminarians in Ireland were unsuccessful, his search for assistance in Europe may not have been in vain. Shortly after his return, the bishop began to accept displaced priests from Eastern Europe into his diocese, many of them Lithuanian, and by 1952 an exiled bishop and seventeen displaced priests were serving in the Grand Rapids diocese.[47]

It was to remedy this shortage of clergy and to assist in the spread of the Catholic faith in western Michigan that Bishop Haas decided to undertake a special diocesan fund-raising campaign each spring. Each elementary and high school sponsored its own campaign for this "Fund for the Faith," and the major drive consisted of a door-to-door solicitation of each Catholic home. Haas explained the purpose of this annual campaign in early 1950:

> It may come as a surprise to many of our people to learn that the Diocese of Grand Rapids with its nearly 17,000 square miles and its population of more than a million is, when all is said and done, only a missionary Diocese. Actually, the ratio of our Catholic population to the total is much less than ten percent. Less than one out of every ten persons is Catholic. The true figure is perhaps one out of every twelve or thirteen. Indeed, there is a missionary job to be done. And this job is not merely for 1950, but for many years to come.
>
> There is no need to go into the reasons why our Catholic population in the Diocese is as small as it is. One obvious reason is that we do not have enough priests to send into smaller communities, to live with the people, and give them daily Mass, instructions, and the sacraments. In many areas where there is a mission church, Mass is offered only once a month. In still others, there is not even a mission church, and, of course, no Mass, no instructions, and no Sacraments. It would be a veritable godsend to such places if we could provide them with a mission chapel and maintain it with a priest until such time as the people themselves could support priest and mission. Under existing conditions the Faith can hardly, if at all, get a foothold in such areas. The result is that whole districts are shut out from the light and grace of God's truth....
>
> The two annual collections of previous years—one for Seminarians and one for Orphans—will not be taken up this year. In their place a campaign will be held during Pentecost week in every parish, consisting of a house-to-house solicitation, for a two-fold purpose. One will be to secure revenue to care for the needs met in previous years by the Seminary and Orphan Collections. The other will be to provide funds for the orderly and vigorous extension of the Faith throughout the Diocese.[48]

The campaign was carefully organized each year, with workers in each parish recruited and assigned in advance and with specific quotas for each area, and the effort proved most successful. The campaign collected approximately $200,000 each year and enabled the bishop not only to provide for St. John's Home and to assist the education of his seminarians but to undertake special works such as construction of Our Lady of Guadalupe Church in Grant for Mexican Americans and the importation of displaced priests from Europe. For someone uncomfortable with daily financial problems, the successful "Fund for the Faith" each year was indeed a blessing.[49]

Even before his ordination as bishop of Grand Rapids, friends had encouraged Haas to revise and republish his *Man and Society*, but it was not until 1949 and 1950 that he felt able to do this. He understood better than others, of course, the need for revision. The data and statistics in the 1930 edition had come from the middle or late twenties, an era brought to a close by the Great Depression and World War II. The book had recommended minimum wage legislation and public works programs and had urged greater government responsibility for the economy, but the Fair Labor Standards Act of 1938, the WPA of 1935, and the legislation of World War II had altered the whole context of the discussion. The bishop realized that he could not undertake a minute revision personally and he therefore asked several professional acquaintances to assist. He urged Regina Flannery Herzfeld of the Catholic University Department of Anthropology to suggest revisions for chapter I, "The Origin of Man." "Last November," he wrote in May 1949, "you kindly agreed to read Chapter I of my *Man and Society* and to patch it up wherever it needs patching up. Well, here it is, and I ask you to do whatever you think should be done with it— short of throwing it in the ash can." He asked Catherine Schaefer of the NCWC Office of United Nations Affairs to revise the chapter on international relations. He suggested that she retain as much as possible of the original but correct whatever was false and bring the data and references up to date and in line with recent studies. He also asked her to note her revisions in the margins, so that he could compare them with the original text and make the final decisions himself.[50]

The bishop devoted many hours throughout 1950 and early 1951 to this revision, and when it was republished in 1952 it retained, as he wanted, most of the material from the original. In the chapter "The Problem of Wages" he noted that minimum wage legislation was now the law of the land, and he included further discussion of the mechanics of wage determination, the role of conciliation and arbitration, and the economic lessons of the National Recovery Administration and other New Deal agencies. Since the 1930 edition preceded Pope Pius XI's encyclical *Quadragesimo Anno* by one year, Haas included in the 1952 revision two new chapters, "An Organized Society" and "Functions of an Industry Council System." In the section "The State in Its Relation to Other States," he elaborated on the work of the League of Nations in the 1930s, included a favorable discussion of the United Nations, and expanded his earlier arguments in favor of some form of world organization.[51] But these were the only major changes he made, indicating that, after a quarter of a century, his views had remained approximately the same, and perhaps that he had been ahead of his time in the 1920s in championing such issues as social secutity, minimum wage legislation, federal protection of the right to organize, increased government intervention in the economy, and the need for a stronger and more effective world organization. But the book was a work of social ethics as much as sociological investigation, and for Haas, ethical and moral precepts did not change.

By 1953, Bishop Haas could look back on ten busy but satisfying years in Grand Rapids. That period throughout the country had been one of reconstruction, rebuilding, and returning to normal living after unsettled years of depression and war. Servicemen returned to college campuses or civilian employment, families were reunited, wives and mothers left industrial jobs to return to their homes and families, and stability was gradually reestablished throughout society—at least as much stability as the inflation of 1946, the recession of 1949, and the Korean War of 1950 would permit. Bishop Haas presided over this postwar reconstruction of his diocese effectively. New churches were constructed, schools were expanded, long-delayed renovations were undertaken, and special efforts were made to cope with the problems of a shortage of priests and an increasingly mobile population. His administration was not innovative or original, but neither were most other diocesan administrations throughout the country. In fact, stability, prudent reconstruction, and a return to familiar religious practices, not innovation and originality, may have been what the people of Grand Rapids desired.

The bishop could be proud of the progress that had been made. The Catholic population had increased from 93,000 to 127,000, the number of priests from 190 to 240, and the number

258

of pupils in Catholic schools from 13,500 to over 19,000.[52] The annual diocesan congresses, the Catholic Service Bureau, the enlarged Catholic Central High School System, the Catholic Information Center, St. Ann's Home for the Aged, the Fund for the Faith, and the *Western Michigan Catholic* were tangible evidence of growth and vitality. The bishop bore final responsibility for a network of churches, schools, hospitals, and other facilities valued in the tens of millions of dollars. He visited parishes, administered the sacraments, presided at religious celebrations, and as the highest official of the Catholic Church in western Michigan, he represented the diocese at countless interfaith gatherings, civic receptions, and other public ceremonies. Guidance of the sprawling diocese was an absorbing responsibility, and since Haas had no auxiliary bishop during his ten years in Grand Rapids, he could delegate very few of his episcopal duties to others.[53] He had not sought the bishopric, he had accepted the assignment to Grand Rapids out of a sense of duty and obedience to the Holy See, and he was rarely comfortable with the duties of administration, but after ten years he could be satisfied that he had acquitted his responsibility well.

12

Social Justice's Elder Statesman, 1943-1953

Soon after the Vatican's announcement of Haas's selection as bishop of Grand Rapids, a reporter asked if he thought he would have to withdraw from government service. "In my new work as Bishop of Grand Rapids," Haas replied, "I will continue to do as I have in the past. I will be available and if I am drafted and feel that I can do a job, I will attempt insofar as I can without interference with my regular duties."[1] These "regular duties," however, could easily have absorbed his attention full time. He was responsible for the religious needs of the more than 90,000 Catholics of his diocese; he oversaw the work of the diocese's many schools, hospitals, and social welfare agencies; he represented the diocese at innumerable public functions throughout western Michigan; and he attempted to coordinate his activities and decisions with those of other members of the American hierarchy, especially those of Michigan, to present a consistent and unified administration.

Although these numerous responsibilities could easily have occupied his years in Grand Rapids full time, Bishop Haas was able to return occasionally to public service at the request of state and federal officials. As one of the Department of Labor's most successful conciliators, he was asked to serve as impartial arbitrator in several industrial disputes in 1944 and 1946; he took part in various labor conferences and conventions (the most notable of which was the ILO conference in Philadelphia in 1946); he was a member of President Truman's Committee on Civil Rights in 1947; and he was chairman of the State Advisory Committee on FEPC Legislation in Michigan in the late 1940s and early 1950s.[2] These government assignments, of course, absorbed much less of his time and attention than those of the preceding years. During his years in Washington and Milwaukee he had been able to delegate many of his ecclesiastical responsibilities and had fre-

259

quently devoted himself almost entirely to public service. After 1943, this was impossible. "Needless to add," Haas had written President Roosevelt in late 1943, "I stand ready to assist you as in the past, in whatever way I can in my new duties as Bishop of the Diocese of Grand Rapids."[3] From 1943 to 1953, however, his "new duties" as bishop had to be the primary concern of his life, and everything else, including government service, was necessarily secondary.

The first arbitration case in which he intervened while bishop of Grand Rapids involved a dispute over seniority rights on the Gulf, Mobile, and Ohio Railroad. When the Mobile and Ohio Railroad merged with the Gulf, Mobile, and Northern in the fall of 1940, some workers had to be released, and the companies decided to retain a proportionate number from each line and to merge departments on this "ratio basis." The Brotherhood of Railway and Steamship Clerks, however, objected to this procedure and demanded that workers be retained according to strict seniority, regardless of the proportion of each company's employees retained.[4] When negotiations failed to resolve the difference, both sides (in October 1943) agreed to submit the controversy to arbitration. The company and the union each selected one member of the arbitration board immediately—D. S. Wright, the company's general solicitor, and L. W. Reigel, union vice president—but when these two could not agree on the choice of a neutral arbitrator, they requested the National Mediation Board to make the selection. The secretary of the Board contacted Haas and the bishop agreed to accept, if the hearings could be delayed until late February. On February 7, 1944, within three months of his episcopal ordination, the National Mediation Board announced the selection of Bishop Haas.

The arbitration board assembled in Mobile, Alabama, on February 25 to begin two days of hearings, with Bishop Haas as chairman. The hearings continued for six hours each day and the testimony seemed to indicate that the majority of workers preferred the strict seniority system. This was the final ruling of the arbitrators. The award, signed by all three, but with Wright dissenting, stated: "The Board finds that the 'chronological' basis will work to the seniority disadvantage of far fewer employees involved in the present controversy than would the 'ratio' basis," and it directed that rosters "be consolidated by dovetailing the names of employees on the basis of their 'chronological' seniority dates." Haas, the neutral arbitrator, had voted with the labor representative, acceding to the union wishes but without imposing serious inconvenience on the railroad.[5]

The second arbitration case that spring, a wage dispute between the Hudson and Manhattan Railroad and the CIO's Utility Workers Organizing Committee, was even less complicated. Only twenty-six workers were involved and the negotiators were less than two cents apart, the union demanding a raise of nine cents an hour and the company offering seven and one-half. When arbitration was agreed upon as the only satisfactory solution, the company selected its general superintendent, J. C. Gieson, as its arbitration member; the union chose Eugene Teeter, national representative of the UWOC; and these two selected Haas. Haas had intervened in a more serious dispute between these same parties over wage rates, overtime, leaves of absence for military service, and grievance machinery a year earlier, and he had impressed both sides with his impartiality. Because of the Gulf, Mobile, and Ohio hearings in Mobile and several commitments in Grand Rapids, Haas announced that he could not be free until April, but the two sides agreed to postpone the hearings to assure his availability.[6]

The bishop presided at public hearings in New York on April 10 and met in executive session with the other members of the arbitration board for the next three days. The union had originally requested an increase of twenty cents an hour and had eventually reduced it to nine cents, while the company would offer no more than seven and a half cents. It was noted during the discussions that a nine-cent increase was not uncommon in this and similar industries (a four-cent-an-hour increase with an additional five cents in lieu of overtime) and that President Roosevelt had approved such a settlement in the rail industry the previous December. On April 13, consequently, Haas announced the board's decision, with the industry representative again dissenting. The award stated that the workers' wage demand seemed justified and would not unduly burden the company, and it therefore granted a nine-cent increase, retroactive to December.[7]

A third controversy broke out in the spring of 1946, a dispute between Detroit's Department of Street Railways and the Street Car Maintenance Workers Association, and Bishop Haas was again asked to intervene. At least twelve issues were in dispute, ranging from paid vacations and night shift differentials to grievance machinery and survivor's insurance, and some were mired in unexpected complications. The workers demanded higher wages, for example, but the department noted that it was prohibited by law from issuing revenue bonds if its property was in debt, and thus it had to avoid a precipitous wage increase which might unbalance its budget. According to the city's charter, such disputes were to be submitted to arbitration, and by agreement of the contending parties Bishop Haas was appointed neutral arbitrator in mid-January. Following his usual procedure, Haas asked the other members—Richard Sullivan for the city and Arnold Dale for the union—to prepare a letter over their signatures, stating the precise issues to be decided and the agreed-upon procedure for voting, and confirming that the award would be accepted by both sides. The letter was drafted and signed on January 31.[8]

The bishop presided at public hearings from February 11 to 15 and spent the next ten days studying the nine hundred pages of transcript and conferring with department and union representatives. On February 26 he announced the board's award. The union won its demand for paid vacations, grievance machinery, and prior notice of all upgrading and demoting, while paid holidays, night shift differentials, and the method of determining overtime were resolved in favor of the department. The wage increase, fifteen cents, was a compromise. The whole award, in fact, was a compromise, and the fact that the union and company representatives dissented from only two of the twelve provisions indicated that, as bishop, Haas was still a successful industrial troubleshooter.[9]

In mid-April 1944, just four days after his return to Grand Rapids from the Hudson and Manhattan Railroad hearings in New York, Bishop Haas was appointed adviser to the American delegation to the International Labor Organization Conference to be held in Philadelphia from April 15 to May 12. The American delegation was composed of Secretary of Labor Frances Perkins and Senator Elbert Thomas of Utah for the government, Henry I. Harriman for industry, and Robert Watt for labor, with Arthur Altmeyer, Charles Taussig, Nelson Rockefeller, and Carter Goodrich (among others) assisting. Two crucial issues before the convention were the relationship between the ILO and any postwar United Nations organization and the jurisdiction of the ILO in discussions of monetary stabilization and national and international fiscal policies, questions which some delegates felt belonged exclusively to national governments. Other topics on the agenda were the right of all peoples to full employment, minimum living standards throughout the world, lifelong medical coverage, and the rights of women in the economy.[10]

The most important accomplishment of the convention was clearly the drafting and approval of the "Declaration of Philadelphia," a statement of the conference's basic goals and principles. The statement opened with the reaffirmation that "labor is not a commodity," that "freedom of expression and of association are essential to sustained progress," and that "poverty anywhere constitutes a danger to prosperity everywhere." The conference affirmed that all human beings, "irrespective of race, creed, or sex," have the right to seek their material and spiritual growth in freedom and dignity and that realization of this goal must be a basic aim of national and international policy and a central concern of the International Labor Organization. The declaration listed among the ILO's specific objectives "full employment and the raising of standards of living," "the employment of workers in occupations in which they can have the satisfaction of giving the fullest measure of their skill and attainments," "the effective recognition of the right of collective bargaining," "the extension of social security measures to provide a basic income to all in need of such protection," and "the assurance of equality of educational and vocational opportunity."[11]

Bishop Haas took a more active part in the deliberations of this conference than in the Havana meeting five years earlier, chiefly through his appointment to the conference's Committee on Dependent Territories.[12] At the first meeting of this committee, the British delegate suggested that a thorough study of the question of dependent nations be undertaken, even if it took three or four years to complete, but other delegates, fearing that this might be a delaying tactic by one of the world's largest colonial powers, opposed the recommendation. Joining some of the smaller nations, Haas spoke in favor of immediate action. On the following day, one of the delegates moved a resolution to encourage all peoples to adopt social and economic progress as an immediate and specific goal, again Haas spoke in favor of it, and the motion carried.

Bishop Haas's major contribution to the conference, however, came toward the end of the sessions. When the Committee on Dependent Territories adopted a report condemning slavery, oppressive labor standards, and racial and religious discrimination, Carter Goodrich asked Haas to make a seconding speech for the United States before the full convention. The former chairman of the FEPC refused to overlook the evils of his own country in his criticism of the shortcomings of others. He began with the admission that he seconded the committee's report "with full consciousness of certain embarrassing facts." "We in the United States," he acknowledged, "have, within our boundaries—and mind you not in distant lands—a tenth of our whole population to whom the other nine-tenths of us deny in varying degrees the exercise of their full rights as human beings. The vast majority of us subject 13,000,000 Negroes endowed by God with an origin and destiny no less sacred than our own to various forms of discrimination, all ending in the same result that these oppressed people are treated [as] less than men and women." He noted, however, that congressional action could establish an agency "which would assure economic equality as a minimum," and he added, overoptimistically, "I am happy to say that sentiment is growing for the creation of such an agency, a permanent Fair Employment Practice Committee."[13]

In the main portion of his speech, the bishop declared that he was not "one of those who hold that imperialism has brought no benefits whatsoever to mankind," and acknowledged that today "countries with empires are making more and more effort to take the peoples of their dependencies into partnership with themselves and to accord them greater and greater measure of their God-given prerogatives." He insisted, however, that much was still to be done and he strongly supported the committee's resolutions. "The forty-six articles of the Committee's report," he concluded, "fall considerably short of the ideal, notably in their failure to provide for inspection. I for one should like to see the articles much more forthright than they are. But while holding to the ideal, we must also be reasonably practical and without saying more, I add my second to the motion."

It was Bishop Haas's opinion, furthermore, that the conference's goals of racial equality, industrial peace, and international cooperation could be satisfactorily guaranteed only if they were founded on religious principles. "The ultimate basis of human dignity," Haas had written fifteen years earlier in *Man and Society*, "is man's eternal destiny." The bishop was disturbed that the ILO conference nowhere affirmed belief in or dependence on a Supreme Being, and he recommended that the name of God be inserted in the charter under discussion. He suggested the simple phrase "invoking the blessing of God on its work," but Miss Perkins and other officials preferred the even shorter "with trust in God." Robert Watt, labor representative on the American delegation, agreed to present the motion to the convention, provided there was no serious opposition. Haas noted in his diary, however, that nine of the eleven South American delegations "threatened to wreck the conference if the name of God is included in the preamble." They cited a provision in the Mexican constitution prohibiting the name of God in any public document. "To which I smiled," Haas's diary continues, "and told Toledano and Carrillo [two of the Latin American delegates] that I was ashamed of Latins."[14] Haas, who had founded his social philosophy on the God-given dignity of every human being, could not disguise his disappointment that the Philadelphia Declaration's excellent program of social justice could not be similarly founded on religious principle and a statement of belief in a Supreme Being.

On his return to Grand Rapids at the close of the conference, the bishop praised the organization's work:

> The Philadelphia ILO conference is over and it has done a good day's work. The three weeks' conference has not done all it set out to do, but I believe that it did do more than it had hoped could be done. There is no point in asking whether it was 95 or 65 or 55% successful because in view of world conditions there is no way of telling what 100 percent is.
>
> The Conference adopted the Philadelphia Charter on Wednesday and it is indeed hopeful that 41 world nations can agree on the splendid principles it set forth. The reports of the committee on social security and territorial dependencies were also adopted, and while their recommendations were not completely adequate, the fact is they were agreed to by the Conference.
>
> One should not forget that the ILO is hewing out its program against terrific odds. Not the least of the obstacles is that the conference is endeavoring during war to make plans as if peace were already here. There are other great drawbacks in the different countries. Nevertheless, the Conference continues with its work and continues to get increasing support for what it is doing.[15]

The praise was guarded, but at a time when many Americans, especially Catholics, openly disapproved of the ILO, the active participation of an American bishop and his public commendation were significant.

Bishop Haas's most important work for the government during these ten years in Grand Rapids, however, was his service on President Truman's Committee on Civil Rights. This committee was established by executive order on December 5, 1946, "to inquire and to determine whether and in what respect current law-enforcement measures and the authority and means possessed by Federal, State, and local governments may be strengthened and improved to safeguard the civil rights of the people." There had been no federal civil rights legislation since 1875, the New Deal had benefited Black Americans only indirectly, the Fair Employment Practices Committee had not been renewed in 1946, and President Truman now insisted that the increasing demands of Black Americans be given conscientious consideration. The fifteen-member committee included Charles E. Wilson of General Electric as chairman; Presidents Frank P. Graham of the University of North Carolina and John S. Dickey of Dartmouth; religious leaders Dorothy Tilly of the Methodist Church, Episcopal Bishop Henry Knox Sherrill, Rabbi Roland B. Gittelsohn, and Bishop Haas; industrialist Charles Luckman of Lever Brothers; attorneys Morris L. Ernst, Francis P. Matthews, and Franklin D. Roosevelt, Jr.; James B. Carey and Boris Shishkin from organized labor; Sadie T. Alexander, assistant city solicitor of Philadelphia; and Channing Tobias, director of the Phelps-Strokes Fund. "The preservation of civil liberties is a duty of every Government—state, Federal, and local," the president told the committee. "Wherever the law enforcement measures and authority of Federal, state, and local governments are inadequate to discharge this primary function of government, these measures and this authority should be strengthened and improved."[16]

The committee met for the first time on January 15 and held nine further meetings throughout the year. The members decided at the first meeting to divide the work, and three subcommittees were appointed in early February: subcommittee 1, with Bishop Sherrill as chairman, was to investigate the adequacy of federal legislation and to recommend new legislation as needed; subcommittee 2, with Charles Luckman as chairman and Bishop Haas, James Carey, Channing Tobias, and Rabbi Gittelsohn as members, was to consider recommendations for additional social, economic, and educational programs; and subcommittee 3, with Morris Ernst as chairman, was to study the work of private organizations whose activities had (or could have) an impact on civil rights. It was further decided that committee meetings would be scheduled on two successive days, with one day devoted to subcommittee meetings and the second to plenary sessions. With one exception, all meetings were held in Washington, usually in the East Wing of the White House or in the National Archives. John Dickey and Franklin D. Roosevelt, Jr., were appointed vice chairmen of the committee in early February and Professor Robert Carr of Dartmouth was named executive secretary.[17]

Bishop Haas worked chiefly as a member of subcommittee 2. At its meeting in early March, the members singled out four main areas for investigation and study: (1) equality in employment and the need for an FEPC; (2) equality in private and public education and the feasibility of withholding federal funds from schools guilty of discrimination; (3) discrimination in the armed services; and (4) inequality in community services, such as housing, recreation, and health facilities.[18] The subcommittee members discussed these issues in three meetings in March and early April, listened to testimony from government and labor officials, supervised the investigations of their research staff, and on April 17 submitted twelve recommendations to the full committee. These recommendations, drafted in part by Bishop Haas and, in the absence of Charles Luckman, presented by him to the full committee, endorsed both state and federal fair employment practices legislation and urged more effective nondiscriminatory hiring and promotion policies within the federal government. They urged full investigation of all federal grant-in-aid programs—to health and social welfare agencies, to veterans' organizations, and to housing and educational programs—and even the withholding of federal funds from institutions that continued to discriminate. They encouraged state legislatures to ban discrimination in "public and private employment, education, health, housing and recreation and places of public accommodation" and urged the "banning of racial restrictive covenants by the courts or by legislation as contrary to public policy." They suggested that preliminary steps be taken in the armed forces "to the end that discrimination in all policies and programs be terminated" and, finally, that some "permanent agency" be established to continue these efforts in civil rights after the work of the committee was completed.[19]

The full committee's final report, published later as *To Secure These Rights*, was submitted to the president on October 29. Almost a century after the Emancipation Proclamation, the committee discovered incidents of involuntary servitude in Alabama, Mississippi, and California, and it noted that even in 1947 "lynching remains one of the most serious threats to the Civil Rights of Americans." The committee decried the use of the poll

tax, the "white primary," and the literacy test to disfranchise
Black voters in many areas of the South. Discriminatory employment practices were also prevalent. "A minority job seeker often
finds that there are fields of employment where application is
futile no matter how able or well trained he is," the report stated,
and it noted further that discrimination did not cease after employment was found. "The average weekly income of white
veterans," it continued, "ranges from 30 to 78 per cent above the
average income of Negro veterans." Discrimination in education
was equally severe: "Therè is a marked difference in quality
between the educational opportunities offered white children and
Negro children in the separate schools. Whatever test is used—
expenditure per pupil, teachers' salaries, the number of pupils per
teacher, transportation of students, adequacy of school buildings
and educational equipment, length of school term, extent of
curriculum—Negro students are invariably at a disadvantage."[20]

The committee's report, after lengthy discussion of discrimination in housing, employment, recreational facilities, public
accommodations, and the armed forces, concluded with thirty-five
recommendations to the president. It urged elevation of the Civil
Rights Section of the Department of Justice to full division status
and establishment of a permanent Civil Rights Commission and of
state and federal Fair Employment Practice committees. It recommended home rule for the District of Columbia, abolition of
the poll tax, and prohibition of lynching by federal statute.
Federal aid to education, public health centers, and similar programs, the committee suggested, should be conditioned "on the
absence of discrimination and segregation based on race, color,
creed, or national origin."[21] The committee urged early statehood
for Alaska and Hawaii, greater self-government for our island
possessions, and removal of all distinctions of race, color, and
national origin from our naturalization laws. The report recommended, finally, a strong presidential mandate abolishing racial
discrimination in the armed forces and in all government employment.

Undoubtedly, the committee's most important recommendation concerned the abolition of racial segregation. The committee
rejected the doctrine, prevalent since *Plessy* v. *Ferguson* in 1896,
that segregation alone does not constitute discrimination:

> The separate but equal doctrine has failed in three im-
> portant respects. First, it is inconsistent with the fundamental
> equalitarianism of the American way of life in that it marks

groups with the brand of inferior status. Secondly, where it has been followed, the results have been separate but unequal facilities for minority peoples. Finally, it has kept people apart despite incontrovertible evidence that an environment favorable to civil rights is fostered whenever groups are permitted to live and work together. There is no adequate defense of segregation.[22]

The committee anticipated objections that desegregation would interfere with personal freedom:

> The Committee is not convinced that an end to segregation in education or in the enjoyment of public services essential to people in a modern society would mean an intrusion upon the private life of the individual. In a democracy, each individual must have freedom to choose his friends and to control the pattern of his personal and family life. But we see nothing inconsistent between this freedom and a recognition of the truth that democracy also means that in going to school, working, participating in the political process, serving in the armed forces, enjoying government services in such fields as health and recreation, making use of transportation and other public accommodation facilities, and living in specific communities and neighborhoods, distinctions of race, color, and creed have no place.[23]

The committee's report was generally well received. President Truman predicted that "it will take its place among the great papers on Freedom." The *New Republic* called it a "magnificent report... a program loftily conceived and brilliantly set forth." "The Committee did a courageous job," the *Harvard Law Review* declared, "and to its members much credit is due."[24] By far the greatest tribute to the committee's work, however, was gradual implementation of most of its recommendations in American public life. In early February 1948, President Truman sent a special message to Congress urging the adoption of many of its proposals, and a similar pledge was inserted in the Democratic platform that fall. The president issued an executive order that year prohibiting racial discrimination in the armed forces and saw commendable progress by the time of the outbreak of the Korean War in 1950. The Supreme Court, in *Brown* v. *Board of Education*, in 1954 struck down the "separate but equal" doctrine in public education. In 1957 a permanent Civil Rights Commission was established, the Civil Rights Section of the Department of Justice was raised to division level, and by 1961, nineteen states had enacted Fair Employment Practice legislation. Racial discrimination in employment, voting, and public accommodations was forbidden in the Civil Rights Act of 1964 and the Voting Rights Act of 1965. Federal funds were ordered withheld from schools and hospitals guilty of discrimination in 1964, and the Equal Employment Opportunity Commission was established that same year. Bishop Haas's contribution to this realization of more complete racial equality, through his work on the President's Committee on Civil Rights, was undoubtedly his most satisfying government service during his ten years in Grand Rapids.

Although the elevation of Haas to the bishopric in 1943 greatly limited his opportunities for public service, it may have increased his influence as an elder statesman of the social justice movement. With John A. Ryan, Peter Dietz, John J. Burke, Robert E. Lucey, Frederick Kenkel, and Raymond McGowan, he was a veteran of the Church's crusade to adapt the teachings of *Rerum Novarum* and *Quadragesimo Anno* to American public life in the 1930s and early 1940s and more than these others, he had been a high government official in the New Deal administration of President Roosevelt. From 1943 to 1953, consequently, he was in ever increasing demand as a speaker at labor conventions, civil rights gatherings, and interfaith conferences, and honored with the dignity of the Catholic bishopric and removed from partisan controversies of government office and the bargaining table, his words were given wide hearing. His social and economic philosophy had not changed over the years. Whether addressing a UAW convention, the Friendly Sons of St. Patrick, the National Council of Catholic Women, or the Grand Rapids Dunkers' Club, he was still concerned with the God-given dignity of every human being, his natural right to life and economic security, the equality of all men and women before God, and the responsibility of the government to promote the common good. As the Depression years of the 1930s gave way to the prosperity of the 1940s, however, the emphasis in Haas's speeches shifted. He did not ignore the key issues of the 1930s—the right to organize, a living wage, a more equitable distribution of wealth, and the need for social legislation—but newer issues received equal attention: the problems of postwar reconstruction, the spread of communism, union responsibility, and fair employment opportunities for all. Throughout the final years of his life, the bishop returned consistently to the need for a major reorganization of society according to the Industry Council Plan of Pope Pius XI.

In one of his first major addresses as bishop, a speech before the Catholic Conference on Industrial Problems in Chicago in February 1944, Haas outlined the basic needs of postwar demobilization. "To the Christian," he declared, "the first objective in post-war planning is the acceptance of Christ as King of the world." This meant that "men accept and be guided by the concept of society that God is the Father of all men and that all men are brothers through his Son," and also accept the principle that "human beings in every part of the world have the same stature in the sight of God that he has, are as dear to Christ and are as capable of eternal life as he is." As a result, he continued, "the Christian expects each to treat every other not merely as someone to be reckoned with because he is stronger or perhaps to be plundered because he is weaker, but as his own brother through the Sonship of Jesus Christ."[25]

The second objective of postwar planning, the bishop stated, was "bread." "By bread," he explained, "I mean all things that are necessary for man's physical life and comfort. My thesis is that they should be produced in sufficient quantity and be so distributed that no one need go without. In other words, the grand total should be enough to go around, and it should be justly parcelled out." The bishop explained in greater detail: "Before all else, the returning soldier as well as every able-bodied civilian has the right . . . to have a job in a useful occupation throughout his productive life . . . the right in city or on farm to compensation sufficient to secure him and his family adequate food, clothing, shelter and medical care . . . the right to security against the vicissitudes of sickness, accidents, unemployment and old age, [and] still more . . . the right to work and live as a free man under a system that will permit him a voice in determining the conditions under which he works from day to day." This was the goal that American industry, labor, and government must seek to implement in the postwar world, the only goal worthy of the innate dignity of a human being as a child of God.

Despite the large number of women employed in industrial production throughout World War II, the bishop hoped that few would be needed in industry after the war. "Sound social policy," he had stated in *Man and Society*, "dictates that the movement of women to factories should not be encouraged either by state intervention or by public opinion." He admitted that there were a "comparatively small number of girls who do not intend to marry and establish families" and that these had a place in industry and should receive a living wage equal to men who perform the same work. The majority of women in industry in the years after the war, however, were married, and Haas saw this as undesirable. As a Catholic sociologist, he accepted "the priority of the family over every other consideration" and he emphasized the "evil effects on child life caused by the employment of mothers," adverse effects on children's health, on the development of their personalities, on their sense of security, and even on their educational standards and motivation. The presence of married women in industry was economically undesirable, according to Haas, because it unnecessarily increased job competition: some husbands and fathers might remain unemployed because of the number of jobs held by women, or they might be forced to work for less than adequate wages because the increased supply of available workers lowered wage rates. Haas admitted that most women held outside employment out of economic necessity, but he saw an alternative. Wages should be raised sufficiently to support a man and his family in reasonable comfort and security and to permit married women to give their home and family highest priority. In all of this, the bishop was simply repeating the directive of Pope Pius XI in *Quadragesimo Anno:* "Mothers should especially devote their energies to the home and the things connected with it. Most unfortunate, and to be remedied energetically, is the abuse whereby mothers of families, because of the insufficiency of the father's salary, are forced to engage in gainful occupations outside the domestic walls to the neglect of their own proper cares and duties, particularly the education of their children."[26]

Postwar reconstruction in international affairs, Bishop Haas insisted, had to be founded on increased cooperation among nations and on some form of world organization. "Looking back to 1920," he suggested in 1952, "was it not tragic that our Congress rejected the great opportunity it had in that year to enroll our country in the League of Nations?" The lesson of the 1920s, however, had not been learned by all. "The tradition of isolationism—abetted by a not too high level of politics—still perdures in our country. Fortunately, in the interval since 1920 we had the services of certain statesmen like Senator Arthur S. Vandenberg who had the courage to break away from isolationism and to urge the need of working with other nations for world security. What Senator Vandenberg saw is what every clear-thinking American must see. It is that it is impossible for us to go it alone in the world. But he saw more. He saw that it is impossible for us to survive if the rest of the world cannot survive. He pleaded for common effort to resolve the common problems of the family of nations."[27]

For Bishop Haas, the specific implementation of this in the postwar world was the United Nations. In the second edition of *Man and Society*, he strongly supported the UN's work of "negotiation, mediation, and conciliation of international disputes" and its efforts toward "lessening the economic causes of war and ... promoting the material welfare of peoples." He praised its admittedly limited success in bringing into sharper focus "respect for human rights" and its "progress in the development and codification of what is called international law." As always, Haas's motive was not simply political. "There is need indeed to meet the challenge of one world today," he declared in 1950. "One means is to eliminate from ourselves all sentiments of stuffy groupiness. Another is to abolish out of our midst every disposition to shut ourselves up in air-tight compartments, in order to oppose others who do the same. Such fragmentation is the formula of death.... The eye of the natural man sees all this. The eye of the supernatural man sees it much clearer. It recognizes in humility, the Father in Heaven above, who has made all men brothers, and has given them commandment to live as brothers, and as brothers even to love one another."[28]

Throughout his twelve years of government service before his appointment to Grand Rapids, Haas had frequently been accused of underestimating the danger of communism. He was a strong supporter of social welfare legislation, both in the United States and in Europe; he defended American participation in the International Labor Organization and other world forums on which Communist nations could have equal representation; and he was criticized in the late 1930s for his association with Harold Christoffel of the Milwaukee UAW and other leftist officials of the International CIO. In a widely publicized Columbus Day address in Canton, Ohio, in 1942, he had paid tribute to "our allies, the British, the Russians, the Chinese, and other free nations." This speech, reprinted in the *Congressional Record*, evoked a storm of protest.[29] "Where did you get that nutty expression, 'Russia and other free nations'?" wrote an alumnus of Catholic University. Another Catholic stated that "it is very unbecoming for one in your position to be preaching politics." A third critic was more blunt: "It costs us taxpayers $123.75 to see that speech in the November 19 *Congressional Record*—and honestly, Monsignor, it wasn't worth 30 cents." Many conservative Catholics clung to the name "Red" Haas long after the bishop's hair began turning gray.

Haas, of course, was not "soft on communism." In a speech before the Detroit Family Life Conference in 1950, he declared: "For fear that anyone may think that I am unduly tender towards Communism, let me say as firmly as I can that any possible dealings with Communism are out of the question, based as it is on lying, duplicity, espionage, and as Asia and Europe know only too well, on slave-prison camps and murder." As might be expected of a Catholic bishop, he spoke out frequently and forcefully against Communist persecution of the Church behind the Iron Curtain and especially against Hungary's treatment of Cardinal Mindszenty. In an address before the 34th Annual Convention of the American Federation of Teachers in Grand Rapids in 1951, the bishop insisted that "the Communist military must be dealt with with might, no different from the way that we are compelled to deal with violent inmates in mental hospitals. The Communist is irresponsible in his disregard of truth, in his contempt of human dignity, and in his resort to any means to obtain his ends. The only course open to the free nations is to repel force with force." In the second edition of *Man and Society*, published just one year before his death, he spoke of "the insane powers that the Communist government has arrogated to itself" and he admitted the "grotesque but real threat" it posed for free nations.[30]

Despite this hatred of communism, however, Bishop Haas refused to succumb to the anti-Communist frenzy of the post-war decade and he had little sympathy for those, even his fellow Catholics, who, in his words, "saw a Communist under every rock." Answering a questionnaire from the NCWC in 1945, he insisted that Communist influence within his diocese, especially in labor unions and among Black American organizations, was minimal.[31] In fact, the bishop seemed more deeply concerned about the extremism of some anti-Communist movements. When Senator Karl Mundt introduced restrictive legislation in 1948, Haas expressed his opposition in a telegram to Congresswoman Mary Norton:

> As one who believes in the widest measure of individual freedom consistent with the public interest, I beg to register my emphatic opposition to this bill.
> This bill contradicts itself. While it professes to combat totalitarian dictatorship, it gives the federal government such

arbitrary powers over personal freedom as to make the government in effect a totalitarian dictatorship.

It is hard to see how anyone who really believes in private enterprise—unless, perhaps, he is talking with his tongue in his cheek—can risk giving Government such wide discrimination over individual conduct as does this bill.

Communism is an evil to be removed, but it would be folly to destroy ourselves in removing it. The slower, but surer, methods of reason and Christian regard for others, rather than a bill such as this, are the instruments best suited to the task of stamping out Communism.[32]

"We should not forget," the bishop declared at a Marian Congress in 1948, "that Communism is a result, rather than a cause. Fundamentally, its cause is hunger and oppression. Remove the cause and Communism will wither and disappear.... While we pray to the Blessed Virgin today for the conversion of Russia, let our prayers be no less insistent that men will have the courage to face the causes that create Communism and manfully remove them."[33]

Bishop Haas saw little serious threat of Communist domination of the American labor movement, and in fact viewed the labor movement as a check to Communist advancement. "We cannot combat Communism," the bishop declared in 1951, "by force of arms alone—necessary as arms are now—unless we stamp out the force that produces Communism. That force, I hardly need to say, is at bottom injustice.... We should not forget that Soviet ideology is at bottom born of hunger, and hunger will not be argued with." The threat of communism would be greatly increased, Haas declared in Boston a few weeks later, if America were to suffer another economic collapse, but it was precisely a strong labor movement, with its advocacy of high wages and adequate purchasing power, that prevented such a disaster. In an address titled "Communism and Organized Labor," delivered before the 1950 convention of the Michigan Federation of Labor, Haas pleaded for greater unionization of American industry. "Roughly, only one-fourth, that is, less than fifteen million of the sixty million workers in the labor force of the country are now in unions," he asserted. "You still have a long road to travel. I hope that you will not delay on the journey but will follow in the great tradition of the American Federation of Labor, together with the Congress of Industrial Organization and the Railroad Brotherhoods. In this way you can hope to do your part in increasing the riches of our country, and help to communicate its blessings of freedom to the rest of the world." "Unionism is an indispensable ingredient in any democratic society," the bishop declared in 1952.[34]

Haas was not unmindful of Communist infiltration in union leadership, however. He warned workers in a Labor Day address in 1948:

> Organized labor, too, should examine its conscience on Labor Day. Labor officials know that the labor movement is by no means perfect. They know, too, and I can vouch for the truth of their claim, that the enemies of labor are all too prone to exaggerate the sins of labor. Nevertheless, there is one evil that labor should lose no time in driving out of any place of authority or influence in the union. I refer to the evil of Communism. The clear-headed unionist will see that the greatest enemy of the labor movement is Communism. He will readily perceive that the Communist brings into the union a "line" from outside, and thereby seeks to defeat the possibility of decisions being made by the union from within. Moreover, he will perceive that if the Communist "line" should come to control, the union would be only a sounding board for the Comintern. Even more, he will understand that if the Comintern should come into world power, it would seek to erase from men's minds all idea of the Supreme Being, the source and foundation of all freedom and liberty. Here, then, is a matter which the few unions that are bitten with the Communist virus should on a day like this thoughtfully consider.[35]

Bishop Haas was aware of the abuses tolerated by many labor organizations, and throughout the 1940s he emphasized not only labor's rights but also its duties and responsibilities. "A union must give as well as get," he told the delegates to the International Typographers Convention in 1944. "Before all else it is the obligation of a union and its members to do everything in their power to make the business in which they are a part prosper." He branded as a "false notion" the idea "that a union is essentially a fighting machine, and that it should do all it can to nag and annoy and antagonize the employer.... Obviously, such an attitude defeats itself as it can end only in ruin both to employers and workers alike." He reminded the delegates that "another plain responsibility that a union has is to live up to its contracts. This simply means that a union should keep its word and carry out what it agrees to do." "No one can condone the racketeering and underworld connections existing in some unions," Haas declared in a speech in Portland, Oregon, in 1952. "Neither can anyone approve of the deliberate restriction of output practiced by some unions seeking to create employment by creating scarcity."[36]

Despite admitted failings in some unions, Haas strongly opposed the Taft-Hartley Act of 1947, which prohibited the closed shop, permitted state right-to-work laws, and authorized the president to impose a mandatory "cooling off" period before a strike could be called. "Whatever excesses organized labor has indulged in in the past," the bishop declared in 1949, "could have and should have been checked by outlawing such excesses. But the Taft-Hartley act goes much further. It does not merely remove alleged abuses. It seeks to destroy—if such were possible—the labor movement." The right to organize, he told the Michigan CIO convention of 1950, "comes from Almighty God Himself.... Accordingly, I can and do say that the Taft-Hartley Act which is designed not merely to put limits on the freedom of labor organizations, but to hamstring and destroy them, is a tyrannous usurpation by government of a worker's God-given rights."[37]

The American labor movement's most pressing responsibility in the 1940s, in the opinion of Bishop Haas, was the admission of Black Americans and other minority groups to full union membership and equal employment. The CIO was more open and advanced in this than the older AFL, and Haas lost few opportunities to commend the CIO for its racial policy. "I cannot refrain from expressing my happiness," he told the Michigan CIO council in 1944, "in the fine position your state and national bodies have taken in opposing all racial discrimination.... You are doing a long delayed pioneer work in industry and your officers in particular are to be commended for their courage and foresight." Before the annual UAW convention two months later, he declared: "I am happy to speak a word of commendation on the splendid policy of your International Union regarding Negroes. Your policy is at once human, American, and Christian. You accept Negroes into the Union with Whites, with full Union status and full Union rights. You insist that they be hired and upgraded whenever they have the skills equal with whites, and you resort to no subterfuge.

It took courage and a true sense of humanity, and I will say of Christianity, to put that policy into effect." But equality of opportunity was not the responsibility of union leaders alone, as he noted in his address to the state CIO council in 1944: "I beg of you delegates to this Convention to use every legitimate means to persuade your rank and file members to set aside their prejudice and to support their officers in the splendid stand they have taken, to the end that the ugly thing of discrimination against Negroes and other minority groups be rooted out from American life."[38]

As might be expected of a former FEPC chairman, Bishop Haas was an outspoken advocate of stringent Fair Employment Practice legislation. "Unequal treatment of Negroes and other minority groups represents the great paradox and dilemma in American life," he wrote to Representative Mary Norton in 1944. "The opportunity to work according to one's skill, regardless of race, creed, color or national origin, is a fundamental American right which should be written into our laws by Congress. Denial of this right to any man or woman is un-American, un-democratic and un-Christian." The pending FEPC bills, he declared publicly one year later, "do not in any sense provide measures to remove all the evils of discrimination.... They provide only the barest minimum of justice, that is, free opportunity to work and earn one's livelihood.... Every self-respecting American demands this minimum as his right and should insist that it be accorded to all others." The bishop had little sympathy for those who counseled delay. "Frankly, I become a bit impatient," he wrote Senator Robert Taft of the Senate Committee on Labor and Public Welfare in 1947, "with persons who insist that the whole matter of securing fair employment opportunity for all people without distinction, is solely the business of 'education.' In too many instances their position amounts to holding that a just social order is to be built, brick by brick, but that only one brick is to be laid every hundred years. We may not resign ourselves to such a policy of defeatism and of doing nothing. Education and more education, indeed, we need. But it may well be doubted whether in the field of fair employment we can educate unless we also legislate."[39]

In discussing Fair Employment Practice legislation, Bishop Haas could not forget the lesson of the Detroit riot of 1943. During deliberations on voting rights at a meeting of the President's Committee on Civil Rights in 1947, the bishop raised a cautious objection. "The discussion the last ten minutes brought out the importance of voting," he began. "I wouldn't want to leave unchallenged the statement that it is most important. To me, most important is job opportunity. If we get people accustomed to work together they're going to get accustomed to living together. I certainly think it would be a tragedy if we play down this importance." "In my observation," he stated in 1952, "we should begin in the places where people work. I am convinced that if we can banish this evil from shops, from factories, and from offices, we will be on the way toward banishing it from our schools and churches and restaurants and places of recreation." "I can suggest only one thing," he declared before a meeting sponsored by the Catholic Interracial Council of Detroit. "It is to examine and extend the successful experiments that we carried on in the defense plants during the war, in which whites and Negroes worked side by side, with a maximum of harmony, even to their own surprise. These experiments prove that the idea is not academic, but when sincerely tried, it works."[40]

Throughout these years in Grand Rapids, Bishop Haas continued to plead for the reorganization of society according to the Occupational Group System or Industry Council Plan of Pope Pius XI. "I repudiate private initiative, alone and unassisted," Haas declared in his first major address as bishop of Grand Rapids, "as the formula for reconstructing the post-war world." "Our entire economic order," he stated before the National Catholic Conference on Family Life three years later, "should be reorganized, planned and administered by the representatives of management, and the representatives of workers in each industry and profession, with such guidance from government as may be necessary to keep them working together. Call this not a dreamer's dream. Since 1926 this system has been operating, at least in germ, with more than ordinary success in railroad transportation, and since 1938 in the tripartite Industry Committees of the Wage and Hour Administration, and more recently in the War Labor Board." "Popes Leo XIII, Pius XI, and Pius XII," Haas declared in the first John A. Ryan Memorial Lecture in 1949, "have urged that necessary steps be taken to secure full production, and a fair apportionment of what is produced. They stress, however, that little or nothing can be expected in this direction unless the economy is made to function as a tri-partite system of organized employers, united with organized workers, and assisted by the government serving as mediator, but in no sense as dictator or even arbitrator." Such a system, the bishop declared in a speech in Portland, Oregon, less than a year before his death, "would help to keep the whole economy working for the good of all the people.... The Industry Council Plan assures freedom for all and contains within it the mechanism to make freedom a reality."[41]

As elder statesman of the social justice movement from 1943 to 1953, Bishop Haas received numerous civic, religious, and industrial testimonials in recognition of his contributions to labor relations and civil rights. "In all the posts of responsibility in which you have served your government," President Roosevelt stated in the fall of 1943, "you have shown a humanity and skill which both church and country greatly need in these difficult days.... You have served your nation well." One year later, Haas was awarded the Certificate of Recognition from the national CIO Committee to Abolish Racial Discrimination for his work as FEPC chairman. In August 1949 he received the National Civic Service Award from the Fraternal Order of Eagles in recognition of his "attainments as an eminent Churchman" and his "activities in labor relations work enhancing the welfare of our country and particularly your community which holds you in highest respect and esteem." Detroit's Workmen's Circle the following year presented him with its Distinguished Service Award "for conspicuous leadership in the field of human relations, for tireless efforts... in developing ever widening public support for the concept of equality among diverse ethnic groups, and for service in many other capacities over many years to the cause of democracy." Two years later, he was honored with the Michigan CIO's Achievement Award for "distinguished service to the cause of human rights." In June 1952, finally, one year before his death, the bishop was given the Order of B'nai B'rith Interfaith Award in recognition of his "lifetime of activity in the field of bettering human relations, which has added to the well-being of all persons who have come within the influence of his work." "His life work," the citation continued, "has been bound up with the ideals of peace, of culture, of conciliation, of fair employment practices, assistance to the aged, and the preaching of tolerance. Because Bishop Haas has fulfilled the injunction of God to Abraham, 'Be Thou a Blessing,' and because Bishop Haas has been a blessing to himself and to humanity, this B'nai B'rith Lodge, whose ideals he has exemplified, hereby proclaims and acclaims him with this award."[42]

These final years of Bishop Haas's life, however, were also saddened by the loss of many close friends and associates in his work for social justice. Like millions of other Americans, the bishop was shocked by the sudden death of President Roosevelt in the spring of 1945. "President Franklin Roosevelt did not belong to the United States alone," he declared, "but rather to the whole human race. He loved people because he loved God.... He will be remembered with affection as long as there are men on earth."[43] Five months later, he journeyed to St. Paul to preach the final eulogy for his mentor and friend, John A. Ryan, "one of the few great men of our generation." When Sidney Hillman died in the summer of 1946, the bishop sent Mrs. Hillman a note of sympathy: "In Mr. Hillman's death not only the labor movement but our whole country lost an outstanding citizen. Sidney Hillman had the rare gift of seeing that the well-being of the public and the well-being of the workers were inseparable and that one cannot be without the other. To this high principle he gave his fine talents and dedicated his whole life. He will be long remembered with gratitude and even affection by all our people." In November 1952, Bishop Haas delivered the funeral sermon for Philip Murray in Pittsburgh, and a few weeks later, with countless other Americans, he mourned the death of William Green, the "grand old man" of the American labor movement. In May 1953, less than four months before the bishop's own death, Senator Robert Wagner of New York passed away. "I am pained to learn of the death of your dear father," he wrote the senator's son. "Somehow I felt he was a father to me. He was not merely a part of the New Deal but in a sense its very soul. So history will remember him. Above all he felt deeply for the weak and distressed and they will not forget him. God will love him because he loved God's poor."

In the late spring of 1953, Bishop Haas's life was drawing to a close. Except for his bout with tuberculosis in 1907, the bishop's health had been excellent throughout his life. He spent a few days at the Mayo Clinic in July 1941, and was in Georgetown Hospital in Washington in early 1943 (perhaps with pneumonia), but on both occasions he was able to return to his work almost immediately.[44] Haas was a big man, six feet tall and somewhat overweight during his years in Grand Rapids, and the often hectic pace of his numerous government and ecclesiastical responsibilities may have put too great a strain on his heart. On May 27, 1953, just three weeks after the death of Senator Wagner, the bishop's health broke and he was rushed to St. Mary's Hospital in Grand Rapids with a heart attack.

Bishop Haas remained in the hospital six weeks and apparently made a satisfactory recovery. On July 14, he was released and returned home, only to reenter the hospital in two weeks with pains in his chest. This second heart attack, if that is what it was, was minor, and the bishop left the hospital again on August 4. Although pictures of the bishop at this time show him much thinner and his face drawn and wrinkled, he insisted the he was fully recovered and he resumed his normal activities. On August 5 he attended a diamond jubilee celebration of the Dominican Sisters at Marywood Chapel and began to make final preparations for a National Liturgical Conference to be held in Grand Rapids later that month. He met regularly with his advisers and gradually resumed full diocesan administration. He attended three sessions of the Liturgical Conference from August 17 to 20 and delivered a short address to the delegates on the final day. But this was the bishop's last public appearance. On Friday, August 28, a friend noted that the bishop's strength "seemed greatest since his return from the hospital," but he may have exerted himself too much.[45] Near midnight, he suffered a third and final attack. His personal physician was summoned immediately, the pastor of nearby St. Stephen's parish administered the Last Rites, and at one o'clock, Saturday morning, the bishop passed away at age sixty-four.

13

Epilogue: "The Big Friend of the Little Guy"

The funeral services for Bishop Haas in early September were an impressive tribute to a well-known churchman and public servant.[1] On Tuesday afternoon, September 1, a procession of sixty priests and monsignors escorted the bishop's body from the episcopal residence on Lake Drive in southeast Grand Rapids to St. Andrew's Cathedral, thirty blocks away. Monsignor Raymond Baker, vicar general of the diocese and recently elected apostolic administrator until a new bishop could be appointed, met the procession at the door of the cathedral and, after a brief service of prayers and readings, accompanied the casket down the long center aisle into the sanctuary, where ten years before Monsignor Haas had been consecrated sixth bishop of the diocese. The body was placed between rows of lighted tapers near the communion rail, the accompanying priests and seminarians filed into the front pews to recite the Office of the Dead, and the solemn vigil began.

A Requiem Mass was sung at the high altar of the cathedral on Wednesday and Thursday mornings, while the body lay in state, and similar Masses were offered in other parishes throughout the diocese. Representatives of each parish kept prayerful watch beside the casket hour by hour; children stopped to recite the rosary on their way home from school, and thousands of mourners, from every walk of life, filed past the bier to pay their final respects to a man they had first known by reputation and had later come to admire and love. Numerous lay organizations, including the Serra Club and Te Deum International, only recently introduced into the diocese, sponsored memorial services each evening. For many non-Catholics it was the first time they entered a Catholic cathedral. The crowds were so large that a special Mass was offered at nine o'clock Friday morning, the day of the funeral, to accommodate the hundreds of school children and others who could not attend the funeral.

More than 1,200 persons, many from long distances, crowded into the cathedral for the funeral that Friday morning and others braved a steamy rain to stand outside and listen to the services through amplifiers. Secretary of Labor Martin Durkin and his executive assistant, George Brown, represented President Eisenhower. Governor G. Mennen Williams was present, as were numerous city and county officials. The CIO was represented by Walter Reuther, John Brophy, and David McDonald, and the AFL by state and local officers.[2] More than a dozen bishops attended, including Haas's seminary classmate, Bishop William O'Connor of Madison; his successor as rector of St. Francis Seminary, Bishop Albert Meyer; and Cardinal Mooney of Detroit. The NCWC was represented by its executive secretary, Monsignor Paul Tanner, and by Father Raymond McGowan, Haas's collaborator in translating the social encyclicals of Pope Leo XIII and Pope Pius XI. The vice rector of Catholic University was present and also the aging Monsignor John O'Grady, secretary of the National Conference of Catholic Charities and director of Haas's doctoral dissertation over thirty years before. Throughout the congregation were officials of the National Urban League and the NAACP, representatives of neighboring Catholic dioceses, and several ministers and rabbis from Grand Rapids and western Michigan.

The services began at 10:30 with recitation of the Office of the Dead by the more than one hundred priests and seminarians in attendance. Immediately following, the Solemn Funeral Mass was sung by Bishop Stephen Woznicki of Saginaw, assisted by Father Robert Haas, the bishop's nephew, and Father George Higgins of the NCWC's Social Action Department. Cardinal Mooney presided from the episcopal throne. The words of the liturgy expressed well the sentiments of the bishop's countless friends and associates: "May eternal light shine upon him, O Lord, with your saints forever. . . . Grant him to pass from death to that life which you promised to Abraham and his descendants. . . . May the angels lead you into Paradise; may the martyrs receive you at your coming, and lead you into the holy city, Jerusalem; may the choir of angels receive you and with Lazarus may you have eternal rest."[3] At the end of the Mass, Bishop Woznicki turned from the altar to recite the closing prayers with the congregation, and a tearful Cardinal Mooney, his voice cracking with emotion, then slowly circled the black-draped casket of his dear friend and pronounced a final benediction.

The Most Reverend Thomas L. Noa, bishop of Marquette and former rector of St. Joseph's Seminary in Grand Rapids, delivered the funeral sermon. "Bishop Haas has left his mark in varied fields of action," the prelate began.[4] "In the eyes of various minority groups in our country, especially racial minorities, he was a sturdy, reliable champion in the vindication of their rights. Many leaders working in the international field for world peace sought his advice and counsel. . . . To the public at large, both on the national and international scene, Bishop Haas was known as an authority on labor relations and questions. The great pioneer of Catholic Action in our country, Monsignor Ryan, referred to him as 'one of the most competent authorities on labor questions in the United States and one of the most valued advisers to government officials in that field.' " The prelate summarized Haas's accomplishments as educator, ecclesiastical administrator, government mediator, and champion of civil rights, but emphasized that none of these was the bishop's primary concern. Above all else, Bishop Noa declared, Haas was "a priest, a Bishop, a man of God. . . . With simplicity and self-effacement, Bishop Haas brought the rich treasure of his talents and research abilities to his work for the Church and for men. But his qualities as a priest, shepherd and father were always dominant. Men of all walks of life, leaders, teachers, workers, politicians, sought him for guidance, not so much because he was an expert in economics and the social sciences, but because he was a holy priest, a man of God—a man who took the problems of men 'from within,' who made their problems his own." "Today," Bishop Noa concluded, "we mourn the loss of a distinguished leader in the national and international field of human activity for peace and order towards the betterment of man's life on earth. Today we mourn the loss of an illustrious scholar and teacher in the field of justice, equity, and charity among men. But, above all, we mourn the loss of a great bishop and priest, a man of God."

Civic and religious leaders across the country echoed the bishop's sentiments. Secretary Durkin called the death of Bishop Haas "a great loss to the Church and to the nation. His counsel and guidance to labor and management will be sorely missed. As a man he distinguished himself not only by his intellectual attainments but also by his integrity, by his kindness and by his humility."[5] "Father Haas rendered outstanding service to the Church and to the working people of this nation," John L. Lewis declared. "His benign influence, friendly guidance and personal participation in the collective bargaining field endeared him to all who had the good fortune to associate with him." Floyd Skinner of the Grand Rapids NAACP pronounced him "unequivocal in his determination that there must be no second-class citizenship."

"All Negro Americans," he asserted, "must mourn the passing of one who imparted so much to the realization of true brotherhood." "A staunch friend of labor, he stressed the obligations as well as the rights of the working man," Cardinal Mooney noted in the *Michigan Catholic.* "And it is significant that men in management who thus came to know him personally were impressed with the broad, calm outlook that enabled him to see both sides of the question in dispute. To us it is still more significant that in all he said and did in reference to social questions no one could fail to discern the mind and the heart of the priest."

As Bishop Noa suggested, Bishop Haas had been a distinguished churchman. As educator—in the classroom, as director of the National Catholic School of Social Service, as rector of St. Francis Seminary, and as dean of the School of Social Science at Catholic University—he influenced countless priests, seminarians, and laymen and women, striving to impart to all his deep respect for the social teachings of the Church. He had been a founder of the Catholic Conference on Industrial Problems and the Commission on American Citizenship, and he had helped organize the first Summer Schools of Social Action for Priests in 1937. He was a frequent participant in seminars and workshops on civil rights, labor relations, and family life sponsored by the National Conference of Catholic Charities, the Catholic Rural Life Conference, and the Social Action Department of the NCWC. As bishop of Grand Rapids, his liberal social justice views, expressed often in pastoral letters read from parish pulpits, seemed to carry the official approval of the Church and, as a result, were given more sympathetic reception by priests and laity alike.

Haas was also an influential author. Several of his pamphlets—*The Wages and Hours of American Labor, The American Labor Movement, The Why and Whither of Labor Unions*, and *Catholics, Race and the Law*—were widely sold on parish book racks and the frequent articles he contributed to popular magazines, like *The Sign* and *The Missionary*, were read in thousands of Catholic homes. His *Man and Society* was one of the most widely used sociology textbooks in Catholic universities before World War II, and its republication a few months before his death attested to its popularity even in the 1950s. Haas had collaborated with Father Raymond McGowan in translating the encyclicals *Rerum Novarum* and *Quadragesimo Anno* and had a major role in drafting the influential statement of the American bishops, *The Church and Social Order*, in 1940. His published books and articles, from his dissertation in 1922 to the second edition of *Man and Society* thirty years later, numbered close to one hundred.

Haas served the Church in other capacities as well. He was a trusted adviser to several members of the American hierarchy, drafting speeches for the apostolic delegate, for Archbishop Stritch, and for Bishop Corrigan at Catholic University, and counseling others on economic trends and on developments in the American labor movement.[6] As an ecclesiastical administrator, he strove to maintain high academic standards at the National Catholic School of Social Service, St. Francis Seminary, and the School of Social Science at Catholic University, and he guided each successfully through periods of financial uncertainty. As bishop of Grand Rapids, he administered a diocese of 16,000 square miles competently and effectively, encouraging in his people the traditional values and virtues he held sacred.

Like Pope Leo XIII, Pope Pius XI, and John Ryan before him, Haas was a political and economic liberal but a theological conservative. He championed liberal causes in industrial relations, international organization, racial equality, and government responsibility for the welfare of the poor; he strongly supported the CIO, the Carnegie Association for International Peace, and the International Labor Organization; and he was outspoken in his praise of the New Deal and Fair Deal legislation of Franklin Roosevelt and Harry Truman. But he was theologically conservative and unsympathetic to changes in accepted Church doctrine and structures. As an ecclesiastical administrator, his outlook was traditional rather than innovative, and he may have been more intent upon continuing an honored past than upon preparing for an uncertain future. There were faint stirrings and questions in the late 1940s and early 1950s which would become public issues in the American Church a decade later—reforms in seminary education, the changing role of the laity, celibacy of the clergy, challenges to the Church's regulations on birth control, divorce, and remarriage, collegial participation in ecclesiastical authority—but Haas gave little encouragement to their supporters.[7] In fact, he was out of sympathy with them. But none of these emerged as major issues before 1953 and thus his conservatism was not a source of public controversy. To some, his may have seemed a dated liberalism, and he probably would have been increasingly uncomfortable with the liberal Catholicism of the 1960s and the immediate post-Vatican II years, but he almost certainly would not have changed. He and other champions of social justice felt free to range widely in social and economic affairs, even against strong opposition, because they were confident of their firm base in a traditional and unquestioned theology. Haas never doubted that this dual position as a theological conservative and a social liberal was appropriate for a minister of Christ, who, two thousand years earlier, had also preached both a strict moral code and service to the poor.

As Bishop Noa stated, Bishop Haas was not only a distinguished churchman but an outstanding public servant. Although many American Catholics, especially those of recent immigrant backgrounds, tended at times to live more secluded and self-contained lives (in "Catholic ghettoes," some said), Haas had turned outward, took an active part in American public life, and was eventually appointed to high government positions. He was a member of the National Recovery Administration, the National Labor Board, the WPA, and the Wisconsin Labor Relations Board, was one of President Roosevelt's chief mediators in the AFL-CIO split, and after 1938 chaired several industry committees in the Department of Labor's Wage and Hour Division. He was a successful conciliator for the Department of Labor, the National Labor Relations Board, the National Mediation Board, and the National War Labor Board; was chairman of the reconstituted Fair Employment Practices Committee in 1943; and was appointed to President Truman's Committee on Civil Rights three years later. Several other priests held high government offices in the 1930s—John Ryan served on the NRA's Industrial Appeals Board, John P. Boland on New York's Labor Relations Board, and John O'Grady on several District of Columbia welfare agencies—but Father Haas surpassed them in the number and importance of the positions he held and in the influence he exerted in public life.[8]

Such influence, however, should not be exaggerated. Historians have noted that President Roosevelt frequently used federal patronage to guarantee the political loyalty of ethnic and religious minority groups, and Father Haas is almost certainly a case in point.[9] Many of Haas's government appointments were less significant than their titles might indicate. President Roosevelt was undoubtedly sincere in his efforts to promote industrial recovery in 1933 by establishing the NRA, but his unwillingness to risk concerted business opposition by insisting upon higher wages, shorter hours, and complete freedom of organization often rendered the work of the Labor Advisory Board and even the National Labor Board ineffective. Both the Robert Committee and the WPA's Labor Policies Board were established in part to placate leaders of the AFL, and administration officials may not have intended them to exert significant influence on public policy. Monsignor Haas did not have the full support of President Roosevelt during his short term as chairman of the FEPC, and it is doubtful that the president was confident of success when he asked Haas to intervene in the AFL-CIO controversy. With the exception of his mediation for the National Labor Board, the U.S. Conciliation Service, the Wisconsin Labor Relations Board, and his membership on President Truman's Committee on Civil Rights, Haas's government service was probably not wholly satisfying. One explanation may be that many of these assignments were dictated in part by political expediency, rather than by a single-minded purpose to promote social justice or remedy economic ills. Despite Haas's best intentions and dedicated service, consequently, some of his public offices probably were never intended, or permitted, to achieve full success.

Haas's influence as a government servant, however, was not insignificant. As a member of the Labor Advisory Board of the NRA and the Labor Policies Board of the WPA, he served as an official adviser to Hugh Johnson and Harry Hopkins, and as chairman of the FEPC in 1943 he was an influential civil rights strategist. He was a confidant of high government and labor officials—Secretary Perkins, Senator Wagner, David K. Niles, Sidney Hillman, John L. Lewis, Francis Biddle, and many others—and his frequent participation in government and labor conferences indicated the esteem in which he was held. Although the contributions of advisers to government policy are difficult to determine, it seems probable that several accomplishments of the New Deal—establishment of the National Labor Board, organization of the first NLRB, drafting of the second FEPC order, the wage-and-hour standards of several NRA codes, and the minimum wages established in many industries after the Fair Labor Standards Act of 1938—were achieved with the aid of his counsel and assistance.

Haas's contribution to government policy, furthermore, was more than advisory. Although he rarely served on the highest administrative level of New Deal agencies and may therefore have exerted little direct influence in the formulation of major policies, his role in implementing these policies was at times significant. The New Deal that most immediately touched the lives of thousands of Americans was the New Deal as interpreted and adapted by government officials on subordinate, subcabinet boards, such as the NLRB and the FEPC. Workers owed many of the benefits they received under the NRA codes to the dedication and persistence of the members of the Labor Advisory Board. Father Haas and other members of the National Labor Board and the Wisconsin Labor Relations Board consistently defended labor's right to organize and bargain collectively, and they helped to incorporate government-supervised elections, the secret ballot, and majority rule into the nation's "common law" of labor relations. As chairman of the FEPC and member of the President's Committee on Civil Rights, he strove to remove the barriers of religious bigotry and racial discrimination from government employment, private industry, and all of public life. Most important, he served as one of the New Deal's most successful labor mediators, and in hundreds of disputes throughout the 1930s and 1940s he was instrumental in restoring industrial peace and protecting workers' right to an adequate wage, reasonable hours, unrestricted unionization, and steady employment. "He has given all his time, his efforts, his ability, to help the cause of the common man and the cause of labor," Sidney Hillman declared in 1936. "If we only had more men of his devotion, ability, understanding, and readiness to serve the cause of labor, we would have entirely different conditions in the country today."[10]

Historians have pointed out that Franklin Roosevelt's New Deal had no coherent social and economic philosophy, that it was pragmatic, opportunistic, and inconsistent—"bold, persistent experimentation," the president called it.[11] But if the New Deal had no consistent philosophy, individual New Dealers did, and Bishop Haas was undoubtedly one. Basing his social philosophy on the belief in the God-given dignity of every human being, he insisted that everyone has fundamental rights to private property, a living wage, and equal employment opportunities. He was convinced that the rights of workers could be guaranteed best through unionization or, if this proved insufficient, through government intervention. In fact, the common good of all could be most effectively achieved, according to Haas, through a reorganization of society whereby industry, labor, and government had an equal voice in determining economic life. He supported the New Deal and Fair Deal programs of Franklin Roosevelt and Harry Truman, therefore, and was willing to serve in various government offices because he saw in such programs opportunities to further his ideal of higher wages, shorter hours, unrestricted unionization, equal opportunity, and a reorganization of society to ensure greater justice for all. "Bishop Haas exemplified in a singular degree the moral content and drive of the New Deal," the *Washington Post* noted. "He was a teacher and priest who believed that religious values needed to be introduced into secular life."[12]

Although Bishop Haas was an outstanding churchman and a distinguished public servant, these were not distinct careers. In *Rerum Novarum*, Pope Leo XIII declared that "every minister of holy religion must throw into the conflict [for social justice] all the energy of his mind and all the strength of his endurance." In 1920, Pope Benedict XV had written: "Let no member of the clergy imagine that such activity is outside his priestly ministry on the ground that it lies in the economic sphere. It is precisely in this sphere that the salvation of souls is in peril." Pope Pius XI repeated this concern in 1937: "To priests in a special way we recommend anew the oft-repeated counsel of Our Predecessor, Leo XIII, to go to the workingman. We make this advice Our own, and faithful to the teachings of Jesus Christ and His Church, we thus complete it: 'Go to the workingman, especially where he is poor.'"[13]

Father Haas chose to serve the workingman and the poor through teaching, writing, and especially government service, and thus he fused his priestly calling and his public life into one career—a crusade for social justice. As teacher, author, and ecclesiastical administrator, he endeavored to make the social teachings of the Church better known and better practiced by his fellow Catholics, and as a government official he strove to assure broader economic benefits to workers, equal rights to minorities, and greater justice and harmony to industrial relations. His influence on American public life was thus significant and in many ways unique. Few New Deal officials had his clear and consistent social philosophy to guide and support their government service, and few priests were called to fill such high positions of public trust. In all he did, his constant concern was social justice and assistance to the poor and needy. "Bishop Haas had a deep and abiding faith in the little fellow," Walter Reuther declared in 1953, "a sincere trust in his fellow man, and a perfect appreciation of the dignity of the individual. He served well his God, his nation, and his state. But most of all, he served his fellow man."[14] As a priest and public servant, he was, as newspapers noted at the time of his death, "the big friend of the little guy."[15]

Notes

Preface

1. *Michigan Catholic*, Sept. 3, 1953.

1. Early Wisconsin Years, 1889-1919

1. *New World*, Sept. 21, 1945; *Catholic Action*, 27 (Oct. 1945), 27; and *Michigan Catholic*, Sept. 20, 1945.

2. This eulogy was reprinted in the *Congressional Record*, 79th Cong., 1st sess., 1945, XCI, part 12, A4055-A4057, and in *Catholic Action*, 27 (Oct. 1945), 24-27.

3. The best biography of John A. Ryan is Francis L. Broderick, *Right Reverend New Dealer: John A. Ryan* (New York, 1963). See also Aaron I. Abell, "Monsignor John A. Ryan: An Historical Appreciation," *Review of Politics*, 8 (Jan. 1946), 128-134; David J. O'Brien, *American Catholics and Social Reform* (New York, 1968), pp. 120-149; and John A. Ryan, *Social Doctrine in Action* (New York, 1941).

4. Raymond A. McGowan, "An Appreciation," *Catholic Action*, 27 (Oct. 1945), 5.

5. *Grand Rapids Press*, Aug. 31, 1953.

6. Among the best and most accessible surveys of this period are John A. Garraty, *The New Commonwealth* (New York, 1968); Harold U. Faulkner, *Politics, Reform and Expansion* (New York, 1959); George Mowry, *The Era of Theodore Roosevelt* (New York, 1958); Arthur Link, *Woodrow Wilson and the Progressive Era* (New York, 1954); Eric Goldman, *Rendezvous with Destiny* (New York, 1952); and Richard Hofstadter, *The Age of Reform* (New York, 1955). .

7. An excellent study of progressive reform in Chicago is Ray Ginger, *Altgeld's America* (New York, 1953). In addition to those listed above, the following works discuss Wisconsin and the Midwest: Herbert F. Margulies, *The Decline of the Progressive Movement in Wisconsin, 1890-1920* (Madison, 1968); Robert S. Maxwell, *La Follette and the Rise of the Progressives in Wisconsin* (Madison, 1956); Horace S. Merrill, *Bourbon Democracy in the Middle West* (Baton Rouge, 1953); Russel B. Nye, *Midwestern Progressive Politics* (East Lansing, Mich., 1959); William F. Raney, *Wisconsin, a Study of*

Progress (Appleton, Wis., 1963); and Bayrd Still, *Milwaukee: The History of a City* (Madison, 1948). Standard works on the American Church in this period are Aaron I. Abell, *American Catholicism and Social Action* (Notre Dame, Ind., 1963); Colman J. Barry, *The Catholic Church and German Catholics* (Milwaukee, 1953); Robert D. Cross, *The Emergence of Liberal Catholicism in America* (Cambridge, Mass., 1958); John Tracy Ellis, *The Life of Cardinal Gibbons*, 2 vols. (Milwaukee, 1958); Thomas T. McAvoy, *The Great Crisis in American Catholic History* (Chicago, 1957) and *A History of the Catholic Church in the United States* (Notre Dame, Ind., 1969), pp. 226-352.

8. Informative histories of Racine are Nicholas C. Burckel (ed.), *Racine: Growth and Change in a Wisconsin County* (Racine, 1977); Eugene W. Leach, *Racine, an Historical Narrative* (Racine, 1920); Racine Daily Journal, *Racine, the Belle City of the Lakes* (Racine, 1900); Alice Sankey, *Racine, the Belle City* (Racine, 1958); and Fanny S. Stone, *Racine, Belle City of the Lakes*, 2 vols. (Chicago, 1916).

9. For family background, the author has relied on Franklyn J. Kennedy, "Bishop Haas," *The Salesianum*, 39 (Jan. 1944), 7; Constance M. Randall, "A Bio-Bibliography of Bishop Francis J. Haas" (unpublished M.A. thesis, Catholic University of America, 1955), pp. 1-2; and interviews and correspondence with several friends and relatives of the bishop. See also the author's shorter study, "Francis J. Haas: Priest and Government Servant," *Catholic Historical Review*, 57 (Jan. 1972), 571-592.

10. Amy to Haas, Feb. 15, 1913, Box 20, Haas Papers, Archives of Catholic University of America. This collection will hereafter be abbreviated HP-ACUA.

11. Much of this description was taken from correspondence of Elizabeth Haas to Francis throughout the 1920s (Box 27, HP-ACUA), from a July 24, 1976 interview with Anthony Marshall, who purchased the building from the Haas family in the 1940s, and from a conversation with Mary Haas Charnon, June 8, 1981.

12. The most convenient family records are preserved in St. Patrick's Church, the Haas family parish, in Racine.

13. See letters of Peter Haas to Francis, beginning in the fall of 1904, in Box 20, HP-ACUA.

14. See Randall, "A Bio-Bibliography of Bishop Francis J. Haas," p. 1.

15. Peter Haas to Francis, Sept. 20, 1904, Box 20, HP-ACUA.

16. See especially letters of Peter Haas to Francis, Oct. 24, 1904, Mar. 3 and 13 and Nov. 7, 1905, Aug. 1, 1907, and Nov. 6, 1911; all in Box 20, HP-ACUA.

17. *Racine Daily Journal*, Mar. 31 and Apr. 3, 1903. There is a family story that when Francis entered St. Francis Seminary the following year, it was necessary to declare a nationality; "half-German and half-Irish" was not acceptable. When he asked his father what he should do, his father thought for a moment and then replied: "In memory of your mother, declare yourself Irish." (Interview with Mary Haas Charon, June 8, 1981).

18. Peter Haas to Francis, May 18, 1905, and July 29, 1907; Box 20, HP-ACUA.

19. For insights into the elder Haas's religious beliefs and practices, see his letters to Francis throughout 1907, and Nov. 16, 1904, and Apr. 1, 1909; Box 20, HP-ACUA.

20. The best history of St. Francis Seminary is Peter Leo Johnson, *Halcyon Days: Story of St. Francis Seminary* (Milwaukee, 1956). Much interesting information is also contained in the "Seminary Locals" section of *The Salesianum;* in the series Studies in the History of St. Francis Seminary, prepared by students and preserved in the Salzmann Library of St. Francis Seminary; in the annual seminary catalogs, *The Provincial Seminary of St. Francis of Sales;* and in John Tracy Ellis, "The Formation of the American Priest: An Historical Perspective," in Ellis, *The Catholic Priest in the United States: Historical Investigations* (Collegeville, Minn., 1971), pp. 30-32. The quotation is from the catalog of 1904-5, p. 8.

21. The theology course was only three years when Haas entered the seminary in 1904 but was extended to four years in 1910, and thus Haas completed a four-year course.

22. *Provincial Seminary of St. Francis of Sales,* 1904-5 (Milwaukee, 1905), p. 7.

23. Peter Haas to Francis, Sept. 20, 1904; Box 20, HP-ACUA.

24. See Rev. Steven Trant to Francis, Nov. 6, 1904; Box 20, HP-ACUA.

25. Notebook diaries for 1904-1906 are in box 27, HP-ACUA. See entries for Dec. 2-5, 1904, and letter of Peter Haas to Francis, Oct. 17, 1906; Box 20, HP-ACUA.

26. Diary, Dec. 31, 1906, and Jan. 1, 1907; Box 27, HP-ACUA.

27. For Haas's nine months in New Mexico, see his diary for 1907, in Box 27, HP-ACUA, and the letters he received from his father, Box 20. Very few of Haas's own letters remain from this period.

28. Francis to Peter Haas, May 31, 1907; Box 20, HP-ACUA.

29. Peter Haas to Francis, June 30, 1907; Box 20, HP-ACUA.

30. Francis to Peter Haas, Oct. 12, 1907; Box 20, HP-ACUA. Haas was given a further medical examination in Milwaukee on Nov. 13, received a clean bill of health, and returned to St. Francis Seminary three days later. See Diary of 1907, Box 27, HP-ACUA.

31. Haas to Nora Wagner, Oct. 5, 1907; Box 20, HP-ACUA.

32. Most of his seminary correspondence and fragmentary diaries are preserved in Boxes 20 and 27, HP-ACUA. See Diary, Feb. 2, 1912, and *The Salesianum,* 7, Apr. 1912, p. 75, and July 1912, p. 74.

33. These quotations are from diary entries for Oct. 17, 1908, Nov. 9, 1910, and Oct. 12 and Nov. 7, 1912; all in Box 27, HP-ACUA.

34. Diary, Feb. 17 and Nov. 17, 1911; Box 27, HP-ACUA.

35. Peter Haas to Francis, Nov. 7, 1906; Box 20, HP-ACUA. See also Francis to Peter Haas, Sept. 20, 1906 (Box 20), and Diary, Feb. 14, 1909 (Box 27, HP-ACUA), and *The Salesianum* 5, Jan. 1910, p. 66.

36. Diary, 1909; Box 27, HP-ACUA. See also Stone, *Racine,* II, 136.

37. Charles Bruehl, "A Course of Social Science at the Salesianum," *Catholic Fortnightly Review,* 18 (min-Dec. 1911), 734-736; interviews with three of Haas's seminary classmates: Bishop William O'Connor, Msgr. Peter

Leo Johnson, and Msgr. Henry J. Schmitt, Jan. 1966; and letter of another classmate, Rev. Frederick C. Dietz, to the author, Oct. 13, 1965. See also James R. Mantsch, "Faculty of St. Francis Seminary, 1906 to 1919," Studies in the History of St. Francis Seminary, vol. 23 (copy in Salzmann Library, St. Francis Seminary).

38. Peter Haas to Francis, Jan. 19 and 25 and May 18, 1905; Box 20, HP-ACUA.

39. Interview printed in *Western Michigan Catholic*, Apr. 10, 1952.

40. *Milwaukee Catholic Citizen*, May 31 and June 14, 1913, and *Racine Journal-News*, June 11, 1913. See also *The Salesianum*, 8, July 1913, p. 74; Kennedy, "Bishop Haas," p. 7; and Diary, May 1 and June 11, 1913; Box 27, HP-ACUA.

41. *Racine Journal-News*, June 12, 1913.

42. See Diary, July 4-8, 1913 (Box 27, HP-ACUA); Albert Paul Schimberg, *Humble Harvest: The Society of St. Vincent de Paul in the Milwaukee Archdiocese* (Milwaukee, 1949), p. 43; and Haas to Rev. James J. McGinnity, Oct. 2, 1935; Box 58, HP-ACUA.

43. Haas recalled this in a letter to Ryan, Sept. 27, 1929; Ryan Papers, Archives of Catholic University of America, hereafter referred to as RP-ACUA. For brief summaries of the life of Father Roche, see Randall, "A Bio-Bibliography of Bishop Francis J. Haas," p. 2, and obituary notices in *Milwaukee Catholic Citizen*, July 29, 1922, and *The Salesianum*, 17, July-Nov. 1922, pp. 88-89.

44. Sister Mary Harrita Fox, *Peter E. Dietz: Labor Priest* (Notre Dame, Ind., 1953); Abell, *American Catholicism*, pp. 174-186; and Marc Karson, *American Labor Unions and Politics* (Carbondale, Ill., 1958), pp. 240-260. Rev. Frederick C. Dietz discussed his brother's relationship with Haas in a letter to the author, Oct. 13, 1965. The quotation is from Abell, *American Catholicism*, p. 177.

45. See St. Francis Seminary catalogs and "Seminary Locals" section of *The Salesianum* for these years.

46. Student Records, Office of the Registrar, University of Wisconsin; Peter Leo Johnson to the author, June 25, 1964; and *Chicago Tribune*, Nov. 9, 1918.

47. There is no record of a Marquette degree in Haas's file in the Records of the Registrar, Marquette University. A copy of this M.A. thesis, dated Dec. 29, 1919, is preserved in the president's office, Aquinas College, Grand Rapids.

2. The Disciple of John A. Ryan, 1919-1933

1. The best studies of Catholic University during this period are Roy J. Deferrari, *Memoirs of The Catholic University of America* (Boston, 1962); Thomas J. Shahan, "The Catholic University of America," *Catholic World*, 102 (June 1916), 365-385; James H. Ryan, "The Catholic University of America," *Ecclesiastical Review*, 85 (July 1931), 25-39; and Rev. Blase

Dixon, T.O.R., "The Catholic University of America, 1909-1928: The Rectorship of Thomas Joseph Shahan" (unpublished Ph.D. dissertation, Catholic University of America, 1972).

2. Biographic information on Haas's professors can be found in *American Catholic Who's Who, 1936-1937* (Detroit, 1937); *New Catholic Encyclopedia* (Washington, 1967); and *Catholic University of America: Year Book*, 1919-20, 1920-21, and 1921-22 (Washington, 1920-1922). See also J.G. Shaw, *Edwin Vincent O'Hara: American Prelate* (New York, 1957).

3. For the best works on John A. Ryan, see footnote 3, chap. 1.

4. Student Records, Registrar's Office, Archives of Catholic University of America. Haas's classnotes from his student days are perserved in the president's office, Aquinas College. Haas to Liz, Apr. 26, 1921; Box 27, HP-ACUA.

5. Liz to Haas, Jan. 21, 1920; Box 20, HP-ACUA.

6. *Shop Collective Bargaining: A Study of Wage Determination in the Men's Garment Industry* (Washington, 1922); the quotations are from pp. 62 and 133. Throughout this work, Haas's name has been omitted from footnote references to his own publications.

7. Correspondence concerning Haas's dissertation is in Box 25, HP-ACUA.

8. *The Salesianum*, 17, July-Nov. 1922, p. 80, and annual catalogs of the seminary, now titled *St. Francis Seminary*. See catalog for 1923-24, p. 6, for a listing of Haas's courses.

9. Haas to O'Grady, Oct. 18, 1923; Box 25, HP-ACUA. See also the annual *St. Francis Seminary* catalogs, 1923-1931; Peter Leo Johnson, *Halcyon Days: Story of St. Francis Seminary* (Milwaukee, 1956), pp. 396-397; *The Salesianum*, 23, Oct. 1928, pp. 73-74, and 24, Oct. 1929, pp. 72-73. For Haas's courses at Marquette, see university and college catalogs: *Marquette University: General Catalog*, 1922-23; *Marquette University: Bulletin: College of Arts and Sciences*, 1923-24; *Marquette University: Bulletin: College of Liberal Arts*, 1924-27; *Marquette University: Bulletin: The Graduate School*, 1925-28; and Haas's personnel file, Faculty Records, Marquette University Archives.

10. For the editorials, see *The Salesianum*, 17, July-Nov. 1922, p. 75; 18, Jan. 1923, pp. 49-51; 19, Jan. 1924, pp. 68-70; 19, July 1924, pp. 51-57; 20, Jan. 1925, pp. 53-61; 22, July 1927, pp. 49-51; and 25, Jan. 1930, pp. 37-41. Haas's addresses are published in volumes 20, July 1925, pp. 29-38; 21, Jan. 1926, pp. 27-29; 22, July 1927, pp. 40-47; and 23, Oct. 1928, pp. 38-48.

11. *Marquette Tribune*, Oct. 22, 1930, and (Bishop) William O'Connor to the author, May 9, 1966.

12. Father Haas's early sermons are preserved in Boxes 1, 3, and 4, HP-ACUA.

13. *Man and Society* (New York, 1930), pp. vii-viii. See also *Marquette Tribune*, Sept. 17, 1925.

14. *Man and Society*, pp. 3-43. Quotations are from pp. 9 and 11.

15. Ibid., pp. 45-107. Quotations are from pp. 67 and 91. See also

Haas's discussion of legal and social justice on p. 76.

16. Ibid., pp. 108-177. Quotations are from pp. 126, 141, 143.

17. Ibid., pp. 178-305. Quotations are from pp. 183 and 278.

18. Ibid., pp. 306-433.

19. Raymond W. Murray, C.S.C., *Introductory Sociology* (New York, 1939), p. 34, note. See also *Man and Society*, p. vii.

20. Kerby to Haas, May 11, 1923; Box 25, HP-ACUA.

21. Newspaper clippings of these activities are preserved in Scrapbook I, HP-ACUA. See also *Current Biography*, 1943 (New York, 1944), pp. 266-267.

22. Rev. Franklyn J. Kennedy, "Bishop Haas," *The Salesianum*, 39 (Jan. 1944), 12; *Milwaukee Journal*, July 21 and 27, 1923; and "Proceedings in Arbitration between Milwaukee Typographical Union No. 23 and Milwaukee Newspaper Publishers, December 4 and 15, 1924" (Milwaukee, 1924) and "Arbitration Award: Milwaukee Typographical Union No. 23 vs. The Journal Company, The Sentinel Company, The Evening Wisconsin Company," Dec. 27, 1924; both in Box 48, HP-ACUA. See also *Milwaukee Leader*, Dec. 27, 1924, and *Wisconsin Typographical Bulletin* (Nov.-Dec. 1924), pp. 7-8, both in HP-ACUA.

23. See "A Steady Job," *Catholic Charities Review*, 8 (Jan. 1924), 13-17.

24. A copy of Haas's testimony has been preserved in Box 1, HP-ACUA. See also a summary of his testimony in *Capital Times* (Madison), Feb. 21, 1923, and Haas's article, "The Huber Unemployment Bill," in *Wisconsin State Journal*, Mar. 4, 1923. For a later discussion of this bill by Haas, see *Man and Society*, pp. 241-242.

25. "Catholic Conference on Industrial Problems Established," *National Catholic Welfare Council Bulletin*, 4 (Feb. 1923), 14, and Linna E. Bresette, "History of the CCIP," unpublished draft (1952), a copy of which is in NCWC Records, ACUA.

26. "Catholic Conference on Industrial Problems," *The Salesianum*, 17, Apr. 1923, p. 71.

27. "Catholic Conference on Industrial Problems Established," p. 14; Bresette, "History of the CCIP"; and R.A. McGowan, "The Catholic Conference on Industrial Problems," *National Catholic Welfare Council Bulletin*, 5 (Aug. 1923), 11-13.

28. *Marquette Journal*, Oct. 16, 1930, and *Milwaukee Catholic Citizen*, Aug. 6, 1932; from clippings in Scrapbook I, HP-ACUA. See also correspondence concerning World Alliance for International Friendship through the Churches; Box 58, HP-ACUA.

29. Patricia F. McNeal, *The American Catholic Peace Movement, 1928-1972* (New York, 1978), pp. 16-21. The quotation, from the CAIP constitution, is on p. 18.

30. *Milwaukee Catholic Herald*, July 25, 1929; *Milwaukee Sentinel*, Sept. 27, 1929, and Sept. 24, 1930; Minutes of Executive Committee Meetings, CAIP, Nov. 11, 1930 (NCWC Papers, ACUA); *Milwaukee Catholic Citizen*, Aug. 6, 1932; and CAIP records in Marquette University Archives.

31. "Material Force versus Moral Right," delivered before Sixth Annual Meeting of CAIP, Apr. 6–7, 1931, a copy of which is in NCWC Papers, ACUA.

32. Outline and extract of address, "The Problems of Peace," before Racine International Club, Dec. 9, 1930; Box 1, HP-ACUA.

33. "World Peace," *The Salesianum*, 21, Oct. 1926, p. 43; "Why a Catholic Peace Movement," address before CAIP, Nov. 11, 1930; Box 2, HP-ACUA; "Material Force versus Moral Right"; "The Problems of Peace"; and comments at meeting of Women's International League for Peace and Freedom, Washington, Jan. 10, 1932, in *Washington Post*, Jan. 11, 1932.

34. Peter to Haas, Oct. 16, 1919 (Box 20); Liz to Haas, Mar. 1 and 15 and May 10, 1922; Allen to Haas, Apr. 5, 1922; Box 27, HP-ACUA.

35. Numerous letters Haas received from members of his family contain information about his father. See, for example, Liz to Haas, May 2, 1920 (Box 20), and Margaret to Haas, Aug. 19, 1933; Box 27, HP-ACUA.

36. Allen to Haas, Jan. 9, 1919, and Liz to Haas, May 17, 1920 (Box 20, HP-ACUA); baptismal and marriage records, St. Patrick's Church, Racine; and *Racine Journal-Times*, Nov. 22, 1943.

37. *Racine Journal-News*, May 12 and 14, 1919; Liz to Haas, Mar. 5, 1920; Box 20, HP-ACUA.

38. Joe Kloss to Haas, Oct. 15, 1919; Liz to Haas, Apr. 24, 1920; and Margaret to Haas, May 9, 1920 (Box 20); Liz to Haas, Jan. 14, 1920 (should be 1921), Apr. 13, 1921, and Mar. 29, 1922; and Margaret to Haas, Nov. 19 and Dec. 5, 1933; Box 27, HP-ACUA. The quotations are from Liz to Haas, Jan. 6 and Apr. 13, 1921; Box 27, HP-ACUA.

39. For the compensation settlement, see Liz to Haas, Nov. 24 and Dec. 16, 1920 (Box 20); Liz to Haas, Jan. 19, and Peter to Haas, Jan. 19, 1921; Box 27, HP-ACUA. Margaret to Haas, Oct. 8, and Liz to Haas, Nov. 8, 1921; Box 27, HP-ACUA. The quotation is from Liz to Haas, Jan. 18, 1922; Box 27, HP-ACUA. For residence locations, see Racine city directories, 1912–1939, in Racine Historical Museum.

40. Liz to Haas, Jan. 21, 1920 (Box 20); Rev. S.J. Dwyer to Haas, Feb. 1, 1922, Rev. H.G. Riordan to Haas, May 24, 1922, and Mary to Haas, June 10, 1934; Box 27, HP-ACUA. A copy of the will of Elizabeth Haas, dated Feb. 19, 1930, is in Box 24, HP-ACUA.

41. Margaret to Haas, May 9, 1920, and Liz to Haas, Mar. 5 and Oct. 17, 1920 (Box 20); Margaret to Haas, Oct. 8, 1921, Apr. 11, 1922, and Apr. 11, 1934, and Liz to Haas, Nov. 8, 1921; Box 27, HP-ACUA.

42. Marriage records, St. Patrick's Church, Racine. Amy to Haas, Feb. 15, 1920, and May 1920 (no day given) (Box 20); and Amy to Haas, Apr. 24, 1934; Box 27, HP-ACUA.

43. Racine city directories, 1935–1939. Peter, Jr., to Haas, Mar. 14, July 15, and Aug. 12, 1935; Box 27, HP-ACUA.

44. Ryan to Haas, Apr. 12, Haas to Ryan, Apr. 23, and Ryan to Haas, May 7, 1929; RP-ACUA.

45. Ryan to Haas, May 28, 29, and June 3; Haas to Ryan, June 6, 1929; RP-ACUA. See also "Excerpt from Minutes of Meeting of the Executive Committee of the Board of Trustees of the University, held May 31, 1929"; Box

63, Rectors Office (1928-1947), ACUA.

46. Haas to Ryan, June 16, 1929; RP-ACUA. See also official correspondence in Box 63, Rectors Office (1928-1947), ACUA.

47. Haas to Ryan, June 16; Ryan to McGowan, June 17; Haas to Rev. Edward Pace, June 16, 1929; and telegram of Haas to Ryan, Oct. 7, 1930; RP-ACUA. Haas never disguised his gratitude and affection for his former teacher. In May 1933, as he was about to begin his long career in public service, he penned a brief note to Ryan: "Let me say again how much I am indebted to you. Although the past is dead and gone, I have by no means forgotten. Your guidance, direction and encouragement will always remain with me. There is no need of using many words; let me just say 'thanks.' " Hass to Ryan, May 26, 1933; RP-ACUA.

48. Haas assumed his new duties in Washington on July 15, 1931. See Daily Journal of the NCSSS, in possession of Dr. Dorothy Mohler of Catholic University of America; *The Salesianum*, 26, July 1931, p. 48; and *Milwaukee Sentinel*, July 8, 1931. The only detailed history of the school is by Loretto R. Lawler, *Full Circle: A Study of the National Catholic School of Social Service* (Washington, 1951). See also Frederick J. Ferris, "The National Catholic School of Social Service," *Catholic University of America Bulletin*, 29 (Jan. 1962), 1-3 ff.

49. The early years of the school are discussed in Lawler, *Full Circle*, pp. 13-28. See also "Memorandum for the Executive Committee of the Board of Trustees, The Catholic University," June 11, 1935, and "Report of the University Committee on the Amalgamation of the University School of Social Work and the National Catholic School of Social Service"; both in Box 4, Departmental Correspondence, 1935-1955, Office of the Vice Rector, ACUA. At the close of the World War, the National Catholic War Council was superseded by the National Catholic Welfare Council, and this name was later changed to National Catholic Welfare Conference.

50. Lawler, *Full Circle*, pp. 29-110 and 126-137.

51. Quoted in ibid., p. 112.

52. Ibid., pp. 57-92. See also "The Report of the Director," Apr. 21, 1934; Box 1, HP-ACUA.

53. "Report of the Director" (Box 1, HP-ACUA) and Daily Journal of the NCSSS, Sept. 20 and 29, 1933, and Jan. 26 and June 12 and 13, 1934.

54. Lawler, *Full Circle*, pp. 103-121, 126-137, 155-165; and Daily Journal of the NCSSS, Jan. 22 and June 9, 1932, Jan. 26 and May 31, 1933, Jan. 26, 1934, and Jan. 25 and June 3, 1935.

55. Lawler, *Full Circle*, pp. 182-187. See also James H. Ryan to Bishop Karl Alter, July 12, 1935; memorandum of John J. Burke, C.S.P., to Executive Committee of Board of Trustees of Catholic University, June 11, 1935; and "Report of the University Committee on the Amalgamation of the University School of Social Work and the National Catholic School of Social Service"; all in Box 4, Departmental Correspondence, 1935-1955, Office of the Vice Rector, ACUA. H. Warren Willis, "The Reorganization of The Catholic University of America under the Rectorship of James H. Ryan" (unpublished Ph.D. dissertation, Catholic University of America, 1971), makes

little mention of the NCSSS in his discussion of the establishment of the School of Social Work (pp. 222-228).

56. Lawler, *Full Circle*, pp. 103-121 and 166-181. The quotation is from page 179.

57. Ibid., pp. 103-121. See also Haas to Rev. H.C. Graham, O.P., Feb. 14, 1935; Box 60, HP-ACUA.

3. The Philosphy of a New Dealer, 1933

1. George Peek, *Why Quit Our Own* (New York, 1936), p. 20; John T. Flynn, *The Roosevelt Myth* (New York, 1948), pp. 10-11; Basil Rauch, *The History of the New Deal* (New York, 1963), p. 33; Forrest Davis, "The Rise of the Commissars," *New Outlook*, 162 (Dec. 1933), 23; and *Literary Digest*, 116 (July 22, 1933), 10.

2. Three early but very readable studies of these New Deal advisers are Stanley High, *Roosevelt—and Then* (New York, 1937); Joseph Alsop and Robert Kintner, *Men around the President* (New York, 1939); and Unofficial Observer, *The New Dealers* (New York, 1934).

3. See, for example, *Milwaukee Sentinel*, Aug. 30, 1953. The following quotation is in James MacGregor Burns, *Roosevelt: The Lion and the Fox* (New York, 1956), p. 157.

4. Mrs. Ida Irene Kitay Lewis, secretary to Sen. Robert Wagner, 1933-1934, in an interview with the author, May 11, 1965.

5. Interview with Msgr. Aloysius Ziegler, June 6, 1966.

6. The most accessible English translation of these encyclicals may be William J. Gibbons, S.J. (ed.), *Seven Great Encyclicals* (Glen Rock, N.J., 1963). Hereafter the encyclicals *Rerum Novarum* and *Quadragesimo Anno* will be abbreviated *R.N.* and *Q.A.*, and will be cited by paragraph rather than page.

7. Louis J.A. Mercier, "Capitalism and the Facts," *Commonweal*, 25 (Jan. 8, 1937), 294-295. See also the excellent study of David J. O'Brien, *American Catholics and Social Reform* (New York, 1968). More recent summaries of this position can be found in Rev. Edward A. Keller, C.S.C., *Christianity and American Capitalism* (Chicago, 1953) and *The Church and Our Economic System* (Notre Dame, Ind., 1947).

8. Charles Bruehl, "The Case against the Capitalistic System," *Homiletic and Pastoral Review*, 35 (Jan. 1935), 337; Virgil Michel, "Facts about Capitalism," *Commonweal*, 25 (Mar. 12, 1937), 542; John F. Prince, *Creative Revolution* (Milwaukee, 1937), p. 15; Frederick P. Kenkel, "The Encyclical 'Quadragesimo Anno' and Social Reconstruction," *Fortnightly Review*, 38 (Aug. 1931), 169-170; and "The President's Program—Whither Directed?" *Central-Blatt and Social Justice*, 26 (June 1933), 80. See also Franz H. Mueller, "The Church and the Social Question," in Joseph N. Moody and Justus George Lawler (eds.), *The Challenge of Mater et Magistra* (New York, 1963), pp. 95-137.

9. John A. Ryan, "The New Things in the New Encyclical," *Ecclesiasti-*

cal Review, 85 (July 1931), 10. See also Ryan's *A Better Economic Order* (New York, 1935) and *Social Doctrine in Action* (New York, 1941), and Patrick W. Gearty, *The Economic Thought of Monsignor John A. Ryan* (Washington, 1953).

10. *Man and Society* (New York, 1930), pp. 25–26 and 27. Although Father Haas published a second edition of this work in 1952, all references in this study will be to this first edition, unless otherwise noted, since this best represents his thought in the 1930s. For the biblical references, see Gen. 1: 26–27, Ps. 8:6, and Matt. 15:34. In this context, of course, "man" is synonymous with "human beings" and includes both men and women.

11. *Man and Society*, pp. 13, 14, 26.

12. Ibid., pp. 51–52. See also *Summa Theologica*, II-II, qq. LVII–LIX; *R.N.*, pars. 5ff. *Q.A.*, pars. 44ff.; and Ryan, *Distributive Justice* (New York, 1916), pp. 56–66. Father Haas quoted the words of Jefferson, for example, in *Man and Society*, pp. 29–30. The following quotation is from *Man and Society*, pp. 52–53.

13. *Summa Theologica*, II-II, q. LXVI, a.2; *R.N.*, par. 5; *Q.A.*, par. 45; and *Man and Society*, pp. 306 and 350.

14. *Man and Society*, pp. 307 and 333.

15. Quoted by Haas in "Freedom of Contract and Legislation," *The Salesianum*, 19, July 1924, pp. 53–54.

16. *Adkins* v. *Children's Hospital*, 261 U.S., 525, 558 (1923).

17. "Freedom of Contract and Legislation," pp. 54–55; "Religion, the Need of Industry," *Missionary*, 46 (Feb. 1932), 39–40; and "Poverty and Wealth," *The Salesianum*, 26, Apr. 1931, p. 53.

18. "Setting Minimum Wages according to Minimum Quantity Standards," *The Salesianum*, 21, Jan. 1926, p. 29.

19. Ibid., pp. 29–30. Quotation is from *Man and Society*, p. 41.

20. "Things and Work," *Missionary*, 47 (June 1933), 188. Father Haas also discussed the causes of the Depression in several other works: *The Wages and Hours of American Labor* (New York, 1937), pp. 8–17; *Jobs, Prices, and Unions* (New York, 1941), pp. 6–18; *Rights and Wrongs in Industry* (New York, 1933), p. 1; "Two Milestones to Social Justice," *Sign*, 15 (May 1936), 585–587; "Toward a Christian Social Order," *Journal of Religious Instruction*, 2 (Mar. 1932), 617–628; "The Vices of Industrialism and Their Remedies," *Ecclesiastical Review*, 92 (Apr. 1935), 352–368; and "Freedom through Unionization," *American Federationist*, 40 (Nov. 1933), 1190–1196.

21. *Man and Society*, p. 324, and *Rights and Wrongs in Industry*, p. 2. See also address titled "Moral and Economic Causes of the Depression," delivered before Catholic Conference on Industrial Problems in Providence, R.I., Nov. 15, 1932, and reprinted in *Providence Visitor*, Nov. 18, 1932; from a clipping in HP-ACUA.

22. Ryan, *A Living Wage* (New York, 1906), pp. 291 and 301.

23. "The Church, Public Opinion, and Industry," *The Salesianum*, 22, July 1927, p. 40.

24. O'Brien, *American Catholics and Social Reform*, pp. 139–140.

25. In an address quoted in *Wilkes-Barre Evening News*, Sept. 30, 1931,

a clipping of which is in HP-ACUA. The following quotation is from "Thinking Out a Catholic Industrial Program," *American Federationist*, 35 (Oct. 1928), 1189–1190.

26. *The Why and Whither of Labor Unions* (Huntington, Ind., 1939), pp. 7, 13, 15–16.

27. *R.N.*, par. 36, and *Q.A.*, par. 31.

28. Labor Day address in Uniontown, Pa., Sept. 3, 1933, quoted in NCWC News Service release, Sept. 4, 1933; address quoted in *Denver Register*, Sept. 8, 1935; and *The Why and Whither of Labor Unions*, pp. 13–15.

29. These and similar letters, often filed in folders marked "Crank Letters," are preserved in Boxes 58, 68, and 69, HP-ACUA.

30. *American Agriculture and International Affairs* (Washington, 1930), pp. 19–20. The following quotation is from pp. 20–21.

31. *The Why and Whither of Labor Unions*, p. 16, and "Freedom of Contract and Legislation," p. 57.

32. "A Steady Job," *Catholic Charities Review*, 8 (Jan. 1924), 113–117; *Man and Society*, p. 375; "The Child Labor Amendment," *The Salesianum*, 20, Jan. 1925, pp. 53–61; "The Child Labor Amendment Again," ibid., Apr. 1925, pp. 29–36; and "Social Insurance and Health," ibid., 23, Oct. 1928, pp. 38–48.

33. *Man and Society*, pp. 375 and 212.

34. *The Why and Whither of Labor Unions*, pp. 27–29. Father Haas discussed this Occupational Group System in several earlier works, as the following footnote indicates, but this description (in 1939) is probably the most complete.

35. "Organized Society: The Remedy for Unemployment," *Proceedings of the Eighteenth Meeting of the National Conference of Catholic Charities* (Sept. 1932), pp. 71–72; *Rights and Wrongs in Industry*, p. 15; *The American Labor Movement* (New York, 1937), pp. 12–13; "Federal Program for Industrial Peace," *American Labor Legislation Review*, 30 (Dec. 1940), 180–188; "Christian Planning for Post-War Reconstruction," *Acolyte*, 20 (Oct. 1944), 9; and "Marks of Social Order," *American Ecclesiastical Review*, 120 (June 1949), 449–457.

36. See, for example, the quotation in *Milwaukee Catholic Herald*, Sept. 3, 1925.

37. *Man and Society*, p. 72. See also this author's "Justice through Organization: The Social Philosophy of Bishop Francis J. Haas," *Social Thought*, 3 (Summer 1977), 41–53; (copyright 1977, National Conference of Catholic Charities).

38. From an interview with Allen P. Haas, Jan. 10, 1966.

4. First Months in Government Service: The NRA, 1933-1934

1. Samuel Rosenman (ed.), *The Public Papers and Addresses of Franklin D. Roosevelt*, 13 vols. (New York, 1938–1950), II, 11–15.

2. Several of the best accounts of the effects of the Depression on American life are Frederick Lewis Allen, *Since Yesterday* (New York, 1961);

Irving Bernstein, *The Lean Years* (Boston, 1960), pp. 247-504; William E. Leuchtenburg, *Franklin D. Roosevelt and the New Deal* (New York, 1963), pp. 1-40; Broadus Mitchell, *Depression Decade* (New York, 1947); Arthur M. Schlesinger, Jr., *The Crisis of the Old Order* (Boston, 1957), pp. 155-169 and 456-485; and Dixon Wecter, *The Age of the Great Depression* (New York, 1948), pp. 1-60.

3. Among the best and most accessible surveys of President Roosevelt's first One Hundred Days are Frank Freidel, *Franklin D. Roosevelt: Launching the New Deal* (Boston, 1973), pp. 196-505; Leuchtenburg, *Franklin D. Roosevelt and the New Deal*, pp. 41-62; Arthur M. Schlesinger, Jr., *The Coming of the New Deal* (Boston, 1958), pp. 1-334; James MacGregor Burns, *Roosevelt: The Lion and the Fox* (New York, 1956), pp. 161-208; and Basil Rauch, *The History of the New Deal* (New York, 1944), pp. 57-84.

4. Some of the best studies of the NRA can be found in Charles D. Dearing and others, *The ABC of the NRA* (Washington, 1934); Freidel, *Launching the New Deal;* Ellis W. Hawley, *The New Deal and the Problem of Monopoly* (Princeton, 1966); J. Joseph Huthmacher, *Robert F. Wagner and the Rise of Urban Liberalism* (New York, 1968); Hugh Johnson, *The Blue Eagle from Egg to Earth* (Garden City, 1935); Leverett Lyon and others, *The National Recovery Administration* (Washington, 1935); Frances Perkins, *The Roosevelt I Knew* (New York, 1964); Charles F. Roos, *N.R.A. Economic Planning* (Bloomington, Ind., 1937); Schlesinger, *The Coming of the New Deal;* and Twentieth Century Fund, *Labor and the Government* (New York, 1935). See also Solomon Barkin, "Collective Bargaining and Section 7 (b) of NIRA," *Annals of the American Academy of Political and Social Science* (hereafter *AAAPSS*), 184 (Mar. 1936), 169-175; Gustav Peck, "Labor's Role in Government Administrative Procedure," ibid., pp. 82-93; Frances Perkins, "A National Labor Policy," ibid., pp. 1-3; and Ruth Reticker, "Labor Standards in NRA Codes," ibid., pp. 72-82. The initials "NIRA" refer to the "National Industrial Recovery Act," while the letters "NRA" refer to the "National Recovery Administration," the government agency set up to administer the act.

5. Keegan to Haas, telegram of Mar. 27; Haas to Keegan, Mar. 27; Keegan to Haas, Mar. 29; and Perkins to Haas, Mar. 28, 1933; Box 60, HP-ACUA.

6. Quotations are from *New York Times*, Mar. 3 and Apr. 1, 1933. See also Haas to Keegan, Apr. 6, 1933; Box 60, HP-ACUA. The best biography of Secretary Perkins is George Martin, *Madam Secretary: Frances Perkins* (Boston, 1976). See especially pages 251-256 for the unemployment conference.

7. Haas to Perkins, Apr. 1, 1933; Box 60, HP-ACUA. See also Haas to R. Dana Skinner, Feb. 27, 1933; Box 62, HP-ACUA.

8. Haas's social and economic philosophy was discussed in the preceding chapter.

9. *New York Times*, June 17, 1933. For information on the Labor Advisory Board, see the works of Dearing, Johnson, Lyon, Perkins, Roos, and the Twentieth Century Fund, mentioned above. See also Irving Bernstein,

"Labor and the Recovery Program," *Quarterly Journal of Economics*, 60 (Feb. 1946), 270–288; John L. Lewis, "Labor and the National Recovery Administration," *AAAPSS*, 172 (Mar. 1934), 58-63; "Reminiscences" of Frances Perkins, Boris Shishkin, and Leo Wolman, The Oral History Collection of Columbia University (hereafter OHC); and "A History of the Labor Advisory Board," Box 3, Rose Schneiderman Papers, Tamiment Library, New York University. This "History" may be the draft commissioned by the Labor Advisory Board at the meeting of June 14, 1935, for which see Hillman Papers, Amalgamated Clothing Workers of America, New York. Since pages are not numbered consecutively, references will be by chapter.

10. Lewis and Berry were not appointed until June 22. See NRA news release of June 20, 1933, and *New York Times*, June 23, 1933.

11. *Milwaukee Catholic Citizen*, July 8, 1933. Correspondence with these officials, chiefly in connection with publication of *Shop Collective Bargaining* in 1922, is preserved in Boxes 25 and 58, HP-ACUA.

12. Leuchtenburg, *Franklin D. Roosevelt and the New Deal*, p. 332; and George Q. Flynn, *American Catholics and the Roosevelt Presidency, 1932-1936* (Lexington, Ky., 1968).

13. Interview with the author, May 11, 1965. See also E.J. Brown to Haas, Dec. 6, 1933, Record Group 25, Records of the National Labor Relations Board, Case No. 208, National Archives; and "Reminiscence of Leo Wolman," p. 26, OHC.

14. Mary Elizabeth Haas to Haas, Apr. 14, 1933; Box 24, HP-ACUA.

15. Haas to Susan M. Kingsbury, Jan. 21, 1933; Box 58, HP-ACUA.

16. Martin, *Madam Secretary*, pp. 56-57 and 279-283; *Washington Post*, June 14, 1933; *New York Times*, June 20, 1933; and *Catholic Action*, 15 (June 1933), 14.

17. *New York Times*, June 17, 21, 23, and 26, 1933. See also Lewis L. Lorwin and Arthur Wubnig, *Labor Relations Boards* (Washington, 1935), pp. 54-58, and "A History of the Labor Advisory Board," chap. III-V.

18. The best discussions of the early days of the NRA are Dearing, *The ABC of the NRA*, pp. 41-108, and Lyon, *The National Recovery Administration*, pp. 83-137.

19. The quotation is from Haas to Rev. Joseph Berg, July 11, 1933; Box 62, HP-ACUA. See also *New York Times*, June 25 and July 11 and 21, 1933, and *Washington Herald*, July 23, 1933, the latter from clipping in HP-ACUA.

20. Haas to Rev. Francis E. Murphy, July 24, 1933; Box 50, HP-ACUA.

21. *Catholic Daily Tribune* (Dubuque), Aug. 2, 1933; from clipping in HP-ACUA.

22. Secretary Perkins's accounts of this visit are in her *People at Work* (New York, 1934), pp. 159-165; *The Roosevelt I Knew*, pp. 214-221; and "Reminiscence of Frances Perkins," V, 330-346, OHC. See also Martin, *Madam Secretary*, pp. 307-310; *New York Times*, July 28-29, 1933; *Pittsburgh Press*, July 29, 1933; and *Homestead Messenger*, July 28-Aug. 1, 1933; letters of Haas to Most Rev. Hugh Boyle, bishop of Pittsburgh, July 29, 1933 (Box

23), and to Rev. Clement Hrtanek (pastor of St. Anne's Church), Aug. 18, 1933; Box 62, HP-ACUA; and Hrtanek to the author, June 6, 1965. The quotation is from *The Roosevelt I Knew*, p. 216.

23. The *Homestead Messenger* (Aug. 1, 1933) quoted Cavanaugh: "I explained the whole situation to her and she agreed with me. I had her interests at heart when I told her [Patrick] Cush would not be allowed at the meeting, that he was not a steel worker and therefore could not have any interest in her presence other than to cause trouble. I told Father Haas a part of the trouble. While he did not agree with me that I should keep Cush out of the meeting, nevertheless I told him that he could not attend the meeting. The matter was dropped at that time and the public meeting in the borough building was then held.... I did not deny the privilege of allowing the Secretary to hold a meeting in the park, but as I knew Cush was not a desirable person to talk about labor conditions, I told her that he was not permitted to address the meeting." The following quotation is from the *Washington Herald*, Aug. 1, 1933 (from clipping in HP-ACUA).

24. Quoted in *Homestead Messenger*, Aug. 1, 1933. Father Haas's papers contain little record of this visit, but the reason for this may be that he gave his files to Miss Perkins at the time she was preparing *People at Work*. See Perkins to Haas, June 7, 1934; Box 58, HP-ACUA.

25. Quoted in *Chicago Tribune*, Aug. 8, 1933.

26. Ready to Haas (undated) and Haas to Ready, Aug. 7, 1933; Box 60, HP-ACUA.

27. Accounts of Haas's speeches are found in the *Pittsburgh Press*, Sept. 4, 1933; *Milwaukee Catholic Herald*, Sept. 14, 1933; *Cleveland Plain Dealer*, Sept. 3, 1933; and *Montreal Gazette*, Aug. 11, 1933; all from clippings in HP-ACUA. See letters in Box 23, HP-ACUA.`

28. Records of these codes are in the National Archives in two files: Consolidated Files (Series 25) and Volumes "A" and "B" (Series 20); both in RG 9, National Recovery Administration.

29. W.J. Woolston (assistant to Labor Advisory Board) to Haas, July 31, 1933 (Box 62, HP-ACUA); transcripts of the public hearings are in RG 9, Consolidated Files, Salt Producing Code; memorandum of Haas to Paddock, Aug. 24, 1933; RG 9, Volume "B," Salt Producing Code, Box 113, National Archives.

30. Woolston to Haas, July 28, 1933 (Box 62, HP-ACUA); transcripts of public hearings are in RG 9, Consolidated Files; records of conferences are in RG 9, Volume "A," Box 120; memorandum of Haas to Muir, Sept. 26; RG 9, Volume "B," Box 120, Retail Lumber and Building Code, National Archives. See also *Monthly Labor Review*, 37 (Sept. 1933), 536–539, and 37 (Nov. 1933), 1046–1047; and *New York Times*, Oct. 4, 1933.

31. See Margaret Stabler (secretary to Labor Advisory Board) to C.C. Williams, July 31, 1933; RG 9, Boot and Shoe Manufacturing Code, Volume "A," National Archives.

32. *New York Times*, Aug. 27, 1933. The best discussion of the merit clause in the Automobile Code is Sidney Fine, *The Automobile under the Blue Eagle* (Ann Arbor, Mich., 1963), pp. 58–74.

33. NRA Release 548, quoted in Lorwin and Wubnig, *Labor Relations Boards*, p. 68.

34. Hearings on the Boot and Shoe Code; RG 9, Consolidated Files, National Archives. See also Lorwin and Wubnig, *Labor Relations Boards*, pp. 79-80, and *New York Times*, Sept. 14 and 16, 1933.

35. Hearings on the Boot and Shoe Code; RG 9, Consolidated Files, National Archives.

36. Hearings on the Salt Producing Industry Code; RG 9, Consolidated Files, National Archives.

37. *Report of Proceedings of the Fifty-third Annual Convention of the American Federation of Labor* (Washington, 1933), p. 257. See also *New York Times*, Sept. 16, 1933; Haas to John Nolan, Sept. 23, 1933 (Box 23, HP-ACUA); and "A History of the Labor Advisory Board," chap. VI.

38. This was the recommendation of General Johnson to President Roosevelt in an undated memorandum (RG 9, Supplementary Volumes "A" and "B," Box 128, National Archives). The following quotations are from Lorwin and Wubnig, *Labor Relations Boards*, p. 81, and Williams to King, Oct. 7, 1933; RG 9, Volume "B," Part II, Box 128, National Archives. See also *New York Times*, Oct. 4 and 6, 1933.

39. *Catholic Daily Tribune*, Aug. 2, 1933. For the Labor Advisory Board's right to nominate labor representatives on code authorities, see Lyon, *The National Recovery Administration*, pp. 458-461, and Sidney Hillman, "The NRA, Labor, and Recovery," *AAAPSS*, 171 (Mar. 1934), 70-75.

40. See Administrative Order X 61, July 10, 1934 (Box 32, HP-ACUA); *New York Times*, Sept. 9, 1934; minutes of General Code Authority meetings (Box 32, HP-ACUA); and "History of the General Code Authority" by William M. Nevins, secretary of the General Code Authority, a manuscript copy of which is also in Box 32, HP-ACUA. The other members of the General Code Authority were Willard Hotchkiss (chairman), DeLancey Kountze, Stacey May, and a fifth member, chosen from the industry the General Code Authority was asked to serve.

41. For activities of the General Code Authority, see minutes of meetings, Box 32, HP-ACUA.

42. "A History of the Labor Advisory Board," chap. VI.

43. Green to Johnson, Sept. 9, 1933 (Box 14, HP-ACUA); Frey to Labor Advisory Board, Dec. 21, 1933 (Box 25, HP-ACUA); Vorse memorandum, Feb. 15, 1935 (Hillman Papers, ACWA, New York); and Twentieth Century Fund, *Labor and the Government*, pp. 262-263.

44. NRA release, "Announcement by the National Recovery Administration," Aug. 5, 1933. Father Haas's membership on the National Labor Board is the subject of the following chapter.

45. Leuchtenburg, *Franklin D. Roosevelt and the New Deal*, p. 69.

46. On labor's advances under the NRA, see Sidney Fine, "Government and Labor Relations during the New Deal," *Current History*, 37 (Sept. 1959), 139-145; Reticker, "Labor Standards in NRA Codes," 72-82; Margaret H. Schoenfeld, "Analysis of the Labor Provisions of N.R.A. Codes," *Monthly Labor Review*, 40 (Mar. 1935), 574-603; Leo Wolman, "Labor under the

NRA," in Clair Wilcox and others (eds.), *America's Recovery Program* (New York, 1934), pp. 89-103; and Alexander Sachs, "National Recovery Administration Policies and the Problem of Economic Planning," in ibid., pp. 133-147.

47. Peck, "Labor's Role in Government Administrative Procedure," p. 88.

5. Mediator for the National Labor Board

1. The inconsistencies of the president's recovery program are discussed in Milton Handler, "The National Industrial Recovery Act," *American Bar Association Journal*, 19 (Aug. 1933), 440-445; Ellis W. Hawley, *The New Deal and the Problem of Monopoly* (Princeton, 1966), pp. 35-52; Hugh Johnson, *The Blue Eagle from Egg to Earth* (New York, 1935), pp. 158-188; William E. Leuchtenburg, *Franklin D. Roosevelt and the New Deal* (New York, 1963), p. 69; Leverett S. Lyon and others, *The National Recovery Administration* (Washington, 1935), pp. 871-885; and Arthur M. Schlesinger, Jr., *The Coming of the New Deal* (Boston, 1958), pp. 167-176. The quotations are from Samuel I. Rosenman (ed.), *The Public Papers and Addresses of Franklin D. Roosevelt* (New York, 1938), II, 253; Schlesinger, *The Coming of the New Deal*, p. 146; and Sidney Fine, "Government and Labor Relations during the New Deal," *Current History*, 37 (Sept. 1959), 141. Donald Richberg was general counsel of the NRA.

2. *Monthly Labor Review*, 37 (Oct. 1933), 870, and 37 (Dec. 1933), 1419. Lewis L. Lorwin and Arthur Wubnig, *Labor Relations Boards* (Washington, 1935), p. 87.

3. Raymond S. Rubinow, *Section 7(a): Its History, Interpretation and Administration* (Washington, 1936), p. 69. In an interview in the *Catholic Daily Tribune* of Dubuque, Aug. 2, 1933 (from clipping in HP-ACUA), Haas revealed that he had taken part in these joint meetings, but neither in this interview nor in his personal correspondence did he discuss the origins of the National Labor Board. The difference of opinion between Johnson and Perkins is seen in Johnson, *The Blue Eagle*, p. 311, and Frances Perkins, *The Roosevelt I Knew* (New York, 1964), pp. 237-238. The quotation is from Johnson, *The Blue Eagle*, p. 311.

4. "Statement by the President, August 5, 1933," a copy of which is in Box 62, HP-ACUA, and "Announcement by the National Recovery Administration," Aug. 5, 1933 (NRA releases).

5. Executive Orders 6511 (Dec. 16, 1933), 6580 (Feb. 1, 1934), and 6612-A (Feb. 23, 1934), in *Decisions of the National Labor Board* (Washington, 1934), I, vi-viii.

6. Johnson's quotation is from Emmanuel Stein and others, *Labor and the New Deal* (New York, 1934), p. 20. See "Announcement by the National Recovery Administration," Aug. 5, 1933; Twentieth Century Fund, *Labor and the Government* (New York, 1935), pp. 195-197; Unofficial Observer,

The New Dealers (New York, 1934); Roosevelt to Haas, Oct. 6, 1933 (Box 6, HP-ACUA); and *New York Times*, Oct. 7, 1933.

7. This fragmentary diary is preserved in Box 62, HP-ACUA; spellings have been corrected and abbreviations have been written out. See *Monthly Labor Review*, 37 (Mar. 1934), 587.

8. Haas to Muench, Nov. 3, 1933; Box 60, HP-ACUA. See, for example, NLB reports of 1934, File XX14, Robert Wagner Papers, Georgetown University. Haas's letters, declining speaking invitations, are also in Box 60.

9. The complete title of the case is *In the Matter of the Ward Baking Company and Baur Brothers' Bakery, and Local #485 of the Bakery Wagon Drivers, Chauffeurs, and Helpers Union and Bakery and Confectionary Workers International Union Local #12*, Case No. 118, *Decisions of the National Labor Board*, I, 37-39. See also Thomas G. Dunn to Perkins, Oct. 19, 1933, and NLB to the bakeries, Oct. 27 and 28, 1933; RG 25, National Labor Relations Board, Case 118, National Archives. The only records of these hearings that have been preserved are apparently unofficial reports sent to the National Labor Board by the companies, one dated Nov. 2, 1933, and the other Jan. 12, 1934; both in RG 25, Case 118, National Archives.

10. The agreement of Nov. 3, 1933, together with memoranda, telegrams, letters, and official releases, are in RG 25, Case 118, National Archives.

11. National Labor Board Release 3522, Feb. 27, 1934; RG 25, Case 118, National Archives.

12. Dairy, Oct. 16, 1933; Box 62, HP-ACUA. The agreement was printed in the *New York Times*, Oct. 17, 1933, and its main provisions are noted in Haas's Diary on Oct. 16. The records of this case are in RG 25, Case 4, National Archives.

13. *New York Times*, Dec. 12, 1933; Lorwin and Wubnig, *Labor Relations Boards*, p. 104; John Larkin and J.J. Young to Wagner, Dec. 8, 1933; RG 25, Case 4, National Archives. See also John D. Ubinger, "Ernest Tener Weir: Last of the Great Steelmasters, Part 2," *Western Pennsylvania Historical Magazine*, 58 (Oct. 1975), 491-494.

14. Quoted in *New York Times*, Dec. 16, 1933. See also minutes of the executive session of the National Labor Board, Feb. 14, 1934; RG 25, Files of the Executive Director, National Archives. See also NLB to Attorney General, Mar. 1, 1934; RG 25, Case 4, National Archives.

15. A copy of Haas's notarized deposition is in Box 15, HP-ACUA.

16. See Lorwin and Wubnig, *Labor Relations Boards*, pp. 104-114.

17. Records of this case are in RG 25, Case 232, National Archives. See especially Buffalo Labor Board to NLB, Dec. 13, 1933; report of Buffalo Labor Board, Mar. 15, 1934; and Wagner to Remington Rand Co., telegram of Apr. 20, 1934.

18. Haas's notes, taken during the Underwood hearings (Apr. 30, 1934), are in Box 62, HP-ACUA. See also NRA Release 4722, Apr. 30; NRA Release 4756, May 1; and agreement of May 3, 1934, signed by Haas, a copy of which is in Box 25, HP-ACUA.

19. NRA Release 5846, June 18; Haas to Remington Rand Co., June 18; and *New York Times*, May 10 and June 6, 9, and 15, 1934. Correspon-

dence and transcripts of telephone conversations from May and June are in
RG 25, Case 232, National Archives.

20. Rev. Paul Stroh, "The Catholic Clergy and American Labor Disputes, 1900–1935" (unpublished Ph.D. dissertation, Catholic University of
America, 1939), p. 139; Haas's Diary, June 3–9, 1934 (Box 62, HP-ACUA);
NRA Releases 5703, 5736, 5754, 5794, 5822, 5844, 5846, 5886, 5939; and
interview with Mrs. Ida Irene Kitay Lewis, May 11, 1965. Through all the
activity, Haas was able to retain a sense of humor. When President W.A. Irvin
of U.S. Steel remarked at one hearing: "As long as I live, my company never
will recognize the United Mine Workers of America," Haas smiled and replied:
"That's too bad. I thought you'd live a lot longer than that" *(Danville Commercial News,* Dec. 2, 1933; from clipping in HP-ACUA). A jingle that cir-
culated in NLB offices at the time is preserved in Box 62, HP-ACUA:

> When plaintiffs grow hysterical
> This man in garments clerical
> Just listens to their ranting
>   with a twinkle in his eyes,
>
> And when their language grows intense
> He feigns the greatest innocence
> But they soon learn—in every way—
>   that Father Haas is wise

21. *Monthly Labor Review,* 38 (Mar. 1934), 527–528, and Wagner to
Roosevelt, Feb. 21, 1934; Official File 716, Franklin D. Roosevelt Library,
Hyde Park, N.Y.

22. Records of these cases are in RG 25 (Cases 153, 52, 9, and 12),
National Archives.

23. Friction between the NLB and the Compliance Division is discussed
in Lorwin and Wubnig, *Labor Relations Boards,* pp. 266–268. See also
memorandum, "Jurisdiction of the National Labor Board," from Milton
Handler to Haas, May 1, 1934; Box 62, HP-ACUA.

24. The best work on this dispute is Sidney Fine, *The Automobile
under the Blue Eagle* (Ann Arbor, Mich., 1963), pp. 213–230. The NLB's
successes and failures are well treated in Lorwin and Wubnig, *Labor Relations
Boards,* pp. 209–230, and Lloyd K. Garrison, "The National Labor Boards,"
Annals of the American Academy of Political and Social Science, 184 (Mar.
1936), 138–146.

25. Labor Disputes bill, S. 2926. See Irving Bernstein, *The New Deal
Collective Bargaining Policy* (Berkeley, 1950), pp. 57–75; D.O. Bowman,
Public Control of Labor Relations (New York, 1942), pp. 34–38; and Twen-
tieth Century Fund, *Labor and the Government,* pp. 338–350.

26. Haas's testimony was reprinted as NRA Release 3842, a copy of
which is in Box 69, HP-ACUA.

27. Ibid. On Feb. 19, 1934, Haas wrote to Margaret Lynch of the
NCWC: "Enclosed is a copy of the Wagner-Lewis Bill now before Congress. I

sincerely hope that the bill will be passed. It is in no sense a basic social reform and is miles away from what the *Quadragesimo Anno* calls for. Nevertheless it is a beginning in the right direction and merits unqualified support"
(Box 60, HP-ACUA).

28. Bernstein, *The New Deal Collective Bargaining Policy*, pp. 57–75;
Bowman, *Public Control of Labor Relations*, pp. 36–68; and Executive Order
6763, June 29, 1934.

29. *Racine Journal-Times*, July 2, 1934, from a clipping in HP-ACUA.

30. Records of this case are in RG 25, Case 208, National Archives. See
also Ruben Levin, "Mass Action Works in Milwaukee," *New Republic*, 79
(July 18, 1934), 261–263; Bayrd Still, *Milwaukee: The History of a City*
(Madison, 1948), pp. 497–499; and *Milwaukee Journal*, June 25–26, 1934.
The union had insisted that this closed shop contract was invalid since the
Employees Mutual Benefit Association was strictly a benevolent society and
had no right to sign a labor contract. See transcript of hearings, Mar. 13,
1934, in RG 25, Case 208, National Archives.

31. Father Haas admitted this difficulty to the *Milwaukee Journal*
(June 29, 1934): "Under the new law we are now in a period of transition
from the old national labor board, of which I am a member and Mr. Moore is
a mediator. While the authority is there, no machinery has been set up so far
to exercise this authority of the new labor board. I am not a member of this
new labor board." Another official was quoted: "We know that if an election
is ordered it will mean a court fight. That is why we want a voluntary submission." Although only 300 workers went on strike, thousands took part in
the rioting, a possible indication of the extent of discontent throughout the
city. Levin, "Mass Action Works in Milwaukee" (pp. 261–263), discusses
Socialist influence in this rioting. The telegram of Moore to NLB, June 28,
1934, is in RG 25, Case 208, National Archives.

32. *Milwaukee Journal*, June 29, 1934, and transcript of telephone conversation between Haas and the NLB, June 29, 1934; RG 25, Case 208, National Archives.

33. The first and second drafts of the agreement, one in Haas's hand
and the other typewritten, are in Envelope 47, HP-ACUA. The earlier quotations are from the *Milwaukee Journal*, July 1, 1934.

34. *Milwaukee Sentinel*, June 30, 1934.

35. *Chicago Tribune*, June 30, 1934, and Haas to Rev. Francis S.
Betten, S.J., July 16, 1934; Box 58, HP-ACUA.

36. *Milwaukee Journal*, July 1, 1934, *Chicago Tribune*, June 30, 1934,
and *Milwaukee Journal*, June 29, 1934; Moore to NLB, July 2, 1934 (RG 25,
Case 208, National Archives); and *Milwaukee Catholic Herald*, July 5, 1934.

37. Lorwin and Wubnig, *Labor Relations Boards*, pp. 220–221; Lyon,
The National Recovery Administration, pp. 482–487; Schlesinger, *The Com-
ing of the New Deal*, pp. 146–151; and Stein and others, *Labor and the New
Deal*, pp. 18–19.

38. Lois MacDonald, *Labor and the N.R.A.* (New York, 1934), p. 16,
and Teagle to Roosevelt, Mar. 27, 1934 (official File 716, FDR Library). The

"Reminiscence of Frances Perkins," OHC, occasionally alludes to the NLB as a "conciliation board" also. Johnson's quotation is from *The Blue Eagle*, p. 265. For criticisms of the NLB, see Lorwin and Wubnig, *Labor Relations Boards*, pp. 225–230; Bernstein, *The New Deal Collective Bargaining Policy*, p. 62; Bowman, *Public Control of Labor Relations*, pp. 46–48; and Garrison, "The National Labor Boards," p. 139.

39. NRA Release 5674, June 11, 1934, and *Monthly Labor Review*, 39 (July 1934), 41–42. These figures do not include the NLB's final month of June.

6. The Minneapolis Truckers' Strike of 1934

1. Two very readable accounts of labor unrest in the summer of 1934 are Irving Bernstein, *Turbulent Years* (Boston, 1970), pp. 217–317, and Arthur Schlesinger, Jr., *The Coming of the New Deal* (Boston, 1958), pp. 385–396. See also Constance Ashton Myers, *The Prophet's Army: Trotskyists in America, 1928–1941* (Westport, Conn., 1977), pp. 59–82.

2. Besides the works of Bernstein and Schlesinger, noted above, other accounts of the Minneapolis strike are Meridel Le Sueur, *North Star Country* (New York, 1945), pp. 289–297, and "What Happens in a Strike," *American Mercury*, 33 (Nov. 1934), 329–335; George H. Mayer, *The Political Career of Floyd B. Olson* (Minneapolis, 1951), pp. 184–222; Seldon Rodman, "A Letter from Minnesota," *New Republic*, 80 (Aug. 15, 1934), 10–12; Sam Romer, "Five Minutes that Changed the Face of Minneapolis," *Minneapolis Sunday Tribune*, July 19, 1964; Anne Ross, "Labor Unity in Minneapolis," *New Republic*, 79 (July 25, 1934), 284–286, and "Minnesota Sets Some Precedents," *New Republic*, 80 (Sept. 12, 1934), 121–123; Donald B. Schewe, "The Minneapolis Truck Drivers' Strike of 1934" (unpublished M.A. thesis, University of Nebraska, 1968); Eric Sevareid, *Not So Wild a Dream* (New York, 1946), p. 58; Herbert Solow, "War in Minneapolis," *The Nation*, 139 (Aug. 8, 1934), 160–161; Philip Taft, *Organized Labor in American History* (New York, 1964), pp. 445–446; "Twin Cities," *Fortune*, 13 (Apr. 1936), 112ff.; "Unionism Wins in Minneapolis," *The Nation*, 139 (Sept. 5, 1934), 274–275; Charles Rumford Walker, *American City* (New York, 1937), pp. 79–183; William F. Dunne and Morris Childs, *Permanent Counter-Revolution: The Role of the Trotskyites in the Minneapolis Strikes* (New York, 1934); James P. Cannon, *The History of American Trotskyism* (New York, 1972), pp. 139–168; and Farrell Dobbs, *Teamster Rebellion* (New York, 1972). See also the author's "Father Haas and the Minneapolis Truckers' Strike of 1934," *Minnesota History*, 42 (Spring 1970), 5–15.

3. Russel Nye, *Midwestern Progressive Politics* (East Lansing, Mich., 1951), p. 229. See also Theodore C. Blegen, *Minnesota: A History of the State* (Minneapolis, 1963), pp. 287–407; Chester M. Destler, *American Radicalism, 1865–1901* (New London, Conn., 1946), pp. 1–31; William Watts Folwell, *A History of Minnesota* (St. Paul, 1930), III, 32–215; John D. Hicks,

The Populist Revolt (Minneapolis, 1931); Lucile M. Kane, *The Waterfall that Built a City* (St. Paul, 1966), pp. 81-113; and Walker, *American City*, pp. 46-59.

4. The first quotation is from Walker, *American City*, p. 40, and the second from "Twin Cities," p. 114. For biographies of Hill, see Stewart H. Holbrook, *James J. Hill: A Great Life in Brief* (New York, 1955); Joseph G. Pyle, *The Life of James J. Hill*, 2 vols. (New York, 1936); and Gustavus Myers, *History of the Great American Fortunes* (New York, 1936), pp. 661-695.

5. This is the title of chap. II of Walker, *American City* (pp. 9-24). See also Folwell, *A History of Minnesota*, III, 272-322; and "Twin Cities," pp. 178-197. The following quotation is from "Twin Cities," pp. 115-116.

6. Cannon, *The History of American Trotskyism*, pp. 20-117; Walker, *American City*, pp. 46-58; Mayer, *The Political Career of Floyd B. Olson*, pp. 17-56; and Herbert Lefkovitz, "Olson: Radical and Proud of It," *Review of Reviews*, 91 (May 1935), 36ff.

7. Bernstein, *Turbulent Years*, pp. 229-231; Mayer, *The Political Career of Floyd B. Olson*, pp. 184-185; Romer, "Five Minutes that Changed the Face of Minneapolis"; Schlesinger, *The Coming of the New Deal*, p. 386; "Twin Cities," p. 113; and Walker, *American City*, pp. 87 and 185-193. The quotations are from Solow, "War in Minneapolis," p. 160, and Walker, *American City*, pp. 85-86.

8. Walker, *American City*, p. 83; Bernstein, *Turbulent Years*, p. 230; and "Twin Cities," pp. 112, 115-116, and 186.

9. For this February strike, see Bernstein, *Turbulent Years*, pp. 233-234; Dobbs, *Teamster Rebellion*, pp. 47-57; Mayer, *The Political Career of Floyd B. Olson*, pp. 188-189; and Walker, *American City*, p. 91. The quotations are from Mayer, *The Political Career of Floyd B. Olson*, p. 189, and Schlesinger, *The Coming of the New Deal*, p. 386.

10. The first quotation is from Schlesinger, *The Coming of the New Deal*, p. 387, and the second from Walker, *American City*, p. 98. This May strike is discussed in Mayer, *The Political Career of Floyd B. Olson*, pp. 192-201; Walker, *American City*, pp. 93-128; Bernstein, *Turbulent Years*, pp. 234-239; and Dobbs, *Teamster Rebellion*, pp. 58-105. See also Schewe, "The Minneapolis Truck Drivers' Strike of 1934," p. 52.

11. *New York Times*, May 27, 1934.

12. Quotations are from "Docket No. 77; Minneapolis General Drivers and Helpers Union Local No. 574 vs. Minneapolis Employers of Truck Drivers and Helpers," a copy of which is preserved in Envelope 48, HP-ACUA, and "Prelminary Report of Commissioner of Conciliation, July 7, 1934," by E.H. Dunnigan; Record Group 25, National Labor Relations Board, Case 38 (New Series), National Archives.

13. *Milwaukee Sentinel*, July 2, 1934, and Diary, July 12-17, 1934; Box 11, HP-ACUA. On July 17 Haas wrote to Rev. Franklyn Kennedy: "I am very sorry that I did not have the opportunity to see you while in Racine. I had to return to Washington as soon as possible in order to help the new Labor

Relations Board get under way"; Box 58, HP-ACUA. Haas resigned this advisory position with the NLRB on Sept. 9, 1934, in order to assume his duties on the General Code Authority.

14. Farrell Dobbs, *Teamster Power* (New York, 1973), pp. 11 and 26-31. See also Ross, "Labor Unity in Minneapolis," pp. 284-286; Dunne and Childs, *Permanent Counter-Revolution*, pp. 3-7; Mayer, *The Political Career of Floyd B. Olson*, pp. 187-188 and 203-205; Schlesinger, *The Coming of the New Deal*, p. 386; Walker, *American City*, pp. 89-90 and 157-160; Bernstein, *Turbulent Years*, pp. 231-234; Donald Schewe, "The Minneapolis Truck Drivers' Strike of 1934," p. 60; Dobbs, *Teamster Rebellion*, pp. 17-35 and 54; Dobbs, *Teamster Power*, pp. 26-31; and Cannon, *History of American Trotskyism*, pp. 143-145.

15. "The International Brotherhood of Teamsters, Chauffeurs, Warehousemen and Helpers of America," *Fortune*, 23 (May 1941), 97ff.; "The Truth about the Truck Drivers' Strikes," unpublished "chronological history" of the strike prepared by Employers' Advisory Committee (copy in Box 20, Citizens' Alliance of Minneapolis, Minnesota Historical Society); and Myers, *The Prophet's Army*, pp. 75-82. The quotations are from J.R. Cochran to Roosevelt, Aug. 8, 1934 (RG 25, Case 38, National Archives), and Mayer, *The Political Career of Floyd B. Olson*, p. 204.

16. Letter to Sheehy, Aug. 10; Sheehy's undated reply; and Sheehy to Haas, Aug. 14, 1934; Envelope 48, HP-ACUA. *Northwest Organizer*, Aug. 9, 1934. Interviews of the author with friends and associates of Haas, Feb. 1966.

17. Proposal of July 19 and Employers' Advisory Committee to Haas, July 20, 1934; both in Envelope 48, HP-ACUA. Dunnigan to Kerwin, July 19, 1934; RG 25, Case 38, National Archives. On the following day, Haas reported to the NLRB: "The collapse of the San Francisco strike has strengthened the employers' position"; "Memorandum, July 20, 1934"; RG 25, Case 38, National Archives.

18. The events immediately preceding the shooting are uncertain. The most objective reporting of the incident is perhaps in the *New York Times*, July 21, 1934. See also *Minneapolis Journal*, July 19, and *New York Times*, *Minneapolis Journal*, and *Northwest Organizer*, July 21, 1934; Le Sueur, "What Happens in a Strike," pp. 329-335; Mayer, *The Political Career of Floyd B. Olson*, pp. 207-211; Sam Romer, "Five Minutes that Changed the Face of Minneapolis"; Walker, *American City*, pp. 155-183; Schlesinger, *The Coming of the New Deal*, pp. 388-389; Sevareid, *Not So Wild a Dream*, pp. 57-58; Dobbs, *Teamster Rebellion*, pp. 124-130; and Bernstein, *Turbulent Years*, pp. 242-244. In "The Truth about the Truck Drivers' Strike" (p. 9), the Employers Advisory Committee insisted that none of the wounded were employees of the firms on strike.

19. Diary, July 19, 1934 (Box 11, HP-ACUA); *Minneapolis Journal*, July 21, and *New York Times*, July 22, 1934. "Memorandum," July 20, 1934; in RG 25, Case 38, National Archives.

20. Dobbs, *Teamster Rebellion*, pp. 130-138; Le Sueur, *North Star Country*, pp. 289-297; Mayer, *The Political Career of Floyd B. Olson*, p. 210;

Solow, "War in Minneapolis," pp. 160-161; Lefkovitz, "Olson: Radical and Proud of It," p. 36; and *Minneapolis Journal*, July 23, 1934.

21. Diary, July 21-25, 1934 (Box 11, HP-ACUA), and "Summary" of events, drafted by Haas, Dunnigan, and P.A. Donoghue of the NLRB, Aug. 28, 1934, in RG 25, Case 38, National Archives. Hereafter this will be referred to as "Summary." Proposal, dated July 23, 1934, is in Envelope 48, HP-ACUA. The same envelope contains replies of the employers' committee and Local President Brown. See also Mayer, *The Political Career of Floyd B. Olson*, p. 211, and transcript of Gov. Olson's radio address on July 30; Box 4, Olson Papers, Minnesota Historical Society.

22. A copy of the Haas-Dunnigan plan is in Envelope 48, HP-ACUA. See also Diary, July 24-25 (Box 11, HP-ACUA); *New York Times*, July 25, 1934; Bernstein, *Turbulent Years*, pp. 244-245; and Dobbs, *Teamster Rebellion*, pp. 144-150.

23. *Minneapolis Journal*, July 26, 1934. The reply of Union President Brown is in Envelope 48, HP-ACUA. This reply is dated July 26, 1934, and consequently the union members may have known, when they voted, that the employers had already rejected the plan. Reply of the employers' committee, dated July 25, 1934, is in the same envelope. Haas's remark is from his Diary, July 26, 1934; Box 11, HP-ACUA. Letters of Haas and Dunnigan to the employers' committee and the committee's reply, all dated July 27, 1934, are also in Envelope 48, HP-ACUA.

24. Proposal of July 30 is in Envelope 48, HP-ACUA, as is correspondence of Haas and Cochran, July 30-Aug. 5. See also Diary, Aug. 1, 1934 (Box 11, HP-ACUA); Bernstein, *Turbulent Years*, pp. 245-247; Dobbs, *Teamster Rebellion*, pp. 151-155; Mayer, *The Political Career of Floyd B. Olson*, p. 217; and Walker, *American City*, pp. 207-208.

25. Olson to General E.A. Walsh, Executive Order 7, Aug. 5, 1934 (copy in Envelope 48, HP-ACUA); *Northwest Organizer*, July 31, 1934; Dunnigan to Hugh Kerwin, Aug. 6, 1934 (in RG 280, U.S. Conciliation Service, Case 176/1539, Box 144, National Archives); Diary, Aug. 5-7, 1934 (Box 11, HP-ACUA); and Donald Schewe, "The Minneapolis Truck Drivers' Strike of 1934," p. 71. The U.S. Conciliation Service was replaced by the Federal Mediation and Conciliation Service in 1947.

26. Haas to Agnes Regan, Aug. 6, 1934 (Box 58, HP-ACUA); Mayer, *The Political Career of Floyd B. Olson*, pp. 217-219; and Bernstein, *Turbulent Years*, pp. 247-249.

27. Quotations from Walker, *American City*, p. 218; *Northwest Organizer*, Aug. 14, 1934; and a letter to the editor, *The Nation*, 139 (Sept. 26, 1934), 352.

28. *Northwest Organizer*, Aug. 14, 1934. John W. Edelman, of the American Federation of Hosiery Workers, defended Haas in *The Nation*, 139 (Sept. 5, 1934), 271: "We have found this priest a real liberal on economic issues and one of the last men in this country who would attempt to trick or deceive a group of labor unionists.... I, for one, resent this sort of loosely worded and unsupported attack on one of the few persons in this country

who are willing to make real sacrifices of time and effort in the cause of peace in industry." See also Dobbs, *Teamster Rebellion*, pp. 171-172, and Diary, Aug. 11, 1934; Box 11, HP-ACUA.

29. "Memo to the Governor," Aug. 14, 1934; Box 2, Day Papers, Minnesota Historical Society.

30. Memorandum, July 26, 1934 (RG 25, Case 38, National Archives); Wolf to Haas, July 28, 1934 (Envelope 48, HP-ACUA); Diary, July 26-Aug. 8, 1934 (Box 11, HP-ACUA); memo of July 31, 1934 (Official File, 407-B, FDR Library); memorandum of Benedict Wolf, Aug. 8, 1934, summarizing telephone conversation with Haas (RG 25, Case 38, National Archives); minutes of RFC meeting of Dec. 8, 1933 (RG 234, Reconstruction Finance Corporation, Series 3, 1933, Vol. XXIII, Part 3, pp. 1774-1775, National Archives); Haas to Wolf, Aug. 7, 1934 (RG 25, Case 38, National Archives); Mayer, *The Political Career of Floyd B. Olson*, p. 218; Bernstein, *Turbulent Years*, pp. 247-250; and Schewe, "The Minneapolis Truck Drivers' Strike of 1934," pp. 82-84.

31. Cochran to Haas, Aug. 15, 1934 (Envelope 48, HP-ACUA); Diary, Aug. 11 and 15, 1934 (Box 11, HP-ACUA); and "Memorandum, August 14, 1934" (RG 25, Case 38, National Archives).

32. Bernstein, *Turbulent Years*, p. 250, and Diary, Aug. 17, 1934; Box 11, HP-ACUA.

33. Diary, Aug. 16, 1934 (Box 11, HP-ACUA); "Twin Cities," p. 112; Diary, Aug. 18-19, 1934 (Box 11, HP-ACUA), and outline of events from Aug. 8 to Aug. 22, 1934, and "Summary," in Envelope 48, HP-ACUA.

34. Quoted in *St. Paul Dispatch*, Aug. 22, 1934; from clipping in HP-ACUA. See also *New York Times* and *Minneapolis Journal*, Aug. 22, 1934, and *Minneapolis Tribune*, Aug. 23, 1934.

35. Haas to Rivers, Sept. 8, 1934 (Box 58, HP-ACUA); telegram of Jones to Roosevelt, Aug. 22, 1934 (Official File, 407-B, FDR Library); minutes of RFC (RG 234, Series 3) meeting of Nov. 22, 1934, pp. 3124-3129.

36. Walker, *American City*, pp. 218-219, and *Minneapolis Journal*, Aug. 22 and 23, 1934. This final statement is not quite accurate, since on July 25 the employers had rejected any minimum wage provisions, reinstatement of strikers involved in the earlier violence, and union elections in many of the 166 firms.

37. *Northwest Catholic*, Sept. 8, 1934; from clipping in HP-ACUA. The following quotation is from Lawson to Perkins, Aug. 29, 1934; Envelope 48, HP-ACUA.

38. Speech reprinted in *Rights and Wrongs in Industry* (New York, 1933), pp. 21-32. The quotation is from pp. 30-31.

39. Quoted from a Toledo, Ohio, speech, in *Toledo Catholic Chronicle*, July 23, 1937; from clipping in HP-ACUA.

7. Return to Milwaukee, 1935-1937

1. Interview in *Catholic Daily Tribune*, Aug. 2, 1933; from clipping in HP-ACUA.

2. Two excellent summaries of the New Deal legislation of 1935 are William E. Leuchtenburg, *Franklin D. Roosevelt and the New Deal* (New York, 1963), pp. 131-166, and Arthur M. Schlesinger, Jr., *The Politics of Upheaval* (Boston, 1960), pp. 211-384.

3. *New York Times*, Aug. 13 and Nov. 8, 1935.

4. *The Salesianum*, 31 (Jan. 1936), 46. The quotation is from NCWC News Service release, Nov. 11, 1935.

5. The best study of St. Francis Seminary is Peter Leo Johnson, *Halcyon Days: Story of St. Francis Seminary* (Milwaukee, 1956). Church regulations pertaining to seminaries are in *Codex Iuris Canonici*, can. 1352-1371. See also John Tracy Ellis, "The Formation of the American Priest: An Historical Perspective," in Ellis, *The Catholic Priest in the United States: Historical Investigation* (Collegeville, Minn., 1971), pp. 3-110. Author's interviews with Rev. William Hennen and Msgr. Alphonse Popek in Milwaukee, July 23-24, 1976.

6. Johnson, *Halcyon Days*, pp. 356-370.

7. Ibid., pp. 222-271, and Seminary of St. Francis de Sales Catalogs, 1934-1937.

8. *Seminary of St. Francis de Sales Catalogue*, 1936-37, p. 37, and *The Salesianum*, 31 (Apr. 1936), 97-99, and 31 (July 1936), 155.

9. From interviews with several friends and former students of Father Haas in Jan. 1966 and July 1976.

10. F.W. Pope, M.D., to Haas, Dec. 11, 1933 (Box 25); Al to Haas, Mar. 7, 1934, and Margaret to Haas, Mar. 8 and May 22, 1934 (Box 27); Mary to Haas, Apr. 7, 1934 (Box 57); and Amy to Haas, Nov. 16, 1934 (Box 27, HP-ACUA).

11. Most of Father Haas's estate correspondence and records are preserved in Box 24, HP-ACUA.

12. Margaret to Haas, May 2 and June 5, 1933, and Apr. 4, 1934; Amy to Haas, Apr. 16 and 24, 1935, and Jan. 22 and June 7, 1935; and Al to Haas, Sept. 11, 1934; all in Box 27, HP-ACUA.

13. Margaret to Haas, Sept. 10, 1932, Nov. 19 and Dec. 5, 1933, and Sept. 6, 1934; Mary to Haas, May 26, 1933, Oct. 29, 1934, Aug. 7, 1935, and June 21, 1937; Billy to Haas, Feb. 24, 1932, Aug. 31, 1933, and Mar. 8, 1934; Dick to Haas, Feb. 14, 1936; all in Box 27, HP-ACUA.

14. Mary to Haas, Oct. 6 and 12 and Nov. 3, 1931, Jan. 13, 1932, and Oct. 29, 1934; all in Box 27. Mary to Haas, Mar. 25, 1934; Box 24, HP-ACUA.

15. Mary to Haas, June 17 and Sept. 26, 1935; Box 27, HP-ACUA.

16. Mary to Haas, Mar. 24, 1936; Box 24, HP-ACUA.

17. Haas to Mary, Mar. 26, 1936; Box 24, HP-ACUA.

18. Mary to Haas, Nov. 3, 1931; Box 27, HP-ACUA.

19. Johnson, *Halcyon Days*, p. 384, and Haas to Roosevelt, Oct. 24, 1935; Box 61, HP-ACUA.

20. From an address titled "More N.R.A.—Not Less"; Box 69, HP-ACUA. The earlier quotation is from *Milwaukee Catholic Herald*, June 29, 1933.

21. "Competition and Social Justice," *The Salesianum*, 30, Oct. 1935, p. 21. See also "The Next Steps to Recovery," *Sign*, 15 (Feb. 1936), 393-395, and an address to the alumnae of NCSSS, quoted in *Catholic Action*, 17 (July 1935), 4.

22. "Lesson of the N.R.A.." *Catholic Action*, 20 (July 1938), 12.

23. *New York Times*, June 7 and 19, 1935; memorandum of A.F. Hinrichs of Bureau of Labor Statistics to Secretary of Labor, June 15, 1935; in Record Group 9, National Recovery Administration, Compliance Division, Robert Committee Data, National Archives. In the same place, see letters of Frank C. Walker to James L. O'Neill, June 20, 1935; Roosevelt to O'Neill, June 17, 1935; and O'Neill to Roosevelt, June 21, 1935. See also NRA release 2-3, June 24, 1935; Box 23, HP-ACUA. Father Haas had been informed of his appointment in a telegram from Gustav Peck on June 21, 1935; Box 61, HP-ACUA. Dickinson was assistant secretary of commerce, Lubin was U.S. commissioner of labor statistics, and Upp was an eastern business executive.

24. *New York Times*, July 4 and 26, 1935. The committee, under General Fries, had met on June 25, 26, 27, 28, and July 1 but then ceased to function, until Robert replaced Fries as chairman, almost a month later. See minutes of the meetings of the Robert Committee, and memorandum of J.H. Ward, assistant division administrator, to state directors, Aug. 20, 1935 (RG 9, Robert Committee Data, National Archives), and mimeographed final report of the committee, released Mar. 17, 1936, a copy of which is in Box 17, HP-ACUA. Hereafter this will be referred to as "Final Report."

25. Haas to Leighton H. Peebles, deputy director, Division of Business Cooperation, Dec. 31, 1935; Box 25, HP-ACUA.

26. "Final Report"; Box 17, HP-ACUA. See a summary of the committee's findings in *Monthly Labor Review*, 42 (May 1936), 1235-1237. Quotations are from "Final Report," pp. 10 and 15. Due to limitations of time, the committee decided to concentrate on labor standards and leave to other government agencies a more detailed investigation of trade practices. On June 27, 1935, O'Neill stated that "the fair-trade practices in voluntary codes of fair competition would be put under the supervision of the Federal Trade Commission, and that the N.R.A. would limit itself to the labor provisions of these Codes"; quoted in *New York Times*, June 28, 1935.

27. Box 21, HP-ACUA, contains three drafts of the committee's final report, with revisions of each draft suggested by Haas.

28. "Executive Order Terminating the N.R.A., December 21, 1935," and transcript of telephone conversation between Chairman Robert and Father Haas, Jan. 3, 1936, signed by Robert; both in Box 23, HP-ACUA. Also Isador Lubin in interview with the author, June 14, 1966.

29. Roosevelt to O'Neill, June 17, 1935 (RG 9, Robert Committee Data, National Archives); Haas to Peebles, Jan. 13, 1936 (Box 25); Haas to Dr. Richard J. Purcell, Jan. 20, 1936, and Haas to Jacob Baker, Jan. 27, 1936 (Box 63); and E.J. Tracy to Haas, Mar. 2, 1936 (Box 25, HP-ACUA). *New York Times*, Mar. 17, 1936, and *Monthly Labor Review*, 42 (May 1936),

1235-1237. Standard New Deal histories of William Leuchtenburg, Raymond Moley, Frances Perkins, Basil Rauch, and Arthur Schlesinger, Jr., apparently make no mention of the committee and its report.

30. This was suggested in the meeting of Aug. 14, 1935; see minutes, RG 9, Robert Committee Data, National Archives.

31. For the WPA, see Searle F. Charles, *Minister of Relief* (Syracuse, N.Y., 1963), pp. 128-158; Harry L. Hopkins, *Spending to Save* (New York, 1936), pp. 160-178; Donald S. Howard, *The W.P.A. and Federal Relief Policy* (New York, 1943), pp. 105-121; Arthur Macmahon and others, *The Administration of Federal Work Relief* (Chicago, 1941), pp. 189-212; and Lewis Meriam, *Relief and Social Security* (Washington, 1946), pp. 345-361. See also *New York Times*, July 25, 1935; *Monthly Labor Review*, 41 (Sept. 1935), 618; and Haas to Hopkins, July 26, 1935 (Box 61, HP-ACUA).

32. WPA release, July 25, 1935; WPA Bulletin 36, Nov. 13, 1935; and Stabler to Roy C. Jacobson, WPA field representative, May 1, 1937; all in Box 28, HP-ACUA. See also *Handbook of Procedures*, Apr. 17, 1937, sec. 7.

33. Overlapping jurisdiction throughout the WPA is discussed in Macmahon, *Administration of Federal Work Relief*, pp. 189-212. The quotation is from minutes of the meeting of the Labor Policies Board, Aug. 27, 1935 (Box 28, HP-ACUA). See also Baker to Wharton, Feb. 1, 1936, also in Box 28.

34. Stabler to Haas, Jan. 28 and Mar. 3, 1936, and Haas to Stabler, Mar. 9, 1936; all in Box 28, HP-ACUA. For Wilson at Geneva, see *New York Times*, Apr. 5, 1936.

35. Minutes of the meetings of the Labor Policies Board in 1936 are in Box 28, HP-ACUA, and in Record Group 69, General Subject Series, 040, National Archives. Minutes of the meeting of Apr. 14, 1936; Nels Anderson to Wharton, Apr. 23, and Haas to Labor Policies Board, May 8, 1936; Haas to Stabler, June 11, 1936; "Memorandum on the Malone, New York Pulpwood Industry" (undated); and Haas's WPA travel vouchers; all in Box 28, HP-ACUA. See also typed draft of interview of Haas with Floyd Dell, Oct. 6, 1936 (in Scrapbook IV), and notes for Washington speech and "summary" of the Cleveland conference; Box 28, HP-ACUA.

36. Minutes of board meetings and Father Haas's correspondence throughout most of 1936 and 1937 mention numerous cases of dismissal which the board was asked to investigate. WPA wage policies are treated by Arthur E. Burns and Peyton Kerr, "Survey of Work-Relief Wage Policies," *American Economic Review*, 27 (Dec. 1937), 711-724; Howard, *The W.P.A. and Federal Relief Policies*, pp. 158-227; Macmahon, *The Administration of Federal Work Relief*, pp. 149-166; and Meriam, *Relief and Social Security*, pp. 382-391. Transcripts of hearings were usually sent to Haas in Milwaukee and he would send his recommendations by return mail. Correspondence is in Box 28, HP-ACUA.

37. Haas to Stabler, Mar. 9, 1937; Envelope 1, HP-ACUA. See also *Michigan Catholic*, Mar. 11, 1937, and Haas's report to Stabler, Mar. 9, 1937; Box 28, HP-ACUA.

38. Box 28, HP-ACUA, contains numerous letters to Haas with complaints of discrimination against WPA workers because of race, religion, or national origin. The files of the Greenberg case are preserved in Envelope 36, HP-ACUA. Especially pertinent are a letter of Dean Brimhall to Haas, Feb. 14, 1938; the transcript of public hearings on Feb. 28 and Mar. 2 and 3, 1938; a union bulletin, "Father Haas to Arbitrate Greenberg Case," Mar. 1, 1938; and the arbitration award of Haas, Mar. 12, 1938. Hopkins at this time was in Mayo Clinic and Williams was acting WPA administrator.

39. Transcripts of hearings; Envelope 36, HP-ACUA.

40. Arbitration Award, "In the Matter of the Dismissal of Bernard Greenberg from the Division of Social Research, Works Progress Administration"; Envelope 36, HP-ACUA. *Washington Star*, Mar. 14, 1938.

41. Elizabeth Wickenden, assistant to Aubrey Williams, to Stabler, Feb. 11, 1938 (Envelope 52); Haas to David K. Niles, June 14, 1938 (Box 28); and Hopkins to Haas, June 28, 1938; Envelope 52, HP-ACUA.

42. Stabler to Haas, Aug. 2, 1938, and Memorandum 13527, from Hopkins to state WPA administrators, Sept. 22, 1938; Box 28, HP-ACUA.

43. The quotation is from Herbert Benjamin, "Organization Is Power," *Work*, Oct. 22, 1938. The author could find no record of a case heard by Haas, either in Haas's papers or in the National Archives. See also Harry L. Kinnear, chief clerk of WPA, to Haas, Feb. 20, 1939; Box 25, HP-ACUA.

44. Forrest Davis, "Father Coughlin," *Atlantic Monthly*, 156 (Dec. 1935), 659-668. Haas's reply is in Box 64, HP-ACUA, and a portion of it appeared in "The Contributors' Column," *Atlantic Monthly*, 157 (Apr. 1936). See also Haas to John J. Burke, Dec. 2, and Burke to Haas, Dec. 6, 1935; Box 64, HP-ACUA. The best studies of Father Coughlin are Charles J. Tull, *Father Coughlin and the New Deal* (Syracuse, N.Y., 1965), and Sheldon Marcus, *Father Coughlin: The Tumultuous Life of the Priest of the Little Flower* (Boston, 1973).

45. Haas to Rev. Raymond J. Miller, Dec. 12, 1937 (Box 65), and Haas to Rice, Feb. 1, 1935 (Box 61, HP-ACUA); Marquette High School *Flambeau*, May 23, 1936, from a clipping in HP-ACUA; and Haas to Mooney, Oct. 28, 1937 (Box 59, HP-ACUA).

46. See "The Next Steps to Recovery," pp. 393-395; "Two Milestones to Social Justice," *Sign*, 15 (May 1936), 585-587; and Loretto R. Lawler, *Full Circle: The Story of the National Catholic School of Social Service* (Washington, 1951), pp. 121-122. Haas was one of the signers of *Organized Social Justice*, a statement issued by the NCWC in 1936, and at about this time he and McGowan began work on a new translation of *Rerum Novarum* and *Quadragesimo Anno*. See the following chapter for this project and Haas's participation in the Summer Schools of Social Action for Priests.

47. The first quotation is from the *Tampa Morning Tribune*, Sept. 20, 1935; from clipping in HP-ACUA. The records of this case are in Envelope 37, HP-ACUA, and Record Group 280, U.S. Conciliation Service, Case 182-295, Box 453, National Archives. Charles A. Ford, director of Evening Extension Division, Temple University, to Haas, Oct. 5, 1935 (Box 62, HP-ACUA);

"Organization, the Need of the Worker and of the Community," *Report of the Proceedings of the Biennial Convention of the Amalgamated Clothing Workers of America* (Cleveland, 1936), pp. 341-344; and "What about the Tampa Convention?" *Milwaukee Catholic Herald-Citizen*, Dec. 5, 1936. The second quotation is from the *Milwaukee Journal*, Nov. 27, 1935.

48. Quoted in *Capital Times* (Madison), June 22, 1936. See also *Milwaukee Catholic Herald-Citizen*, June 27, 1936.

8. The Wisconsin Labor Relations Board, 1937-1939

1. The quotation is from Haas to Perkins, Apr. 1, 1933; Box 60, HP-ACUA.

2. A copy of Haas's speech before the Amalgamated Clothing Workers of America, "More NRA—Not Less," is in Box 69, HP-ACUA. The quotations are from Haas to Wagner, Apr. 12, 1937 (Box 64, HP-ACUA), and *The Why and Whither of Labor Unions* (Huntington, Ind., 1939), p. 11.

3. 49 Stat. 449 (1935), and 29 U.S.C., secs. 151-166; and Wisconsin *Session Laws, 1937,* c. 51 (Apr. 15). The National Labor Relations Act is reprinted in *Monthly Labor Review,* 41 (Aug. 1935), 370-377, and the Wisconsin act in ibid., 45 (Oct. 1937), 859-860.

4. "Report" of Wisconsin Labor Relations Board, Dec. 22, 1938, pp. 3-4. A copy is in Box 23, HP-ACUA.

5. Quoted in *New York Times*, July 6, 1935. See also *Monthly Labor Review,* 41 (Aug. 1935), p. 373.

6. "Report," p. 5; Box 23, HP-ACUA.

7. Edwin Witte to L.A. Lecher, May 5, 1937; Box 63, Witte Papers, State Historical Society of Wisconsin.

8. A speech of Haas, "State Labor Relations Boards," reprinted in *Bulletin of the U.S. Bureau of Labor Statistics,* No. 653 (1938), p. 122.

9. *Milwaukee Journal,* Apr. 23, 1937.

10. *Sheboygan Press,* Apr. 24, 1937; *Labor,* May 9, 1937 (from clipping in HP-ACUA); *Capital Times* (Madison), May 17, 1937; *Wisconsin State Journal,* Apr. 27, 1937; and undated clipping from editor of *Racine Day* to Edwin Witte, May 11, 1937; in Box 63, Witte Papers, State Historical Society of Wisconsin.

11. *Milwaukee Journal,* May 21, 1937. Wrabetz was chairman of the state Industrial Commission and Witte was on the faculty of the state university. Haas was given a salary of $25 per day. Witte confided to a friend in early May: "At this stage the Board has no appropriations and the Governor doubtless selected me because I am already on the state payroll"; Witte to Professor Stewart Scrimshall, May 5, 1937; Box 63, Witte Papers, State Historical Society of Wisconsin. See also *Wisconsin State Journal,* May 20, 1937; Haas to Stabler, May 22, 1937 (Box 28, HP-ACUA); and Haas to Rev. John Maguire, May 3, 1937; Box 23, HP-ACUA.

12. *New York Times* and *Washington Post,* Apr. 21, 1937. For the

story of Haas's acceptance, see *Milwaukee Catholic Herald-Citizen*, May 1, 1937. Witte was reluctant to accept the appointment because he feared he would not have sufficient time to devote to it. See Witte to A.J. Glover, Aug. 11, 1939, and Witte to Charles Bernhard, Jan. 11, 1939; Box 63, Witte Papers, State Historical Society of Wisconsin. Father Haas expressed his view of the problem of overlapping jurisdiction in an article later that year: "Practically speaking, until the matter is decided in the courts, so long as the same policies and decisions are followed by both Federal and State boards, the problem of jurisdiction, always inherent in our Federal form of government, need not be of great concern. The Wisconsin Labor Relations Board and Mr. Nathaniel Clark, regional director of the National Labor Relations Board office in Milwaukee, have worked in closest co-operation, and so long as this mutual confidence continues, the objectives of either Federal or State law cannot be frustrated by charging either board with defect of jurisdiction"; "State Labor Relations Boards," p. 123.

13. Diary, Apr. 26–May 1, 1937 (Box 23, HP-ACUA), and *Capital Times*, Apr. 28, 1937.

14. Diary, Apr. 28, 1937 (Box 23, HP-ACUA); "Report of the Wisconsin Labor Relations Board to the National Labor Relations Board," in Case I-675, R. 61, Series 21/0/1, Archives Division, State Historical Society of Wisconsin. See also Witte to J. Warren Madden, Oct. 20, 1937; Envelope 51, HP-ACUA. Information on the board's early activities is often lacking since the staff was not then organized and complete records were not retained.

15. See Perkins to Haas, Apr. 29, 1937; Haas to Margaret Stabler, May 2, 1937; and Haas to Wrabetz, May 6, 1937; Box 28, HP-ACUA. The quotation is from *New York Times*, May 5, 1937.

16. "Memorandum," signed by Witte, May 10, 1937, and "Report on Efforts at Mediation," undated; in Case I-675, R. 61, Series 21/0/1, Archives Division, State Historical Society of Wisconsin. See also Witte to Madden, Oct. 20, 1937 (Envelope 51, HP-ACUA), and *Milwaukee Journal*, May 13 and 14, 1937. Further disagreements in these two cases were not resolved for several additional weeks.

17. Quoted in *Wisconsin State Journal*, May 14, 1937. See also *Milwaukee Journal*, *Wisconsin News*, and *Milwaukee Leader*, May 11, 1937.

18. Haas to Margaret Stabler, May 22, 1937; Box 28, HP-ACUA. See also *Milwaukee Journal*, May 16, 1937; *Wisconsin State Journal*, May 20, 1937; "Rules and Regulations of the Wisconsin Labor Relations Board," May 22, 1937 (copy in Box 23, HP-ACUA); and Nathan P. Feinsinger and William Gorham Rice, Jr., *The Wisconsin Labor Relations Act* (Madison, 1937), p. 55. On May 5 Witte had written: "As we have no funds, we cannot at this time even reprint the law under which we are acting"; Witte to Stewart Scrimshall, May 5, 1937, Box 63, Witte Papers, State Historical Society of Wisconsin.

19. *Milwaukee Journal*, June 2, 8, 9, 10, and 11, 1937, for this and the following cases. Records of the Milwaukee Athletic Club dispute are in Case I-2, C-3; the Yahr-Lange dispute in Case II, 680, A 26; the Oshkosh contro-

versy in Case I, 305; and the Johnson Company controversy in Case III, 786; Archives Division, State Historical Society of Wisconsin, and Envelope 51, HP-ACUA. See also a report, "Oshkosh, Wisconsin, Woodstock Strike, June 24-25, 1937," written in Haas's hand and preserved in Envelope 38, HP-ACUA. *Monthly Labor Review*, 45 (July-Dec. 1937), lists the number of strikes and disputes by state for April-August in the section "Industrial Disputes."

20. *New York Times*, Aug. 15, 1937. A copy of this report, dated Aug. 1, is in Box 23, HP-ACUA. See also Thomas R. Fisher, *Industrial Disputes and Federal Legislation* (New York, 1940), p. 324.

21. The silk strike and Haas's appointment to Catholic University will be discussed in the following chapter.

22. Aaron I. Abell, *American Catholicism and Social Action* (Notre Dame, Ind., 1963), pp. 260-261; Rev. R.A. McGowan, "Clergy Hail Schools of Social Action," *Catholic Action*, 19 (Aug. 1937), 16-17; Right Rev. Msgr. Thomas O'Dwyer, "Los Angeles School of Social Action," *Catholic Action*, 19 (Sept. 1937), 19; and Paul Tanner, "The Summer School of Social Action for the Clergy," *The Salesianum*, 32 (Oct. 1937), 169-173. The following quotation is from Haas to Lucey, Jan. 28, 1937; Box 64, HP-ACUA.

23. McGowan, "Clergy Hail Schools of Social Action," p. 16.

24. Tanner, "The Summer School of Social Action for the Clergy," pp. 170-171. See also McGowan, "Clergy Hail Schools of Social Action," pp. 16-17, and *Milwaukee Catholic Herald-Citizen*, July 4 to Aug. 7, 1937.

25. Tanner, "The Summer School of Social Action for the Clergy," p. 172. See also McGowan, "Clergy Hail Schools of Social Action," pp. 16-17, and proceedings of the Milwaukee Summer School of Social Action, 1937, (a bound copy in possession of the author).

26. Quoted in *Toledo Catholic Chronicle*, July 23, 1937; from clipping in HP-ACUA.

27. A copy of this address, "Strikes," is in Box 1, HP-ACUA. Catholic opinion on the sitdown strike is summarized in David J. O'Brien, "American Catholics and Organized Labor in the 1930's," *Catholic Historical Review*, 52 (Oct. 1966), 336-337.

28. Although the San Francisco Summer School preceded the one in Milwaukee by a few weeks, Haas's participation in the planning dated at least from January. See Haas to Lucey, Jan. 27, 1937; Box 64, HP-ACUA.

29. *Monthly Labor Review*, 46 (Jan. 1938), 176; 46 (Feb. 1938), 440; 46 (Mar. 1938), 718; and 46 (Apr. 1938), 923.

30. Norman Moe to Haas, Jan. 7, 1938; see also Jack Kyle to Haas, Jan. 14, 1938. Both in Envelope 51, HP-ACUA.

31. Records of this dispute are in Case I, 52, and Case IV, 672, Series 21/0/1, Archives Division, State Historical Society of Wisconsin, and in Envelope 54, HP-ACUA. The most detailed newspaper accounts are in *Milwaukee Journal*, May 4-7; *Milwaukee Sentinel*, May 2-8; and *New York Times*, May 5, 1938. See Harold Christoffel to La Follette, Apr. 27, 1938, and Moe to Kyle, May 10, 1938 (Case IV, 672, Series 20/0/1, Archives Division, State

Historical Society of Wisconsin); and *Milwaukee News*, May 2, 1938 (from clipping in HP-ACUA).

32. Quoted in *Milwaukee Sentinel*, May 4, 1938.

33. Both quotations from *Milwaukee News*, May 4, 1938 (from clipping in HP-ACUA). See also *New York Times*, May 5, 1938.

34. Moe to Kyle, May 10, 1938; Case IV, 672, Series 20/0/1, Archives Division, State Historical Society of Wisconsin. Haas had been appointed domestic prelate, with the title of monsignor, by this time.

35. The terms of this settlement were printed in the *Milwaukee Journal*, May 7, 1938.

36. The quotations are from the *Milwaukee Sentinel* and *Milwaukee Journal*, May 5, 1938; Garrison to Haas, May 9, 1938; and La Follette to Haas, May 16, 1938; all in Envelope 54, HP-ACUA.

37. *Newsweek*, 12 (Oct. 10, 1938), 40.

38. Records of this dispute are in Envelopes 51 and 53 (HP-ACUA) and in Case II, 916 (Series 21/0/1), Archives Division, State Historical Society of Wisconsin. See especially the memoranda of Moe to Kyle, Sept. 1, 1938, and Moe to Norman M. Clapp, Sept. 10, 1938 (both in Archives Division, State Historical Society of Wisconsin), and the memorandum of Moe to Haas, Oct. 11, 1938 (Envelope 51, HP-ACUA). The best newspaper accounts are in the *Kenosha Evening News* and *Racine Journal-Times*; from clippings in HP-ACUA.

39. The major change was that in combining the seniority lists the workers' days of unemployment were not counted, the practice followed in Kenosha but not in Racine. The following quotation is from Moe to Haas, Oct. 10, 1938; Envelope 53, HP-ACUA.

40. Records of this controversy are in Envelope 51 and Box 23, HP-ACUA, and in Box 9, Series 21/0/1, Archives Division, State Historical Society of Wisconsin. In Box 9, see especially Alfred Fernbach to Kyle, Aug. 24, 1938, and Moe to Kyle, Sept. 7 and 17, 1938. In Envelope 51, see Moe to Kyle, Sept. 2, 1938, and transcripts of telephone conversations of Haas with John Steelman (Nov. 7), a staff member of the NLRB (Nov. 9), Steelman (Nov. 9), and Edward Littel, secretary to La Follette (Nov. 9). Records of this case are also preserved in Record Group 280, U.S. Conciliation Service, Case 199/2342, Box 1024, National Archives.

41. Transcripts of many of these telephone calls have been preserved in Envelope 51, HP-ACUA. For some days, there are transcripts for as many as six telephone calls, chiefly to Gov. La Follette, the NLRB, and John Steelman of the Conciliation Service. Although such days may have been exceptional, Haas undoubtedly made other calls for which no transcripts have been preserved. The quotation is from a transcript of a telephone call from Haas to the NLRB, Nov. 9, 1938. For a discussion of the strike vote, see K.H. Tuchscherer to Kyle, Sept. 22, 1938; Box 9, Archives Division, State Historical Society of Wisconsin.

42. Memorandum of H. Herman Rauch, Nov. 19, 1938; Box 9, Series 21/0/1, Archives Division, State Historical Society of Wisconsin. See also Ed-

ward Littel (secretary to the governor) to Haas, Nov. 19, 1938; Envelope 51, HP-ACUA.

43. William F. Raney, *Wisconsin, a Story of Progress* (New York, 1940), pp. 369-370. For the election returns, see *New York Times*, Nov. 9, 1938. The cover story of *Time*, 32 (Jan. 16, 1939), 16-19, describes the new governor and his election. See also the *Milwaukee News*, Dec. 24, 1938; from clipping in HP-ACUA.

44. Haas to Heil, Jan. 1, 1939; Envelope 51, HP-ACUA.

45. The best studies of the Wisconsin Employment Peace Act of 1939 are Mason C. Doan, "State Labor Relations Acts," *Quarterly Journal of Economics*, 56 (Aug. 1942), 545-556, and Charles C. Killingsworth, "Public Regulation of Labor Relations—the Wisconsin Experiment," *American Economic Review*, 33 (June 1943), 247-263. A copy of Haas's affidavit, dated Feb. 28, 1939, is in Envelope 51, HP-ACUA. The quotation is from Heil to Haas, Mar. 29, 1939; Envelope 51, HP-ACUA. See also Witte to Ronald Houghton, Feb. 27, 1939 (Box 5), and Witte to A.J. Glover, Aug. 2, 1939; Box 63, Witte Papers, State Historical Society of Wisconsin. The governor made a temporary replacement for Haas to enable the new board members to sign the final report and transfer the board's assets to the new panel established by the Employment Peace Act.

46. During Haas's years as rector of St. Francis Seminary, he had also served on Milwaukee's Metropolitan Committee on Crime Prevention, the Board of Review of the Trade Practice Department of the Wisconsin Recovery Administration, and other state and local agencies, but none of these exerted significant influence on Wisconsin public life. For these appointments, see La Follette to Haas, Feb. 18, 1936; Charles M. Dow, secretary to the governor, to Haas, Apr. 7, 1936 (Box 63, HP-ACUA); and Haas to Mayor Daniel Hoan of Milwaukee, Feb. 15 and Sept. 18, 1937; Box 64, HP-ACUA.

47. "Report," p. 21; Box 23, HP-ACUA. Similar figures are given in Doan, "State Labor Relations Acts," pp. 507-559.

48. *Wisconsin State Journal*, Aug. 27, 1937; *Capital Times*, Aug. 28, 1938; and La Follette to Haas, Dec. 30, 1939 (Envelope 51, HP-ACUA).

9. The Church's Monsignor and Labor's Troubleshooter: Washington, 1937-1943

1. *Milwaukee Journal*, Aug. 25, 1937, and *Milwaukee Catholic Herald-Citizen*, Aug. 28, 1937.

2. See also *The Salesianum*, 32 (Oct. 1937), 192-193.

3. The first quotation is from NCWC News Service Release 37-2804, Aug. 28, 1937, and the second is from the *Milwaukee Catholic Herald-Citizen* of the same date; the latter also reprinted the letter of Pope Pius XI. Haas knew of the appointment weeks earlier, of course. On July 29, the day on which the Vatican announced Haas's elevation to the rank of domestic pre-

late, Msgr. Corrigan had wired Haas: "The University congratulates the new Domestic Prelate and welcomes him as Dean of its School of Social Science"; Corrigan to Haas, July 29, 1937 (Box 64, HP-ACUA).

4. *Acta Apostolicae Sedis*, 23 (July 1, 1931), 241-262. An interesting commentary on this apostolic constitution is by the rector of Catholic University, James H. Ryan, "Pope Pius XI and the University Education of Priests," *Ecclesiastical Review*, 85 (Oct. 1931), 337-344.

5. See pages 44-45 above for the background of this situation.

6. For these early efforts, see memorandum of Rev. John Burke, C.S.P., to Haas, June 12, 1935, and letter of Bishop James Ryan to Bishop Karl Alter, July 13, 1935; both in Box 4, Office of Vice Rector, Departmental Correspondence, ACUA. Roy J. Deferrari, *Memoirs of The Catholic University of America, 1918-1960* (Boston, 1962), pp. 35-39 and 269-270; and interview with Paul Hanly Furfey, July 17, 1976. Box 58, HP-ACUA, contains several letters of Haas to Stritch, informing him of various proposals at that time for affiliating the NCSSS with Catholic University. See also O'Grady to Archbishop Amleto Cicognani, apostolic delegate to the United States, Aug. 20, 1937, and memorandum of Msgr. O'Grady, probably Sept. 8, 1937; both in NCWC Papers, ACUA.

7. In addition to the works cited in the preceding note, see also *The Statutes of The Catholic University of America* (Washington, 1937), art. 5; John O'Grady to Corrigan, July 25, 1936; John Burke to Corrigan, July 28, 1936; Haas to Corrigan, Oct. 26 and Nov. 2, 1936; and Robert Keegan to Corrigan, Nov. 17, 1936; all in Box 124, Rectors Office (1928-1947), ACUA. The quotation is from Marion Hathway to O'Grady, Oct. 7, 1937; Box 124, Rectors Office (1928-1947), ACUA. Msgr. Corrigan was understandably disturbed that the matter had been referred to the association, apparently without his knowledge; Corrigan to Hathway, Oct. 8, and Hathway to Corrigan, Oct. 11, 1937, also in Box 124, Rectors Office (1928-1947), ACUA. See also Msgr. Corrigan's sermon, "University Faces New Year," in *Catholic University Bulletin*, 6 (Nov. 1937), 2-3ff.

8. Deferrari, *Memoirs*, p. 270, for example, gives Haas and Msgr. Burke major responsibility.

9. Haas to Corrigan, Oct. 26 and Nov. 2, 1936; Box 124, Rectors Office (1928-1947), ACUA.

10. News release of Oct. 21, 1938, "The School of Social Science," a copy of which is in Box 67, HP-ACUA.

11. See pages 40-41 above for a discussion of this 1929 controversy; Richard Purcell to Haas, Aug. 12, 1937 (Box 64, HP-ACUA); and *Milwaukee Journal*, Aug. 25, 1937. Haas had attempted to resign from the Wisconsin Labor Relations Board that fall but his resignation was not accepted until 1939. See pages 168-169 above.

12. Msgr. George Higgins, long-time official of the NCWC and the United States Catholic Conference, was a student of Haas's. The author interviewed several former participants in these "Sunday morning seminars" between 1965 and 1976.

13. Report of the Dean of the Faculty oɩ the School of Social Science," annually between 1938 and 1942, and Haas to Most Rev. Rector, Mar. 31, 1942; Box 124, Rectors Office (1928-1947), ACUA. Haas was also able to persuade several government officials to assist with classes in the new School of Social Science. An announcement for 1937 lists Leon Henderson of the WPA, Marius Parioletti of the Department of Agriculture, and officials of the Bureau of Labor Statistics as part-time faculty. See "Catholic University of America: School of Social Science," Box 124, Rectors Office (1928-1947), ACUA.

14. Loretto Lawler, *Full Circle: The Story of the National Catholic School of Social Service* (Washington, 1951), pp. 121-122; "Report of the Dean of the Faculty of the School of Social Science" (1939-1942) Box 124, Rectors Office (1928-1947), ACUA; *Better Men for Better Times* (Washington, 1943), pp. ix-xiii; Mary Synon, "The University Builds a Curriculum for Elementary Catholic Schools," *Catholic University Bulletin*, 12 (Sept. 1944), 4-5; Sister M. Annunciata, O.P., "The Commission on American Citizenship," ibid., 33 (Oct. 1965), 7-9; and *Commission on American Citizenship: Annual Report*, 1940 (Washington, 1940). The quotation is from the "Report" of 1938-39.

15. See "Report of the Dean of the Faculty of the School of Social Science" (1939-1942); Box 124, Rectors Office (1928-1947), ACUA. "Report of the Commission on American Citizenship" (1942), a bound, mimeographed copy of which is in the Catholic University of America Library. Sister Mary Joan, O.P., and Sister Mary Nona, O.P., *Guiding Growth in Christian Social Living*, 3 vols. (Washington, 1944-1946); Msgr. George Johnson's introduction, "Education for Life," is on pages 1-14 of vol. I. The quotation is from a letter of Sister Mary Nona to the author (undated) in late 1977.

16. "Report of the Commission on American Citizenship" (1943 and 1944), bound, mimeographed copies of which are in the Catholic University of America Library.

17. Haas to Althoff, Apr. 22, 1936; Box 64, HP-ACUA. He expressed the same view in a letter to Bishop Robert Lucey, Jan. 9, 1940; Box 66, HP-ACUA. The following quotation is from Haas to Rev. Paul Stroh, C.SS.R., January 27, 1936; Box 63, HP-ACUA.

18. Haas to Rev. Raymond J. Miller, C.SS.R., May 10, 1940, and Haas to Muench, March 23, 1942; Box 63, HP-ACUA. The apostolic delegate's letter is reprinted in *Two Basic Social Encyclicals* (New York, 1943).

19. Charles Bruehl, "Bishops on the Social Order," *Ave Maria*, 51 (Apr. 13, 1940), 455; Ryan to John R. McCurdy, July 14, 1941, quoted in Francis L. Broderick, *Right Reverend New Dealer: John A. Ryan* (New York, 1963), p. 257; (undated) letter of Luigi Cardinal Maglione, papal secretary of state, to Archbishop Amleto Cicognani, apostolic delegate to the United States, reprinted in *Catholic Action*, 22 (July 1940), 3.

20. Broderick, *Right Reverend New Dealer*, p. 257, and "Reminiscence of Archbishop Karl Alter," University of Notre Dame Archives, pp. 12 and

22-23. A copy of the proposed pastoral letter and the correspondence relating to it are in Box 1, HP-ACUA. See especially Haas to Bishop Stephen J. Donohue, D.D., auxiliary bishop of New York, May 30, 1938. As might be expected, Haas's draft is more specific and detailed in describing the sufferings of labor and the abuses of business, and it seems less fearful of the dangers of socialism. The more centrist tone of the completed statement seems to confirm that the final author was Alter, rather than Haas.

21. This and the following quotations are from *The Church and Social Order* (Washington, 1940), pp. 6, 20, 21, 24, and 32-33.

22. *Racine Journal-Times*, March 9, 1939; from clipping in HP-ACUA. The earlier quotation is from Haas to Stabler, Feb. 12, 1936; Box 28, HP-ACUA.

23. Father Haas's address is published in the *Report of the Fifty-fifth Annual Convention of the A.F. of L.* (Washington, 1935), pp. 676-677. For background on the AFL-CIO break, see Walter Galenson, *The C.I.O. Challenge to the A.F.L.* (Cambridge, Mass., 1950), pp. 3-74; Herbert Harris, *Labor's Civil War* (New York, 1940), pp. 22-61; James O. Morris, *Conflict within the A.F.L.* (Ithaca, N.Y., 1958), pp. 171-290; Philip Taft, *The A.F. of L. from the Death of Gompers to the Merger* (New York, 1959), pp. 140-172. For well-documented but less objective expositions, see American Federation of Labor, *A.F. of L. vs. C.I.O., The Record* (Washington, 1939), and *Proceedings of the First Constitutional Convention of the Congress of Industrial Organization*, Pittsburgh (Nov. 14-18, 1938), pp. 92-113.

24. Galenson, *C.I.O. Challenge to the A.F.L.*, pp. 1-16; Morris, *Conflict within the A.F.L.*, pp. 212-223; and Taft, *The A.F. of L. from the Death of Gompers to the Merger*, pp. 148-160.

25. The best secondary sources are Galenson, *C.I.O. Challenge to the A.F.L.*, pp. 17-28, and Taft, *The A.F. of L. from the Death of Gompers to the Merger*, pp. 162-170. *Washington Star*, July 16, 1936, and *Washington Daily News*, July 17, 1936; from clippings in HP-ACUA.

26. Haas to Margaret Stabler, Nov. 21, 1936 (Box 28, HP-ACUA); *Milwaukee Journal*, Nov. 25, 1936; Haas to P.H. Callahan, Dec. 3, 1936; Box 64, HP-ACUA.

27. "What about the Tampa Convention?" *Milwaukee Catholic Herald-Citizen*, Dec. 5, 1936. Compare this with Secretary Perkins's statement: "The A.F. of L.-C.I.O. split was largely an internal fight for control, in which the idea of vertical unions was only a minor issue," in Perkins, "Eight Years as Madame Secretary," *Fortune*, 24 (Sept. 1941), 79.

28. Haas to Lewis, Mar. 6, 1936 (Box 63, HP-ACUA), and *The Why and Whither of Labor Unions* (Huntington, Ind., 1939), p. 12.

29. The transcript of this telephone conversation is in Box 65, HP-ACUA. In a letter to the author on May 4, 1966, Dr. Robert M. Hutchins, one of those selected, stated that the conference was never held.

30. Harris, *Labor's Civil War*, p. 224. See also James A. Wechsler, *Labor Baron* (New York, 1944), p. 89. On Oct. 16, 1937, Haas wired the Wisconsin Labor Board's Jack Kyle in Madison: "Will leave Washington Saturday night

and arrive Madison Sunday evening"; Envelope 51, HP-ACUA. Haas returned from Madison to Washington on Oct. 31, 1937, according to a letter from Haas to a Miss Ziebarth of the Labor Board staff, Nov. 2, 1937, also in Envelope 51, HP-ACUA. See also "The Haas Plan," *America*, 42 (Feb. 24, 1940), 547-548.

31. Memoranda of telephone conversations between Haas and Secretary Perkins, Jan. 11 and 17, 1938; Box 65, HP-ACUA.

32. Haas's speech was reprinted in *Proceedings of the Thirty-fifth Constitutional Convention of the United Mine Workers of America*, Washington (Jan. 25 to Feb. 3, 1938), pp. 280-286.

33. For the reactions of Lewis and Green, see *New York Times*, Feb. 1, 1938.

34. This and the following quotation are from a letter of Haas to Hillman, Dec. 6, 1938, in Archives of the AFL-CIO, Washington, CIO Historical Files, Reel III, Side 2. Haas had originally planned to meet with Hillman and Harrison in Pittsburgh in November, at the time of the CIO convention, but the seriousness of the Harnischfeger strike in Milwaukee prevented him from leaving Washington at that time. See transcripts of telephone calls from Haas to Steelman and to Gov. La Follette, Nov. 7, 1938; Envelope 51, HP-ACUA. See also Galenson, *C.I.O. Challenge to the A.F.L.*, pp. 43-48; Morris, *Conflict within the A.F.L.*, pp. 267-269; and Haas to William Winter, Dec. 1, 1938, in possession of the author, courtesy of Mr. Winter.

35. "Memorandum of January 24, 1939," Perkins Papers, Reel 8, Columbia University. See also Galenson, *C.I.O. Challenge to the A.F.L.*, pp. 48-49.

36. For these subsequent negotiations, see Galenson, *C.I.O. Challenge to the A.F.L.*, pp. 49-74, and Harris, *Labor's Civil War*, p. 224. In private, Haas was also urging public pressure on government officials for a settlement. "The pressure of the rank and file," he wrote to Father John Maguire of St. Viator's College on Mar. 29, 1939, "can be measured by the telegrams and letters of resolutions, many of them jointly signed by the A.F. of L. and the C.I.O., which have been sent to the White House and to the Department of Labor. The resolutions represent well over 2,500,000 union members. Confidentially, this is the real pressure for peace.... Pass the word along and be sure that the resolutions are sent to the White House and to the Department of Labor. Publicity is essential." Box 59, HP-ACUA.

37. Perkins to Roosevelt, July 21, 1936; Official File 716, FDR Library.

38. Drew Pearson, "Washington Daily Merry-Go-Round," *Washington Times-Herald*, Mar. 29, 1939, and *Washington Daily News*, Mar. 29, 1939; from clippings in HP-ACUA. *New York Times*, Aug. 28, 1940; Perkins to Roosevelt, Aug. 9, 1940, (Official File 716, FDR Library); and Diary, Aug. 28, 1941 (Envelope 3, HP-ACUA). The entry for the following day mentions Carey's visit with Haas at Catholic University.

39. Haas to Stritch, Mar. 29, 1939; Box 59, HP-ACUA.

40. Diary, Sept. 1 and 2, 1941 (Envelope 3, HP-ACUA), and Haas to Kiley, Sept. 4, 1941; Box 66, HP-ACUA. Efforts to amend the Wagner Act

at this time are described in Joseph Rosenfarb, *The National Labor Policy and How It Works* (New York, 1940), pp. 646-675.

41. *New York Times*, Nov. 11, 1939. Haas's diary, Aug. 10 to Sept. 12, 1939, and a copy of Haas's report to the Secretary of Commerce, undated; both in Envelope 15, HP-ACUA. See also Assistant Secretary of Commerce J. Monroe Johnson to Haas, Aug. 15, 1939; also in Envelope 15, HP-ACUA.

42. *New York Times*, Nov. 19, 1939. See Sumner Welles to Haas, Nov. 11, 1939; Isador Lubin to Haas, Nov. 9, 1939; and Lubin to Haas, Nov. 10, 1939; all in Envelope 28, HP-ACUA. See also "The Second Labour Conference of American States Members of the International Labour Organisation," *International Labour Review*, 41 (Mar. 1940), 225-268; and Antony Alcock, *History of the International Labor Organization* (New York, 1971), pp. 147-148.

43. Two helpful studies of the National Resources Planning Board are John D. Millett, *The Process and Organization of Government Planning* (New York, 1947), and Charles E. Merriam, "The National Resources Planning Board: A Chapter in American Planning Experience," *American Political Science Review*, 38 (Dec. 1944), 1075-1088. The quotation is from *United States Government Manual*, 1939 (Washington, 1939), p. 44. The other members of the committee were Will Alexander, Farm Security administrator; Katherine Lenroot, chief of the Department of Labor's Children's Bureau; Clarence M. Bookman of the Cincinnati Community Chest; Corrington Gill, assistant administrator of the WPA; Fred H. Hoehler of the American Public Welfare Association; Thomas J. Woofter, director of research for the Federal Security Agency; and Mary E. Switzer, assistant to the administrator, Federal Security Agency. See Charles W. Eliot, director of the NRPB, to Frederic Delano, Nov. 9, 1939, and Eliot to Monsignor Michael Ready, Nov. 10, 1939 (Record Group 187, National Resources Planning Board, Central Office Correspondence, Relief Committee Minutes, National Archives), and Eliot to Haas, Nov. 10, 1939; Box 68, HP-ACUA.

44. Minutes of all eighteen meetings are in Boxes 44 and 53, HP-ACUA.

45. The full title is *Security, Work, and Relief Policies: Report of the Committee on Long-Range Work and Relief Policies to the National Resources Planning Board* (Washington, 1942). See also "Reminiscence of Eveline Burns" pp. 102-122, OHC.

46. See Haas to Haber, May 5, 1941; Haber to Haas, Mar. 12, 1942; and Haas to Haber, Jan. 23, 1941; all in Box 53, HP-ACUA. For Haas's earlier views on these subjects, see *Man and Society* (New York, 1930), pp. 216-258.

47. Charles E. Meriam, "The National Resources Planning Board," pp. 1082-1083.

48. Records of these committees are in Record Group 155, Wage and Hour and Public Contracts Division, National Archives: Industry Committee No. 6 (Boot and Shoe Industry); No. 10 (Leather Industry); No. 56 (Canned Goods Industry); and No. 8 (Puerto Rican Industries Committee). Two excellent studies of the Fair Labor Standards Act are James M. Burns, *Congress on Trial* (New York, 1949), pp. 68-82, and Paul H. Douglas and Joseph Hack-

man, "The Fair Labor Standards Act of 1938, I and II," *Political Science Quarterly*, 53 (Dec. 1938), 491–516, and 54 (Mar. 1939), 29–55.

49. Transcripts of the public hearings and of the two executive sessions are in Box 51, HP-ACUA. Correspondence and releases relating to these meetings are in RG 155, Industry No. 6, National Archives. See especially U.S. Department of Labor, Wage and Hour Division, Release R-233, Mar. 17, and Release R-367, Aug. 3, 1939.

50. Fleming to Haas, Apr. 24, 1940 (Box 50, HP-ACUA), and *Labor*, Apr. 2, 1940. Fleming succeeded Elmer F. Andrews as wage-and-hour administrator in Feb. 1940. The following quotations are from "Official Report of Proceedings before the Wage and Hour Division of the Department of Labor: Hearings before Industry Committee No. 6," May 25–27, 1939 (Box 51, HP-ACUA); and Rondeau to Haas, May 10, 1940 (Box 59, HP-ACUA). See also Joseph D. Munier, *Some American Approximations of Pius XI's Industries and Professions* (Washington, 1943), pp. 93–117.

51. *Time*, 30 (Sept. 20, 1937), 49; *Northwest Catholic* (St. Paul), Sept. 8, 1934, and *Pittsburgh Press*, Apr. 3, 1941 (from clippings in HP-ACUA); *Milwaukee Journal*, Apr. 23, 1937; "The Washington Merry-Go-Round," *San Francisco Chronicle*, May 14, 1936 (from clipping in HP-ACUA).

52. *Current Biography*, 1943 (New York, 1944), p. 266, notes the report that Haas may have "settled something like 1500 labor disputes since 1935."

53. Although the National Labor Relations Board did not engage in mediation, Haas occasionally settled disputes when assigned as "special examiner" to investigate whether the Wagner Act had been violated. For Haas's appointment to the U.S. Conciliation Service on Dec. 23, 1935, see Samuel J. Gompers, chief clerk of the Department of Labor, to Haas, Jan. 6, 1936; Box 64, HP-ACUA. He was appointed to the Railway Labor Panel on Feb. 18, 1943. Records of these disputes are in Record Group 280, U.S. Conciliation Service, National Archives, and in Envelopes 2, 6, 18, 19, 27, 29, and 49, HP-ACUA.

54. Records of this strike are in Envelope 50, HP-ACUA, and in RG 280, Case 199/327, Box 971, National Archives. See also "Employers Favor Silk Stoppage," *Business Week*, Aug. 7, 1937, pp. 28–30; "Hillman's Silk Workers," *Literary Digest*, 124 (Aug. 28, 1937), 8; "Silent Silk," *Time*, 30 (Aug. 23, 1937), 12; Mary Heaton Vorse, "Bringing Union to Textiles," *New Republic*, 92 (Oct. 27, 1937), 331–333; Matthew Josephson, *Sidney Hillman, Statesman of American Labor* (Garden City, 1952), pp. 418–421; and *New York Times*, Aug. 12–21, 1937. The quotation is from Vorse, "Bringing Union to Textiles," p. 332.

55. *Detroit Free Press*, Nov. 21, 1943, and *Milwaukee Catholic Herald-Citizen*, Aug. 28, 1937. *New York Times*, Aug. 12 and 15, 1937. The early history of the strike is told in "Supplementary Data on Silk Textile Strike: August 9–August 20," by Haas, a copy of which is in Envelope 50, HP-ACUA. See also "Administrative Order," Aug. 13, 1937, in RG 280, Case 199/327-1, National Archives.

56. Progress in the negotiations was revealed in frequent telegrams and

transcripts of telephone conversations between Haas and Steelman; all in RG 280, Case 199/327, Box 971, National Archives. The agreement is contained in "Supplementary Data on Silk Strike," by Haas, Aug. 20, 1937, a copy of which is in Envelope 50, HP-ACUA, and *New York Times*, Aug. 22, 1937.

57. Records of this dispute are in Envelope 44, HP-ACUA, and in RG 280, Case 196/4072, Box 800, National Archives. See also Stanley High, "Rehearsal for Revolution," *Reader's Digest*, 38 (June 1941), 89–93; "Knudsen's Coup," *The Nation*, 152 (Apr. 5, 1941), 396–397; "Showdown Strike," *Business Week*, Mar. 29, 1941, pp. 49–52; Herman L. Klein, "Allis-Chalmers Strike Hits Largest Defense Plants in the Nation," *Iron Age*, 147 (Mar. 27, 1941), 81–88; and *Monthly Labor Review*, 52 (June 1941), 1464–1465. The quotation is from "Showdown Strike," p. 50. See also *Time*, 37 (Mar. 24, 1941), 17, and 37 (Apr. 7, 1941), 26.

58. This and the following quotations are from Stanley High, "Rehearsal for Revolution," p. 89, and La Follette to Haas, May 16, 1938; Envelope 54, HP-ACUA. Christoffel's early years are discussed in *Time*, 37 (Mar. 24, 1941), 17. See also editorials in *Milwaukee Catholic Herald-Citizen*, Mar. 29 and Apr. 5, 12, and 19, 1941.

59. Haas's travel vouchers for this period are in Envelope 44, HP-ACUA. His early activities in this strike are described in "Memorandum for the Record," Dec. 28, 1940; RG 280, Case 196/4072, Box 800, National Archives. See Haas to Steelman, Jan. 3, 1941 (Envelope 44, HP-ACUA); "Memo for the Record," Jan. 11, 1941; "Memo for the Record," Jan. 29, 1941; and Steelman to Perkins, Jan. 23, 1941 (RG 280, Case 196/4072, Box 800); *New York Times*, Jan. 23, 1941. Haas's quotation is from E.J. Cunningham to Steelman, Jan. 23, 1941, RG 280, Case 196/4072, Box 800, National Archives. In fact, Lee Pressman apparently did not enter the negotiations, although Leo Mann attended several conferences as company counsel.

60. The best source of information on this strike is Haas's "Progress Report," a day-by-day summary of events, dated Mar. 26, 1941, in RG 280, Case 196/4072, Box 800, National Archives. The strike can also be followed in the daily newspapers, especially the *New York Times* and *Milwaukee Journal*.

61. "Progress Report," in RG 280, Case 196/4072, Box 800, National Archives, and *New York Times*, Feb. 16, 1941. A copy of this agreement is also in RG 280, Case 196/4072, Box 800.

62. Haas stated in his "Progress Report" (Feb. 28, 1941): "I told Hillman that he would have to withdraw in writing his one-sentence interpretation." See also "Progress Report" for Mar. 3, 1941 (RG 280, Case 196/4072, Box 800, National Archives); *Milwaukee Journal*, Mar. 4, 1941; and *New York Times*, Mar. 4, 1941.

63. *Milwaukee Sentinel*, Mar. 26, 1941.

64. *New York Times*, Mar. 27, 1941; "Knudsen's Coup," pp. 396–397; and Josephson, *Sidney Hillman*, pp. 543–544. Since the vote in January had been approximately six to one in favor of the strike, it is doubtful that the irregularities significantly affected the outcome. The following quotations are from Knudsen and Knox to Murray, Mar. 27, 1941 (RG 280, Case 196/4072,

Box 800, National Archives); "Knudsen's Coup," p. 396; and *Washington Post*, Apr. 2, 1941. For labor's reaction, see *C.I.O. News* (Wisconsin ed.), Mar. 31, 1941.

65. Haas to Rev. H.G. Reardon, Apr. 7, 1941; Box 65, HP-ACUA. The full text of the agreement was printed in the *New York Times*, Apr. 7, 1941. Although union membership was not required, the agreement stated that "it is expected that by union members remaining in good standing, such interference with shop discipline will be reduced."

10. Chairman of the FEPC, 1943

1. *Man and Society* (New York, 1930), p. 30. See also "Thinking Out a Catholic Industrial Program," *American Federationist*, 35 (Oct. 1928), 1187, and "Economic Security," reprinted in *The Salesianum*, 36, July 1931, pp. 37-38.

2. *Man and Society*, pp. 92-93.

3. Quoted in Linna E. Bresette, "Report of the Sixth 'Negro in Industry' Conference," *Interracial Review*, 6 (Oct. 1933), 177.

4. Haas to Roy Wilkins, Aug. 9, 1933; Haas to John Davis, Oct. 30, 1933 (both in Box 23, HP-ACUA); and Haas to Rev. John LaFarge, S.J., Mar. 22, 1934; Box 62, HP-ACUA. See also transcripts of the hearings on the Salt Producing Industry Code, Aug. 14, 1933, and the Boot and Shoe Industry Code, Sept. 13, 1933; Record Group 9, National Recovery Administration, Consolidated Files, National Archives. Haas's WPA correspondence and case records are in Box 28, HP-ACUA.

5. National Resources Planning Board, *Security, Work, and Relief Policies* (Washington, 1942), pp. 159-160.

6. "The Klan," *The Salesianum*, 19, Oct. 1924, pp. 57-63. See also Donald L. Kinzer, "The Political Uses of Anti-Catholicism: Michigan and Wisconsin, 1890-1894," *Michigan History*, 39 (Sept. 1955), 312-326; Herbert F. Margulies, "Anti-Catholicism in Wisconsin Politics, 1914-1920," *Mid-America*, 44 (Jan. 1962), 51-56; and K. Gerald Marsden, "Patriotic Societies and American Labor: The American Protective Association in Wisconsin," *Wisconsin Magazine of History*, 41 (Summer 1958), 287-294. Records of the Bernard Greenberg arbitration case, discussed in chap. 7 are in Envelope 36, HP-ACUA, and records of the Harnischfeger dispute are in Envelope 51. The following quotation is from a speech before the National Conference of Catholics, Protestants, and Jews, quoted in *Washington Times*, Mar. 7, 1932; from clipping in HP-ACUA. The *New York Times*, May 9, 1933, carried a protest, signed by Haas and other religious and civic leaders, condemning Nazi treatment of Jews in Germany.

7. For a general discussion of Black Americans and the New Deal, see John P. Davis, "A Black Inventory of the New Deal," *Crisis*, 42 (May 1935), 141ff; John B. Kirby, *Black Americans in the Roosevelt Era* (Knoxville, 1980); Allan Morrison, "The Secret Papers of FDR," *Negro Digest*, 9 (Jan. 1951), 3-13; Gunnar Myrdal, *An American Dilemma* (New York, 1962),

pp. 251-303 and 409-426; Arthur M. Schlesinger, Jr., *The Politics of Upheaval* (Boston, 1960), pp. 426-438; and Walter White, *A Man Called White* (New York, 1948), pp. 139-194. Throughout the 1930s, *The Crisis*, the publication of the NAACP, contained numerous articles and editorials on Black Americans and the New Deal. Events leading to the establishment of the FEPC are also discussed in John Morton Blum, *V Was for Victory* (New York, 1976), pp. 182-188; Herbert Garfinkel, *When Negroes March* (Glenco, Ill., 1950), pp. 21-61; Lester B. Granger, "Barriers to Negro War Employment," *Annals of the American Academy of Political and Social Science*, 223 (Sept. 1942), 72-80; Louis C. Kesselman, *The Social Politics of FEPC* (Chapel Hill, N.C., 1948), pp. 3-15; James A. Nuechterlein, "The Politics of Civil Rights: The FEPC, 1941-1946," *Prologue*, 10 (Fall 1978), 171-176; Leon A. Ransom, "Combatting Discrimination in the Employment of Negroes in War Industries and Government Agencies," *Journal of Negro Education*, 12 (Summer 1943), 405-416; Thomas N. Roberts, "The Negro in Government War Agencies," *JNE*, 12 (Summer 1943), 367-375; Louis Ruchames, *Race, Jobs, and Politics: The Story of FEPC* (New York, 1953), pp. 9-11; and Robert C. Weaver, "Defense Industries and the Negro," *AAAPSS*, 223 (Sept. 1942), pp. 60-66. The quotation is from Eleanor Roosevelt, *This I Remember* (New York, 1949), p. 162.

8. Samuel Rosenman (ed.), *The Public Papers and Addresses of Franklin D. Roosevelt* (New York, 1950), XII, 420. The following quotations are from the *Chicago Defender*, Jan. 25, 1941 (quoted in Ruchames, *Race, Jobs, and Politics*, p. 13); Myrdal, *An American Dilemma*, p. 412; *Amsterdam News*, Apr. 19, 1941 (quoted in Ruchames, *Race, Jobs, and Politics*, p. 16); and Garfinkel, *When Negroes March*, p. 38. Hillman's directive was further weakened by the fact that William Knudsen, his co-director at OPM, declined to sign it.

9. Quotations are from Ruchames, *Race, Jobs, and Politics*, p. 17; Granger, "Barriers to Negro War Employment," p. 78; and Kesselman, *The Social Politics of FEPC*, p. 3.

10. *New York Times*, June 26, 1941, and Ruchames, *Race, Jobs, and Politics*, p. 22.

11. Executive Order 8823, July 18, 1941. The white members were Ethridge, Sarnoff, Green, and Murray; Webster and Dickerson were Black.

12. See Earl Dickerson's interview in Studs Terkel, *Hard Times: An Oral History of the Great Depression* (New York, 1970), p. 449; John Beecher, "8802 Blues," *New Republic*, 108 (Feb. 22, 1943), 248-250; Herman D. Bloch, "Craft Unions and the Negro in Historical Perspective," *Journal of Negro History*, 43 (Jan. 1958), 10-33; Garfinkel, *When Negroes March*, pp. 77-80; Lester Granger, "Negroes and War Production," *Survey Graphic*, 31 (Nov. 1942), 469-470; Herbert Hill, "Labor Unions and the Negro," *Commentary*, 28 (Dec. 1959), 479-488; Kesselman, *The Social Politics of FEPC*, pp. 15-16; Ray Marshall, *The Negro and Organized Labor* (New York, 1965), pp. 89-207; Herbert R. Northrup, *Organized Labor and the Negro* (New York, 1944); Ruchames, *Race, Jobs, and Politics*, pp. 11-16; and Robert

Weaver, *Negro Labor* (New York, 1946), pp. 97–191. The final quotation is Malcolm MacLean's, quoted in Ruchames, *Race, Jobs, and Politics*, p. 31.

13. See Beecher, "8802 Blues," pp. 248–259; John Temple Graves, "The Southern Negro and the War Crisis," *Virginia Quarterly Review*, 18 (Autumn 1942), 509; Ransom, "Combatting Discrimination in the Employment of Negroes in War Industries and Government Agencies," p. 412; and Roberts, "The Negro in Government War Agencies," p. 373.

14. At this same time, the War Manpower Commission also assumed jurisdiction over the War Production Board's Negro Employment and Training Branch, its Minorities Group Branch, and the U.S. Employment Service. This may have been a simple administrative reorganization, but under the War Production Board the FEPC received its funding from the president while the War Manpower Commission would have to seek FEPC appropriations from Congress. The following statement, issued by Stephen Early, is quoted in Ruchames, *Race, Jobs, and Politics*, p. 47. See also George Q. Flynn, *The Mess in Washington: Manpower Mobilization in World War II* (Westport, Conn., 1979), pp. 149–162.

15. The best discussions of the closing weeks of this first FEPC are Beecher, "8802 Blues," p. 250; Flynn, *The Mess in Washington*, pp. 159–162; Kesselman, *The Social Politics of FEPC*, pp. 23–24; and Ruchames, *Race, Jobs, and Politics*, pp. 49–53. Malcolm MacLean, president of Hampton Institute, had succeeded Ethridge as chairman on Feb. 10, 1942, although Ethridge stayed on as committee member; *New York Times*, Feb. 11, 1942. The above quotations are from the *New York Times*, Jan. 12, 1943, and Ruchames, *Race, Jobs, and Politics*, p. 51. Minutes of FEPC meetings that spring, with Dickerson presiding, are in Record Group 228, Fair Employment Practices Committee, Office of the Chairman, Box 1, National Archives.

16. Ruchames, *Race, Jobs, and Politics*, p. 53. The above quotations are from James Wechsler, "Pigeonhole for Negro Equality," *The Nation*, 156 (Jan. 23, 1943), 122, and "Further Abandonment of the Four Freedoms," *Commonweal*, 37 (Jan. 29, 1943), 363–364.

17. There is a typed list of candidates for the FEPC chairmanship, unsigned and undated, but "in order of preference," in Box 45, HP-ACUA. The above quotations are from the *New Republic*, 108 (May 10, 1943), 621, and "Reminiscence of Will M. Alexander," III, 688, OHC. The following is from Biddle to Roosevelt, Apr. 23, 1943; President's Personal File, FDR Library. See also "Reminiscences" of Benjamin F. McLaurin and John Brophy, OHC.

18. *Washington Star*, May 19, 1943; Haas to Lucey, May 20, 1943, and Haas to Stritch, June 1, 1943; Box 66, HP-ACUA. Lucey had been appointed archbishop of San Antonio in early 1941.

19. *Washington Post*, May 31, 1943; *New Republic*, 108 (June 7, 1943), 750; *America*, 69 (May 29, 1943), 197–198; *Christian Century*, 60 (June 2, 1943), 652; and Felix Frankfurter to Haas, May 20, 1943; Box 46, HP-ACUA.

20. Executive Order 9346, May 27, 1943. For Haas's role in drafting this order, see various drafts, with Haas's suggested corrections, in Box 46,

HP-ACUA; Biddle to Roosevelt, May 25, 1943; and an unsigned memorandum, May 22, 1943; Box 45, HP-ACUA.

21. Shishkin and Brophy had earlier replaced Green and Murray as FEPC members.

22. Marvin McIntyre to Haas, July 1, 1943; Box 46, HP-ACUA. Malcolm Ross, *All Manner of Men* (New York, 1948), pp. 32-33, and Ruchames, *Race, Jobs, and Politics*, p. 56. For a discussion of Dickerson's leftist associations, see Biddle to Haas, June 3 and 9, 1943; Box 46, HP-ACUA. See also Haas to Lucey, May 20, 1943 (Box 66); Lucey to Haas, May 27, 1943, and May 29, 1943; Haas to Marvin McIntyre, June 23, 1943, and Hillenbrand to Haas, June 14, 1943 (Box 46); and Lapp to Haas, June 14, 1943; Box 59, HP-ACUA.

23. Division of Research, Bureau of Special Services, Office of War Information, "Mobile: Race Friction Disrupts War Production." Report No. D1, July 3, 1943, Official File 4245g, FDR Library (hereafter referred to as OWI, Report No. D1). See also Merl E. Reed, "The FEPC, the Black Worker, and the Southern Shipyards," *South Atlantic Quarterly*, 74 (Autumn 1975), 446-467.

24. Ruchames, *Race, Jobs, and Politics*, pp. 40 and 49, and "Summary of the Hearings of the President's Committee on Fair Employment Practice Held in Birmingham, Alabama, June 19, 1942," attached to OWI, Report No. D1, Official File 4245g, FDR Library.

25. *Mobile Register*, May 26-31, 1943; OWI, Report No. D1, Official File 4245g, FDR Library; and Reed, "The FEPC, the Black Worker, and the Southern Shipyards," pp. 454-457.

26. *Mobile Register*, May 29, 1943; minutes of FEPC meeting of July 6-7, 1943 (Box 46, HP-ACUA); and OWI, Report No. D1, Official File 4245g, FDR Library.

27. Haas to Alabama Shipbuilding and Dry Dock Company, June 3, 1943, attached to OWI, Report No. D1, Official File 4245g, FDR Library. See also *Mobile Register*, June 5, 1943.

28. Quoted in *Mobile Register*, June 2, 1943. OWI, Report No. D1, Official File 4245g, FDR Library; minutes of FEPC meeting of July 6-7, 1943 (Box 46, HP-ACUA); Ruchames, *Race, Jobs, and Politics*, pp. 58-59.

29. Ruchames, *Race, Jobs, and Politics*, p. 41. The quotations are from Graves, "The Southern Negro and the War Crisis," pp. 504-505, and *Chicago Defender*, July 25, 1942, quoted in Ruchames, *Race, Jobs, and Politics*, p. 41.

30. Statement of Marvin Cos, director of Office of War Information, in *Mobile Register*, June 8, 1943; OWI, Report No. D1, Official File 4245g, FDR Library; *Mobile Register*, May 28, 1943; Flynn, *The Mess in Washington*, p. 156; and Reed, "The FEPC, the Black Worker, and the Southern Shipyards," pp. 454-455.

31. Minutes of meeting of July 6-7, 1943; Box 46, HP-ACUA.

32. Interview of Haas in *Mobile Register*, July 9, 1943. See also Haas to George A. Wilson, Office of Emergency Management, Aug. 9, 1943; Box 46,

HP-ACUA. For a favorable judgment of this settlement, see Reed, "The FEPC, the Black Worker, and the Southern Shipyards," pp. 454 and 457.

33. Haas to Malcom Ross, Mar. 6, 1944; Archives of the Diocese of Grand Rapids.

34. Quoted in *Washington Star*, May 29, 1943. Haas's early activities in this case are revealed in correspondence between him and Ernest G. Trimble, FEPC examiner; RG 228, Office of the Chairman, Box 41, National Archives. See also Office of War Information, WMC release, Dec. 1, 1942; Ruchames, *Race, Jobs, and Politics*, pp. 55-56; and *Washington Star*, May 19, 1943.

35. Ernest Trimble to Haas, June 21, 25, and 29, 1943; RG 228, Office of the Chairman, Box 41, National Archives.

36. Minutes of meetings of July 6-7, July 26, Aug. 9, 1943; and Haas to Capital Transit Company, Aug. 14, 1943; Box 46, HP-ACUA.

37. Quoted in *Washington Afro-American*, Sept. 25, 1943; from clipping in HP-ACUA. See also Malcolm Ross to Haas, Sept. 9, 1943, and Dorothy E. Alexander to Haas, Sept. 10, 1943 (RG 228, Office of the Chairman, Box 41, National Archives); "Summary of FEPC Meetings," Aug. 28, 1943, and minutes of meeting of Oct. 2, 1943 (Box 46, HP-ACUA); and Ruchames, *Race, Jobs, and Politics*, pp. 152-153.

38. *New York Times*, Oct. 2, 1943. See following chapter for the selection of Haas as bishop of Grand Rapids.

39. Ross, *All Manner of Men*, pp. 156-162.

40. Among the best studies of this Detroit riot are Blum, *V Was for Victory*, pp. 199-205; Earl Brown, "The Truth about the Detroit Riot," *Harper's Magazine*, 187 (Oct. 1943), 488-498, and *Why Race Riots* (New York, 1943); "Defeat at Detroit," *The Nation*, 157 (July 3, 1943), 4; Alfred M. Lee and Norman D. Humphrey, *Race Riot* (New York, 1943); William J. Norton, "The Detroit Riots—and After," *Survey Graphic*, 32 (Aug. 1943), 317-318; Sister Mary Sigmunda Ryniewicz, "Metropolitan Detroit Fair Employment Practice Council" (unpublished M.A. thesis, Catholic University of America, 1952); Thomas Sancton, "The Race Riots," *New Republic*, 109 (July 5, 1943), 9-13; Robert Shogan and Tom Craig, *The Detroit Race Riot* (Philadelphia, 1964); Harvard Sitkoff, "The Detroit Race Riot of 1943," *Michigan History*, 53 (Fall 1969), 183-206; and White, *A Man Called White*, pp. 224-232. See also "The Detroit Race Riots (A Memorandum by Turner Catledge)," June 30, 1943; memorandum of Anthony Luchek to Joseph D. Keenan, July 14, 1943; and memorandum for the attorney general by C.E. Rhetts, July 12, 1943; all in Official File 4245g, FDR Library. The following quotations are from "Detroit Is Dynamite," *Life*, 13 (Aug. 17, 1942), 15; Shogan and Craig, *The Detroit Race Riot*, p. 8; and Brown, *Why Race Riots*, p. 2.

41. Background of the riot is discussed in Brown, *Why Race Riots*, pp. 3-18; Ross, *All Manner of Men*, pp. 219-223; Lee and Humphrey, *Race Riots*, pp. 20-97; Shogan and Craig, *The Detroit Race Riot*, pp. 1-33; Sitkoff, "The Detroit Race Riot of 1943," pp. 187-189; and "The Detroit Race Riots (A Memorandum by Turner Catledge)," June 30, 1943; memorandum of Luchek to Keenan, July 14, 1943; and memorandum for the attorney general by C.E.

Rhetts, July 12, 1943; all in Official File 4245g, FDR Library.

42. Brown, *Why Race Riots*, pp. 3-18; Lee and Humphrey, *Race Riots*, pp. 72-79; Shogan and Craig, *The Detroit Race Riot*, pp. 1-33; and "Memorandum for the Attorney General" by J. Edgar Hoover, July 8, 1943, and memorandum for the attorney general by C.E. Rhetts, July 12, 1943; Official File 4245g, FDR Library.

43. Sitkoff, "The Detroit Race Riot of 1943," pp. 138-190; and "The Detroit Race Riots (A Memorandum by Turner Catledge)," June 30, 1943, and memorandum for the attorney general by C.E. Rhetts, July 12, 1943; Official File 4245g, FDR Library.

44. Lee and Humphrey, *Race Riot*, pp. 26-48, present a day-by-day and often hour-by-hour description of the riot. This quotation is from p. 38. The following quotation is from the *New Republic*, 109 (July 5, 1943), 3.

45. Sancton, "The Race Riots," p. 9, and Sitkoff, "The Detroit Race Riot of 1943," pp. 190-195. See also Thurgood Marshall, "The Gestapo in Detroit," *Crisis*, 50 (Aug. 1943), 232-233 and 246-247; memorandum of Detective Lieutenant George R. Branton of Detroit Police Department, July 2, 1943, and Phillip Nash to Jonathan Daniels, Sept. 28, 1943; both in Official File 4245g, FDR Library.

46. "Memorandum for the Attorney General," July 5, 1943, a copy of which is in Box 46, HP-ACUA. See also Haas's press conference in the *New York Times*, July 8, 1943.

47. A serious riot had broken out in Feb. 1943, for example, when Black Americans attempted to move into the Sojourner Truth Housing Project, built the year before under the auspices of the Federal Public Housing Authority.

48. Attorney general to FDR, July 15, 1943; Official File 4245g, FDR Library.

49. The thousands of man-hours lost in defense industries were not the result of rioting in the war plants but of the refusal of defense workers, white and Black, to leave their homes during the violence. The quotation is from Office of War Information Release 2161; Box 46, HP-ACUA.

50. "Unionist's Duty toward Negroes," *West Michigan C.I.O. News* (Feb. 9, 1944). See also Haas's diary, June 30 to July 2, 1943; Envelope 16, HP-ACUA.

51. Address at Detroit's Interracial Council, Sept. 8, 1946, quoted in *Work*, Oct. 1946 (from clipping in HP-ACUA); and *Catholics, Race and Law* (New York, 1947), p. 22.

52. Northrup, *Organized Labor and the Negro*, p. 34. The following quotations of Randolph are found in Wechsler, "Pigeonhole for Negro Equality," p. 121, and in Garfinkel, *When Negroes March*, p. 140.

53. Office of War Information Release 2439, Sept. 5, 1943. See also minutes of meetings of July 6-7 and July 26, 1943; Box 46, HP-ACUA.

54. A copy of this agreement is in RG 228, Legal Division, Box 320, National Archives.

55. Transcripts of the four days of hearings are in RG 228, Legal Division, Box 304, National Archives. See also "Summary of the Hearing of the

President's Committee on Fair Employment Practice, held in Washington, D.C., September 15-18, 1943"; copy in Box 73, HP-ACUA.

56. Minutes of the meeting of Oct. 2, 1943 (Box 46, HP-ACUA), and of Oct. 18, 1943; RG 228, Office of the Chairman, Box 1, National Archives. See also Ross, *All Manner of Men*, pp. 128-131.

57. *New York Times*, Oct. 2, 1943.

58. The final developments of this case, after the departure of Haas, are discussed in Ross, *All Manner of Men*, pp. 128-141, and Ruchames, *Race, Jobs, and Politics*, pp. 59-86.

59. Ross, *All Manner of Men*, pp. 136-141. Senator Russell is quoted on p. 137.

60. See Haas to Msgr. Patrick McCormick, Aug. 23, 1943 (Box 65, HP-ACUA); memorandum of Will Maslow, dated Aug. 19, 1943 (Box 46, HP-ACUA); *First Report: Fair Employment Practice Committee* (Washington, 1945), pp. 2-3; Ruchames, *Race, Jobs, and Politics*, p. 159; and *The Negro Handbook, 1944*, pp. 211-215. Good summaries of the cases brought before the committee are found in minutes of the FEPC meetings; Box 46, HP-ACUA.

61. Quoted in *Detroit News*, Nov. 17, 1943.

62. Charles Van Devander and William O. Player, Jr., "Washington Memo," *New York Post*, Dec. 30, 1943; from clipping in HP-ACUA.

63. Paul H. Norgren and Samuel E. Hill, *Toward Fair Employment* (New York, 1964), pp. 157-158.

64. Good discussions of the FEPC's successes and failures are in Norgren and Hill, *Toward Fair Employment*, pp. 149-179; *The Negro Handbook, 1944*, pp. 211-215; Louis Kesselman, "The Fair Employment Practice Commission Movement in Perspective," *Journal of Negro History*, 31 (Jan. 1946), 38-46; Neuchterlein, "The Politics of Civil Rights: The FEPC, 1941-1946," pp. 180-191; Stanley Hugh Smith, *Freedom to Work* (New York, 1955), pp. 46-51; R.M. MacIver, *The More Perfect Union* (New York, 1948), pp. 150-163; Michael I. Sovern, *Legal Restraints on Racial Discrimination in Employment* (New York, 1966), pp. 9-17; and Ruchames, *Race, Jobs, and Politics*, pp. 156-164.

65. See Ruchames, *Race, Jobs, and Politics*, pp. 158 and 163; *Final Report: Fair Employment Practice Committee* (Washington, 1947), p. 8; and the statement of Haas to the press, Oct. 7, 1943, a copy of which is in Box 73, HP-ACUA.

11. Bishop of Grand Rapids, 1943-1953

1. For the early history of the Church in western Michigan, see George Pare, *The Catholic Church in Detroit, 1701-1888* (Detroit, 1951), pp. 397-398, 470-471, and 582-614; and John W. McGee, *The Catholic Church in the Grand River Valley, 1833-1950* (Grand Rapids, 1950), pp. 111-125 and 225-238. A shorter account is J.P. Moran, "Diocese of Grand Rapids," *New Catholic Encyclopedia* (New York, 1967), VI, 693. The Apostolic Vicariate

of Upper Michigan, created by Rome in 1853, became the Diocese of Sault Sainte Marie in 1857, and the episcopal seat was transferred to Marquette shortly thereafter.

2. McGee, *The Catholic Church in the Grand River Valley*, pp. 225-235, and Pare, *The Catholic Church in Detroit*, p. 471. Most reliable statistics for the Diocese of Grand Rapids for each year are found in the *Official Catholic Directory*, published annually since the early nineteenth century by P.J. Kenedy and Sons, New York.

3. McGee, *The Catholic Church in the Grand River Valley*, pp. 331-352, and *Michigan Catholic*, Aug. 1, 1918, and Apr. 1, 1926. See also F. Clever Bald, *Michigan in Four Centuries* (New York, 1954), pp. 291-402, and William J. Etten (ed.), *A Citizen's History of Grand Rapids* (Grand Rapids, 1926). For the Ku Klux Klan in Michigan, see David M. Chalmers, *Hooded Americanism* (New York, 1965), pp. 194-197.

4. McGee, *The Catholic Church in the Grand River Valley*, pp. 352-382, and *Michigan Catholic*, Nov. 7, 1940, and Apr. 1, 1943. The quotation is from McGee, p. 357. Of the sixteen counties in the new Saginaw diocese in 1938, thirteen had formerly been in the Diocese of Grand Rapids and three in Detroit.

5. *Acta Apostolicae Sedis*, 8 (Nov. 3, 1916), 402-403. The selection of bishops is a complex procedure. At the beginning of Lent every second year, all the bishops of an ecclesiastical province draw up a list of priests they consider qualified for the episcopacy and then by secret ballot select from that list those they wish to nominate to the apostolic delegate. When a vacancy occurs, the delegate consults with the archbishop of the province in question, and with other persons who know the candidates well, and then submits three names to Rome. See also John Tracy Ellis, "On Selecting American Bishops," *Commonweal*, 85 (Mar. 10, 1967), 643-649.

6. For increasing opposition to the New Deal among American Catholic leaders, especially Patrick Scanlan of the *Brooklyn Tablet*, Paul Blakely of *America*, and James Gillis of the *Catholic World*, see David J. O'Brien, *American Catholics and Social Reform* (New York, 1968), pp. 47-96. Haas's quotation is from the *Washington Afro-American*, Oct. 23, 1943; from clipping in HP-ACUA. In a much-publicized controversy, Father McGlynn was reprimanded and eventually suspended by Archbishop Michael Corrigan of New York because of his outspoken advocacy of Henry George's single-tax proposals and other activities. The best works on Father Coughlin are Charles J. Tull, *Father Coughlin and the New Deal* (Syracuse, N.Y., 1965), and Sheldon Marcus, *Father Coughlin: The Tumultuous Life of the Priest of the Little Flower* (Boston, 1973). For disagreements between Ryan and officials of Catholic University, see Francis L. Broderick, *Right Reverend New Dealer: John A. Ryan* (New York, 1963), pp. 205-208 and 245-246. The view of Haas held by some members of the hierarchy might be suggested by a comment of Bishop John O'Hara of Buffalo to Archbishop Patrick O'Boyle of Washington in late 1950: "I am glad we have no jurisdiction over Bishop Haas. His recent address in Covington hails back to the days of President Roosevelt and is just

as inaccurate now as it was then"; quoted in Thomas T. McAvoy, C.S.C., *Father O'Hara of Notre Dame* (Notre Dame, Ind., 1967), p. 327.

7. After the death of Bishop Corrigan there was growing conviction at Catholic University that the reorganization embodied in the new School of Social Science had not been successful, the school was abolished soon after Haas's departure, and its departments were returned to their former status. See minutes of the 111th meeting of the board of trustees, Catholic University, Apr. 9, 1944, ACUA.

8. From clipping in Box 45, HP-ACUA.

9. Haas to Rev. Charles L. Souvey, Jan. 19, 1936 (Box 63); Haas to Kiley, Sept. 4, 1941 (Box 66); and Diary, July 7 to Sept. 8, 1941 (Envelope 3); all in HP-ACUA. See also Haas to Msgr. Patrick McCormick, Aug. 13, 1943; Rectors Office, ACUA. The author discussed this with several close friends of the bishop, including Msgr. George Higgins of the U.S. Catholic Conference and Msgr. Aloysius Ziegler of Catholic Univerity.

10. On Sept. 14, 1937, Haas wrote Msgr. Corrigan of Catholic University: "I have just received a telegram from the Archbishop of Detroit which is something more than an invitation to see him. You know what is involved. Consequently I shall be in Washington to begin the week of September 20 instead of September 16 as I informed your secretary" (Rectors Office, ACUA). The topic of discussion between Haas and Mooney that fall might have been Father Coughlin or Detroit's labor unrest. In 1941, Haas also asked Mooney's advice about accepting an appointment to the NLRB. See Diary, July 7 to Sept. 8, 1941; Envelope 3, HP-ACUA. The following quotation is from a conversation with Msgr. Anthony Arszulowicz, a close associate of Bishop Haas, in Grand Rapids, in Jan. 1966.

11. Quoted in *Bay City Times*, Oct. 5, 1943; from clipping in HP-ACUA.

12. Roosevelt to Haas, Oct. 15, 1943, released as Office of War Information Release N-671; *Congressional Record*, 78th Congress, 1st sess., 1943, LXXXIX, Part 7, 9645; *Grand Rapids Herald*, Jan. 17, 1944; and *Milwaukee Catholic Herald-Citizen*, Oct. 9, 1943.

13. The best descriptions of this ceremony are in the *Michigan Catholic*, Nov. 18 and 25, 1943, and in the Grand Rapids dailies, the *Herald* and the *Press*.

14. A copy of this sermon is in Box 2, HP-ACUA.

15. Archbishop Cicognani's remarks were published as "In Christo Justitia," *The Salesianum*, 39 (Jan. 1944), 1–6. A copy of Ryan's remarks is in Box 2, HP-ACUA. The *Michigan Catholic*, Nov. 18, 1943, describes other public receptions and tributes of that week.

16. A copy of the luncheon remarks of Bishop Haas is in Box 2, HP-ACUA.

17. For information concerning the bishop's work in Grand Rapids, the author is especially indebted to interviews with Msgrs. Anthony Arszulowicz, Edmund Falicki, Joseph Walen, and Arthur Bukowski, and Father Raymond Drinan, Mr. John Alt, and others in Grand Rapids in Jan. 1966 and July

1976. The following letter is in the Archives of the Diocese of Grand Rapids, hereafter abbreviated ADGR.

18. See, for example, Murray Thorne to Haas, Mar. 8, 1947, and Arszulowicz to Thorne, Mar. 13, 1947; ADGR.

19. In addition to the interviews noted above, the author is also indebted to a conversation with Mrs. Gerald B. Bennett in Grand Rapids in July 1976.

20. Haas to Rev. James Gilmartin, C.SS.R., Oct. 7, 1941 (Box 66, HP-ACUA), and interviews with Msgr. Edmund Falicki, Jan. 1966 and July 1976; Msgr. Alphonse Popek, July 24, 1976; and other friends and acquaintances of the bishop.

21. A further delay had been caused by uncertainty over zoning restrictions. Correspondence, memoranda, and reports pertinent to the establishment of St. Ann's Home are in ADGR. See especially Walter J. Cesarz to Haas, Oct. 14, 1952. *Michigan Catholic*, Aug. 24, 1944, and July 5, 1945. See also *Grand Rapids Herald*, Sept. 8, 1944, Mar. 6, 1945, and Jan. 16, 1951; and letter of Dennis Morrow to St. Ann's Home, June 28, 1976 (ADGR).

22. "Constitutions of the Catholic Service Bureau of the Roman Catholic Diocese of Grand Rapids"; ADGR. See also *Michigan Catholic*, Jan. 24 and June 27, 1946, and May 1, 1947; *Western Michigan Catholic*, Oct. 1, 1953; and McGee, *The Catholic Church in the Grand River Valley*, pp. 486-487.

23. "By-Laws of the Catholic Service Bureau of the Roman Catholic Diocese of Grand Rapids"; ADGR. *Michigan Catholic*, Apr. 22, 1948; *Western Michigan Catholic*, Sept. 16, 1948, and Oct. 1, 1953; and McGee, *The Catholic Church in the Grand River Valley*, pp. 462-463.

24. Ulanowicz to Haas, Aug. 5 and Nov. 11, 1947; Haas to Ulanowicz, Nov. 23, 1947, and May 18, 1948; and Ulanowicz to Haas, Oct. 16, 1952 (ADGR). See also *Michigan Catholic*, Feb. 19, 1948, and *Western Michigan Catholic*, Apr. 6, 1950, and Oct. 1, 1953; and McGee, *The Catholic Church in the Grand River Valley*, p. 395.

25. *Michigan Catholic*, May 18, 1944, Aug. 1 and Dec. 19, 1946, and Aug. 21, 1947; and *Western Michigan Catholic*, Jan. 5, 1950. It might be noted, however, that according to the *Official Catholic Directory* for 1944 the ratio of diocesan priests to Catholic population was higher in Grand Rapids than in the surrounding dioceses of Detroit, Fort Wayne, Lansing, or Saginaw.

26. *Michigan Catholic*, Oct. 19 and 26, 1944, and "Why Catholic Schools," address of Bishop Haas at the formal opening of the campaign; copy in Box 2, HP-ACUA.

27. "Why Catholic Schools." See also a second address, "The Catholic School and Citizenship," delivered in Grand Rapids on Dec. 7, 1944, and published in 1945 by Central Bureau Press of St. Louis.

28. *Michigan Catholic*, Oct. 19, Nov. 23, and Dec. 7, 1944. The bishop's remarks are quoted from issues of Oct. 26 and Dec. 21, 1944. In fact, only $631,000 of this was apparently collected—still an excellent drive. See *Western Michigan Catholic*, Sept. 3, 1953.

29. *Michigan Catholic*, Jan. 25, 1945, Aug. 28, 1947, Mar. 8 and May 24, 1951, and Sept. 3, 1953. There was criticism that so much of the money, collected primarily for school expansion, was expended on the convents, but most admitted that renovations in the convents were sorely needed. There was also some criticism, in the early 1950s, that Haas was overemphasizing the importance of patronizing Resurrection Cemetery, because the diocese had gone into debt to renovate it.

30. *Michigan Catholic*, Jan. 9 and 16 and Feb. 13, 1947. *Western Michigan Catholic*, Mar. 8 and May 17 and 24, 1951; Sept. 18 and Oct. 9 and 16, 1952; and Jan. 8 and 15, Apr. 2, and Sept. 3, 1953. See also *Grand Rapids Press*, Aug. 2, 1953.

31. *Michigan Catholic*, June 17, 1948, and *Western Michigan Catholic*, Feb. 22, 1951. Sister M. Rosella, O.P., to Haas, July 3, 1952; ADGR.

32. *Michigan Catholic*, Mar. 9, May 18, July 20, Aug. 24, Sept. 14, and Oct. 12, 1944; Mar. 22 and 29, June 7, Sept. 20, and Dec. 20 and 27, 1945; and June 13, July 11 and 25, Oct. 17, and Nov. 21, 1946.

33. The best studies of the Paulists are James M. Gillis, *The Paulists* (New York, 1932); Joseph McSorley, *Father Hecker and His Friends* (2nd ed.; St. Louis, 1953); and Vincent F. Holden, *The Yankee Paul: Isaac Thomas Hecker* (Milwaukee, 1958). "Memo of agreement between His Excellency, the Bishop of Grand Rapids, Michigan, and the Missionary Society of St. Paul the Apostle, known as the Paulist Fathers," Feb. 19, 1947; ADGR. See also *Michigan Catholic*, Nov. 11, 1946, Apr. 17, 1947, and Sept. 16, 1948. There was some concern that Grand Rapids was not as large as New York, Boston, Baltimore, Chicago, and these other cities, and therefore may not have needed the same kind of information center.

34. McGee, *The Catholic Church in the Grand River Valley*, pp. 391-393. *Michigan Catholic*, Apr. 22, June 3, and Sept. 16, 1948, and *Western Michigan Catholic*, Oct. 1, 1953. The quotation is from Sept. 16, 1948. See also "Grand Rapids Chapel Dedicated," *Paulist News*, 8 (July-Aug. 1948).

35. *Michigan Catholic*, June 5, Aug. 21, and Sept. 4 and 18, 1947. Haas is quoted in the issue of June 5, 1947.

36. Quoted in *Michigan Catholic*, Sept. 2, 1948. See also Aug. 12, 1948, and *Western Michigan Catholic*, Oct. 14, 1948.

37. *Western Michigan Catholic*, June 9 and Sept. 1 and 15, 1949; Sept. 7 and 20 and Oct. 4 and 18, 1951; and Oct. 2 and 16, 1952.

38. "Serra International," *New Catholic Encyclopedia* (New York, 1967), XIII, 125. *Michigan Catholic*, Sept. 9, 1948; and *Western Michigan Catholic*, Mar. 31, 1949, and Oct. 1, 1953.

39. *Michigan Catholic*, July 1, 1948. The following quotation is from *Western Michigan Catholic*, Sept. 16, 1948.

40. "Synodal Statutes: Official Translation of the Second Synod at Grand Rapids"; ADGR. The quotations are from Statutes 12, 13, and 16. See also *Western Michigan Catholic*, Dec. 23 and 30, 1948.

41. *Codex Iuris Canonici*, Canons 340-342. See also James J. Carroll, *The Bishop's Quinquennial Report* (Washington, 1956).

42. Edwin Haas to Haas, undated, and Haas's reply, June 10, 1948; ADGR. The Hug family was the family of Haas's paternal great-grandmother.

43. This letter was published in *Western Michigan Catholic*, June 2, 1949.

44. The *Official Catholic Directory* (1944 and 1950) gives the most accessible statistics on the growth of the diocese during these years. McGee, *The Catholic Church in the Grand River Valley*, pp. 389-391.

45. *Western Michigan Catholic*, Apr. 21 and 28 and June 2 and 9, 1949. The quotation is from a letter published in the issue of June 2, 1949.

46. Haas to Joseph Patrick Walsh, July 23, and Haas to Mrs. P. Flannery, June 30, 1949; ADGR. See also *Western Michigan Catholic*, June 9, 1949, and John M. Kelly, "Bishop Haas Views Europe," *Western Michigan Catholic*, June 30, 1949.

47. Charles A. Salatka to Haas, Mar. 5, 1952; ADGR, and *Western Michigan Catholic*, Mar. 29, 1951. Bishop Joseph Rancans, exiled from Latvia, served as chaplain to St. Ann's Home for the Aged during his final years in Grand Rapids.

48. Letter published in *Western Michigan Catholic*, Jan. 5, 1950.

49. *Western Michigan Catholic*, Feb. 16, Mar. 2, and June 8, 1950; Feb. 8 and May 3, 1951; Apr. 10 and June 12, 1952; and May 14 and Sept. 3, 1953.

50. *Man and Society* (New York, 1930), and *Man and Society* (2nd ed.; New York, 1952). Haas to Regina Flannery Herzfeld, Apr. 23, and Haas to Miss Catherine Schaefer, July 27, 1949; ADGR.

51. Compare, for example, chap. XV of the first edition, "The Problem of Wages," with chap. XI of the second, "Wages, Prices, and Organized Life." Chaps. XIII and XIV in the second edition are new. The "Industry Council System" was another expression for the "Occupational Group System" of *Quadragesimo Anno*.

52. Statistics are from the *Official Catholic Directory*, 1944 and 1954. The increase in the number of priests is explained in part by the number of immigrant priests from Eastern Europe.

53. Bishop Rancans occasionally confirmed and attended ecclesiastical functions as Haas's delegate or representative, but because of cultural and language differences he rarely made official public appearances.

12. Social Justice's Elder Statesman, 1943-1953

1. *Bay City Times*, Oct. 5, 1943; from clipping in HP-ACUA.

2. For Haas's appointments to state agencies and committees, chiefly in the area of civil rights, see *Michigan Catholic*, Jan. 9, 1947, *Grand Rapids Herald*, Dec. 24, 1948, and *Western Michigan Catholic*, Mar. 24, 1949.

3. Haas to Roosevelt, Oct. 7, 1943; released as Office of War Information Release N-671.

4. The complete title of this union is Brotherhood of Railway and Steamship Clerks, Freight Handlers, Express and Station Employees. Records

of this case are in Record Group 13, National Mediation Board, Case A-1495, Arb. 27, Box 19, National Archives, and in Envelope 12, HP-ACUA. See especially Thomas Bickers to R.C. Lauten, Oct. 26, 1943; D.S. Wright and L.W. Reigel to Bickers, Jan. 26, 1944; and "Transcript of Proceedings of the Arbitration Board"; all in RG 13, Case A-1495, National Archives. Bickers to Haas, Jan. 31, and Haas to Bickers, Feb. 1, 1944; Envelope 12, HP-ACUA. Haas's letter of appointment is reproduced in the "Transcript."

5. "Transcript of Proceedings of the Arbitration Board"; RG 13, Case A-1495, National Archives. Diary, Feb. 25-26, 1944; Haas to clerk of District Court, Feb. 29, 1944; and Haas to Bickers, Mar. 6, 1944; all in Envelope 12, HP-ACUA.

6. Records of the 1943 case are in RG 13, Case 1362, Arb. 23, Box 15, National Archives, and Envelopes 13 and 24, HP-ACUA. Records of the 1944 case are in RG 13, Case A-1592, Arb. 33, Box 22, National Archives, and Envelope 34, HP-ACUA. See especially Thomas Bickers to William Leiserson, Feb. 24, 1944 (RG 13, Case A-1592, National Archives), and Bickers to Haas, Mar. 11 and 18; Haas to Bickers, Mar. 19; and Bickers to Haas, Mar. 20, 1944; Envelope 34, HP-ACUA.

7. Diary, Apr. 10-12, 1944 (Envelope 34, HP-ACUA), and "Arbitration Award" and "Transcript of Proceedings of the Arbitration Board"; RG 13, Case A-1592, National Archives. For the earlier decision, see *New York Times*, Dec. 27 and 28, 1943.

8. Records of this case are in Envelopes 10, 11, and 17, HP-ACUA. See especially Sullivan to Haas, Jan. 18; Dale to Haas, Jan. 19; Haas to Dale, Jan. 23; and Dale and Sullivan to Haas, Jan. 31, 1946; all in Envelope 10, HP-ACUA.

9. Arbitration award, Feb. 26, 1946, and Diary (Envelope 10); and "Transcripts of Hearings," Feb. 11-15, 1946; Envelopes 11 and 17, HP-ACUA.

10. Cordell Hull to Haas, Apr. 18, 1944; Envelope 33, HP-ACUA. The *New York Times*, Apr. 18 to May 18, 1944, carried almost daily articles on the conference. See also Antony Alcock, *History of the International Labor Organization* (New York, 1971), pp. 171-187; G.A. Johnston, *The International Labour Organisation* (London, 1970), passim; Albert Le Roy, S.J., *The Dignity of Labor* (Westminster, Md., 1957), pp. 35-41; and David A. Morse, *The Origin and Evolution of the I.L.O. and Its Role in the World Community* (Ithaca, N.Y., 1969), pp. 28-30. The declaration is reprinted in G.A. Johnston, *International Labour Organisation*, pp. 302-304.

11. See G.A. Johnston, *International Labour Organisation*, pp. 302-304.

12. Haas was also a member of the Committee on Application of Conventions, but this assignment occupied little time. For Haas's work on both of these committees, see his diary, Apr. 25-May 12, 1944, and "Third Report on the Selection Committee: Composition of the Committees," Apr. 25, 1944; both in Envelope 33, HP-ACUA.

13. A copy of this speech is in Envelope 33, HP-ACUA. See also Diary, May 10-11, 1944 (Envelope 33); *Philadelphia Inquirer*, May 12, 1944; and, for the conference in general, "The Twenty-Sixth Session of the International

Labor Conference," *International Labour Review,* 50 (July 1944), 1-39.
      14. *Man and Society* (New York, 1930), p. 26, and Diary, May 10,
1944; Envelope 33, HP-ACUA.
      15. A copy of Haas's remarks, dated May 8, 1944, is in Box 2, HP-
ACUA.
      16. Executive Order 9808, Dec. 5, 1946, reprinted in President's Com-
mittee on Civil Rights, *To Secure These Rights* (New York, 1947), p. viii;
see also p. vii; William C. Berman, *The Politics of Civil Rights in the Truman
Administration* (Columbus, 1970), pp. 50-73; Robert K. Carr, *Federal Protection of Civil Rights* (Ithaca, N.Y., 1947); Alonzo L. Hamby, *Beyond the
New Deal: Harry Truman and American Liberalism* (New York, 1973), pp.
188-215; Milton R. Konvitz, *The Constitution and Civil Rights* (New York,
1947) and *A Century of Civil Rights* (New York, 1961); and Harry S. Truman,
Memoirs (New York, 1956), II, 179-182.
      17. Wilson to Haas, Feb. 3, 1947 (Box 19, HP-ACUA), and minutes of
committee meetings; Boxes 18 and 19, HP-ACUA, and Box 12, President's
Committee on Civil Rights, Harry S. Truman Library. Hereafter, this latter
will be abbreviated PCCR.
      18. Minutes of this subcommittee's meetings are in Boxes 18 and 19,
HP-ACUA. See also "Interim Report of Subcommittee No. 2," Apr. 17,
1947; Box 18, PCCR, Truman Library. Haas, James Carey, and one of the
Black members of the committee would occasionally eat together at different
hotels and restaurants in Washington, on days the committee met, to determine for themselves the treatment Black Americans received in the District of
Columbia; from an interview with James Carey, Aug. 10, 1966.
      19. See "Proceedings" of Subcommittee 2, Apr. 17, pp. 8-19; Box 12,
PCCR, Truman Library.
      20. *To Secure These Rights,* pp. 23, 35-40, 56-57, and 63-64.
      21. These recommendations are listed in ibid., pp. 151-173. The quo-
tation is from p. 166.
      22. Ibid., p. 166.
      23. Ibid., p. 87.
      24. Truman to Haas, Nov. 3, 1947 (Box 19, HP-ACUA); James R. New-
man, review of *To Secure These Rights* in *New Republic,* 117 (Nov. 17,
1947), 24, and review by Thomas H. Eliot in *Harvard Law Review,* 61 (May
1948), 899-903. For Truman's message to Congress, see *New York Times,*
Feb. 3, 1948.
      25. "Christian Planning for Postwar Reconstruction," Feb. 21, 1944;
copy is in Box 2, HP-ACUA.
      26. *Man and Society* (2nd ed.; New York, 1952), pp. 191-206. Quota-
tions are from pp. 201 and 203. *Quadragesimo Anno,* par. 71. See also Haas's
remarks before the Grand Rapids Council of Catholic Women, in *Michigan
Catholic,* Oct. 12, 1944. In a letter to the Committee on Labor of the Michigan legislature, Mar. 14, 1945, Haas suggested that coverage of the proposed
state FEPC bill be limited to "race, creed, color, and national origin," and not
include "sex." A copy of this letter is in Box 2, HP-ACUA.

27. "Working Together," address to B'nai B'rith Houseman Lodge No. 239, June 5, 1952, a copy of which is in Box 2, HP-ACUA. Senator Vandenberg, of course, was from Grand Rapids. See also Haas's remarks on the "Dumbarton Oaks World Organization" before the Grand Rapids Chamber of Commerce, Dec. 11, 1944, a copy of which is in Box 2, HP-ACUA.

28. *Man and Society*, p. 521, and "One World," address in Detroit on Apr. 16, 1950, a copy of which is in Box 2, HP-ACUA.

29. *Congressional Record*, 77th Congress, 2d sess., 1942, LXXXVIII, Part 10, A4004-A4006. The quotation is from A4005. Postcards and letters in reaction, most of them unsigned, are in Box 68, HP-ACUA. See also address of Victor Ridder, noted in *Brooklyn Tablet*, Feb. 20, 1937, and an article by George E. Sullivan in *Baltimore Catholic Review*, Feb. 4, 1938.

30. *Western Michigan Catholic*, Mar. 16, 1950, and Jan. 6, 1949; "Building Our Internal Defenses," address before 34th annual convention of American Federation of Teachers, Grand Rapids, Aug. 21, 1951 (Box 2, HP-ACUA); and *Man and Society*, pp. 387-388.

31. "Answers to Questionnaire on Communism," Feb. 1945, a copy of which is in Box 2, HP-ACUA.

32. Quoted in *Grand Rapids Herald*, May 19, 1948.

33. *Michigan Catholic*, May 6, 1948.

34. "Building Our Internal Defenses" (Box 2, HP-ACUA); "Controls and the Encyclical Forty Years After," address at 3d Boston meeting of Catholic Conference on Industrial Problems, Oct. 9, 1951; and "Communism and Organized Labor," address before annual state convention of Michigan Federation of Labor, Grand Rapids, June 5, 1950 (all in Box 2, HP-ACUA); and *Seven Pillars of Industrial Order* (Washington, 1952), pp. 14-15.

35. "Labor, Management and Government," *Catholic Mind*, 47 (Jan. 1949), 8.

36. "A Union, Its Rights and Duties," address at national convention of International Typographical Union, Grand Rapids, Aug. 19, 1944 (Box 2, HP-ACUA), and *Seven Pillars of Industrial Order*, p. 14.

37. Labor Day address in Steubenville, Ohio, titled "Labor Day, Yesterday and Today," Sept. 5, 1949, and "The Right to Organize," May 8, 1950; both in Box 2, HP-ACUA.

38. "Labor and the Postwar World," July 14, 1944, and "Union Politics and Union Leadership," Sept. 12, 1944; Box 2, HP-ACUA.

39. Haas's letter to Congresswoman Norton was published in the *Michigan Catholic*, June 22, 1944; *Milwaukee Catholic Herald-Citizen*, Sept. 22, 1945; and a copy of Haas's letter to Sen. Taft, June 10, 1947; Box 7, PCCR, Truman Library. The following quotation is from the *Michigan Catholic*, Nov. 28, 1946.

40. Minutes of meeting of Feb. 5, 1947 (Box 12, PCCR, Truman Library); "Rights for Negroes in Industry," June 2, 1952 (Box 2, HP-ACUA); and *Michigan Catholic*, Sept. 12, 1946.

41. "Christian Planning for Postwar Reconstruction," Feb. 21, 1944 (Box 2, HP-ACUA); *Grand Rapids Herald*, Mar. 12, 1947; "The 'Marks' of the

Social Order," *American Ecclesiastical Review*, 120 (June 1949), 453 and 454; and *Seven Pillars of Industrial Order*, p. 16.

42. Roosevelt to Haas, Oct. 15, 1943; reprinted as Office of War Information Release N-671. The Certificate of Recognition is in Box 18, HP-ACUA. See also *Grand Rapids Herald*, July 13, 1944. Remarks of Eagle President De Vere Watson, quoted in *Grand Rapids Herald*, July 21, 1949. *Detroit News*, Apr. 19, 1950; *Grand Rapids Press*, Feb. 11, 1952, and *Western Michigan Catholic*, Feb. 14, 1952. The award and citation of Julius Houseman Lodge 238, B'Nai B'rith, are in Scrapbook VII; HP-ACUA. The *Grand Rapids Herald* and *Grand Rapids Press*, June 5, 1952, reported the event.

43. This and the following quotations are from the *Grand Rapids Herald*, Apr. 13, 1945; *Catholic Action*, 27 (Oct. 1945), 24; *Milwaukee Catholic Herald-Citizen*, July 20, 1946; and *Grand Rapids Press*, Nov. 22, 1952, and May 5, 1953. Haas's funeral sermon for Philip Murray is noted in the *New York Times*, Nov. 14, 1952.

44. Haas to Dr. Andrew Rivers of Mayo Clinic, July 24, 1941 (Box 59, HP-ACUA), and Judith Barrett, secretary to Haas, to Steward Hooker, Feb. 3, 1943; Envelope 32, HP-ACUA. Friends and relatives of the bishop whom the author interviewed agreed that Haas's health throughout most of his life seemed good.

45. Quoted in *Western Michigan Catholic*, Sept. 3, 1953. During the bishop's days in the hospital, the *Grand Rapids Herald* published daily bulletins on the state of his health.

13. Epilogue: "The Big Friend of the Little Guy"

1. The most detailed accounts of the bishop's funeral are in the *Western Michigan Catholic*, Sept. 10, 1953, and the *Grand Rapids Herald* and *Grand Rapids Press*, Sept. 2-5, 1953.

2. The story has been told that George Meany and Walter Reuther, presidents of the rival AFL and CIO, put aside their differences long enough to attend the bishop's funeral together, but George Meany did not attend; he was represented by other AFL officials. Through a mistake in scheduling, Governor Williams attended the 9:00 Mass rather than the funeral.

3. Quoted from the Requiem Mass and Burial Service in the official Catholic Ritual.

4. The *Western Michigan Catholic*, Sept. 10, 1953, reprinted this sermon in its entirety.

5. Quoted in *Western Michigan Catholic*, Sept. 3, 1953. The following quotations are from the *Western Michigan Catholic*, Sept. 10, 1953, and the *Michigan Catholic*, Sept. 3, 1953.

6. Haas's correspondence with members of the American hierarchy is in Boxes 59, 61, 63, 65, and 66, HP-ACUA. See also Haas to Msgr. Joseph Corrigan, June 30, 1938; Rectors Office, ACUA.

7. For American Catholicism and postwar challenges, see Paul E. Czuchlewski, "The Commonweal Catholic: 1924-1960" (unpublished Ph.D dissertation, Yale University, 1972); "How U.S. Catholics View Their Church," *Newsweek*, Mar. 20, 1967, pp. 67-75; Thomas T. McAvoy, C.S.C., "American Catholicism and the Aggiornamento," *Review of Politics*, 30 (July 1968), 275-291; Gary MacEoin, *New Challenges to American Catholics* (New York, 1965); David J. O'Brien, *The Renewal of American Catholicism* (New York, 1972); Thomas F. O'Dea, *American Catholic Dilemma* (New York, 1958); Walter J. Ong, S.J., *Frontiers in American Catholicism* (New York, 1957); Joseph Roddy, "Catholic Revolution," *Look*, Feb. 9, 1965, pp. 21-27; Edward R.F. Sheehan, "Not Peace but the Sword," *Saturday Evening Post*, Nov. 28, 1964, pp. 21-42; and Donald J. Thorman, *The Emerging Layman* (New York, 1962).

8. The work of other priests in government service during these years has been discussed by George Q. Flynn, *American Catholics and the Roosevelt Presidency, 1932-1936* (Lexington, Ky., 1968); David J. O'Brien, *American Catholics and Social Reform* (New York, 1968); and Paul Stroh, "The Catholic Clergy and American Labor Disputes, 1900-1937" (unpublished Ph.D. dissertation, Catholic University of America, 1939).

9. George Q. Flynn, in *American Catholics and the Roosevelt Presidency*, p. xi, writes: "My major thesis is that it was under Franklin Rosevelt and the New Deal that American Catholics were given recognition as a major force in society." See also William E. Leuchtenburg, *Franklin D. Roosevelt and the New Deal* (New York, 1963), pp. 328-333.

10. *Report of the Proceedings of the Biennial Convention of the Amalgamated Clothing Workers of America*, Cleveland, pp. 340-341.

11. Samuel Rosenman, *The Public Papers and Addresses of Franklin D. Roosevelt* (New York, 1938), I, 646. See also James M. Burns, *Roosevelt: The Lion and the Fox* (New York, 1956), pp. 179-182, and Broadus Mitchell, *Depression Decade* (New York, 1947), p. 368.

12. *Washington Post*, Sept. 1, 1953.

13. Pope Leo XIII, *Rerum Novarum*, par 45; letter of Pope Benedict XV to the bishop of Bergamo, in *Acta Apostolicae Sedis*, 12 (1920), 112; and Pope Pius XI, *Divini Redemptoris*, par. 61.

14. *C.I.O. News*, Sept. 7, 1953.

15. The *Grand Rapids Herald*, August 30, 1953.

Selected Bibliography

Manuscript sources for this study of the life and work of Francis J. Haas are abundant. The major collection of Haas's papers is in the Department of Archives and Manuscripts of the Catholic University of America. Other Haas materials are in the Archives of the Diocese of Grand Rapids and in the Office of the President, Aquinas College, Grand Rapids. The Department of Archives and Manuscripts at Catholic University contains the Papers of John Brophy, Monsignor William Kerby, and Monsignor John A. Ryan; the Records of the Board of Trustees; the Records of the Offices of the Rector and the Vice Rector; the Records of the Dean of the School of Social Science; the Student Records of the Office of the Registrar; the Records of the National Catholic School of Social Service; and the Records of the National Catholic Welfare Conference. At the Franklin D. Roosevelt Library the author consulted the President's Personal File, the President's Secretary File, the Official File, and the Papers of Harry L. Hopkins. Various Record Groups in the National Archives were beneficial: the National Recovery Administration (RG 9), the National Mediation Board (RG 13), the National Labor Relations Board (RG 25), the Works Progress Administration (RG 69), the Wage and Hour and Public Contracts Division (RG 155), the National Resources Planning Board (RG 187), the National War Labor Board (RG 202), the President's Fair Employment Practice Committee (RG 228), the Reconstruction Finance Corporation (RG 234), and the United States Conciliation Service (RG 280). The Records of the Wisconsin Labor Relations Board and the Papers of William Leiserson and Edwin Witte are preserved in the State Historical Society of Wisconsin in Madison, and the Papers of Vince A. Day, Governor Floyd B. Olson, and the Citizens Alliance of Minneapolis in the Minnesota State Historical Society in St. Paul. The Records of the Faculty, the Records of the Office of the Registrar, and the Records of the Catholic Association for International Peace are in the Department of Archives of Marquette University. St. Francis

Seminary School of Pastoral Ministry in ~~Milwaukee~~ contains the
unpublished "Studies in the History of St. Francis Seminary." The
author was privileged to consult the Sidney Hillman Papers at the
Amalgamated Clothing Workers of America in New York, the
Frances Perkins Papers at Columbia University, the Rose Schneid-
erman Papers at New York University, and the Robert F. Wagner
Papers at Georgetown University. The Student Records of the
Office of the Registrar of the University of Wisconsin, Madison;
the Archives of the Archdiocese of Milwaukee; and the CIO
Historical Files of the Archives of the AFL-CIO in Washington
were also helpful. The Records of the President's Committee on
Civil Rights are preserved in the Harry S. Truman Library in
Independence, Missouri. The Columbia University Oral History
Collection has preserved the Reminiscences of Will Alexander,
John Brophy, Eveline M. Burns, Benjamin McLaurin, Frances
Perkins, Boris Shishkin, Florence Calvert Thorne, and Leo Wolman.
The Reminiscence of Archbishop Karl J. Alter is in the University
of Notre Dame Archives.

The author interviewed approximately forty personal friends
and associates of Bishop Haas. Very helpful were interviews with
Bishops Jerome Hastrich and William O'Connor; Monsignors
Anthony Arszulowicz, Arthur Bukowski, Edmund Falicki, Paul
Hanly Furfey, George Higgins, Peter Leo Johnson, Alphonse
Popek, Henry J. Schmitt, Joseph Walen, and Aloysius Ziegler; and
Fathers Raymond Drinan and William Hennen. Government and
labor officials who shared their recollections include James Carey,
Milton Handler, Paul Herzog, John L. Lewis, Isador Lubin, Gustav
Peck, Jacob Potofsky, Rose Schneiderman, and Benedict Wolf.
Members of the Haas family were especially helpful: Allen, Arthur,
and Dorthy Haas, Mary Haas Charnon, and Mrs. Peter (Irene)
Haas. Others whose reminiscences supplied important information
include John Alt, Mrs. Gerald Bennett, Roy J. Deferrari, Mrs. Ida
Kitay Lewis, Anthony Marshall, Dorothy Abts Mohler, and Domini-
can Sisters Euphemia Popell, Agnes Dominic Roberge, and Casimir
Zukowski.

Bishop Haas was the author of two books, nine pamphlets,
more than fifty major articles, and innumerable editorials and
commentaries. His published doctoral dissertation, *Shop Collective Bargaining: A Study of Wage Determination in the Men's Garment Industry* (Washington: Catholic University of America Press,
1922), and *Man and Society* (New York: Century, 1930; rev. ed.,
Appleton-Century-Crofts, 1952) shed essential light on his think-

ing, as do several of his popular pamphlets: *American Agriculture and International Affairs* (Washington: Catholic Association for International Peace, 1930), *Rights and Wrongs in Industry* (New York: Paulist Press, 1933), *The American Labor Movement* (New York: Paulist Press, 1937), *The Wages and Hours of American Labor* (Huntington, Ind., Our Sunday Visitor Press, 1937), *The Why and Whither of Labor Unions* (Huntington, Ind., Our Sunday Visitor Press, 1939), *Jobs, Prices, and Unions* (New York: Paulist Press, 1941), *The Catholic School and Citizenship* (St. Louis: Central Bureau Press, 1945), *Catholics, Race and Law* (New York: Paulist Press, 1947), and *Seven Pillars of Industrial Order* (Washington: Catholic Conference on Industrial Problems, 1952). His most important articles on the rights of labor are "A Steady Job," *Catholic Charities Review*, 8 (Jan. 1924), 13-17; "Freedom of Contract and Legislation," *The Salesianum*, 19 (July 1924), 51-57; "Setting Minimum Wages according to Minimum Quantity Standards," *The Salesianum*, 21, Jan. 1926, pp. 27-39; "The Church, Public Opinion, and Industry," *The Salesianum*, 22, July 1927, pp. 40-47; "Thinking Out a Catholic Industrial Program," *American Federationist*, 35 (Oct. 1928), 1185-1190; "Poverty and Wealth," *The Salesianum*, 26, Apr. 1931, pp. 49-55; "Toward a Christian Social Order," *Journal of Religious Instruction*, 2 (Mar. 1932), 617-628; "Organized Society: The Remedy for Unemployment," *Proceedings of the Eighteenth Meeting of the National Conference of Catholic Charities* (Omaha, 1952), pp. 68-74; "Freedom through Unionization," *American Federationist*, 40 (Nov. 1933), 1190-1196; "The Vices of Industrialism and Their Remedies," *Ecclesiastical Review*, 92 (Apr. 1935), 352-368; "Two Milestones to Social Justice," *The Sign*, 15 (May 1936), 585-587; "Federal Program for Industrial Peace," *American Labor Legislation Review*, 30 (Dec. 1940), 180-188; "Christian Planning for Post-War Reconstruction," *The Acolyte*, 20 (Oct. 1944), 7-10; "Bishops Speak on Labor," *Catholic Mind*, 43 (Nov. 1945), 665-674; and "The 'Marks' of Social Order," *American Ecclesiastical Review*, 120 (June 1949), 449-457.

Three articles on the rights of Black Americans and other minority groups are "Justice for All," *American Federationist*, 50 (Aug. 1943), 18-20; "Unionist's Duty toward Negroes," *West Michigan C.I.O. News*, Feb. 9, 1944; and "Rights for Negroes in Industry," *Interracial Review*, 25 (July 1952), 102-104. Other important topics were treated in "Equal Rights for Women," *Proceedings of the Fourth Annual Meeting of the Catholic Conference* on *Industrial Problems* (Cleveland, 1926), pp. 43ff.; "Social Insurance and Health," *The Salesianum*, 23, Oct. 1928, pp. 38-48; "Necessitarianism in Contemporary Ethics," *The Salesianum*, 26 (Jan. 1931), 55-61; "Why Nations Should Disarm," *The Missionary*, 47 (Feb. 1933), 46-49; "Training the Priest for Leadership in the Social and Economic Field," *National Catholic Education Association Bulletin*, 30 (Nov. 1933), 599-609; and "Authority," *Catholic Mind*, 49 (Apr. 1951), 230-238.

Three standard histories of American Catholicism are John Tracy Ellis, *American Catholicism* (Chicago: University of Chicago Press, 1956); Theodore Maynard, *The Story of American Catholicism*, 2 vols. (Garden City: Doubleday 1961); and Thomas T. McAvoy, *A History of the Catholic Church in the United States* (Notre Dame, Ind.: University of Notre Dame Press, 1969). Excellent works on more specific topics are Colman Barry, *The Catholic Church and German Catholics* (Milwaukee: Bruce, 1953); Robert Cross, *The Emergence of Liberal Catholicism in America* (Cambridge, Mass.: Harvard University Press, 1958); John Tracy Ellis, *The Life of Cardinal Gibbons*, 2 vols. (Milwaukee: Bruce, 1952), and his edited work, *The Catholic Priest in the United States: Historical Investigations* (Collegeville, Minn.: St. John's University Press, 1971); William Halsey, *The Survival of American Innocence: Catholicism in an Era of Disillusionment, 1920-1940* (Notre Dame, Ind.: University of Notre Dame Press, 1980); and Thomas T. McAvoy, *The Great Crisis in American Catholic History, 1895-1900* (Chicago: Regnery, 1957).

American Catholics in the New Deal period are discussed in Monroe Billington, "Roosevelt, the New Deal, and the Clergy," *Mid-America*, 54 (Jan. 1972), 20-33; Paul Czuchlewski, "The Commonweal Catholic: 1924-1960" (unpublished Ph.D. dissertation, Yale University, 1972); George Q. Flynn, *American Catholics and the Roosevelt Presidency, 1932-1936* (Lexington: University of Kentucky Press, 1968); Paul Kiniery, "Catholics and the New Deal," *Catholic World*, 112 (Apr. 1935), 10-20; David O'Brien, *American Catholics and Social Reform* (New York: Oxford University Press, 1968), and "American Catholics and Organized Labor in the 1930's," *Catholic Historical Review*, 52 (Oct. 1966), 323-349.

For the American Church since World War II, see Gary MacEoin, *New Challenges to American Catholics* (New York: P.J. Kenedy, 1965); Thomas McAvoy, "American Catholicism and the Aggiornamento," *Review of Politics*, 30 (July 1968), 275-291;

David O'Brien, *The Renewal of American Catholicism* (New York: Paulist Press, 1972); Thomas O'Dea, *American Catholic Dilemma: An Inquiry into the Intellectual Life* (New York: Sheed and Ward, 1958); Walter Ong, *Frontiers in American Catholicism* (New York: Macmillan, 1957); Joseph Roddy, "Catholic Revolution," *Look*, 29, Feb. 9, 1965, pp. 21-27; Edward Sheehan, "Not Peace but the Sword," *Saturday Evening Post*, Nov. 28, 1964, pp. 22-42; and Donald Thorman, *The Emerging Layman* (Garden City: Doubleday, 1962).

Good historical studies of the Catholic University of America during this period are Roy Deferrari, *Memoirs of the Catholic University of America, 1918-1960* (Boston: Daughters of St. Paul, 1962); Blase Dixon, "The Catholic University of America, 1909-1928" (unpublished Ph.D. dissertation, Catholic University of America, 1972); James H. Ryan, "The Catholic University of America," *Ecclesiastical Review*, 85 (July 1931), 25-39; Thomas J. Shahan, "The Catholic University of America," *Catholic World*, 103 (June 1916), 365-383; and H. Warren Willis, "The Reorganization of the Catholic University of America under the Rectorship of James H. Ryan," (unpublished Ph.D. dissertation, Catholic University of America, 1971). Two other educational institutions are discussed in Peter Leo Johnson, *Halcyon Days: Story of St. Francis Seminary* (Milwaukee: Bruce, 1956); Frederick J. Ferris, "The National Catholic School of Social Service," *Catholic University of America Bulletin*, 29 (Jan. 1962), 1-3ff.; and Loretto Lawler, *Full Circle: The Story of the National Catholic School of Social Service, 1918-1947* (Washington: Catholic University of America Press, 1951). See also Sister M. Annunciata, "The Commission on American Citizenship," *Catholic University of America Bulletin*, 33 (Oct. 1965), 7ff.; "Catholic Conference on Industrial Problems Established," *National Catholic Welfare Council Bulletin*, 4, (Feb. 1923), 14; Raymond A. McGowan, "The Catholic Conference on Industrial Problems," *National Catholic Welfare Council Bulletin*, 5 (Aug. 1923), 11-13; and Patricia McNeal, *The American Catholic Peace Movement, 1928-1972* (New York: Arno Press, 1978). For the Summer Schools of Social Action for Priests, see Raymond McGowan, "Clergy Hail Schools of Social Action," *Catholic Action*, 19 (Aug. 1937), 16-17; Thomas O'Dwyer, "Los Angeles School of Social Action," *Social Action*, 19 (Sept. 1937), 19; and Paul Tanner, "The Summer School of Social Action for the Clergy," *The Salesianum*, 32 (Oct. 1937), 169-173.

In addition to Haas's writings, other studies of Catholic social teaching at the time are Aaron Abell, *American Catholicism and Social Action* (Notre Dame, Ind.: University of Notre Dame Press, 1963); Thomas Blantz, "Justice through Organization: The Social Philosophy of Bishop Francis J. Haas," *Social Thought*, 3 (Summer 1977), 41-53; Charles Bruehl, "A Just Social Order," *Homiletic and Pastoral Review*, 35 (Mar. 1935), 561-569, "A Course of Social Science at the Salesianum," *Catholic Fortnightly Review*, 17 (mid-Dec. 1911), 734-736, "Bishops on the Social Order," *Ave Maria*, 51 (Apr. 13, 1940), 455-460, "The Case against the Capitalistic System," *Homiletic and Pastoral Review*, 35 (Jan. 1935), 337-345, and "The Catholic Church and Social Order," *Homiletic and Pastoral Review*, 35 (Dec. 1934), 225-233; Edward A. Keller, *Christianity and American Capitalism* (Chicago: Heritage Foundation, 1953), and *The Church and Our Economic System* (Notre Dame, Ind.: Ave Maria Press, 1947); Frederick Kenkel, "The Encyclical 'Quadragesimo Anno' and Social Reconstruction," *Fortnightly Review*, 38 (Aug. 1931), 169-170, and "The President's Program—Whither Directed?" *Central-Blatt and Social Justice*, 26 (June 1933), 80; Virgil Michel, "Facts about Capitalism," *Commonweal*, 25 (Mar. 12, 1937), 541-543; Joseph Munier, *Some American Approximations of Pius XI's "Industries and Professions"* (Washington: Catholic University of America Press, 1943); Franz Mueller, "The Church and the Social Question," in Joseph Moody and Justus George Lawler (eds.), *The Challenge of Mater et Magistra* (New York: Herder and Herder, 1963); J.F.T. Prince, *Creative Revolution* (Milwaukee: Bruce, 1937); James Roohan, "American Catholics and the Social Question, 1865-1900," *Historical Records and Studies*, 43 (1955), 3-26; and John A. Ryan, *A Better Economic Order* (New York: Harper, 1935), *A Living Wage* (New York: Macmillan, 1906), *Distributive Justice* (New York: Macmillan, 1916), "New Deal and Social Justice," *Commonweal*, 19 (Apr. 13, 1934), 657-659, "The New Things in the New Encyclical," *Ecclesiastical Review*, 85 (July 1931), 1-14, and "Roosevelt and Social Justice," *Review of Politics*, 7 (July 1945), 297-305.

Three short biographical studies of Haas are Thomas Blantz, "Francis J. Haas: Priest and Government Servant," *Catholic Historical Review*, 57 (Jan. 1972), 571-592; Franklyn Kennedy, "Bishop Haas," *The Salesianum*, 39 (Jan. 1944), 7-14; and Constance Randall, "A Bio-Bibliography of Bishop Francis J. Haas" (unpublished M.A. Thesis, Catholic University of America, 1955). Philip

Land discusses Haas and Ryan in "Bishop Haas and Monsignor Ryan," *America*, 89 (Sept. 12, 1953), 573-574. Of Haas's contemporaries in the priesthood, see John Sheerin, *Never Look Back: The Career and Concerns of John J. Burke* (New York: Paulist Press, 1975); Forrest Davis, "Father Coughlin," *Atlantic Monthly*, 156 (Dec. 1935), 659-668; Sheldon Marcus, *Father Coughlin: The Tumultuous Life of the Priest of the Little Flower* (Boston: Little, Brown, 1973); Charles Tull, *Father Coughlin and the New Deal* (Syracuse: Syracuse University Press, 1965); Sister Mary Harrita Fox, *Peter E. Dietz, Labor Priest* (Notre Dame, Ind.: University of Notre Dame Press, 1953); Saul Bronder, "Robert E. Lucey: A Texas Paradox" (unpublished Ph.D. dissertation, Columbia University, 1979); Thomas Tifft, "Toward a More Humane Social Policy: The Work and Influence of Monsignor John O'Grady" (unpublished Ph.D. dissertation, Catholic University of America, 1979); J.G. Shaw, *Edwin Vincent O'Hara: American Prelate* (New York: Farrar, Straus and Cudahy, 1957); Thomas McAvoy, *Father O'Hara of Notre Dame* (Notre Dame, Ind.: University of Notre Dame Press, 1967); Aaron Abell, "Monsignor John A. Ryan: An Historical Appreciation," *Review of Politics*, 8 (Jan. 1946), 128-134; Francis Broderick, *Right Reverend New Dealer: John A. Ryan* (New York: Macmillan, 1963); Patrick Gearty, *The Economic Thought of Monsignor John A. Ryan* (Washington: Catholic University of America Press, 1953); and John A. Ryan, *Social Doctrine in Action* (New York: Harper, 1941). Biographical studies of Haas's government and labor associates are also valuable: Matthew Josephson, *Sidney Hillman: Statesman of American Labor* (Garden City: Doubleday, 1952); J. Michael Eisner, *William Morris Leiserson: A Biography* (Madison: University of Wisconsin Press, 1967); Melvyn Dubofsky and Warren Van Tine, *John L. Lewis: A Biography* (New York: Quadrangle/New York Times, 1977); James Wechsler, *Labor Baron* (New York: Morrow, 1944); George Martin, *Madam Secretary: Frances Perkins* (Boston: Houghton Mifflin, 1976); Frances Perkins, "Eight Years as Madame Secretary," *Fortune*, 24 (Sept. 1941), 77ff.; Theron Schlaback, *Edwin E. Witte: Cautious Reformer* (Madison: State Historical Society of Wisconsin, 1969); Joseph Alsop and Robert Kintner, *Men around the President* (New York: Doubleday, Doran, 1939); and Unofficial Observer, *The New Dealers* (New York: Literary Guild, 1934).

Essential for any study of Franklin Roosevelt or the New Deal is Samuel Rosenman (ed.), *The Public Papers and Addresses of Franklin D. Roosevelt*, 13 vols. (New York: Harper, 1938-

1950). New Deal studies most helpful for this work include Irving Bernstein, *The Lean Years* (Boston: Houghton Mifflin, 1940); Forrest Davis, "The Rise of the Commissars," *New Outlook*, 162 (Dec. 1933), 23-24; Harold Ickes, *The Secret Diary of Harold L. Ickes*, 3 vols. (New York: Simon and Schuster, 1953); Richard Kirkendall, "Franklin D. Roosevelt and the Service Intellectual," *Mississippi Valley Historical Review*, 49 (Dec. 1962), 456-471; William E. Leuchtenburg, *Franklin D. Roosevelt and the New Deal* (New York: Harper and Row, 1963); Broadus Mitchell, *Depression Decade* (New York: Rinehart, 1947); George Peek, *Why Quit Our Own* (Princeton: Van Nostrand, 1936); Frances Perkins, *People at Work* (New York: John Day, 1934); Basil Rauch, *The History of the New Deal* (New York: Capricorn, 1963); Eleanor Roosevelt, *This I Remember* (New York: Harper, 1949); Arthur M. Schlesinger, Jr., *The Age of Roosevelt*, 3 vols. (Boston: Houghton Mifflin, 1957-1960); Studs Terkel, *Hard Times: An Oral History of the Great Depression* (New York: Pantheon, 1970); and Dixon Wecter, *The Age of the Great Depression* (New York: Macmillan, 1948). The best biographies of Roosevelt are James M. Burns, *Roosevelt: The Lion and the Fox* (New York: Harcourt, Brace, 1956); Frank Freidel, *Franklin D. Roosevelt*, 4 vols. (Boston: Little, Brown, 1952-1973); Frances Perkins, *The Roosevelt I Knew* (New York: Harper and Row, 1963); and Rexford Tugwell, *The Democratic Roosevelt* (Garden City: Doubleday, 1957). Stanley High, *Roosevelt—And Then* (New York: Harper, 1937), is of interest but John T. Flynn, *The Roosevelt Myth* (New York: Devin-Adair, 1948) is almost wholly negative. Some of the social thinking behind the New Deal is discussed in Adolf Berle, Jr., "The Social Economics of the New Deal," *New York Times Magazine*, Oct. 29, 1933, pp. 4ff.; Daniel Fusfeld, *The Economic Thought of Franklin D. Roosevelt and the Origins of the New Deal* (New York: Columbia University Press, 1956); and Thomas Greer, *What Roosevelt Thought* (East Lansing: Michigan State University Press, 1958).

Works that examine American labor in the early years of the twentieth century or in the New Deal period include Irving Bernstein, *Turbulent Years* (Boston: Houghton Mifflin, 1969) and *The New Deal Collective Bargaining Policy* (Berkeley: University of California Press, 1950); David Brody, "Labor and the Great Depression: The Interpretive Prospects," *Labor History*, 13 (Spring 1972), 231-244; Milton Derber and Edwin Young (eds.), *Labor and the New Deal* (Madison: University of Wisconsin Press,

1957); Sidney Fine, "Government and Labor Relations during the New Deal," *Current History*, 48 (Winter 1964-65), 111-126; Marc Karson, *American Labor Unions and Politics* (Carbondale: Southern Illinois University Press, 1958); Joseph Rosenfarb, *The National Labor Policy and How It Works* (New York: Harper, 1940); Emanuel Stein and others, *Labor and the New Deal* (New York: Crofts, 1934); Philip Taft, *The A.F. of L. from the Death of Gompers to the Merger* (New York: Harper, 1959) and *Organized Labor in American History* (New York: Harper and Row, 1964); and Twentieth Century Fund, *Labor and the Government* (New York: McGraw-Hill, 1935). Three good studies of the AFL-CIO split in the 1930s are Walter Galenson, *The CIO Challenge to the AFL* (Cambridge, Mass.: Harvard University Press, 1960); Herbert Harris, *Labor's Civil War* (New York: Knopf, 1940); and James O. Morris, *Conflict within the AFL* (Ithaca: Cornell University Press, 1958).

There are many excellent studies of American history during Haas's pre-New Deal years: Harold Faulkner, *Politics, Reform, and Expansion* (New York: Harper, 1959); John Garraty, *The New Commonwealth* (New York: Harper and Row, 1968); Ray Ginger, *Altgeld's America* (New York: Funk and Wagnalls, 1958); Eric Goldman, *Rendezvous with Destiny* (New York: Random House, 1956); John Hicks, *The Populist Revolt* (Minneapolis: University of Minnesota Press, 1931); Richard Hofstadter, *The Age of Reform* (New York: Random House, 1960); Arthur Link, *Woodrow Wilson and the Progressive Era* (New York: Harper, 1954); Horace Merrill, *Bourbon Democracy in the Middle West* (Baton Rouge: Louisiana State University Press, 1953); George Mowry, *The Era of Theodore Roosevelt* (New York: Harper, 1958); and Russel Nye, *Midwestern Progressive Politics* (East Lansing: Michigan State College Press, 1951). For Wisconsin, Milwaukee, and Racine, see Nicholas Burckel (ed.), *Racine: Growth and Change in a Wisconsin County* (Racine: Racine County Board of Supervisors, 1977); Donald Kinzer, "The Political Uses of Anti-Catholicism: Michigan and Wisconsin, 1890-1894," *Michigan History*, 39 (Sept. 1955), 312-326; Eugene Leach, *Racine, an Historical Narrative* (Racine, 1920); Herbert Margulies, "Anti-Catholicism in Wisconsin Politics, 1914-1920," *Mid-America*, 44 (Jan. 1962), 51-56, and *The Decline of the Progressive Movement in Wisconsin, 1890-1920* (Madison: State Historical Society of Wisconsin, 1968); Robert Maxwell, *La Follette and the Rise of the Progressives in Wisconsin* (Madison: State Historical Society of Wisconsin, 1956);

A Priest in Public Service

Racine Daily Journal, *Racine, the Belle City of the Lakes* (Racine: Press of the Journal Publishing Company, 1924); William Raney, *Wisconsin, a Story of Progress* (New York: Prentice-Hall, 1940); Alice Sankey, *Racine, the Belle City* (Racine: Board of Education, 1958); Albert Schimberg, *Humble Harvest: The Society of St. Vincent de Paul in the Milwaukee Archdiocese* (Milwaukee: Bruce, 1949); Bayrd Still, *Milwaukee: The History of a City* (Madison: State Historical Society of Wisconsin, 1948); and Fanny Stone, *Racine, Belle City of the Lakes*, 2 vols. (Chicago: S.J. Clarke, 1916).

Of numerous studies of the NRA, the following were most helpful: Solomon Barkin, "Collective Bargaining and Section 7 (b) of NIRA," *Annals of the American Academy of Political and Social Science (AAAPSS)*, 184 (Mar. 1936), 169-175; Irving Bernstein, "Labor and the Recovery Program," *Quarterly Journal of Economics*, 60 (Feb. 1946), 270-288; Charles Dearing and others, *The ABC of the NRA* (Washington: Brookings Institution, 1934); Sidney Fine, *The Automobile under the Blue Eagle* (Ann Arbor: University of Michigan Press, 1963); Milton Handler, "The National Industrial Recovery Act," *American Bar Association Journal*, 19 (Aug. 1933), 440ff.; Ellis Hawley, *The New Deal and the Problem of Monopoly* (Princeton: Princeton University Press, 1966); J. Joseph Huthmacher, *Robert F. Wagner and the Rise of Urban Liberalism* (New York: Atheneum Press, 1968); John L. Lewis, "Labor and the National Recovery Administration," *AAAPSS*, 172 (Mar. 1934), 58-63; Leverett Lyon and others, *The National Recovery Administration* (Washington: Brookings Institution, 1935); Lois McDonald, *Labor and the N.R.A.* (New York: Affiliated Schools for Workers, 1934); Gustav Peck, "Labor's Role in Government Administrative Procedure," *AAAPSS*, 184 (Mar. 1936), 83-92; Ruth Reticker, "Labor Standards in the NRA Codes," *AAAPSS*, 184 (Mar. 1936), 72-82; Charles Roos, *NRA Economic Planning* (Bloomington, Ind.: Principia Press, 1937); Raymond Rubinow, *Section 7 (a): Its History, Interpretation and Administration* (Washington: National Recovery Administration, 1936); Margaret Schoenfeld, "Analysis of the Labor Provisions of N.R.A. Codes," *Monthly Labor Review*, 40 (Mar. 1935), 574-603; John D. Ubinger, "Ernest Tener Weir: Last of the Great Steelmasters," part 2, *Western Pennsylvania Historical Magazine*, 58 (Oct. 1975), 487-507; and Clair Wilcox and others (eds.), *America's Recovery Program* (New York: Oxford University Press, 1934).

Basic studies of the National and Wisconsin Labor Relations boards include Dean Bowman, *Public Control of Labor Relations* (New York: Macmillan, 1942); Mason Doan, "State Labor Relations Acts," *Quarterly Journal of Economics*, 56 (Aug. 1942), 507-559; Thomas Fisher, *Industrial Disputes and Federal Legislation* (New York: Columbia University Press, 1940); Lloyd Garrison, "The National Labor Boards," *AAAPSS*, 184 (Mar. 1936), 138-146; Charles Killingsworth, "Public Regulation of Labor Relations—The Wisconsin Experiment," *American Economic Review*, 33 (June 1943), 247-263; Lewis Lorwin and Arthur Wubnig, *Labor Relations Boards* (Washington: Brookings Institution, 1935); and James Patterson, *The New Deal and the States* (Princeton: Princeton University Press, 1969).

For the history of Minneapolis and the background of the truckers' strike of 1934, see Theodore Blegen, *Minnesota: A History of the State* (Minneapolis: University of Minnesota Press, 1963); Chester Destler, *American Radicalism, 1865-1901* (New London: Connecticut College, 1946); William Folwell, *A History of Minnesota*, 4 vols. (St. Paul: Minnesota Historical Society, 1921-1930); Steward Holbrook, *James J. Hill: A Great Life in Brief* (New York: Knopf, 1955); Lucile Kane, *The Waterfall that Built a City* (St. Paul: Minnesota Historical Society, 1966); Meridel Le Sueur, *North Star Country* (New York: Book Find Club, 1945); Gustavus Myers, *History of the Great American Fortunes* (New York: Random House, 1936); Joseph Pyle, *The Life of James J. Hill*, 2 vols. (New York: Peter Smith, 1936); "Twin Cities," *Fortune*, 13 (Apr. 1936), 112ff.; and Charles Walker, *American City* (New York: Farrar and Rinehart, 1937). Informative works on the strike are Thomas Blantz, "Father Haas and the Minneapolis Truckers' Strike of 1934," *Minnesota History*, 42 (Spring 1970), 5-15; James Cannon, *The History of American Trotskyism* (New York: Pathfinder Press, 1972); Farrell Dobbs, *Teamster Power* (New York: Monad Press, 1973), and *Teamster Rebellion* (New York: Monad Press, 1972); William Dunne and Morris Childs, *Permanent Counter-Revolution* (New York: Workers Library Publishers, 1934); "The International Brotherhood of Teamsters, Chauffeurs, Warehousemen, and Helpers of America," *Fortune*, 23 (May 1941), 97ff.; Herbert Lefkovitz, "Olson: Radical and Proud of It," *Review of Reviews*, 91 (May, 1935), 36ff.; Meridel Le Sueur, "What Happens in a Strike," *American Mercury*, 33 (Nov. 1934), 329-335; George Mayer, *The Political Career of Floyd B. Olson* (Minneapolis: University of

Minnesota Press, 1951); Constance Myers, *The Prophet's Army: Trotskyists in America, 1928-1941* (Westport, Conn.: Greenwood Press, 1977); Selden Rodman, "A Letter from Minnesota," *New Republic*, 80 (Aug. 15, 1934), 10-12; Sam Romer, "Five Minutes that Changed the Face of Minneapolis," *Minneapolis Sunday Tribune*, July 19, 1964, pp. 10-11; Anne Ross, "Labor Unity in Minneapolis," *New Republic*, 79 (July 25, 1934), 284-286, and "Minnesota Sets Some Precedents," *New Republic*, 80 (Sept. 12, 1934), 121-123; Donald Schewe, "The Minneapolis Truck Drivers' Strike of 1934" (unpublished M.A. thesis, University of Nebraska, 1968); Eric Severeid, *Not So Wild a Dream* (New York: Knopf, 1946); and Herbert Solow, "War in Minneapolis," *The Nation*, 139 (Aug. 8, 1934), 160-161.

Other labor disturbances in which Haas was involved are discussed in "Employers Favor Silk Stoppage," *Business Week*, Aug. 7, 1937, pp. 28-30; Stanley High, "Rehearsal for Revolution," *Reader's Digest*, 38 (June 1941), 89-93; "Hillman's Silk Workers," *Literary Digest*, 124 (Aug. 28, 137), 8; Herman Klein, "Allis-Chalmers Strike Hits Largest Defense Plants in the Nation," *Iron Age*, 147 (Mar. 27, 1941), 81-88; "Knudsen's Coup," *The Nation*, 152 (Apr. 5, 1941), 396-397; Ruben Levin, "Mass Action Works in Milwaukee," *New Republic*, 79 (July 18, 1934), 261-263; "Showdown Strike," *Business Week*, Mar. 29, 1941, pp. 49-52; "Silent Silk," *Time*, 30 (Aug. 23, 1937), 12; and Mary Heaton Vorse, "Bringing Union to Textiles," *New Republic*, 92 (Oct. 27, 1937), 331-333.

Literature on other New Deal agencies and activities is plentiful. For the WPA, see Arthur E. Burns and Peyton Kerr, "Survey of Work-Relief Policies," *American Economic Review*, 27 (Dec. 1937), 711-724; Searle Charles, *Minister of Relief* (Syracuse: Syracuse University Press, 1963); Harry L. Hopkins, *Spending to Save* (New York: Norton, 1956); Donald Howard, *The W.P.A. and Federal Relief Policy* (New York: Russell Sage Foundation, 1943); Arthur Macmahon and others, *Administration of Federal Work Relief* (Chicago: Public Administration Service, 1941); and Lewis Meriam, *Relief and Social Security* (Washington: Brookings Institution, 1946). The Wages and Hours Act is discussed in James M. Burns, *Congress on Trial* (New York: Harper, 1949), and Paul Douglas and Joseph Hackman, "The Fair Labor Standards Act of 1938, I-II," *Political Science Quarterly*, 53 (Dec. 1938), 491-516, and 54 (Mar. 1939), 29-55. Good studies of the National Resources Planning Board are Eveline Burns, "Freedom from Want: The NRPB Report," *Survey Midmonthly*, 79 (Apr. 1943), 106-109; Charles Merriam, "The National Resources Planning Board: A Chapter in American Planning Experience," *American Political Science Review*, 38 (Dec. 1944), 1075-1088; John Millett, *The Process and Organization of Government Planning* (New York: Columbia University Press, 1947); and the NRPB's own report, *Security, Work, and Relief Policies* (Washington: U.S. Government Printing Office, 1942). American participation in the ILO is discussed in Antony Alcock, *History of the International Labor Organization* (New York: Octagon Books, 1971); George Johnston, *The International Labour Organisation* (London: Europa Press, 1970); Albert Le Roy, *The Dignity of Labor* (Westminster, Md.: Newman Press, 1957); David Morse, *The Origin and Evolution of the I.L.O. and Its Role in the World Community* (Ithaca: New York State School of Industrial and Labor Relations, Cornell University, 1969); Gary Ostrower, "The American Decision to Join the International Labor Organization," *Labor History*, 16 (Fall 1975), 495-504; "The Second Labour Conference of American States Members of the International Labour Organisation," *International Labour Review*, 41 (Mar. 1940), 225-268; and "The Twenty-sixth Session of the International Labour Conference," *International Labour Review*, 50 (July 1944), 1-39.

A few of the many informative works on civil rights during the Roosevelt years are Linna Bressette, "Report of the Sixth 'Negro in Industry' Conference," *Interracial Review*, 6 (Oct. 1933), 176-178; David Chalmers, *Hooded Americanism* (New York: Doubleday, 1965); John P. Davis, "A Black Inventory of the New Deal," *Crisis*, 42 (May 1935), 141ff.; Leslie Fishel, Jr., "The Negro in the New Deal Era," *Wisconsin Magazine of History*, 48 (Winter 1964-65), 111-126; John Kirby, *Black Americans in the Roosevelt Era* (Knoxville: University of Tennessee Press, 1980); Allan Morrison, "The Secret Papers of FDR," *Negro Digest*, 9 (Jan. 1951), 3-13; and Gunner Myrdal, *An American Dilemma* (New York: Harper and Row, 1962). For President Truman's Committee on Civil Rights, see William Berman, *The Politics of Civil Rights in the Truman Administration* (Columbus: Ohio State University Press, 1970); Robert Carr, *Federal Protection of Civil Rights* (Ithaca: Cornell University Press, 1947); Milton Konvitz, *A Century of Civil Rights* (New York: Columbia University Press, 1961) and *The Constitution and Civil Rights* (New York: Columbia University Press, 1947); the committee report, *To Secure These Rights* (New York: Simon and Schuster, 1947); and Harry Truman, *Years of Trial and Hope* (Garden City: Doubleday, 1956).

The wartime FEPC and the employment of Black Americans are the subject of many excellent works. Among the most helpful are John Beecher, "8802 Blues," *New Republic,* 108 (Feb. 22, 1943), 248-250; I. George Blake, *Paul V. McNutt: Portrait of a Hoosier Statesman* (Indianapolis: Central Publishing Company, 1966); Herman Bloch, "Craft Unions and the Negro in Historical Perspective," *Journal of Negro History,* 43 (Jan. 1958), 10-33; John M. Blum, *V Was for Victory* (New York: Harcourt Brace Jovanovich, 1976); George Q. Flynn, *The Mess in Washington* (Westport, Conn.: Greenwood Press, 1979); "Further Abandonment of the Four Freedoms," *Commonweal,* 37 (Jan. 29, 1943), 363-364; Herbert Garfinkel, *When Negroes March* (Glencoe, Ill.: The Free Press, 1959); Lester Granger, "Barriers to Negro War Employment," *AAAPSS,* 223 (Sept. 1942), 72-80, and "Negroes and War Production," *Survey Graphic,* 31 (Nov. 1942), 469-470; John Temple Graves, "The Southern Negro and the War Crisis," *Virginia Quarterly Review,* 18 (Autumn 1942), 500-517; Herbert Hill, "Labor Unions and the Negro," *Commentary,* 28 (Dec. 1959), 479-488; Louis Kesselman, "The Fair Employment Practice Movement in Perspective," *Journal of Negro History,* 31 (Jan. 1946), 30-46, and *The Social Politics of FEPC* (Chapel Hill: University of North Carolina Press, 1948); R.M. MacIver, *The More Perfect Union* (New York: Macmillan, 1948); Ray Marshall, *The Negro and Organized Labor* (New York: Wiley, 1965); Paul Norgren and Samuel Hill, *Toward Fair Employment* (New York: Columbia University Press, 1964); Herbert Northrup, *Organized Labor and the Negro* (New York: Harper, 1944); James Nuechterlein, "The Politics of Civil Rights: The FEPC, 1941-1946," *Prologue,* 10 (Fall 1978), 171-191; Leon Ranson, "Combatting Discrimination in the Employment of Negroes in War Industries and Government Agencies," *Journal of Negro Education,* 12 (Summer 1943), 405-416; Thomas Roberts, "The Negro in Government War Agencies," *Journal of Negro Education,* 12 (Summer 1943), 367-375; Malcolm Ross, *All Manner of Men* (New York: Reynal and Hitchcock, 1948); Louis Ruchames, *Race, Jobs and Politics* (New York: Columbia University Press, 1953); Stanley H. Smith, *Freedom to Work* (New York: Vantage Press, 1955); Michael Sovern, *Legal Restraints on Racial Discrimination in Employment* (New York: Twentieth Century Fund, 1966); Robert Weaver, "Defense Industries and the Negro," *AAAPSS,* 223 (Sept. 1942), 60-66, and *Negro Labor* (New York: Harcourt, Brace, 1946); James Wechsler, "Pigeonhole for Negro Equality," *The Nation,* 156 (Jan. 23, 1943), 121-122; and Walter White, *A Man Called White* (New York: Viking Press, 1948).

The Detroit riot of 1943 and its background are treated in Earl Brown, "The Truth about the Detroit Riot," *Harper's Magazine,* 187 (Oct. 1943), 488-498, and *Why Race Riots* (New York: Public Affairs Committee, 1944); "Defeat at Detroit," *The Nation,* 157 (July 3, 1943), 4; "Detroit Is Dynamite," *Life,* 13 (Aug. 17, 1942), 15-23; Alfred Lee and Norman Humphrey, *Race Riot* (New York: Dryden Press, 1943); Thurgood Marshall, "The Gestapo in Detroit," *Crisis,* 50 (Aug. 1943), 232ff.; William Norton, "The Detroit Riots—and After," *Survey Graphic,* 32 (Aug. 1943), 317-318; Thomas Sancton, "The Race Riots," *New Republic,* 109 (July 5, 1943), 9-13; Robert Shogan and Tom Craig, *The Detroit Race Riot* (Philadelphia: Chilton Books, 1964); and Harvard Sitkoff, "The Detroit Race Riot of 1943," *Michigan History,* 53 (Fall 1969), 183-206.

Of additional interest for Haas's years as bishop of Grand Rapids are F. Clever Bald, *Michigan in Four Centuries* (New York: Harper, 1954); John Tracy Ellis, "On Selecting American Bishops," *Commonweal,* 85 (Mar. 10, 1967), 643-649; William Etten (ed.), *A Citizen's History of Grand Rapids, Michigan* (Grand Rapids: A.P. Johnson Co., 1926); James Gillis, *The Paulists* (New York: Macmillan, 1932); Alonzo Hamby, *Beyond the New Deal: Harry S. Truman and American Liberalism* (New York: Columbia University Press, 1973); Vincent Holden, *The Yankee Paul: Isaac Thomas Hecker* (Milwaukee: Bruce, 1958); John McGee, *The Catholic Church in the Grand River Valley, 1833-1950* (Grand Rapids, 1950 [printed by Franklin Dekleine Co., Lansing, Mich.]); Joseph McSorley, *Father Hecker and His Friends* (St. Louis: B. Herder Book Co., 1952); and George Pare, *The Catholic Church in Detroit, 1701-1888* (Detroit: Gabriel Richard Press, 1951).

Index

Rerum Novarum, 49, 51, 53, 57, 188, 270, 286, 291; Haas-McGowan translation of *Rerum Novarum*, 177-178
Lewis, John L., 73, 125, 146, 156, 234, 285, 289; appointed to Labor Advisory Board, 72; and National Labor Board, 91, 94, 105; and AFL-CIO split, 181-187
Locke, John, 29
Lord, Robert, 42
Loyola University (Chicago), 32, 241
Lubin, Isador, 136-140
Lucey, Robert (archbishop), 34, 208, 210, 248, 270; and Summer Schools of Social Action, 160, 161
Luckman, Charles, 266, 267

MacLean, Malcolm, 207
Madden, Warren, 187
Mann, Leo, 196
Manton, Martin, 34
Marquette University, 20, 26-27, 35, 36, 37, 148
Martin, Homer, 166
Marywood Academy (Grand Rapids), 245, 282
Maslow, Will, 224
Matthews, Francis P., 266
Matz, Nicholas (bishop), 14
Mayne, Joseph, 234
Mayo, William and Charles, 119
McCabe, David R., 32, 42
McCormick, Patrick, 231
McDonald, David, 284
McGowan, Raymond A., 32, 48, 113, 126, 147, 270, 284; on John A. Ryan, 3; and Summer Schools of Social Action, 159-160; with Haas, translates encyclicals, 177-178, 286; and *The Church and Social Order*, 179
McGlynn, Edward, 230
McGrady, Edward, 193, 197
McIntyre, Marvin, 208
McNutt, Paul V., 207, 208, 210
Messmer, Sebastian (archbishop), 18, 20, 33
Meyer, Albert (cardinal), 232, 284

Michel, Virgil, 50-51
Militia of Christ, 19
Mill, John Stuart, 55
Miller, George, 18
Millis, Harry, 25, 73, 112; and NLRB appointment, 187, 188
Milwaukee County Association for the Promotion of Old Age Pensions, 30-31
Milwaukee County Civil Service Commission, 30
Milwaukee Newspaper Publishers' Association, 31
Milwaukee Railway and Light Company strike (1934), 101-104
Mindszenty, Joseph (cardinal), 274
Minneapolis truckers' strike, 100, 107-124; background, 107-111; strike in May, 111-112; early mediation efforts, 113-116; "Battle of Bloody Friday," 114-115; Haas-Dunnigan plan, 116-121; martial law declared, 118; appeal to Strike Committee of One Hundred, 118-119; settlement, 121; effects of strike, 122; *see also* Dunnigan, E.H.; General Drivers and Helpers Union; Olson, Floyd B.; and Reconstruction Finance Corporation
Minnesota Law and Order League, 111
Mitchell, Clarence, 212
Moon, Parker, 34
Mooney, Edward (cardinal), 147, 234, 248, 286; and appointment of Haas, 232-233; at Haas's funeral, 284
Moore, John D., 102-104
Moore, Thomas Verner, O.S.B., 44
Muench, Aloysius (cardinal), 25, 26, 31, 93, 171-172, 178, 232; appointed bishop, 126
Muir, Malcolm, 80
Mundelein, George (cardinal), 231
Mundt, Karl, 274
Murray, Philip, 205, 248; and AFL-CIO split, 184, 186; and Allis-Chalmers strike of 1941, 198; funeral, 281